D1756273

Irish Women
and
Street Politics
1956–1973

'This could be contagious'

TARA KEENAN-THOMSON
Foreword by PAUL ARTHUR

IRISH ACADEMIC PRESS
DUBLIN • PORTLAND, OR

First published in 2010 by Irish Academic Press

2 Brookside,	920 NE 58th Avenue, Suite 300
Dundrum Road,	Portland, Oregon,
Dublin 14,	97213-3786
Ireland	USA

www.iap.ie

© 2010 Tara Keenan-Thomson

British Library Cataloguing in Publication Data
An entry can be found on request

ISBN 978 0 7165 3026 8 (cloth)
ISBN 978 0 7165 3027 5 (paper)

Library of Congress Cataloging-in-Publication Data
An entry can be found on request

All rights reserved. Without limiting the rights under copyright reserved alone, no part of this publication may be reproduced, stored in or introduced into a retrieval system, or transmitted, in any form or by any means (electronic, mechanical, photocopying, recording or otherwise) without the prior written permission of both the copyright owner and the above publisher of this book.

Printed by Good News Digital Books, Ongar, Essex

Contents

List of Illustrations

1. Republican women and men at Bodenstown in 1954. Photo courtesy of Noel Kavanagh.
2. Homeless Citizens League in Dungannon, c. 1963. *Left to right*: Bernie Hill, Jean Mohan, Patricia McCluskey, Angela McCrystal, Margaret McArdle, Ann Dunlop and son, Maureen Fearon, Susan Dinsmore and son. Photo courtesy of Ann Dunlop and Susan Dinsmore.
3. Recent photo of Angela McCrystal. Photo by Tara Keenan-Thomson.
4. Women march in Derry against Internment without trial, 18 August 1971. Photo courtesy of Edwina Stewart for NICRA.
5. Betty Sinclair addressing demonstration outside Mulhouse Street RUC/army barracks in Belfast, 21 September 1974. Photo courtesy of Edwina Stewart for NICRA.
6. Newry march, 6 February 1972, one week after Bloody Sunday. *Left to right*: Ann Hope, NICRA treasurer (bearing wounds she received in the Derry march now known as Bloody Sunday), Jimmy Doris, past Chairman of NICRA, Madge Davison, assistant organizer for NICRA, Hugh Lough, then NICRA member, Margo Collins, and Paddy O'Hanlon, Stormont MP. Photo courtesy of Edwina Stewart for NICRA.
7. Bernadette Devlin mural also depicting women sounding the alarm by bashing bin lids and children taking part in the Battle of the Bogside. Mural painted by the Bogside Artists, Derry, in 1996. Photo courtesy of Martin Melaugh, CAIN (cain.ulster.ac.uk).
8. Brandywell women marching against internment without trial c. 1971. Photo courtesy of Eamon Melaugh, CAIN (cain.ulster.ac.u/melaugh).
9. Cumann na mBan mural in West Belfast. Photo courtesy of Martin Melaugh, CAIN (cain.ulster.ac.uk).
10. Cumann na mBan poster. n.d., courtesy of *An Phoblacht*.
11. Female members of the Official IRA, Derry, c. 1972. Photo courtesy of Eamon Melaugh, CAIN.

List of Tables

1. Founders of the Irish Women's Liberation Movement with occupation and/or political identification.
2. Information on contraceptives gathered by Minister for Justice from Irish Embassies, 1971.

Acknowledgements

The completion of such a comprehensive research project necessarily requires endurance and patience both on the part of the researcher and on the part of those closest to him or her. Over the past ten years this research has required me to constantly refocus my energies, all the while teaching, working, visiting a host of archives and conducting interviews. All of the people I have encountered along the way have been critical to the formation of my analysis through their shared knowledge and willingness to discuss and debate history. I would like to thank the following people for their crucial contributions to the success of this project: the staff at the national archives of Dublin, London, Belfast and the United States, the staff at the Linen Hall Library's Political Collection, and those at the National Library of Ireland, Trinity College, University College Dublin, the Morris Library in Delaware, University College Cork's Boole Library and the New York Public Library.

I would also like to thank Lynda Edgerton, Noel Kavanagh, Michael MacEvilly, Chrissie McAuley, Eamonn McCann, Angela McCrystal, Seán O'Mahony, Dolours Price and Edwina Stewart for being so generous with their time during this long period of research. I am also indebted to my interviewees, whose bravery and trust allowed me to shed light on events discussed in this book. Likewise, those who assisted me to locate images for this book proved invaluable. They include *An Phoblacht,* the Bogside Artists, Dr Anna Bryson, Susan Dinsmore and Ann Dunlop for the Homeless Citizens League, Noel Kavanagh, Dr Michael Kennedy, executive editor of the Documents on Irish Foreign Policy series, Eamon Melaugh (cain.ulster.ac.uk/ melaugh), Dr Martin Melaugh of CAIN (cain.ulster.ac.uk), Carol Quinn of University College Cork and Edwina Stewart for NICRA.

I owe a tremendous debt of gratitude to members of the staff and faculty at Trinity's School of Histories and Humanities, particularly to my supervisor Professor Eunan O'Halpin of the Centre for Contemporary

Irish History and Dr Maryann Valiulis of the Centre for Gender and Women's Studies. Professor Paul Arthur has offered valuable ideas and suggestions along the way. Dr Simon Prince's critical insight was pivotal in challenging my assumptions and helping me frame my analysis. Many thanks also to Lisa Hyde, Hilary Hammond, Mark Wells and Guy Holland at Irish Academic Press for their helpful suggestions. Though all of these people leant their insight and expertise to this project, any mistakes, opinions and interpretations are my own.

I could not have completed the project without the support of my friends like Danny Bach, Kate Blackwell, Francesca Breccia, Dr Anna Bryson, Dr Andrea Comencini, Laurel Coston, Dr Christopher Farrington, Susan and Dan Fritz, Dr John Gibney, Ignacio Gomez, Dr Ciara Hogan, Liselotte Keogh, Dr Chiara Lucarelli, Nina Malkevitch, Dan O'Grady, the O'Malley family, Dr Enrico Terrinoni, Ami Trivedi, Heather Walker, Dr Ian Russell and Melissa Scannell. I must also thank Dr Kate O'Malley, whose enduring friendship I will forever treasure. The board of the Nassau Chapter of the New York Civil Liberties Union provided key encouragement during a difficult period by validating my work and encouraging me to pursue my dreams, however outrageous they might have sounded to Barbara! I must also thank Ed Schmieder, Catherine Oriani and Carlo Rebolini for their support at the beginning of this project and for letting me know it was okay to stay. Gail and Robert Thomson, my in-laws, have no idea how critical their nurturing and care were throughout the entire project.

Finally, I would like to thank my parents, Maura Donoghue and Jerry Keenan, and my sisters, Patricia Sharp, Kathleen Yoo and Maura Slavens, without whom I could not have attempted this project. Most of all, I thank my husband, Brian Thomson, who embarked on this journey alongside me and with patience listened to my midnight ravings, debated them, and raved a little himself. Though doing our work at the same time has been a challenge, it has also been, at times, the only thing that has kept me going. Thank you for your love, your support and, above all, your understanding.

Tara Keenan-Thomson
November 2009

Abbreviations

ACIF	American Conference for Irish Freedom
CDU	Campaign for Democracy in Ulster
CPNI	Communist Party of Northern Ireland
CSJ	Campaign for Social Justice
CSW	Commission on the Status of Women
DHAC	Dublin Housing Action Committee
ECSC	European Coal and Steel Community
EEC	European Economic Community
HCL	Homeless Citizens League
IAW	International Alliance of Women
ICA	Irish Countrywomen's Association
ICFTU	International Confederation of Free Trade Unions
ICTU	Irish Congress of Trade Unions
IHA	Irish Housewives Association
IRA	Irish Republican Army
NAIJ	National Association for Irish Justice
NAWI	National Association of Widows in Ireland
NCCL	National Council for Civil Liberties in Britain
NICRA	Northern Ireland Civil Rights Association
NOW	National Organization of Women
NSA	Nursery School Association
PD	People's Democracy
RUC	Royal Ulster Constabulary
TUC	Trade Union Congress
UCD	University College Dublin
UDR	Ulster Defence Regiment
WTS	Wolfe Tone Society

Foreword

Over the past forty years Ireland has seen a phenomenal growth in the creation of summer schools. Merriman began in 1968, a celebration of the eighteenth century poem *The Midnight Court*. In 2008 the McCluskey Civil Rights Civil Rights Summer School was established. The contrast could not have been greater. The former has a somewhat Rabelaisian feel about it, fun-loving, self confident and sophisticated. The latter was a much more sombre affair coming on the back of an incipient little civil war in Northern Ireland. It was named after the founders of the Campaign for Social Justice (CSJ), Patricia and Conn Mc Cluskey, in 1964. One of the themes of the School was a reflection on the state of human rights in Ireland in the new millennium and particularly on the status of women, a debate that had been ongoing in the Republic of Ireland for many decades.

When the civil rights movement began in Northern Ireland in the late 1960s it was inconceivable that women's rights would be discussed. The slogans said it all: 'One *Man* One Vote'; One *Man* One Job, although the role of the family was acknowledged with 'One Family One House'. Indeed as the author of one of the earliest studies of the radical civil rights movement, *The People's Democracy*, I was (rightly) criticised for ignoring the part that had been played by many women activists – with the obvious exception of Bernadette Devlin. In a much more recent memoir, Austin Currie examines the origins of the civil rights movement with the creation of the Homeless Citizens League (HCL)[1] in 1963. Save for a mention of Patricia Mc Cluskey's position as Chair*man* of the HCL the innocent reader would not realise that the HCL was an organisation founded and led by ordinary working class women.

The roles of the HCL and CSJ – and many other like-minded organisations – are analysed, dissected and celebrated in Tara Keenan-Thomson's fascinating multi-layered study of the origins of the second wave of feminism by examining island-wide and transnational activist trends and overlapping networks of nation, class and gender. She attempts to explain the shift from first-wave feminism (concerned with attempting to enter into the political system to establish equal citizenship) to second-wave feminism (interested in radically changing society through a renegotiation of gender roles) in the critical years 1956 to 1973.

The dates are important because it includes the period from 1956 up to the mid 1960s that belongs to the history of the hidden Ireland, largely ignored save for the IRA's failed campaign; and as the somnambulant interlude before the dark of communal conflict descended on Northern Ireland and spread its wings into other corners of Britain and Ireland. Equally it concludes in 1973 by which time the political boundaries in Ireland had been staunched by violence and both the UK and Ireland were coordinate members of the EEC.

Multi-layeredness produces a mosaic of contradictory trends, of uneven levels of development, and of competing aspirations in a book that is necessarily culturally specific when set against general international trends. It is not that the history of feminism in Ireland is *sui generis* – after all the author quotes Juliet Mitchell's 1966 observation that British experience demonstrated that the subordination of women had become a 'subsidiary, if not an invisible element in the preoccupations of socialists'. And that view was reinforced in 1980 by that doughty class warrior of the Communist Party of Northern Ireland (CPNI), Betty Sinclair, who resorted to Lenin, no less, that women's equality 'can only be solved on the basis of class struggle ... Feminism is not a working class outlook'.

A later generation might have been expected to challenge that iron law but as Keenan-Thomson demonstrates prominent individuals such as Máirín de Burca had to struggle to find a place for a feminist agenda in official republicanism; and groups like the courageous HCL in Dungannon had to subordinate their female working class background to allow for male-centred middle class interests to present a political alternative to the status quo. Even the emblematic Bernadette Devlin is defined in this study by the ethno-sectarian conflict that produced her:

> She could never hold a place among the emergent international second-wave feminist leaders of the period because she was limited by her politics to working for change within the traditional male-oriented framework of Northern Irish political expression'... But that is not to demean her contribution because 'she provided a crucial link between social/political conservatism and the tentative articulation of feminist goals that would emerge in the groups that proliferated after this germination period ....

Essentially this book is about establishing that link. It is less concerned with personality and more with general trends spreading from the aspirational nature of Art. 119 of the Treaty of Rome (1957) on women's position in employment through to the connection between women's issues, journalism and activism that created a space for the emergence of second-wave feminism in the Republic of Ireland. It is about putting this in its Irish context 'where nationalism is a key context of *difference* in the women's movement'. It is about understanding the nature of feminist history which, as Joan Wallach Scott argues is not simply 'recounting great deeds performed by women' but that it entails 'the exposure of the often silent and hidden operations of gender that are nonetheless present and defining forces in the organisation of most societies'.

That is one of the great services that Tara Keenan-Thomson delivers in this book. She rescues the parts played by many ordinary women operating in extraordinary circumstances and gives them their place in history – women like Angela McCrystal, Susan Dinsmore and Ann Dunlop from the HCL. She explains the difficulties in developing a women-centred political consciousness, she traces the emergence of the tyranny of structurelessness, of the rise of women's anti-state activism and of their use of the myth of innocence. In short this is a brilliant contextualisation of the appearance of the second-wave of feminism against particularly difficult occurrences.

Her conclusion that the emergence of a culture of street politics in Northern Ireland contrasts with the rise of a feminist lobby in the Republic set in a European integration context encapsulates the complexity of an incredibly detailed and subtle commentary built on considerable ingenuity and originality. All of this she explains in a highly accessible style and in a research output that spans the spectrum from archival searches and highly revealing interviews with many of the key players, through to social movement analysis and to media studies.

Tara Keenan-Thomson asserts that Irish women's history is still in a process of recovery. This is a hugely significant contribution to that recovery. While it acknowledges that the time scale of the research does not allow for an examination of the part played by Protestant working class women in Northern Ireland (their political consciousness developed in later years), nevertheless it belongs to the mainstream of contemporary Irish historiography, to the study of the Northern Ireland conflict and its overflow and to international feminist studies. It deserves to be read by practitioners and academics alike because it is a work of advocacy that maintains the highest scholarly standards.

Paul Arthur
18 January 2010

NOTE

1. Austin Currie, *All Hell Will Break Loose* (Dublin: The O'Brien Press, 2004)

Introduction

In the period between 1956 and 1973 the island of Ireland underwent a rapid, if uneven, transformation in its gender regime. On both sides of the border a women's activist agenda emerged that was inextricably linked to each region's historical and political development. One factor that profoundly influenced these changes was the development of new types of radical street politics characterized by public protest, confrontational pressure tactics and a comprehensive critique of the status quo. This particular brand of advocacy attracted a diverse assemblage of activists attempting to restructure the state using a variety of means to achieve a variety of goals. These activists, from feminists to republicans to civil rights campaigners, shared a common tactic: the use of street politics to effect political change. This type of extra-parliamentary activity proliferated during the period and served to forge links between hitherto disjointed movements. This is not to imply that all extra-parliamentary political groups got swept up in the new momentum; women's groups such as the Irish Housewives Association and the Irish Countrywomen's Association, unionists as well as loyalists eschewed this emerging political discourse because they did not seek such comprehensive structural changes. This book, however, will tell the story of some of those who did.

Though women who participated in radical politics in the 1950s did not call for the re-evaluation of women's roles within their own groups, their work as domestic and supporting activists provided a strong sense of continuity during a difficult period for radical politics in Ireland. By the late 1960s the proliferation of radical groups and the media coverage about those groups pushed the boundaries of Irish discourse towards breaking social taboos by embracing heretofore unspoken topics such as family breakdown, reproductive rights and equality in the workplace. This contributed to the redefinition of women's roles in Irish society. This book traces the development of a women's activist agenda in both parts of Ireland, from their participation in radical anti-state

Leabharlanna Fhine Gall

action in the 1950s to their increased involvement in republicanism
and street politics in the early 1970s. Specifically, it will consider how
the changing roles of women within radical politics contributed towards redefining gender roles throughout Irish society.

The relevant research indicates that women did indeed experience
significant changes in their roles throughout this period and more recent and comprehensive histories have sought to integrate that aspect
of the Irish experience with varying amounts of success into the Irish
historical narrative.[1] Beale and Hill have documented changes in familial and social roles; Trewsdale and Daly have explored changes in
the labour market; Gardiner, Galligan and Wilford have looked at
women's changing attitudes towards political activity; and Eileen Connolly has traced a transformation in public policy and how that impacted on redefining the Irish gender regime.[2] Linda Connolly and
Rosemary Cullen Owens have documented the feminist movement in
the Republic during this period in their studies of the continuities between first-wave and second-wave feminism and the social history of
women in Ireland, respectively.[3] These studies have provided substantial background material for this book, which seeks to broaden the
scope of discourse on the transformation of social roles by looking at
how radical political activism and specifically street politics have contributed to the mainstreaming of those changes. Historians of the
1960s outside Ireland have shown how radical activist networks have
worked to create a climate for the renegotiation of gender roles in
wider society.[4] Ireland, however, has escaped such analysis.

Linda Connolly and Tina O'Toole point out that there is a paucity
of research on socialist politics in this period as it relates to feminism.[5]
There is also little on the convergence of the tactics employed by these
networks and on how this convergence helped set the stage for a
reimagining of gender roles. Historical treatments of Irish republicanism have also lacked any significant analysis of women's changing
roles.[6] Though most recently Richard English and Ed Maloney have
widened the narrative to include an account of women's roles, none of
these histories have attempted to grapple with how gender relations
have contributed to defining the republican movement and its power
structures. This book addresses how these sex/gender roles have
changed over time throughout the radical political milieu and how
these groups have contributed to the formation of a new social contract
within mainstream society. It must be pointed out, however, that their
tactics, successes and failures are only a chapter in the story of how
women's roles have changed throughout recent history in Ireland. This

book is meant to supplement the stories told by the writers mentioned above in order to create a more comprehensive picture of social change in Irish society during this period.

This study focuses primarily on how power structures governing gender relations have operated from the time of the Republican border campaign in the 1950s through the civil rights movement in Northern Ireland. Robert Connell and Sylvia Walby use the concept of the 'gender regime' to describe the interactions of multiple systems of inequalities (e.g., social systemic, domestic, public, economic, political, civil) that rule social relations.[7] I will chart the evolution of Irish gender regimes within a variety of radical groups active in this period, ranging from feminists to republicans to left-wing campaigners. These structures, or set of relations that buttress how people function within a group or society at any given time, provide a framework for the examination of the transformations of women's roles in the radical political milieu and how that transformation eventually impacted on Irish society at large. Specifically, I will look at a variety of factors that have contributed to the overall structure of gender regimes throughout Irish society. By examining gender relations and the social rules that inform their construction in the domestic sphere, the workforce and the public and political/legislative spheres (including the formal and informal political arena), this study will tease out how women's activism in radical politics began to challenge prevailing notions of normative gender relations throughout Irish society. In discussing changes to Irish gender regimes, it is necessary to comprehensively lay out both the factors that have comprised the prevailing gender regimes as well as the benchmarks against which change is measured. Consequently, gender regimes in 1950s Ireland must be located in a postwar European and post-partition context, as discussed in Chapter 1.

One of the most pronounced changes to the gender regime in 1950s Ireland took place within the domestic sphere. Until this period the power structures of rural Ireland's gender regime had remained relatively static and organized along traditional familial roles, with the woman running the home and its environs and the man working the farm. Communal in structure, the rural economic system was characterized by visits to market, the sharing of farm equipment and informal bartering to supplement familial income. Catriona Clear demonstrates that by this time women's roles had increasingly become more isolated as farming technology advanced and their activities transitioned from communal labour structures to domestic managerial duties.[8] Mary E. Daly, in discussing the collapse of the rural demographic system, points out that women flooded into urban centres or emigrated in response to the constant hard work, isolation and lack of basic amenities that characterized life on the farm.[9] In this period, within the cities and towns, traditional gender regimes began to buckle under the weight of women's increasing role in the workforce and rising levels of emigration.

Changes in the domestic sphere bore a close relationship to changes in the workforce in the 1950s. In the Republic women faced impediments to achieving equality due to policies such as the marriage bar and unequal pay legislation. Among the Catholic community of Northern Ireland, workplace gender regimes had similar structures to those in the Republic, but these inequalities were compounded by chronic male unemployment and the effective segregation of the workforce.

Much of these inequalities in the workplace gender regime began to change due to state-led initiatives and European integration legislation. For example, policies such as the public sector marriage bar began to outlive their economic purpose, especially in professions such as teaching and nursing, where staffing crises plagued schools and hospitals. As the 1950s drew to a close these types of shortages left policy makers in the Republic with little choice but to rethink the constitution's endorsement of a woman's place in the home. During this period European integration measures such as the Treaty of Rome likewise forced legislators on both sides of the border to begin the process of abandoning unequal pay policies.

As Ireland began to modernize in the 1960s, the gender regime in the public sphere began to change as well. Consumer culture mushroomed and combined with women's increasing engagement in formal and informal politics, television and film to allow for a reimagining of womanhood. A combination of greater educational attainment among Irish women and a proliferating international and radical media presence in Ireland encouraged an increasingly vocal cohort of women to locate domestic and workplace gender regimes in an international context (see Chapter 3). Cast in this light policies such as the marriage bar and restrictive fertility control laws grew increasingly anomalous. The debates surrounding these issues led to a change in the public sphere's gender regime to include a more prominent role for women in politics, and indeed in Irish society at large, than had been the norm in the 1940s and 1950s.

These factors set the stage for a comprehensive re-evaluation of the gender regime throughout the domestic sphere, the workplace and the public and political/legislative spheres in Irish society. By utilizing the

1950s as a benchmark to begin the analysis of gender regime changes, this book charts a dynamic re-evaluation of women and their varied roles in Irish life by radical activists and then by Irish society as a whole.

I will use the word *radical* to describe those who utilized street politics to push for a comprehensive restructuring of the state. These feminists, left-wing activists, civil rights campaigners and republicans sought to exert pressure on the establishment from outside the political structure and they employed a variety of tactics from staging marches and sit-ins to pickets. None of these tactics were new, however. The Ulster Women's Unionist Council was out canvassing against home rule in 1911, Cumann na mBan took part in 1916, and the women of Springtown had taken over Derry's Guildhall as recently as 1959. The period of this inquiry is significant then, not due to any ground-breaking tactics these radical groups employed but rather because of an overlapping pattern of island-wide and international networks that allowed activists to share information and innovative ideas. These movements proliferated throughout the world in the 1960s and utilized shared modes of advocacy to gain ground quickly. Like the overlapping networks active throughout the independence movement – populated by women such as Charlotte Despard, Maud Gonne, Countess Markiewicz and Hannah Sheehy-Skeffington – the groups in this study represent a second wave of a kind of activism that was at once indicative of an international momentum and at the same time uniquely Irish.

Amitai Etzioni argues that radical protest ensues when people perceive that a 'lack of responsiveness on the part of the current leadership is not accidental but endemic to the system'. He argues: 'it reflects the monopolization of resources by the privileged classes and the control of the society by a small power elite'. For the radical, that responsiveness could only be achieved when this system is uprooted following a revolution or at least a fundamental redistribution of resources.[10] It is necessary to maintain an awareness that the groups in this study represent the fringes of political thought and not the mainstream; the goal is to find out how these radical groups, and specifically the women in these networks of street activists, influenced and, in some cases, transformed mainstream politics and gender regimes in Ireland.

This book charts the emergence among women street activists of what Guida West and Rhoda Lois Blumberg call a women-centred consciousness, or a sensitivity of the multiple types of oppression experienced by women in mixed-sex organizations.[11] This consciousness is an awakening to the material reality of the gender regime. Under some circumstances that consciousness develops into a feminist consciousness, which offers solutions and alternatives to the prevailing sex/gender-based hierarchies. Like the word *radical* the term *feminist* can have multiple meanings. Gerda Lerner describes a feminist consciousness as an awareness that women

> belong to a subordinate group; that they have suffered wrongs as a group; that their condition of subordination is not natural, but is societally determined; that they must join with other women to remedy these wrongs; and finally that they must and can provide an alternative vision of societal organization in which women as well as men will enjoy autonomy and self-determination.[12]

In the Republic this consciousness was a direct result of decades of institutionalized inequalities, consciousness-raising, advocacy and, in some instances, progressive legislation. Indeed, Catriona Clear makes a convincing case that Irish women fared better than many of their European counterparts in terms of their access to the parliamentary vote, certain professions and political career choices.[13] I argue that in the period of this study a feminist consciousness evolved out of a combination of the Republic's piecemeal approach to equality legislation and the proliferation of pressure groups and radical activism.

Northern Ireland followed a different trajectory. As in the Republic, women possessed a similar lexicon of Independence-era role models, but since Partition the region's development had diverged from its neighbour to the south. By the 1950s segregation along sectarian lines had grown entrenched and institutionalized discrimination (real and perceived) infused public and private spheres with a unique experience (see Chapter 1). This book demonstrates how women organized from 1956 to 1973 to take stock of that. Women's increased participation in republicanism and street politics in the 1960s was a direct result of this sectarianism and community division. Though this participation was influenced by the rise of civil rights activism and international student movements, it was inextricably linked to the germination of tribalism and the political conflict that ensued. A feminist consciousness, as Lerner defines it, did not thrive in such a tumultuous environment but, as explored in this book, the gender regimes of a significant amount of political groupings were none the less transformed by the influx of women into these radical street movements by the early 1970s.

By looking at the period between the first wave of western feminist activism, which focused on equal citizenship rights, such as women's suffrage, for example, and the second wave of western feminist activism, which focused on a combination of equal citizenship rights as well as psychoanalysis, sexuality and gender differences, this study traces the development of second-wave feminism in Ireland. The work of what Linda Connolly calls 'abeyance' organizations during the early part of this study, in activities such as lobbying for a Commission on the Status of Women, set the stage for a more comprehensive critique of the gender regime by demonstrating that a core group of women were still committed to obtaining equal citizenship legislation and that the government was also willing (however reluctantly) to rethink its position on some aspects of women-as-mothers.[14] It was these groups, Galligan and later Connolly argue, because of their activity between the first and second waves of feminism, that built the foundation upon which much of the second wave of Irish feminism could stand.[15] A key argument I make is that there is no one recipe to follow or time line to which to adhere that results in a feminist consciousness taking root in a society or activist group, that consciousness does develop in very different manners depending on a country's geopolitical, social, cultural and economic trajectory. Therefore I will avoid terms that retain an implicit sense of time line or linear progression, like 'pre-feminist' and 'post-feminist', etc.

The favoured terminology of this study is a complicated matter; I am aware that all descriptive terms of the two regions convey certain political undertones. Generally, I have used the term *Northern Ireland* and the *Republic of Ireland* or the *Republic* for the sake of expediency, and *North* and *South* for the same reason. I have made an effort to use the term *Ireland* when discussing issues that could be applied to communities on both sides of the border. Similar issues come up when one uses words like *Catholic* and *Protestant* or *republican* and *loyalist* to describe different groups. When discussing members of the Nationalist or Unionist parties I use a capital letter, whereas when describing a general school of thought I use lower-case.

So while we pare down the language, we must widen the scope. It is necessary to look beyond geographic boundaries and narrow time frames in order to expose the factors that influenced the formation of these groups. On the spectrum of historical, political and sociological studies of women and second-wave feminism, most of the work done to date deals with only one of the Irish states, with muted reference to the fact that strong cultural, political, social and religious connections crossed borders and impacted on the development of the activist movements of the period.[16] While this approach makes for a straightforward study, Connolly in her study of second-wave feminism in the Republic cites Kearney to acknowledge that 'Although feminism as theory and activism sprang from within Irish society in distinctive shape and form, it is organically an element of a movement that is global and moves across national borders.'[17] Some studies of second-wave feminism in Ireland have attempted to look at both parts of Ireland,[18] but Connolly and O'Toole are careful to highlight the need for a more comprehensive study like this one, unwieldy as it may be.[19] In terms of the time frame, this study begins before the main surge of radicalism that took place in the late 1960s. By beginning a decade earlier, I will trace the emergence of a re-evaluation of women's activities in republicanism and in radical activism, in general. The 1950s provides a backdrop to examine social change and to evaluate the types of gender roles that women of the late 1960s and early 1970s questioned.

There are very few examples of studies that attempt to connect radical networks of this period on an island-wide basis to show how they converged to influence political and popular discourse by the late 1960s. The overlapping membership between groups throughout the island and the networks that grew out of these memberships can go some distance towards explaining how a progressive notion of women's participation in street politics was advanced relatively quickly and without a significant amount of resistance from some of the groups in which they operated. This problematizes the cliché about Irish society's highly developed patriarchy, though it does not dispute that a level of patriarchy did exist within each group and throughout Irish society. As Linda Edgerton and Lorraine Dowler demonstrate, Irish women held a special position as strong leaders within the domestic sphere, which gave them a degree of latitude in entering the public sphere as street activists.[20] Accordingly, this study demonstrates that activists, security forces and members of the administration in both parts of Ireland generally perceived Irish women to be political innocents who were unlikely to bring their activism to significant fruition. A pivotal argument of this study is that this perceived political innocence among Irish women temporarily pre-empted calls for a feminist movement, especially in a period of rapidly deteriorating communal relations. Women could assume roles equal to their male counterparts more easily because of gendered security tactics, such as internment, which was initially adopted for men only. This revitalized women's special position within a significant portion of Northern Irish society and eventually led to the birth of an equality agenda without the feminist discourse that would emerge later in response to years of internment, strip searches and hunger strikes. Second-wave feminism gained a foothold in a much more stable Irish Republic, and even there it was rapidly subsumed by the overarching prerogatives of republican politics.

Some of the scholarly research on women in this period has looked at the development of second-wave feminism in Ireland as a manifestation of an international phenomenon or a product of external influences.[21] While international feminism and civil rights agitation was indeed profoundly significant to Irish activism, modernization, the growth of a secular discursive field, local political developments and other specifically *Irish* factors all helped to shape second-wave feminism as it evolved in Ireland. The abeyance feminist groups' dogged attempts at promoting an equality agenda in the lean years between the two waves of feminism certainly primed the political elite for what was to come.[22] The Republic's experience of gender regime transformation came about initially through the legislative reform of marriage and family law utilizing pieces of legislation such as the Married Women's Status Act and the Succession Act. Similar to other European countries, these reforms sought to re-evaluate women's position within the social fabric of the country. Eileen Connolly makes the point that these changes may have created the space for women to assert themselves to agitate for further changes to the gender regime.[23]

In her study of European feminism, Joni Lovenduski concludes that first-wave and second-wave feminist movements were influenced by international trends, but that they were culturally specific.[24] Similarly, Margaret L. Inglehart's research on European women and political participation suggests that women's interest levels depend largely on their national history.[25] This study seeks to build on this idea by looking at the nature of Irish women's roles in street politics. I will examine the relationship between feminism and radical politics by focusing in on Irish republicanism, the emergence of the New Left in Ireland, and the proliferation of the civil rights movement in Northern Ireland. A major question I will be asking is how radical politics encouraged women to redefine themselves in the late 1960s and early 1970s in Ireland. If each country's experience of the transformation of women's roles was a product of both international influence and its own historical development, then what happened in Ireland in the late 1960s must be viewed in the context of the national question, which played a significant part in political discourse in both parts of Ireland, as well as the political activism and legislative reform that also took place during this period.

This book demonstrates that due to the contested questions of Partition and citizenship in this region, one cannot evaluate the changes in women's roles by simply applying 'one size fits all' theories of international activism to Ireland. It deals specifically with republicanism, radicalism and street activism in an attempt to widen the prevailing account of the development of women's agendas in these two regions. The discussion on Northern activism is limited to the Catholic population (with obvious exceptions among the civil rights community), because Protestant women did not engage in street activism in significant numbers until 1974; more research into this area is necessary in order to begin to explore this equally significant history of activism that began in earnest with the Loyalist workers' strike that year.[26] It was at this point that paramilitarism had subsumed much of street activism on both sides of the border and old political paradigms had succumbed to the binaries of sectarianism.

By 1974 the nature of street activism had changed in vastly different ways on both sides of the border. The South experienced a phase of proliferation and diversification of service-oriented advocacy groups such as AIM, Cherish, Adapt and the Rape Crisis Centre, to name but a few. Some groups remained engaged in street politics. Irish Women United continued to break social taboos through imaginative protests such as invading a male-only swimming area. The Contraception Action Programme brought education and services to communities in need by establishing a mobile unit that visited suburbs and rural areas. All of these groups belong to a vibrant phase of the Irish feminist movement that warrants its own study. This study does not focus on the Northern Ireland Women's Rights Movement, established in 1975, the Peace People in 1976, and the Relatives Action Committee that same year. More groups were to follow in quick succession – the Socialist Women's Group and Women Against Imperialism, etc. In the North, political discourse had changed dramatically, with the Loyalist workers' strike and the increase in paramilitarism and sectarianism in both communities. Accounting for this dramatic shift in political discourse would mean pushing the parameters of this study too far from its original intent. This book is meant to continue the process of recovering the origins of this second wave by looking at island-wide and transnational activist trends and overlapping networks up to the early period of the Troubles. I focus in on the formation of a women-centred consciousness, the process of awakening to one's segregated and subordinated position within a gendered society. The women in this study generally identified themselves as Irish, sought to destabilize or revolutionize the state, and came from a left-leaning nationalist or republican tradition. I anticipate the sea change in political expression that took place after 1973 but cannot chronicle it as well. The period from 1974 forwards, with its entirely transformed set of political developments functioning as a backdrop to a revolutionized concept of street activism, demands its own analysis and thus lies outside the scope of this present project.

Echoing the Greek sceptics, Dale Spender, in her discussion of feminist research, comments that 'there is no one truth, no one authority, no one objective method which leads to the production of pure knowledge'.[27] What one can construct is a narrative that contributes to the creation of an overall history – one that may challenge or confirm prevailing notions of the past. Historians strive to tap source material from archives and publications that may inform and focus their perspective on their subject. They are trained to read the sources and let them determine how their narrative progresses. Out of this process grows an argument or conclusion, which goes back to Spender – there is no one authority. The aspiration for many a researcher is the ability to spark debate and to engage multiple 'authorities', after which the historian hopes to arrive at a better understanding and portrayal of the period in question.

Archival research underpins the work of most empirical historians, and this history is no different. But the adversarial nature of the relationship between street activists in this study and the authorities has necessitated a study of both governmental records and activist groups' records. In order to assess the contribution of women to republicanism, radicalism and street politics in Ireland, I have spent significant periods at the following archives and libraries: Derry City Council Archives; Linen Hall Library's Political Collection; Morris Library's Archives Department at the University of Delaware; National Archives and Records Administration in the United States; National Archives in England; National Archives of Ireland; New York Public Library; Public Records Office of Northern Ireland; University College Cork Archives. At these archives I have studied key categories of records in order to track the development of each of the relevant governments' attitudes towards women as political activists. Britain's National Archives has proved to be the most rich in this respect. The National Archives of Ireland has been helpful in elucidating the perspective of the governing elite, but the dearth of the files available on this subject has been disappointing. American diplomatic reports have presented a valuable third perspective of the main personalities and radical groupings during the period. I have also looked at papers that some of the activist groups have deposited in these archives, to uncover evidence of their own experience with engaging authorities in street politics. What I have found in these archival records and collections has been critical to framing my interpretation of the transformation of women's roles in republicanism and street activism. The records available reveal the evolution of this relationship and how each group and set of authorities influenced the development of their counterparts.

However, there is a general paucity of archival sources dealing with women as actors in radical movements. This dearth of records is instructive in and of itself; it illustrates a general lack of consciousness or consideration of the subject of women's participation in street activism. Though I have made considerable use of the archival records available, this lack of consideration of women activists and indeed the lack of official papers of many of these groups (Official and Provisional republican groups, the People's Democracy and the Irish Women's Liberation Movement, to name a few) has given me the opportunity to widen the scope of my research methodology.

Contemporary press coverage of these personalities, groups and issues has contributed to a more comprehensive picture of the period. An advantage of utilizing press coverage to complement archival work on adversarial groups and movements is that it can offer another perspective on the event. The *Irish Echo*, stored at the New York Public Library, for example, has been critical to understanding how political splits and debates have or have not spilled over to the Irish emigrant community in the United States. A survey of the republican movement's own *United Irishman* (and later *An Phoblacht* and *Republican News*) between the years 1956 and 1973 has been instructive; its focus on women's traditional roles and its conspicuous failure to cover feminism reveals the publication's complicated relationship with certain aspects of women's changing roles, even in the face of increasing egalitarianism within the movement itself. Of course, researchers must always be conscious of an editorial agenda that might underpin coverage of these issues. They must also acknowledge the subjectivity of this type of source when drawing conclusions or constructing arguments. Other such sources are the semi-structured interview and living memory source material, which can be used to supplement a rigorous analysis of the available documentary evidence.

Shulamit Reinharz makes the point that engaging with living memory 'is invaluable for historians who seek information unlikely to be contained in written records. To the extent that men's lives are more likely to produce written documentation, men are more likely to be the subject of analysis by historians who use archival data.' In this way, engaging with living memory 'is useful for getting information about *people* less likely to be engaged in creating written records and for creating historical accounts of *phenomena* less likely to have produced archival material'.[28] Reinharz cautions her readers, however, that the researcher's interpretive perspective can impact on the transmission of the historical experience.[29] Paul Thompson agrees, raising other questions about authenticity, subjectivity, emphasis, and changes in political perspective over time.[30] Because of this, it is important to properly interrogate interviews and corroborate as much as possible.

Living memory documents, including personal interviews, correspondence and witness statements, have helped augment the research for this study. In all, I have examined and compiled twenty-two such documents from members of various movements across the Irish political spectrum. For this aspect of the research I chose to spend most of my time with less-documented political leaders who could offer different insights into the germination of these groups. While this study certainly charts the work of the most prominent leaders, those who have written on their experiences and who have been quoted extensively in the media already have a body of work to offer on the subject. The purpose of these interviews was less about present-day glosses on past events as it was about uncovering a variety of contributions to the story of the development of these groups. Still, this method of inquiry was not without its challenges. Rachel Ward, in her important study of unionism and loyalism in Northern Ireland, discusses the difficulties in gaining access to closed communities through 'gatekeepers'.[31] I experienced similar difficulties in some instances. Thus, this study was certainly augmented by the living memory documents derived from interviewees who, for the most part, were more than generous with their time and insight. But while interviews can lend a richness and depth to a document-based study, I treated them as a supplement to the existing work, not as the basis for this historical inquiry.

In Chapter 1 the scene is set for an examination of women in radical politics in the late 1960s, by documenting their activism in both parts of Ireland a decade earlier. It locates Ireland and Irish women within the context of postwar Europe and America and teases out the political activity in which women engaged, from mainstream activity such as lobbying for the Irish Housewives Association, to joining radical groups such as the republican movement and the Communist Party.

The analysis of the activity women did do within the private sphere to support the family's radical political activity challenges prevailing notions among these women that their own work was not as significant to the movement as their male counterparts' work. Taking stock of European trends in the 1950s, this chapter demonstrates that in contrast to much of the scholarly research on women's activism, Irish women in this period did not develop a women-centred consciousness. However, they emerged from this period with a more egalitarian point of view; to them, their work was simply an extension of their role as mothers, wives and women involved in agitating for radical political change.

Chapter 2 looks at women in housing agitation and civil rights activism in Northern Ireland during a period of republican restructuring. It presents an example of radical activism within the nationalist community that did not evolve into anti-state activity, but rather became a group of Catholic citizens of Northern Ireland seeking their rights as citizens. It documents the development of this early rights-based activism by focusing on the Homeless Citizens League and the Campaign for Social Justice. The chapter tells the story of a working-class, women-led protest movement whose members defied the traditional notions of femininity and political inertia dominant within the nationalist community in order to engage in civil disobedience. It also documents how this movement was co-opted by a middle-class, mixed-sex reform group with connections to a socially conservative group of Irish Americans as soon as its initial demands were met by the Northern Irish government. The main argument of this chapter focuses on the gendered nature of both groups and how they utilized a myth of women's political innocence to articulate a comprehensive critique of the prevailing institutionalized discrimination against the Catholic population in Northern Ireland. The chapter also documents a lack of any developed women-centred consciousness emerging from this experience and proposes that the evolution of this kind of awareness required a different coalescence of experience.

Chapter 3 analyzes an emerging radical press to chart how new ideas concerning the gender regime and the proliferation of social movements were portrayed. During this period the republican movement shifted towards left-wing political activity in order to attract a more diverse membership. A main argument of this chapter is that the republican movement in both parts of Ireland and America, despite some high-profile female activists, failed to address the changing role of women by not restructuring its women's section and by not taking on the issue in its newspapers. By failing to do so, it lost an opportunity to broaden its base to include women and Protestants concerned about the Republic's legislation against birth control. This chapter also traces the growth of women's magazines, student magazines and the women's page of the *Irish Times*, demonstrating women's frustration with slow-to-reform social legislation regarding contraception, equal pay and housing. The chapter's main argument is that a women-centred consciousness began to emerge through a non-republican radical press that brought international ideas and causes into Ireland from abroad, but also tailored them to fit an Irish paradigm.

Chapter 4 examines how women's increasing role in parliamentary and street politics at the advent of the civil rights movement constituted a surge in activity, but did not lend itself to a call for the restructuring of the gender regime in Northern Ireland. It argues that feminist concerns rarely even made it on to the radar of civil rights groups due to growing violence and state repression of rights-based political activity. This movement, though strongly influenced by the growing republican movement, presented an alternative to it and an outlet for women to ascend to powerful positions. The chapter also focuses on the rise to prominence of Bernadette Devlin, presenting her as a problematic icon of feminist politics. While she easily weaved internationalist left-wing rhetoric into a damning critique of the state, she pointedly refused to integrate feminist concerns into her speeches anywhere but in America in this period. This chapter charts her tour of America in the aftermath of the battle of the Bogside and her willingness to engage with race relations and later feminism in order to expose Irish America's social conservatism. This chapter argues that women's rapid integration into active street politics once again forestalled the emergence of a women-centred consciousness. Though this does not surface, the emergence of women's dual roles as activists in both the domestic sphere and the public sphere sets the stage for a re-evaluation of the gender regime by the Northern Ireland Women's Rights Movement and other groups.

Chapter 5 examines the Irish Women's Liberation Movement in the Republic of Ireland and the ways in which it challenged the prevailing gender regime. Though the state was well on its way towards ushering in significant equality legislation due to impending European integration, this movement, pioneered by seasoned political organizers and journalists, burst on to a scene that had already been ripened by the drumbeat among the radical press for Irish feminism to take root in the Republic. This chapter charts how international movements as well as domestic events factored into its development and eventual demise. By looking at how the persistence of women such as Máirín de Burca forced the official republican movement to reluctantly embrace a feminist analysis, it charts how a critique of the gender regime was beginning to make its way into a comprehensive left-wing understanding of systemic oppression in Ireland. The chapter also argues that the short-lived nature of a movement that sky-rocketed to fame only to diverge into issue-oriented offshoots just as quickly, accomplished its goal of breaking the final taboos in establishing a women-centred consciousness and ultimately a feminist outlook. It also argues that by doing so and giving way to offshoots like Women's Aid, Cherish, AIM and the Dublin Rape Crisis Centre, the movement remained vibrant and accomplished more than the founders of the group anticipated.

Chapter 6 argues that for women in the Catholic community in Northern Ireland, the first few years of the 1970s saw a renegotiation of the gender regime in ways that were heavily informed by their experience of the unfolding conflict in Northern Ireland. The transition undertaken by women to challenge the gender regime within both strands of republicanism, Official and Provisional, coincided with the advent of second-wave feminism, yet, at the time, it was rarely couched in feminist rhetoric. It argues that in joining the IRA as full members instead of the auxiliary Cumann na mBan, women were beginning to express (but not verbalize) a dissatisfaction with the limits of traditional roles. Had it been a less chaotic period, there may have been more resistance to the integration of women, which may in turn, have forced women to begin to articulate feminist demands within the movement. A main argument of this chapter is that initially women were able to manipulate the tacit acceptance among security forces of their political innocence to serve the movement, but by entering into the paramilitary paradigm women eroded that unique status. Likewise, by introducing gendered tactics such as the internment of men and imposing the Falls Road Curfew, the state ironically worked in conjunction with republicans to ensure an increasing number of women were no longer content to serve as auxiliaries. The chapter concludes by making the point that a women-centred consciousness does not emerge, but that this activity set the stage for it to do so as the conflict wore on and strip searches, no-wash protests and relatives action committee demonstrations became the order of the day.

This book sheds light on the development of women's street activism in both parts of Ireland by tracing how their political activity on the margins worked alongside parliamentary initiatives, international trends and domestic sociopolitical activities to encourage challenges to the gender regime within the activist paradigm and set the stage for Irish society to engage with second-wave feminism.

NOTES

1. D. Ferriter, *The Transformation of Ireland, 1900–2000* (London: Profile, 2004); A. Jackson, *Ireland 1798–1998* (London: Basil Blackwell, 1999); D. Keogh, *Twentieth-Century Ireland: Nation and State* (Dublin: Gill & Macmillan, 1994).
2. J. Beale, *Women in Ireland: Voices of Change* (Indiana: Indiana University Press, 1987); E. Connolly, 'The State, Public Policy and Gender: Ireland in Transition, 1957–1977' (Dublin City University, Ph.D. thesis, 1998); E. Connolly, 'Durability and Change in State Gender Systems', *European Journal of Women's Studies*, 10 (2003); M.E. Daly, 'Women in the Irish Workforce from Pre-Industrial to Modern Times', *Saothar*, 7 (1982); Y. Galligan, *Women and Politics in Contemporary Ireland: From the Margins to the Mainstream* (London: Pinter, 1998); F. Gardiner, 'Political Interest and Participation of Irish Women, 1922–1992: The Unfinished Revolution', *Canadian Journal of Irish Studies*, 18 (1992); M. Hill, *Women in Ireland: A Century of Change* (Belfast: Blackstaff Press, 2003); J.M. Trewsdale 'The Role of Women in the Northern Ireland Economy', in R.J. Cormack and R.D. Osborne (eds), *Religion, Education and Employment: Aspects of Equal Opportunity in Northern Ireland* (Belfast: Appletree Press, 1983); J.M. Trewsdale and M. Trainor, 'Womanpower: A Statistical Survey of Women and Work in Northern Ireland' (Belfast: Equal Opportunities Commission for Northern Ireland, 1979); R. Wilford, 'Women and Politics in Northern Ireland', in J. Lovenduski and P. Norris (eds), *Women and Politics* (Oxford: Oxford University Press, 1996).
3. L. Connolly, *The Irish Women's Movement: From Revolution to Devolution* (New York: Lilliput Press, 2002); R.C. Owens, *A Social History of Women in Ireland: 1870–1970* (Dublin: Gill & Macmillan, 2005).
4. D. Bouchier, *The Feminist Challenge: The Movement for Women's Liberation in Britain and the USA* (London: Macmillan, 1983); A. Coote and B. Campbell, *Sweet Freedom: The Struggle for Women's Liberation* (Oxford: Basil Blackwell, 1987); S. Evans, *Personal Politics: The Roots of Women's Liberation in the Civil Rights Movement and the New Left* (New York: Vintage, 1979).
5. L. Connolly and T. O'Toole, *Documenting Irish Feminisms* (Dublin: Woodfield Press, 2005), p.198.
6. J.B. Bell, *The Secret Army: The IRA, 1916–1979* (Dublin: Poolbeg, 1990); T.P. Coogan, *The IRA* (London: Harper Collins, 2000); R. English, *Armed Struggle: The History of the IRA* (London: Macmillan, 2003); E. Maloney, *A Secret History of the IRA* (London: Allen Lane, 2002); P. Bishop and E. Mallie, *The Provisional IRA* (London: Heinemann, 1987); P. Taylor, *Provos: The IRA and Sinn Féin* (London: Bloomsbury, 1997).
7. For recent accounts see R. Connell, *Gender* (Cambridge: Polity Press, 2002); S. Walby, 'The European Union and Gender Equality: Emergent Varieties of Gender Regime', *Social Politics*, 11, 1 (2004), pp.4–29.
8. C. Clear, *Women of the House: Women's Household Work in Ireland: 1922–1961* (Dublin: Irish Academic Press, 2000), pp.5–6.
9. Daly, 'Women in the Irish Workforce from Pre-Industrial to Modern Times'.
10. A. Etzioni, *Demonstration Democracy: A Policy Paper Prepared for the Task Force on Demonstrations, Protests and Group Violence of the President's National Commission on the Causes and Prevention of Violence* (New York: Gordon & Breach, 1970), p.49.
11. G. West and R.L. Blumberg, 'Reconstructing Social Protest from a Feminist Perspective', in G. West and R.L. Blumberg (eds), *Women and Social Protest* (Oxford: Oxford University Press, 1990), p.20.
12. G. Lerner, *The Creation of a Feminist Consciousness* (Oxford: Oxford University Press, 1993), p.274.
13. Clear, *Women of the House*, pp.5–6.

14. Connolly, *Irish Women's Movement*, p.58.
15. Ibid., Galligan, *Women and Politics*.
16. B. Aretxaga, *Shattering Silence: Women, Nationalism and Political Subjectivity in Northern Ireland* (Princeton, NJ: Princeton University Press, 1997); Connolly, *Irish Women's Movement*; Galligan, *Women and Politics*; R. Ward, *Women, Unionism and Loyalism in Northern Ireland* (Dublin: Irish Academic Press, 2006).
17. Connolly, *Irish Women's Movement*, p.27; R. Kearney, *Postnationalist Ireland: Politics, Culture, Philosophy* (London: Routledge, 1997).
18. Connolly and O'Toole, *Documenting Irish Feminisms*; Y. Galligan, E. Ward and R. Wilford (eds), *Contesting Politics: Women in Ireland, North and South* (Oxford: Westview Press, 1999); Hill, *Women in Ireland*.
19. Connolly and O'Toole, *Documenting Irish Feminisms*, p.145.
20. L. Dowler, '"And they think I'm just a nice old lady": Women and War in Belfast, Northern Ireland', *Gender, Place and Culture*, 5 (1998); L. Edgerton, 'Public Protest, Domestic Acquiescence: Women in Northern Ireland', in R. Ridd and H. Calloway (eds), *Caught up in Conflict: Women's Responses to Political Strife* (Basingstoke: Macmillan Education in association with Oxford University Women's Studies Committee, 1986).
21. F. Gardiner, 'The Impact of EU Equality Legislation on Irish Women', in Y. Galligan, E. Ward and R. Wilford (eds), *Contesting Politics: Women in Ireland, North and South* (Oxford: Westview Press, 1999); E. Mahon, 'From Democracy to Femocracy: The Women's Movement in the Republic of Ireland', in P. Clancy, S. Drudy, K. Lynch and L. O'Dowd (eds), *Irish Society: Sociological Perspectives* (Dublin: Institute of Public Administration, 1995).
22. Connolly, *Irish Women's Movement*; Galligan, *Women and Politics*.
23. Connolly, 'State, Public Policy and Gender', p.4.
24. J. Lovenduski, *Women and European Politics: Contemporary Feminism and Public Policy* (Brighton: Wheatsheaf, 1986), p.6.
25. M. Inglehart, 'Political Interest in West European Women', *Comparative Political Studies*, 14 (1981), p.329.
26. Hill, *Women in Ireland*, p.174.
27. D. Spender, *For the Record: The Meaning and Making of Feminist Knowledge* (London: Woman's Press, 1985), pp.5–6.
28. S. Reinharz, *Feminist Methods in Social Research* (Oxford: Oxford University Press, 1992), p.131; italics the author's own.
29. Ibid., p.137.
30. P. Thompson, *The Voice of the Past: Oral History* (Oxford: Oxford University Press, 2000).
31. Ward, *Women, Unionism and Loyalism*, p.5.

Leabharlanna Fhine Gall

CHAPTER ONE

'Sure, I didn't do much':[1] Women, Republicanism and Radical Activism in the 1950s

We applaud women who want to redefine their role but we can't blame their position entirely on men. Some women don't want to leave the 'Doll's House'. It is little to our credit that our heroes are so little known. It is less to our credit that our heroines are hardly known at all. (Terence MacSwiney from *Principles of Freedom*, republished in the *United Irishman* in November 1962)

When one thinks of women participating in armed resistance or agitating for a radical change of the political structure, images of 1950s housewives do not normally come to mind. Indeed, one would be hard pressed to cite even one woman who took part in radical agitation in Ireland during the 1950s. Somehow, though, women began to engage in collective action and street politics in the 1960s. If, as Joni Lovenduski contends, each social movement is a product of both international influences *and* regional historical development, then we must scrutinize the political and social development of Ireland in the period leading up to the proliferation of street politics in the 1960s.[2] By locating this study in a European, Irish and gendered context, we can begin to explore how women's apparent invisibility in street politics and collective action in the 1950s gave way to a heightened level of political engagement among women in the 1960s and early 1970s.

POSTWAR EUROPE

Throughout the western world, the postwar period was characterized by the drive for stability above all else. Individual governments sought ways to ensure security for a bitterly divided continent. If former adversaries in Western Europe had difficulties mending relationships, they needed only to look to their eastern neighbours to convince themselves of the wisdom of broad alliances; the spectre of communism was growing taller as the days progressed. Due to the massive economic growth rate that initially accompanied communism, it was not until the 1960s that capitalism pulled ahead.[3] To insulate themselves against communist influence, individual states began to cobble themselves together in a broad security alliance aimed at 'keeping the Americans in, the Russians out, the Germans down and the French calm', according to a popular saying at the time.[4] The North Atlantic Treaty Organization, encompassing North American powers, Iceland and other European states was established for this purpose; old European divisions could be offset by its transcontinental membership. This alliance created room for a hugely significant European economic venture: the European Coal and Steel Community (ECSC). Linking the two main building blocks of the French and German economies in a mutually beneficial relationship, the goal was that this forerunner of the European Economic Community (EEC) would ensure peace between these long-time adversaries.

A third component in the drive against communism was the Anglo-American enforcement of a free-market system enshrined in the Bretton Woods Agreement, which emphasized uniformity at the expense of home-grown political and economic innovation. The order of the day was getting back to business and the most effective way to do this included enabling the most economically profitable structures to thrive. Taken altogether, the adoption of this triple-pronged strategy to rebuild Europe left the United States with a strong military and economic interest in seeing a nascent Western European free market succeed. Equally important was the idea of a European federation of states, which would one day be so inextricably linked that a declaration of war on another state would be tantamount to suicide.

By 1957 the scope of the ECSC partnership was revised and expanded to allow for a harmonization of labour markets, agricultural strategies, atomic energy initiatives and social policies. The Treaty of Rome would pave the way for an expanded market and a 'phasing in' process in order to afford countries the time to standardize their labour practices and economic infrastructure. The advent of atomic energy meant that member countries were much less willing to go to war, and, as McAllister points out, this created room for bold ideas. The Treaty of Rome set in train the gradual federalization of Western Europe.[5] It was this idea, in itself, that became the main debate surrounding the community's first decade of life: would Europe be, as France's president, Charles de Gaulle, hoped, a Europe of states? Or would it be a union of people, as one of his top advisers, Jean Monnet, had sought? This debate became the most significant at the EEC's inception, and on many levels the argument continues today. France's discomfort with the potential adverse effects of economic union dominated European politics throughout the early years of the EEC leading to – among many palliatives designed to assuage French anxiety – the insertion of Article 119 of the Treaty of Rome. Enshrining the principle of equal pay, Article 119 was included to assure France that cheap female labour from other countries would not be allowed to undercut France's significantly higher female wage rates, which, Hoskynes reminds us, owed their legacy to the first wave of feminism in France.[6]

WOMEN IN EUROPE

Gisela Kaplan identifies 1957 as one of the most significant periods in the destabilization of women's legal inferiority in Western Europe, because of such sweeping legislation adopted during integration negotiations.[7] The significance of Article 119 lay not in its demonstrable effects; savvy employers would find ways to evade the legislation. Rather, its importance lay in its aspiration. The article formalized women's position in employment and, to an extent, the public sphere. The call for equal pay laid the groundwork for a Europe-wide rethink of women's status as citizens and workers. Moreover, this labour market legislation inadvertently prompted a move towards the renegotiation of women's roles in general throughout European society. Common 'European' values would somehow have to infuse themselves into each state's local gender contract – and judging from the debates emerging from Leinster House and its European counterparts, that is exactly what was beginning to happen.

The business of getting back to normality involved cultivating two things: business and traditional definitions of normality. After the war many Europeans threw themselves into the reconstruction effort, which resulted in rapid economic growth rates throughout both parts of Europe. A major goal for the average citizen was to establish a dependable income, which dovetailed nicely with a regional drive to rebuild. Another major component in the drive for stability was the resurgence of traditional familial structures and middle-class aspirations, which allowed for a male-centred household income in return for married women's withdrawal from the workforce. Women who could afford to were generally willing to take up these traditional roles, which saw the birth rate rise and the marriage age for women fall.[8] In addition to this trend, women's representation in third-level education soared during this period, fuelling the middle-class aesthetic.

The wartime surge in labour-saving technology meant that both paid work and the unpaid work of household labour could be restructured to increase household efficiency. However, though labour-saving devices like washing machines and refrigerators were helpful, the rise in consumer culture simply meant that more washes could be done and more food could be bought. Furthermore, this technology had little impact on the household gender regime; maintenance of the household remained chiefly the responsibility of the woman of the house, regardless of class, according to Ann Oakley.[9] Consumer culture was not confined to household products either; the pop cultural trinity of music, movies and magazines gripped Western Europe as more and more people made use of their newfound disposable income. Mary Grieve, editor of Britain's *Woman* magazine, confirmed this:

> After years of strictures, rations and restraints a whole new world of commodities flowed in on the flood tide of the 1950s. Younger women had never known such joys, few older women had been able to afford them pre-war. The women's magazines with their close understanding of women, their sympathy with the situation, and their printing techniques, carried this new life straight into the homes and hearts of millions.[10]

Pop culture, more than anything else in daily life, transgressed national borders in a way few things could. This served to widen people's perspectives by challenging prevailing notions of culture and identity.

Though European countries have undergone differing political and historical development, Eileen Connolly points out their gender regimes displayed marked similarities during the 1950s and 1960s.[11] Most countries, with the exception of those in Scandinavia, which underwent earlier reforms, made noises about equal rights legislation but did little to ensure the implementation of specific laws. The feeble equality legislation they did enact was designed to do no more than harmonize the EEC economy and placate those who might threaten the status quo by applying their mother's suffragist rhetoric and tactics to the contemporary situation. This was a success for the governments involved; few women agitated for changes to the gender regime or more comprehensive legislation. The prevailing point of view was that women's equality lay in their status as managing director of their own private domestic economy; without their crucial contribution to the family structure, the state could not replicate its workforce and cultivate good citizens. Many Europeans, regardless of their sex, believed that women's prime social importance lay in their willingness to stabilize the domestic sphere. Prevailing ideology dictated that the ultimate success lay in the middle-class aesthetic of man-as-worker and woman-as-homemaker.

This traditional ideology allowed Europeans at large to believe that their mothers had won all that was to be won and that feminism was now a 'spent political force'.[12] West Germany, for example, guaranteed equal rights after the war, which pre-empted any widespread call for the mobilization of a militant women's movement, but it remained socially conservative throughout the 1950s. And though there were moderate reforms of family law in 1957 and 1959, women's practical experience of the family hierarchy remained unaffected.[13] Italy, heavily influenced by Catholic doctrine, failed to shed its fascistic legislation throughout the decade. Characterized by its acceptance of women's legal inferiority, Italy's leniency towards 'crimes of honour' and its discriminatory adultery legislation meant that while the constitution stipulated equal rights among the sexes, the state did little to support this provision.[14] In England a mixture of welfare reform, economic opportunities and political rights seemed to render any sort of women's movement redundant.[15]

Some states, such as France, Belgium and Italy, nominally recognized women's contributions during the war years by giving women the vote and expressing a move towards equality. But overall, traditional family-centred legislation dominated most Western European countries in the 1950s, and any legislation adopted by the governments tended to echo that ideology. Across the spectrum, from the more progressive countries of Scandinavia to the most authoritarian regimes to the south of Western Europe, the equality legislation that existed left a traditional gender structure intact by failing to fundamentally critique prevailing notions of sex and gender roles.[16] In French family law, for example, the Napoleonic codes deemed women to be subordinate to their husbands. This view was not uncommon throughout Europe: Ireland, Italy and Austria, West Germany and others, waited until the second half of the 1950s and the 1960s to begin the process of family law reform. But despite this, at the height of the postwar drive for stability, Kaplan points out that a slow process of re-evaluating the importance of traditionalism began to take place throughout Europe, which set the stage for the conflict over gender roles that would emerge in the late 1960s.[17]

CONTEXTUALIZING THE TWO IRELANDS

In terms of historical development, a significant turning point for the two Irelands emerged when the South declared itself neutral at the onset of the Second World War. Politically, the policy of neutrality was a difficult path for Taoiseach Eamon de Valera to steer for a variety of reasons that have been discussed in detail elsewhere.[18] It is important to remember that though Ireland 'had a relatively cosy war' when compared to belligerents and other neutral states, it did attempt to eliminate all unnecessary spending by instituting rationing and price and wage controls.[19] Also, due to Ireland's unique proximity and strategic importance to Britain, one of the main combatants, de Valera, endorsed a rigid policy of censorship. These two measures meant that the neutral South did not remain entirely unaffected by the war. In basic terms, however, Éire had escaped some of the defining fundamental experiences of warfare: devastating air raids and massive loss of life. This was probably the most significant factor dividing Éire from its European counterparts. Another consequence of the neutrality policy, according to Brown, was that it effectively copper-fastened the partition of the island of Ireland in the minds of many on both sides of the border.[20] O'Halpin points out that this consequence had been 'largely anticipated in 1939'; the rationale for the adoption of this policy was based on '*realpolitik*, defencelessness, the likelihood of republican insurrection if the state attempted to participate on Britain's side, and fear of the consequence of modern warfare'.[21]

As the war drew to a close Europe embarked on a period of restructuring and economic growth. Southern Ireland fell out of step with the rest of Europe as continental governments began to rebuild their economic and social systems. Between 1945 and 1957 the growth rate of income in the Republic stagnated at a rate that was one-fifth that of the rest of Western Europe.[22] During this period it seemed that even Northern Ireland, hands outstretched towards Britain's purse, pulled away from a languishing South in all but geography. Indeed, one need only look at accounts of the South's history to discover that the words 'stagnation'[23] and 'morass'[24] appear time and again when discussing the postwar South. In most arenas the South remained devoid of momentum: as other countries experienced a surge in the standard of living, Éire did not; as they experienced a mass drive towards industrialization, Éire did not; as they struggled to fill vacant jobs during postwar reconstruction, Éire did not. Daly points out that a failure in social policy innovation during this period rendered the

South more akin to the Britain and Northern Ireland of the 1920s than its contemporary counterparts, which served to further cement social differences between North and South.[25]

In 1949 both regions consolidated their constitutional positions. On a trip to Canada, Taoiseach John Costello announced his intention to declare the Republic. Eamon de Valera had previously refrained from raising the political stakes to this level in the belief that the Republic could only be declared when the British fully withdrew from the island of Ireland. In response Westminster enacted the Ireland Act, which proclaimed that Northern Ireland would remain part of the United Kingdom for as long as the majority of its people wished. As the sun set on the 1940s, the two states within Ireland began to define themselves in fundamentally different ways.

Life in Northern Ireland was characterized by segregation based on religious identity. Educational institutions, public and private employment, and social institutions suffered under what Rosemary Harris calls a 'dichotomization' of the community. Her *Prejudice and Tolerance in Ulster*, researched in the 1950s and published in 1972, underlines how this 'dichotomization' impacted negatively on the development of the province. She points out that much of this segregation in the 1950s was voluntary and based on recognizing boundaries based on religious difference. Though later surveys have pointed out that in certain areas the level of discrimination was exaggerated, Harris's research suggests that segregationist attitudes were critical to the formation of such a divided community.[26] So while the welfare state was beginning to draw Northern Ireland away from its southern neighbour economically, socially little was changing.

In the Republic of Ireland successive waves of emigration and a near economic collapse had taken its toll, and by 1958 civil servants and government ministers alike were searching for a way to inject new life into the Irish economy. When senior civil servant T.K. Whitaker presented his report entitled *Economic Development* that year, his radical suggestions regarding dropping protectionism in favour of attracting multinational investment were seen as the push that the Irish economy so badly needed in order to pull itself out of the 'morass'. But this was not just an Irish phenomenon: Connolly points out that as much as the '1958 turn' was led by governmental personalities, it was also a product of its time; Spain and Portugal were also experimenting with trying to attract foreign investment.[27] As both states found their feet in the wake of the war, Britain's welfare reform forced Ireland into restructuring its own systems. Northern Ireland began to rethink its social structures as a province of the United Kingdom and the Republic began to realize it would continue to experience increased emigration if it failed to do something along those lines. Daly notes that in light of the increasing gap between British and Irish wages in this period, it can be no surprise that Irish emigration rates were soaring.[28] Northern Ireland's industrial production rate in this decade increased by 50 per cent, which highlighted the South's sluggish performance and brought into sharp relief the economic divergence of the two regions.[29]

CATHOLICISM IN BOTH PARTS OF IRELAND

In terms of the Republic's gender regime, we can observe patterns of sociopolitical development in the 1950s that are tied to the development of religion. Liam O'Dowd points out that we must contextualize the narrowing of women's roles in light of Catholic social teaching and the right-wing nationalist and fascist politics that gripped Europe at large in the period.[30] Moreover, continental Catholicism, due to its experience of forced integration with left-wing political groups during and after the war, pulled away from Irish Catholicism in the 1950s, making Irish Catholicism appear 'increasingly right wing' compared to its continental counterparts.[31] Catholicism in Ireland exercised a strong impact on the cultural development of the nation, which helped it to develop along a different trajectory than Britain, and indeed other European states. Coupled with the fact that Catholic morality and social values underpinned the Irish constitution and propelled much of the social legislation until the 1950s, it is fair to conclude that socially conservative thought characterized Irish society in the postwar period. Marianne Elliott, in *The Catholics of Ulster* expands on this idea of Catholic identity by arguing that in Northern Ireland Catholicism became more than a cultural identity: 'For Catholics their religion *was* their political identity, and the Church provided all the necessary institutional infrastructure. This is why secular nationalist institutions, including the Nationalist Party itself, remained so weak in Northern Ireland. There was no need for them.'[32] In both parts of Ireland, evolving from different circumstances, Marian Catholicism shored up its support base in the 1950s and informed much of what is known today as Irish culture.

This strengthening of Catholic support also led to power struggles; both governments in Ireland wrangled with the Roman Catholic hierarchy in their attempts to develop health service provisions in this period. Belfast's Roman Catholic Mater hospital became embroiled in controversy when it refused to accept state funding in 1948, fearing that government money meant government control. In the South in 1951, the Church came out firmly against the 'Mother and Child' health scheme, fearing that socialized medicine would mean that women could receive advice on fertility control, though many today concede that a major reason for the rejection of the scheme was due to the Minister for Health's political inexperience. Whyte points out that the real significance of this controversy lay in the fact that for the first time church–state relations entered public discourse.[33] This episode is also instructive in that it illustrates the absence of women from public discourse, even on an issue that concerned them. Save the protestations of the Irish Housewives Association,[34] this controversy did not provoke a significant element of resistance among Irish women at large. A cursory exploration of the big controversies throughout the decade shows the bishops coming down squarely in favour of pub closures, censorship and dance hall closures and in opposition to issues such as socialized medicine and the formalization of the adoption process. If Irish Catholicism was becoming isolated from the continent, it was also becoming uniquely Irish, both as a response to Irish political developments and the modernizing forces in Ireland.

In both parts of Ireland religious institutions ruled primary and secondary education. This, combined with both religious and, in many cases, sex segregation meant that children experienced their formative years in an artificially homogenous environment. The segregationist credo of both the dominant religions on the island stunted social relations between communities in the North[35] and had far-reaching ramifications for those on both sides of the border. Whyte makes the point when discussing Northern Ireland that segregated education was a primary factor in dividing the community.[36] Both Catholic and Protestant religious leaders saw the primary purpose of education to be the indoctrination of children into the morality of religious teaching. After independence the South continued the pattern of clerical religious control of education, which had germinated under the union with Great Britain. One of the best examples of the South's acquiescent attitude towards religious education is a statement by General Mulcahy, Minister for Education from 1948 to 1951 and 1954 to 1957. He remarked that the state 'accepts that the foundation and crown of youth's entire training is religion. It is the desire that its teachers, syllabuses and textbooks in every branch be informed by the spirit underlying this concept of education'.[37] Catholic schools in Northern Ireland took much the same attitude and because, as Thomas Hennessey points out, state funding for capital expenditure involved a degree of local (and in many cases non-Catholic) control, Catholic education remained financially disadvantaged in the 'voluntary schools' sector.[38]

The Republic's Council for Education supported Mulcahy's vision of Catholic social teaching as late as 1960, when it published a report that stated the purpose of education was the 'inculcation' of religious morality. The report went on to say that this task was outside the scope of the state.[39] Considering the historical context and the power the Church wielded, this report is unremarkable. However, it underlines the state's failure to take responsibility for its youth as well as highlighting its complicity in reinforcing the existing gender regime: children learned their place in the family and ultimately in the state by learning about the hierarchal gender relations of the Bible. In Northern Ireland the Catholic schools developed in much the same way. Until the late 1960s Catholic schoolteachers maintained strict discipline by promoting rote memorization. One woman's experience at a Dublin convent school in the early 1960s exemplifies this type of educational philosophy:

> I remember in one class being told, 'Right girls, take out your pens and write this down: Communism is ...' I put up my hand and said, 'Why don't you just give us the facts and figures and we can decide for ourselves what communism is?' I almost took my life in my hands, I felt, because it wasn't done to ask any questions.[40]

This account of one woman's experience is illustrative of the broad educational philosophy that devalued debate and dialectics in Catholic Ireland.

The impact of religion extended into many aspects of life. Island-wide, clerical influence was a powerful force in dictating social, familial and personal priorities. If we look to the interwar period to get our bearings, we can see the Irish Catholic Church looking to grow and rebuild after the chaos of the Irish Revolution. We can also see a hierarchy struggling to cope with the modernization process, Irish militarism and first-wave feminism. Maryann Valiulis argues that the Irish bishops 'chose women as their group with which to make their stand not simply against the modern world, as is often said, but against the forces of modernisation'.[41] As guardians of Irish Catholic morality, the bishops interpreted women's changing identity with alarm. The forces of modernization helped to redefine Irish womanhood in the context of suffragism and republicanism, and this filled the hierarchy with dread. The bishops' determination to keep patriarchal authority intact informed many of their pastoral decisions from the Independence period through to the 1950s.

The cult of Mary, though experienced in other countries, held a particular appeal to Irish Catholics in the 1950s. Pope Pius XII decreed that 1954 was 'the Marian year', and this appealed to countries where women were subject to what Connolly calls 'enforced domesticity', where they were viewed as wives and mothers.[42] Ireland, which defined women as mothers and placed them firmly within the domestic sphere in its 1937 constitution, had already begun to take up the worship of Mary with fervour since the famine, MacCurtain points out.[43] One element that made this type of worship appeal to Irish people is the development of Ireland's symbolism and rhetoric. The personification of Ireland has rarely been a challenge to Irish artists. She has been portrayed as Dark Rosaleen or Cathleen Ní Houlihan, a sad old woman, by dramatists, poets and illustrators alike.[44] So when the Pope signalled the glorification of Mary, Irish Catholics simply superimposed the crying woman in blue on top of the crying woman in green. Mary Holland points out: 'We have apostrophised the country itself as a mother [*sic*]. The concept of Mother Ireland has met with wholehearted approval. The message has been unequivocal. The proper place for a woman apart from the convent is the home, preferably rearing sons for Ireland.'[45]

The 1950s can be viewed as a decade that saw Mary and Mother Ireland complete their amalgamation in their own shared suffering and that of their sons; a trinity was formed – Mary, Mother Ireland, and all Irish women. The arrested development of women's roles outside the home in Catholic communities on both sides of the border became symptomatic of the acceptance of this trinity as a natural relationship to benefit family and country.

WOMEN IN THE REPUBLIC

As enshrined in the Irish constitution of 1937, women's roles were limited to mothering within the home. The man, as the provider, remained at the head of the house, assuming much of the official decision-making power. Connolly has identified four components to what she calls 'the Irish state's gender regime':

> An emphasis on gendered difference
> A hierarchal ranking of male and female
> Clear divisions between the public sphere and the private/

> domestic sphere
> A subjugation of individual rights within the family[46]

The Republic followed a pattern many European countries adhered to: women may have possessed elements of political equality, such as the parliamentary vote, but overall they would remain subordinate to their male counterparts. This is not to say that women's groups failed to take part in public discourse; groups such as the Irish Country-women's Association (ICA), which was founded in 1910, the Irish Housewives Association (IHA), established in 1942, and the Ulster Women's Unionist Council, founded in 1911, all provided a forum for women to express their activism. But even the trade union movement in this period shied away from tackling gender inequality in a mean-ingful way. In 1951 Helen Chenevix, as president of the Irish Trades Union Congress, did name the issue of equal pay as a pressing concern, but gave priority to other issues.[47] Though these groups and individuals did, at times, seek to change some aspects of the role of women in Irish society, they 'did not engage in a fundamental critique of the existing gender regime', and so women's position in formal politics 'remained static throughout the decade', according to Eileen Connolly.[48] Though the IHA had strong roots and links with the first-wave feminist movement in Ireland, it focused primarily on equal citizenship rights, seeking to enter into the system rather than to radically change it.

Probably one of the more visible challenges to the gender contract that surfaced towards the end of the1950s was the Married Women's Status Act. This was one of the first public attempts at reconciling the gender inequalities that permeated public policy in the South.[49] Granted, the legislation was enacted due to economic concerns: the government proposed it in order to prevent women who had previ-ously lacked the right to enter legally binding contracts from engaging in fraud. But the ensuing debates reveal a gender-biased Orieachtas be-fuddled with a transforming concept of social roles. One major fear was that women could use their new-found legal independence to sue their husbands, thereby securing a *de facto* legal separation. Another fear involved inheritance laws: women would now be able to legally disinherit their husbands. Connolly points out that throughout the debate it is 'women and not men who are described as likely to frus-trate the real purpose of the legislation by using the courts against their husbands, thereby weakening the marriage contract'.[50] This fear, that women would inundate the courts with an endless barrage of lawsuits against their husbands, betrays an overarching fear of women's equality within marriage and ultimately within the state.

Catriona Clear generously argues that legislators in the Republic did not hold anti-female ideologies, but, rather, their attacks on women's roles were inconsistent and piecemeal.[51] Certainly it seems de Valera, the prime architect of so much of the state's legislation, did indeed have a coherent philosophy about women's roles. Moreover, when one analyzes the parliamentary debates of the time, it is difficult to see anything other than a patriarchal ideology at work. The debate around the inclusion of women into the Garda Síochána in 1958 is an interesting case study. Introduced by Fianna Fáil largely as a formalization of policing procedure on the ground, the conservative bill made the provision for hiring twelve female gardaí on a trial basis. The rationale was that female gardaí would be better suited to deal with survivors of sexual assaults and with children. Dáil members expressed fears that policing was outside the purview of proper women's roles, that women would feminize the profession, that women would become masculine, that female gardaí would be quick to raid pubs because they lacked male discretion, that their cheaper wage rates could affect male recruitment, and that they would retire on marriage. Again, the fact that only the IHA protested this thinking exposes an underlying acceptance of the existing gender regime. In general men *and* women failed to question a main assumption of the Garda Act debate – that women were better suited to social work than men and less able to take part in more dangerous policing activity.[52]

Throughout most of Ireland, women encountered obstacles to pursuing an independent lifestyle. Their choice to leave farms and rural areas, while a step towards independence itself, helped speed up the collapse of the rural system, making life far more difficult for those women who chose to remain.

> In Ireland, most farming was still done with horses, and in Connacht only one farm in forty-five had a tractor in 1951. Only one in thirty people owned a car, only one in nine had a radio. Rural electrification was under way, but incomplete. The standard of living on small farms had changed little since the turn of the century, a period of fifty years in which the material quality of life in Britain had improved dramatically.[53]

Emigration held one of the few viable opportunities for country girls who did not stand to inherit the farm. As one woman who left a small Irish farm for New Jersey in 1948 explained: 'Well, it was the understood thing then, there was nothing else in Ireland really. Only emigration. Very few did get jobs in Ireland.'[54] Letters supported such generalizations as they arrived in Ireland laden with dollars and sterling and boasting of work, money, films and late-night dance halls and pubs. The Republic, with little to offer to counter these tantalizing accounts of life 'across the water', could not compete. Between 1951 and 1956, 200,000 people left the Republic and the number was increasing each year.[55] In the next six years 400,000 left, which in rural demographic terms meant that for every 1,000 men there were 868 women left in these areas.[56] According to Mary E. Daly, it was this decade that marked the 'decay and near collapse of the demographic system'. As a result farmers increasingly found themselves single and middle-class homes increasingly found themselves without domestic servants. Daly infers that 'many women no longer found traditional Irish living conditions and the status which they afforded tolerable'.[57] A government report on emigration supports this idea: 'Particularly to the young mind, rural areas appear dull, drab, monotonous, backward and lonely.'[58] Out of those who left, approximately half were women, which was a significantly higher proportion than other European averages.[59] Those women who remained increasingly looked to towns and cities for work. But in urban areas new challenges to carving out a life awaited them.

Marriage bars, or compulsory retirement upon marriage, had been accepted practice throughout the first half of the century in many European countries, but the pressure to fill jobs during and after the Second World War forced these countries to reconsider the policy. The Republic's wartime neutrality and sluggish economy did not demand this rethink, however, so the marriage bar remained intact in many white-collar professions. The 1958 decision to repeal the bar for married women teachers constitutes one of the few exceptions to this widespread discriminatory practice in public employment. The Department of Education rationalized that teaching would not interfere with the 'fulfilment of [women's] duties and obligations in regard to the creation and maintenance of a home'.[60] The rhetorical side-stepping required of the government to justify dispensing with the ban in the education sector concealed just how acute the teacher shortage was. The main reason for the repeal of the bar was economic, not because the teaching profession leant itself to housewifery. This fact could not be mentioned too loudly; the next logical conclusion would be that, should the need arise, marriage bars in other areas of employment would be dropped. This flew in the face of Catholic social teaching, trade unionist job protectionism and the concept of the family wage. Working-class women who engaged in public employment, such as night cleaners, did not face the same types of restrictions, which further demonstrates the inconsistencies inherent in the practice.

Overall, women in the Republic faced two general issues in the lead up to the 1950s: legal inferiority to their male counterparts and emigration. Their role as second-class citizens was enforced by a number of pieces of legislation designed to confine them to domestic roles. Rural life held very few opportunities for women in terms of economic and social prospects. Increasingly rural women moved to urban centres to seek employment and carve out a new kind of life, which further perpetuated the collapse of the demographic system. Those who remained in Ireland faced dismissal upon marriage if they worked in white-collar public sector employment. By the middle of the 1950s, however, the Irish state found itself under increasing pressure to re-evaluate women's legal status by reforming marriage and family law. As the Dáil took up issues regarding women's legal inferiority, it also introduced a radical policy change in an effort to curb emigration and spur the economy.

WOMEN IN NORTHERN IRELAND

In Northern Ireland during the 1950s public policy regarding women was largely a non-issue for two reasons. First, on both sides of the sectarian division, political and religious conservatism reigned supreme, ensuring that women remained squarely in the domestic sphere. Another reason why women remained well out of the public sphere is that some elements of Stormont's welfare legislation short-circuited calls for alterations to the gender contract. Jonathan Bardon aptly labels the 1950s 'The quiet years' in his history of Northern Ireland, because it was a period characterized by maintaining the status quo.[61] What lurked beneath the surface of the 'quiet years', to differentiate the North from its southern neighbour, was also the ideology of sectarianism and segregation that permeated many aspects of Northern Irish society.

Economically, one of Northern Ireland's most successful markets – linen – experienced an initial postwar boom, which seemed to herald a renaissance for the traditional industries. But by 1953 it became clear that the demand for linen was unsustainable, which sent legislators and economists scrambling for new ideas. Then, when it seemed it could not get worse, as international shipping implemented more efficient systems and Belfast failed to innovate, the shipping industry began to buckle. Stormont failed to replace its cash cows despite both direct and indirect financial incentives to attract investment; eventually the two major traditional industries capsized, leaving many to tread water 'on the brew'.[62] This put pressure on working-class women to increase their hours at the remaining factories, if they were fortunate enough to have a job. Because the gender regime remained intact, working-class women tended to find themselves faced with the double burden of daytime work and evening housework.

The most crushing pressure working-class women faced was not the collapse of industry, however. If the Northern Irish housing crisis had been bad before the war, it was now catastrophic. In order to repair both the substandard housing and the damage done by German bombs, some 200,000 new houses were needed.[63] In the wake of the war Stormont established housing trusts and the Northern Irish bureaucracy began to grind into action to respond to this challenge. One element, however, that was either neglected or ignored was an equality stipulation. This resulted in local authorities having carte blanche to distribute the new houses as they saw fit. Consequently they were distributed unevenly (for a detailed discussion of this see Chapter 2). This meant that as the crisis was slowly dissipating for the Protestant community, it was becoming more acute for the Catholics. While Catholics did hold a greater portion of public housing, Daly makes the point that 'they may have deserved an even greater portion' owing to their larger family size and their prevalence among lower socioeconomic groups.[64]

Northern Ireland's employment profile was not much better than its housing policy. The striking thing about the Northern Irish economy during this period was the amount of people perilously attached to the collapsing traditional industries of shipbuilding, textiles, linen and agriculture.[65] Even though, as Daly points out, the region was embarking on a period of rapid economic growth,[66] unemployment remained at the alarmingly high level of between 5 and 10 per cent throughout the 1950s. This level exceeded both Scottish and Welsh levels, which had shared the same rates as Northern Ireland before the war.[67] Due to institutionalized discrimination and some Catholic reluctance to engage in public employment, Catholics were particularly affected by soaring unemployment despite their high rates of emigration, which peaked at a rate more than double non-Catholic emigration in the 1950s.[68] During the war women experienced a kind of social and workforce repositioning, as they were encouraged to join wartime industries and auxiliary military forces. Betty Sinclair, for example, a long-time trade unionist and communist, wrote a pamphlet calling on women to 'man the factories' to help Soviet Russia against Hitler.[69] Some did find this period ripe with opportunity. Women took to the Northern factories, some eager to prove their patriotism and some simply eager to work. This new state-sponsored drive for women's employment meant the introduction of day nurseries. Thirteen were opened during the war and only closed when the linen market collapsed in 1955.[70] This situation provides a unique glimpse into Northern Ireland's gender regime: the nurseries had outlasted the war and could have outlasted the collapse of the linen industry, because there was still significant demand. So, like the decision to revoke the marriage bar for teachers in the Republic and like the equal pay provision in the Treaty of Rome, the demise of the NSA demonstrated that financial policy tends to supersede social concerns. Yet this whole episode proved something else as well: Northern Ireland, like its British and American counterparts, was willing to bend the rules and send women out of the house when the economic or wartime demand was sufficient. However, until the early 1970s a marriage bar still functioned in the civil service and banking sector,[71] and a governmental commitment to housewifery dangled from Stormont's pocket threads, similar to the experience of other European countries.

Though the war had created some employment opportunities for women, war industries petered out and women turned back to what they had been doing before the war. Disappointingly, the war had not translated into prosperity for all in the region. Women's employment rates during this period remained 5 per cent lower than other regions of the United Kingdom.[72] One area of employment that had some success in outlasting the collapse of linen and shipbuilding was factory work. In Derry, where 90 per cent of the factory workers were female, the factory workforce peaked at approximately 7,000 in 1951.[73] Looking at a female-dominated factory workforce such as Derry, unique as it was, can be instructive in understanding how even in areas with significant demand for female employment, women's economic vulnerability remained pronounced. In the Derry factories the conditions were poor, women made less money than men, there was less opportunity for promotion, and women had no job security. Moreover, women's hours were subject to the whims of the market, which was constantly in a state of flux. The evidence that women were the breadwinners in this period seems to be largely anecdotal, though unemployment was indeed high among Derry men. In light of the intermittent nature of the shirt factories' employment practices, Andrew Finlay makes the point that in the woman-as-breadwinner scenario family income was hugely unreliable due to the vulnerability of women's economic status.[74]This boded ill for the other parts of the North that did not count on women's employment to make ends meet.

Even though the skies remained dark over the employment landscape in Northern Ireland, a small break in the clouds gave people hope: education. The Butler Act of 1944, though marred by controversy for three years, and denounced by the Roman Catholic bishops, was finally shepherded through Stormont by Samuel Hall-Thompson a few years later. Both Protestants and Catholics opposed the bill on the grounds that religious instruction would have to be nondenominational, a provision designed to draw Catholic schools into the state education system. The bill increased capital grants for voluntary schools to 65 per cent to be administered by committees, but the Catholic bishops opposed the scheme by claiming that this was tantamount to state control of education, that 100 per cent funding without a provision for committee administration would be more appropriate.[75] After much wrangling, the bill was finally passed and the plans for expanding the education system got underway. The youth profited – academically, but not in terms of social integration. With more children remaining in school, the number of students in grant-aided schools increased by more than 80,000 between 1948 and 1964.[76] Despite this promising news, we must remember that the segregationist ethos the schools' administrators cultivated on both sides of the sectarian divide remained intact, which meant under the new act children were actually deprived of the possibility of integrating with other religious backgrounds for a longer period of time, should they remain in school. It was not until students attended university at Queen's (if they got to that level) that they began to mix with students from other traditions. Overall though, it was the Catholic community that was most positively affected by this new drive for educational reform. Their numbers at Queen's rose by 500 in the late 1950s.[77]

For the working classes, life in Northern Ireland in this period was characterized by sky-rocketing unemployment, the collapse of traditional industries and the housing crisis. It is noteworthy therefore that so few aside from trade union officials were making a noise about them. During the war Northern Irish people had learned to put up with many hardships, and life in the 1950s was an extension of this practice. Due to a combination of sectarianism, segregation and limited welfare reform, the records available demonstrate that a women's agenda did not surface in any public forum. But while few questioned the position of women, an increasingly sullen Catholic population began to question its position within the political and economic structure of Northern Irish society.

REPUBLICANISM AND THE BORDER CAMPAIGN

Militant republicanism has had a long history in Ireland, but with the success of Seán MacBride's Clann na Poblachta and Eddie's McAteer's modest gains with the Anti-Partition League, by the mid-1950s in both parts of Ireland a significant number of republicans were rethinking the wisdom of armed struggle. This corresponded with a general mood throughout postwar Europe that yearned for the security of peace and the stability of private life. Thus, the Irish Republican Army (IRA) faced an uphill battle in reinventing itself after the 1940s campaign. In 1956 the action of fringe groups forced the IRA into commencing a poorly planned campaign targeting British security installations and symbols of British rule throughout Northern Ireland. Dubbed the 'border campaign', the ''50s campaign' or even 'Operation Harvest', in reference to the codename of its opening operation, the main tactic involved IRA men penetrating the border from the South, attacking British targets and quickly withdrawing back over the border. Eunan O'Halpin points out that in the years leading up to the border campaign republican militants could operate with near impunity in the South for two practical reasons: Costello's coalition government depended on a small group of republicans in Clann na Poblachta and the IRA's weak numbers and aversion to confronting Southern security forces rendered their operations a negligible threat at best.[78]

In December 1956 the IRA commenced the campaign in the North and Sinn Féin addressed the people:

> Irish men have again risen in armed revolt against British aggression in Ireland. The Sinn Féin organization states to the Irish people that they are proud of the risen nation and appeal to the people of Ireland to assist in every way they can the people of the occupied area ... It was obvious that the young men of this generation would have to rise as the young men of other generations have risen against such tyranny ... Sinn Féin appeals to the people to support Sinn Féin policy.[79]

This statement, signed by Máire Ní Gabhann and Michael Traynor on the eve of a new campaign, betrays the gender regime that characterized the republican movement. Men were seen to be the soldiers and women were only included in the equation as possible supporters or victims of an occupation, even in this case when a woman played an equal part in penning the communique.

The border campaign consisted of flurries of arms raids and explosions followed by long lulls in operation. Brookeborough, one of the best-known raids at the onset of the campaign, produced two martyrs: Seán South and Fergal O'Hanlon. For a short while the republican movement was able to propagandize their deaths in song and poetry, but overall this failed to inspire many outside the fold to join up. Moreover, the Southern government was giving every indication that their days of looking the other way were over. Despite senior IRA figure Thomas MacCurtain's public assurance on 12 January 1957 that the IRA posed no physical threat to Southern security forces, he and other crucial members of the IRA leadership were arrested the very next day in what can only be interpreted as a shot across the boughs from heretofore quiescent Southern security forces. On 18 January the IRA blew up an army barracks in Dungannon and the clergy came out against the campaign, deeming it a mortal sin for the men of Ireland to participate: 'With paternal insistence we warn young men to be on their guard against any such organisation.'[80] Predictably, even the most devout members of the republican leadership, such as Patrick McLogan and Anthony Magan, simply chose to ignore the statement.[81]

Though McLogan and Magan took hierarchal pronouncements like these with a grain of salt, they slavishly followed other aspects of Catholic doctrine and social teaching. Through their influence, social and political conservatism became pivotal to the prevailing ethos of the republican movement in this period. Brian Feeney explores this in his study of Sinn Féin. He points out that the organization's social and economic policy during this period drew heavily on the 1891 papal encyclical *Rerum Novarum*, which attempted to tackle industrialization and declared that the Church had the right to pronounce on social issues and relate them to moral issues.[82] The leadership joined the Church in arguing against anything that smacked of socialism, including welfare legislation and the Mother and Child health scheme, as well as anything that encourage a loosening of social mores. To illustrate his point Feeney cites an apocryphal story that circulated after the border campaign: the republican leadership rejected the idea of using condoms as bomb timing devices, so strong was the feeling against the use of contraceptives for any purpose.[83] Feeney argues that regardless of the veracity of the story, had the issue arisen, the leadership would have indeed rejected the idea out of hand, judging from the conservative nature of the leadership. Condoms, it must be noted, would have made little difference to the plummeting trajectory of the campaign.

When Fianna Fáil returned to government in March 1957, de Valera decided to leave no question of his commitment to security by crushing the IRA in a July swoop that netted most of the remaining men in the Sinn Féin Ard Comhairle. J. Bowyer Bell points out that the republican movement's failure to anticipate the July arrests proved to be their major weakness because it pointed to larger failures in their ability to read the political landscape: 'Despite all the evidence, the leadership held fast to the illusion that their simple promise to remain quiescent in the South would be sufficient surety for the Irish government, a government whose legitimacy they publicly denied.'[84] A combination of the July arrests, military tribunals, cross-border security liaisons and the introduction of internment without trial had effectively broken the back of the IRA. The campaign hobbled along for another five years of intermittent attacks in the North and finally sputtered to a halt in 1962 with a dump arms order and a denunciation of Irish popular political indifference. As observed by the Irish ambassador in London, Con Cremin: 'the spasmodic outbreaks of the IRA activities ... proved scarcely more than a minor irritation' to the British government.[85] Though the campaign was a spectacular failure, Richard English warns us not to dismiss it; the one hundred active IRA members engaged in more than 500 incidents, more than ten people had been killed and more than thirty had been wounded throughout the six years of attacks.[86]

Demoralized and divided by 1962, the republican movement, as conceived of by the IRA and Sinn Féin, looked set to fade into the dusty tomes of history. Many of the leaders moved on and the few who remained seemed to be at a loss about where to go from there. On both sides of the border republican-minded people had made a resounding push towards formal politics in the elections that had taken place during the campaign. Now there was almost no new blood of which to speak. The significance of the campaign's failure was that it created room for sweeping changes in policy and bold ideas from within the movement. This could conceivably spell the end for single-minded militant traditionalists, if the ideas sought to take the movement in a new direction.

REPUBLICAN WOMEN DURING THE BORDER CAMPAIGN

Joan Wallach Scott argues that feminist history is not simply 'recounting great deeds performed by women'. Rather, it entails 'the exposure of the often silent and hidden operations of gender that are nonetheless present and defining forces in the organization of most societies'.[87] We must be careful then to steer clear of a kind of 'add-women-and-stir'[88] approach to writing women into history. Yet, because a comprehensive analysis of women's roles in the border campaign has not been done, it is necessary to document their activities.

In the years running up to the border campaign senior republicans began to engage in a debate about the future direction of the movement. The controversy lay in the debate over what kind of action to take – formal political engagement or militant activism? Some who had survived the previous campaign were eager to pursue a less violent path, but the militants won the day and the IRA began to take control over Sinn Féin's leadership. One of their first acts was the demotion of the elderly Margaret Buckley from president to an untitled position on the Ard Comhairle.[89] Buckley, one of the 'old guard', had provided a link with prewar republicanism, but she was unlikely as president to acquiesce to this consolidation of IRA rule led by Padraig MacLogan. Buckley's presidency and subsequent demotion reveal two things: that a woman president was possible (though not at this time a female IRA member) and that the militants seeking to take over viewed her as a significant barrier to their planned domination of the group.

Aside from a handful of female leaders like Buckley, the highest concentration of women in the republican movement lay in Cumann na mBan, the women's auxiliary to the IRA. Margaret Ward points out in her study of the group's formation, that 'at no stage were the women critical of their exclusion from the volunteers; the only alternative ever considered was the creation of a female equivalent, not a merger of forces'.[90] This remained the attitude of the Cumann na mBan leadership into the period of our study. The belief that an army could not function without a support staff dovetailed easily with members of Cumann na mBan's domestic commitments, which many of them considered equally important to the movement.

Rosemary Ridd builds on Michelle Rosaldo's observations that women may wield power within the domestic sphere through their influence over relatives, by pointing out that their power can be covert and symbolic when they do not appear to step out of the domestic role.[91] In Algiers and Cyprus their assumed domestic role allowed them to smuggle arms and act as couriers, because they were less likely to be body searched. Ridd writes: 'Women seen as political innocents can on occasion use this immunity to take initiatives and responsibilities of a covert political nature.'[92] Monica E. Neugebauer goes further in her analysis of domestic activism by describing how these activities can affect and indeed propagate domestic activism:

> The politicizing of domesticity consists of women baking bread, preparing food and tending to the wounded. Reproductive politics is embodied in the 'mother of the martyr' … It is her duty to educate her children to be nationalists. These forms of action do not challenge domesticity, but expand the tasks and political significance associated with them. Remaining in the domestic sphere may keep women from making certain contributions to public struggle, but it strengthens the bonds of cooperation among women which can be mobilized in a way that brings women into meaningful participation.[93]

These observations support the research carried out for this study; oftentimes the simple act of preparing a home to act as a 'safe house', and teaching children about family connections to a nationalist cause, or even mundane acts like preparing dinner for relatives before political meetings or providing laundry services for imprisoned relatives were pivotal in supporting the movement in a difficult period.

Dolours Price, a woman who would one day become one of the first female IRA members, recalled growing up in the 1950s and 1960s in a staunchly republican family; two generations of women in her family had been to prison and she would become the third in the 1970s. She remembered her aunts enlisting her help to pack food parcels with 'big slabs of chocolate' for those imprisoned friends and family. She was brought to commemorations by these women and taught that republicans like themselves were an elite group, 'in possession of all of the truth' about Irish history.[94] Noel Kavanagh, Officer Commanding of the Teeling Column of the IRA during the border campaign who would go on to play a significant role in various prison break operations,[95] has pointed out that women played a significant role in Sinn Féin and in an Cumann Cabhrach, the group that raised funds for prisoners and their families. 'While a somewhat hum-drum activity, fundraising, etc., was of paramount importance to married prisoners with mortgages and family dependents as well as to prisoners, though single, [who] had dependents, as the main bread winner in a family.'[96] But for the women, this kind of activism was simply an extension of their role, and because it was often confined to the domestic sphere, they oftentimes minimized the fact that their activity had any bearing on the development of the movement.[97] It would be left to their children and the next generations, perhaps as a consequence of second-wave feminism, to acknowledge the activism of these women.

Outside the home, in the public sphere Cumann na mBan's activities as auxiliaries were also helpful to the militants most significantly in the act of providing cover for covert activities. Mae Smith posed as a soldier's girlfriend and went to a Gough Barracks dance in Armagh, where she met Seán Garland, an army infiltrator, who would take her outside to 'court' in order to facilitate intelligence-gathering operations.[98] Smith's work providing cover for the operation exemplified the more dangerous aspects of Cumann na mBan agency. While this raid was successful due to this kind of supplementary assistance, other joint operations were not. As it became clear that the IRA was going to commence the border campaign, senior activists decided to aid Cathal Goulding in escaping from Wakefield prison in England. A series of aborted plans culminated in Terry Cronin, the wife of border campaign architect Seán Cronin, hiring an Aer Lingus DC-3 airplane. Ten men and five women posed as the 'Skellig Players' and boarded the plane, smuggling broken-down Thompson guns in the women's wardrobe.[99] In England the women took in a film – their activity of providing initial coverage for the men having been completed – while most of the men made their way to the prison. The attempt was aborted when Goulding and a few others could not make it over the prison wall. The operation was a colossal waste of time and money, and as Coogan points out, could have cost the IRA most of its leadership only weeks before the start of the campaign.[100] Noel Kavanagh, who had accompanied the women to the cinema during that operation, later pointed out about Mae Russell and the women in the prison-break attempt: 'the principle aspect of their bravery is that, had they been arrested at that time they would have spent many years in a British jail and they accepted that possibility'.[101]

Other than these two minor joint efforts, Cumann na mBan's role in the campaign is largely undocumented if, indeed, the group played much of a role at all. By its own public admission in *United Irishman*, it was ineffective in its role as an auxiliary to the IRA. The group collected clothes, funds and food, which they stored in Dublin. The Special Branch quickly found the 'depot' and confiscated everything.[102] The other activities in which Cumann na mBan took part, helping Sinn Féin during elections and selling copies of *United Irishman*, had even less of an impact. Like the rest of the republican movement, Cumann na mBan's support base had crumbled, leaving wives and members of the 'old guard' in its place to continue on with the name for tradition's sake.

The group had become the atrophied appendage to a ghost – so much so that one woman wrote to *United Irishman* asking where the women were within the republican movement. 'For some time I have been wondering where the Irish women are being put in this struggle for freedom. In past generations women have played an active part. Are the women of this generation to be left in the background?'[103] This letter assumes that women wanted to be in the foreground, but were being held back. It also implies that at one point women had played an equal role in political militancy, shoulder to shoulder with their male counterparts, which is not reflected in the historical record.[104] For the most part domestic responsibilities, combined with a popular drive for stability, limited republican women's choices. One of those who did not have domestic commitments was sceptical of its effectiveness given the political climate: 'I think I left Cumann na mBan before the end of the border campaign. It got very silly.'[105] Her judgement that the organization had become 'silly' reflects a frustration with the kind of supportive activity asked of the group, which was proving itself so ineffective in furthering the republican cause. It also reflects a growing dissatisfaction with the stagnation of the republican movement. She only returned after the campaign, when the republican movement had begun to engage with left-wing politics, and at that point she joined Sinn Féin. But Cumann na mBan was taken seriously, if not by some of its own members but by the government it was committed to bringing down.

On 10 May 1958 America's *Irish Echo* reported that Northern Ireland Home Minister, Colonel Topping, authorized the closing of Armagh prison for 'civilian females' so that it could be used instead to intern Cumann na mBan members. The minister explained that some women had been discovered to be spying on British soldiers and smuggling bombs for IRA members. On 21 November 1959 the *Irish Press* reported that Bridie O'Neill had been interned and that the police had a list of women that they were seeking out. Though Cumann na mBan tried to capitalize on her internment, claiming that to free her women should join the organization,[106] there was no perceptible attempt to propagandize this woman's internment in the mainstream press, and as far as increasing their membership, Cumann na mBan failed to make significant use of the opportunity. One newspaper reported at the time that Stormont was so acutely aware of a possible backlash in negative publicity that it discussed the internment of women at cabinet level, though the relevant records available do not support this assertion.[107] Yet, Bridie O'Neill's case dropped off the pages of even the republican press rather quickly. This could be because the internment policy was nothing more than insurance against renewed IRA action. It is possible that being aware of the prevailing gender regime in Northern Ireland, the Royal Ulster Constabulary (RUC) interned this one mother as a message to the movement, which would explain why more women were not interned.

Some of the more visible women in the republican movement fared better than Bridie O'Neill. A raid on the Sinn Féin headquarters in July 1957 netted many members of the republican leadership. Significantly, the only one to escape the round-up was 78-year-old Margaret Buckley, who, as discussed earlier, had been stripped of her title as President of Sinn Féin by militants seeking to take over the Ard Comhairle. A few days later, in an interview with a *Sunday Dispatch* reporter, Buckley pointed out that she was left at the Sinn Féin headquarters the night of the swoop because she was a woman,[108] and now she was the only one left of the Sinn Féin leadership to remain free.[109]

Though Stormont was willing to risk a backlash for interning a woman, de Valera, recently restored to power, was not. Throughout his very public life de Valera made no secret of his traditional view of women, and this situation would be no different. Even a few years later, after he became president, de Valera still maintained that women's only significant role within the republican movement was to gather intelligence.[110] The republican movement was quick to adapt to this policy by sending women to the press to argue their case. On 2 September Mae Russell (née Smith) spoke for Sinn Féin, criticizing the decision to intern and reaffirming the party's commitment to ending partition.[111] By November Sinn Féin had finally rebuilt its executive, predictably with Margaret Buckley brought back into the senior leadership as co-vice president with Tom Doyle and Mae Russell as co-secretary with Michael Traynor. Now if there were any more swoops, following from the logic of the last one, there would be two high-ranking members of Sinn Féin left to keep the continuity, even if they were not members of the IRA army council. Buckley, who had been president of Sinn Féin between 1937 and 1950, had kept the movement alive during internment in the war years because the government decided against interning a woman in her sixties. Brian Feeney makes the point that 'it would have been rather difficult for the State to intern her as a threat to its existence'.[112]

Guida West and Rhoda Lois Blumberg point out that 'various feminist scholars have observed that women-centred political consciousness frequently evolves through women's participation in gender-integrated struggles, whether revolutionary or reformist in nature'.[113] What is clear from this study, however, is that there are times when women do *not* develop a women-centred political consciousness. Women who engaged in the 1950s campaign rarely, if ever, expressed dissatisfaction with their auxiliary status, and Buckley and Russell were more than happy with their role in this shrewd arrangement designed to keep continuity within the movement should more arrests take place. They were only admitted into senior positions within the Ard Comhairle at this stage because their sex could be useful to the men that had stripped (at least one of) them from power only a year before. One of the aims of this chapter and the one that follows is to document and analyze how women could be involved with organizing protest movements and not develop this women-centred political consciousness. Building on Lovenduski[114] and Inglehart's[115] respective theories that developing that kind of consciousness is culturally specific and that political interest among women is influenced by national development, I argue that the act of *not* developing a women-centred consciousness is also influenced by historical development and its interaction with prevailing notions of gender regimes. We must be careful in this analysis to avoid dismissing the traditional nationalist consciousness these women displayed as less important or less worthy of study simply because the women of this movement did not find it necessary to destabilize their roles as women within the movement.

As more and more men were interned and kept from their families, some became acutely aware of the special position women held in Irish society. Frank Driver, famed for his imaginative if unrealistic methods of escape, came up with two plans that made use of this position. The first plan involved his wife dropping off their ten children on the doorstep of Archbishop McQuaid in Dublin to exert pressure on the Church to influence the government to release the internees. Another plan required wives and female relatives to march on the Curragh internment camp. They would bring wire cutters and try to cut through the fences. 'Think of the publicity if one of them got shot!' Driver is reported to have exclaimed.[116] In both scenarios, unlikely as they were, he played on the prevailing gender regime to expedite his release. Many at the camp dismissed Driver's imaginative schemes, but at a basic level his awareness of how the movement could manipulate perceptions of gender roles was very much in keeping with some of the more innovative tactics the IRA has become famed for. As if taking a cue from Driver, women in Belfast spontaneously stormed the Crumlin Road jail when they were denied access to their husbands, sons and fathers on 17 March 1958. A few months later a poem appeared in *United Irishman* applauding the women for their short-lived protest:

> May God bless the soldiers of Ireland
> In battle for freedom today;
> May God bless the mothers who bore them
> Their prayers giving them strength in the fray.
> But blessing I pray in abundance
> On Ulster's proud women and true
> For Crumlin Road Jail fell before them
> Its strong gates they bravely swept through.
> Their children were there beside them
> Their mothers to help and cheer.
> The RUC cried for assistance –
> Ye gods! How they trembled with fear!
> The women and children retreated
> – Against them the odds were too great.
> The 'chivalrous' minions of England
> Were glad when they opened the gate.
> Then over the Crumlin jail railings
> A Tricolour proudly was hung
> And while its fold flashed in the breezes
> The songs of the Rebels were sung.
> May God bless the women of Ulster –
> They're bravest were thickest the fray.
> We'll never forget how you captured
> The jail on St Patrick's own day.[117]

Though just a small blip on the state security radar, the storming of Belfast jail demonstrated what Driver knew to be true: women could transgress boundaries and commit security breaches with relative impunity. Notably, no feminist awareness grew out of this event and the women, though buoyed by their actions, did not undergo a collective identification with women-centred politics. The poem, itself, followed in a long line of gendered nationalist rhetorical tributes focusing on motivating men to fight and women to support them. Part of the humour of this poem is that women asserted themselves in a non-traditional aggressive manner.

Republican rhetoric is particularly instructive in studying the prevailing ideology surrounding women's position within the movement. For example, during the campaign *United Irishman* reran Padraig Pearse's decades-old call to arms:

Before we can do any work, any *men's* work, we must first realize ourselves as men. Whatever comes to Ireland, she needs men.
And we of this generation are not in any real sense men, for we
suffer things that men do not suffer and we seek to redress grievances by means, which men do not employ. We have, for instance,
allowed ourselves to be disarmed ... We may make mistakes in
the beginning and shoot the wrong people; but bloodshed is a
cleansing and sanctifying thing, and the nation which regards it as
the final horror has lost its manhood.[118]

The reprinting of Pearse's words suggests that gender roles had changed
very little within republicanism over the years. Men were the fighters
and political violence was the ultimate way to prove their virility.
Women, on the other hand, were generally portrayed as the personified
national territory. Under the prevailing gender regime, reconstituting
the land as a woman could easily explain how she had been subjugated
and dominated for so long. Eamonn O Murchadha's poem 'Róisín
Dubh', printed in *United Irishman*, is probably one of the most demonstrative of this kind of rhetoric:

As I was walking one evening fair
Among the bushes of green Tyrone
I met a maiden of beauty rare
Who sighed and mourned as she walked along
St Patrick bless you, my gentle girl;
Why do you grieve so my colleen dhoun?
'Alas', said she, 'I have lost a pearl,
And now it adorns a foreign crown.'
Said I: 'Remember in '57
The call resounded from sea to sea
And some who answered are now in heaven –
They died to win back that gem for thee.'
'And even today there are soldiers dwelling
In Belfast jail and across the sea,
Because they love you with fond hearts swelling
They've given all that you may be free.
Take courage maiden and cease your crying,
There are still brave soldiers to hear your call;
And soon our flag will be proudly flying
From Derry City to Cushendall.'
She smiled and said: 'Now my heart is joyful
For hope is burning in me anew;

While I have guardians with sword and rifle
I fear no tyrant or Saxon crew.'[119]

The poem personifies Ireland and speaks of the loss of her pearl, symbolic of her virtue. Freudian imagery aside, this poem functioned to
help shape its readership's perception of gender roles. It was designed
to be a tribute to those who fought in the border campaign by placing
them firmly within the continuum of Irish martyrs who had come
before them. This was nothing new to *United Irishman* readers, who
were well used to the personification of Ireland. However, it is her
youth that serves to heighten the effect of the poem. It serves to
dichotomize its readership while simultaneously calling them to
action. Men are asked to ready their arms to guard the woman; if every
man had a woman like Róisín Dubh to protect, armed resistance would
seem an adequate response to any assault on her. This poem also asks
women to *be* their husband's Róisín Dubh and in so doing, they would
play their part in furthering the cause.

It was not only poetry that set forth what was expected of republican women. The *United Irishman* also printed prose that analyzed
womanhood in the context of republicanism. Throughout the second
half of the campaign Gerard McKeown wrote full-page articles about
famous Irish heroines.[120] With the exception of two or three, all of
them treated the women in a perfunctory manner for a paragraph
or two before launching into a summary of the careers of the men
connected to them. Each article conveyed the message that to be
a good republican woman one's primary goal should be to further the
republican goals of her husband. This type of rhetoric, directed at
establishing acceptable parameters for women in republican households, continued in republican newspapers throughout the border
campaign and into the Troubles.[121]

Women occupied a kind of auxiliary position within the republican
movement with which very few, if any, voiced dissatisfaction. Gender
roles played a significant part in the division of labour, at points serving to retain movement structure in the face of mass internment of
men. The women of Cumann na mBan were a spent auxiliary force
in the 1950s and their contribution in the public sphere to further the
cause was negligible. More work needs to be done in order to determine the extent to which their contributions in the private sphere fur-
thered the goals of the republican movement, though hard
documentation that addresses this is scanty at best. Overall, their
secondary status generally benefited the patriarchal hierarchy of the

movement. Their portrayal as symbols of the national territory, which was probably the most significant contribution to the movement in this period, fed into that patriarchal hierarchy by cultivating a passive demeanour. Women in 1950s republican politics developed no significant women-centred consciousness. But most likely, this is more a product of their history, political development, and culture than any other mitigating factors.

PARTITION POLITICS ABROAD

Probably the most notable cross-border pressure group was the Anti-Partition League. Established in 1945 in Dungannon by Nationalist MPs, senators, priests and citizens, it sought, with the tacit approval of the Southern government, to counter the South's perceived acquiescence to the realities of partition. But a combination of poor organization and a lack of public enthusiasm for the cause saw the group disband by 1951, having achieved very little. The one thing it managed to do was spawn related groups abroad. These groups survived through sheer determination and quiet support from Leinster House. League members resident in Britain travelled between Northern Ireland and Dublin to report to the department of External Affairs on how partition was affecting those in the North.

On one such mission in 1955 the British Anti-Partition League recommended that the Republic publicly clarify its concern for the nationalist community in the North as a gesture to Northern nationalists.[122] Their vague suggestions went largely ignored and by the late 1950s the British League acted as nothing more than a mouthpiece to vent the frustration of Ireland's Department of External Affairs in Britain. Occasionally the group wrote responses to anti-nationalist articles in the British press under the main organizer's wife's name; these responses were broadly representative of the Irish government's position on the issue of partition.[123] This group continued its quixotic attempt to set the record straight throughout the 1950s, but by 1960 it had gone the way of its Irish counterpart. It was reportedly down to 102 members, most of whom had not paid their dues.[124]

Other Irish-focused radical groups fared similarly in Britain. The Irish National Union seemed to garner the antipathy of the more moderate groups. Scotland Yard Inspector Cunningham reported to the Irish Embassy in London that the leader of this group was a 'professional agitator, devoid of sincerity' who passed around the hat at meetings and lived off of those earnings and the income of prostitutes.[125]

Cunningham also reported that the communist Connolly Association had no sway over the Irish in London and that Sinn Féin did have some influence, which it wielded to gather intelligence for the IRA.[126] The Easter 1958 commemoration passed without incident and from the platform the Movement for Colonial Freedom made a speech contextualizing Northern Irish politics into the geopolitics of contemporary colonial struggles.[127] This commemoration provoked a quick spark of republican fervour in London when a hoax bomb threat against the Irish Embassy was called into the *Irish Independent*.[128] Overall though, very little radical and republican spillover occurred on the streets of London. Of the few events that did take place among the emigrant community, the records reveal women played an insignificant role in pressure tactics and radical agitation.

Emigrants and second-generation and third-generation Irish Americans fared somewhat better in terms of their activism. Places such as New York and California demonstrated their support both financially and rhetorically, limited though it was. The rhetorical support usually involved one or two fervent republican personalities rather than strong cohesive groups. Most of the support seemed to coincide with the commencement of the border campaign and the most vociferous in these groups were women such as Maureen Mulcahy, executive secretary of the United Irish Counties Association of New York, and Anne B. Kearns, president of the MacSwiney chapter of the American League for an Undivided Ireland. Their letters supporting the objectives of the republican movement and their campaign appeared frequently in government records and in the *United Irishman*.[129] Kearns single-handedly deluged the Irish Consulate, the Department of External Affairs and *United Irishman* with letters expressing concern for imprisoned or interned IRA members and contempt for the Republic's mode of handling the campaign. In a characteristic letter to *United Irishman*, she strongly urged the Irish government, the Dublin courts and all public bodies to 'extend justice to the young men of Ireland who have national aspirations for their country'.[130] Acting in her capacity as the secretary of the resolutions committee of the Saint Patrick's Day Convention of the United Irish Societies in San Francisco, she also sent a letter to the United Nations deprecating the treatment of Catholics in Northern Ireland. Lord Brookeborough, Prime Minister of Northern Ireland, publicly referred to Kearns's letter on 19 March 1958 by stating that those who wrote the resolution 'sympathized with' if not 'actively supported' those taking part in the border campaign.[131] Kearns would not have disputed this.

There was further evidence of Irish-America's support for militant republicanism in the columns and advertisements in local Irish-American newspapers. Throughout this period the *Irish Echo*, based in New York, routinely carried advertisements taken out by mixed-sex groups as well as female-based support groups such as the IRA Field Day Schedule Committee, the IRA Prisoners Aid Committee of New York, the Northern Republican Ladies Auxiliary, the Benevolent IRA Ladies and Cumann na mBan Inc. of New York.[132] The most significant issue to all of the governments concerned was Irish America's capacity to raise funds. Early on during the campaign Sean G. Ronan of the Chicago Consulate sent word back to Ireland that support in Chicago was growing and the IRA stood to make great sums of money from harnessing that support.[133] In 1959 an American embassy memorandum to the US State Department outlined how a 'major portion of IRA funds [were] derived from the contributions by Irishmen and other sympathizers in the United States'.[134] There is little doubt American money did go towards funding the campaign, but judging by its failure, it could not have been as significant as this correspondence indicates.

Though this issue worried the Department of Foreign Affairs, the activism that drew most comment was the power of celebrity. The fact that highly regarded entertainers such as Carmel Quinn and Siobhan McKenna were scheduled to appear at a New York dinner honouring the two main martyrs of the border campaign, Seán South and Fergal O'Hanlon, set off alarm bells in the Department of External Affairs in 1957. A directive was sent to John Conway, Consul General of New York, that they should be discouraged from attending: 'While we realize the full delicacy of the position it occurs to us that a personal approach to either or both the young ladies asking them to withdraw their support from these proceedings might be worth trying ... It occurs to me, however, that some of your staff or the staff of the Permanent Representative may be personally acquainted with either or both young ladies and might approach them informally.'[135]

A few years later McKenna voiced the republican line in a BBC interview, thus provoking angry responses from politicians in Northern Ireland. Most notably Prime Minister Brookeborough's sexist remarks provoked headlines: 'Normally I would not pay attention to this lady, but if she were put across someone's knee and spanked, it would do her some good.'[136] The *Irish Echo* in New York heartily supported her both in the aftermath of this interview and following her subsequent appearance at Dublin's Gaiety theatre wearing a gag in reference to the controversy generated by her statements.[137]

Overall, the few available archival records and contemporary press accounts indicate that though emigrant communities maintained an interest in Irish affairs, radical politics and pressure tactics regarding Ireland were generally weak. Linda Dowling Almeida contends that during this period interest in Irish political affairs 'remained solid among a core segment of the immigrant and ethnic community', but the evidence suggests that this interest did not translate into substantive support for the border campaign.[138] The women who involved themselves in this activity were of little significance to the general picture of activist groups and the money raised had little impact on the campaign. This trend in the emigrant community mirrors the trend on the island of Ireland itself, where women played a vocal but secondary role in a movement that itself was ailing.

WOMEN AND OTHER STRANDS OF RADICALISM

Though republicanism was a concern for the security community on both sides of the border and in Britain and America, the possibility of the spread of communism also preoccupied many intelligence gatherers. To contextualize this threat we must remember that in the 1950s the idea of a communist takeover was a powerful force in itself, which meant that many Irish communists had been driven underground. In the South, a combination of censorship, trade union and labour party red scares and strong Catholic opposition to communism rendered any type of communist organization redundant. In spite of this a few stalwarts lingered in the Communist Party of Northern Ireland (CPNI) based in Belfast and remained active in the trade union movement. Interestingly, the most useful records on the CPNI from this period were generated by the United States Department of State.[139] These memorandums generated in the embassy and consulate kept tabs on the general political situation in Ireland. In January 1955 the CPNI was already down to only 255 people, of which no more than twenty were serious members, according to the US State Department representatives.[140] A report sent back to Washington, DC acknowledged: 'Although admittedly the CP directs its appeals to the malcontents of all shades and descriptions, it is difficult for them to cut across both sides of the partition fence.'[141] Indeed, the CPNI had difficulty appealing to the Catholic community in general and therefore had even more difficulty discussing the unification of the working class. But the CPNI is worth looking at, regardless of its one-sided membership, because of its prominence; despite its insignificant numbers, it was well placed within the radical scene – disproportionately well placed.

The strength of the party was not in its numbers but in its ability to utilize its few members who retained strategic positions within the constellation of left-wing movements. Emmet O'Connor's research on Irish communism between 1919 and 1943 supports this assertion: in Northern Ireland, 'though membership fell sharply in 1944, and had withered to 172 by 1949, [it retained] positions of influence, in the engineering unions especially'.[142] There is little evidence that Moscow was directing operations or providing for local action on either side of the border; Comintern and then Cominform, the logical links between Moscow and international organizations, were dissolved by 1943 and 1956, respectively.[143] But the 'hard-core' of the CPNI were career politicos deeply committed to communist ideology, who hung on to their organization despite this breakdown in association. The Menzies family seemed to bind left-wing politics together during this period. Atheists coming from a Protestant tradition, both Sadie and her husband Edward had helped found the communist movement in its contemporary form, and their daughter, Edwina, was following in the tradition by directing the Young Workers League. Sadie was treasurer of the CPNI and was influential in the Belfast Assembly of Women and the Tenants' Defence Association, which had been established by the Belfast and District Trades Union to provide advice on housing and slum clearance. Edward was on the CPNI executive and also worked with the Tenants' Defence Association, according to the American State Department.[144] Betty Sinclair was another CPNI workhorse. She had dedicated her life to communism and the labour movement, which resulted in her retaining a seat on the CPNI executive and simultaneously holding the position of secretary of the Belfast and District Trades Union Council. Having made her name in the Outdoor Relief Workers' strike of 1932, she was by now a veteran of working-class politics.

Sadie Menzies, Betty Sinclair and Edwina Stewart (Sadie Menzies' daughter) would at different points wield considerable power within the CPNI,[145] but they were big fish in a small pond. The negligible membership of the party most likely played a factor in the ease at which these women ascended to powerful positions. They were suspicious of feminist politics in the same way that they would be suspicious of any other identity politics – it distracted from what they thought to be the more important struggle of uniting the working classes. In an interview conducted in 1980 Betty Sinclair summed up the prevailing distaste for feminism among those in the Party:

> Lenin put it plainly that in order to give women complete equal-
> ity we must be able to give her the economic conditions to express
> this equality ... It can only be solved on the basis of class strug-
> gle. I don't like feminism ... that the men are all wrong and the
> women are all right ... Feminism is not a working class outlook.[146]

Similar then, to women in the republican movement, women within
this radical movement did not develop a women-centred consciousness
during this period. This was compounded by the practicalities of working within such a small organization. The main goal had always been the
unification of the working classes. This, in a sectarian society, would
prove to be a Sisyphean effort.

   These figures would dominate the Communist Party for years to
come and would be instrumental in arguing for a broad-based radical
coalition to move publicly against the government. The American State
Department observed of them: 'The general view is that the organization will renew its activity in another form and may become a radical
party in the fuller sense of the term with an "abolish partition" platform.'[147] In 1962 the CPNI printed 'Ireland's path to Socialism'; it
would become crucial to teaching a new generation about the wisdom
of overlapping membership in broad-based activist groups.

CONCLUSION

Europe in the 1950s was characterized by a drive for stability. This led
to the formation of alliances and the establishment of wide-ranging
trade agreements. The main goals of these political and economic agreements were to counter the threat of communism and to render another
European war unlikely, if not impossible. Within this political paradigm,
European women experienced similar trends in terms of citizenship
status and legislative rights. Throughout this decade, however, many
European countries began to reassess their gender regimes initially with
the goal of economic reform.

   In both parts of Ireland women were becoming dissatisfied with
their prospects and they began to move to cities or emigrate to other
countries. The collapse of the rural demographic system contributed to
a self-perpetuating population crisis throughout the Irish countryside.
Social change was afoot most noticeably in public power struggles with
the Catholic hierarchy. We can trace the first utterings of social change
through the modernization process and the rise of popular culture.
In both parts of Ireland there was relatively little public pressure to

establish a women's agenda though changing international attitudes combined with transforming economic concerns would soon necessitate a re-evaluation of women's roles in society. Generally Irish women, similar to their European counterparts, focused on political lobbying and letter-writing, even within abeyance feminist organizations such as the Irish Countrywomen's Association and the Irish Housewives Association. These activities, however, did not represent a significant challenge to the status quo.

Within radical politics, and specifically republicanism, women were not well represented, nor were they vocal in seeking increased representation, though a few were able to secure senior positions in Sinn Féin specifically because of their perceived immunity to security force action and internment. The republican movement remained socially conservative in this period and tended to assign them to auxiliary roles with a handful of notable exceptions. The available records indicate that often women were content to remain in these roles due to their domestic commitments and a prevailing vision of sex-role propriety. This practice was typical of most political organizations of the period and should be looked at in the context of the abeyance of the feminist movement itself. The records indicate that women's issues was only on the radar of the republican leadership insofar as it focused on their auxiliary nature in reality and their victimhood in the abstract. Nowhere were these issues on the political agenda and even if they were, the high degree of religious observance, social conservatism and consensus meant that the movement remained organized along patriarchal lines. This rendered women's most critical role within the republican movement during this period domestic activism, with notable exceptions such as Margaret Buckley and Mae Russell. The few available records indicate that the emigrant community failed in its goal of garnering support for the republican movement's border campaign. Women within these groups though strong voices of republicanism themselves, could not marshal the kind of support that would turn the campaign towards success.

Within the Communist Party of Northern Ireland the handful of women involved worked as equals to men in the group, but this was most likely due to the emaciated state of the organization and not due to women's explicit agitation for equality. Rhetorically, Vladimir Lenin, the Russian communist leader and philosopher, emphasized equality among all members of the working class in working towards a socialist revolution. To members of the CPNI this obviated the need for a comprehensive discussion on sex roles.

Largely reflective of European trends in the 1950s, women within the radical political scene in either part of Ireland did not develop a women-centred consciousness, despite working in mixed-sex political organizations. If women did not develop this kind of consciousness within the mixed-sex but male-dominated republican movement, we should consider how women fared in a female-dominated movement. This next chapter explores the trajectory of what began as a woman-centred housing action committee and what turned into a male-dominated pressure group.

NOTES

1. Interview with border campaign-era republican activist Rita Whelan, Dublin, 2 April 2003.
2. J. Lovenduski, *Women and European Politics: Contemporary Feminism and Public Policy* (Brighton: Wheatsheaf, 1986), p.72.
3. E. Hobsbawm, *The Age of Extremes: The Short Twentieth Century, 1914–1991* (London: Abacus, 1994), p.259.
4. P. Thody, *An Historical Introduction to the European Union* (London: Routledge, 1997), p.8.
5. R. McAllister, *From EC to EU: An Historical and Political Survey* (London: Routledge, 1997), p.16.
6. C. Hoskynes, 'The European Union and the Women Within: An Overview of Women's Rights Policy', in R. Amy Elman (ed.), *Sexual Politics and the European Union: The New Feminist Challenge* (Oxford: Berghahn, 1996), p.15.
7. G. Kaplan, *Contemporary Western European Feminism* (London: UCL Press, 1992), p.26.
8. E. Sullerot, *Women, Society and Change,* trans. Margaret Scotford Archer (New York: McGraw Hill, 1971), p.225.
9. A. Oakley, *Subject Women* (New York: Pantheon, 1981), pp.250–1.
10. M. Grieve, *Millions Made My Story* (London: Victor Gollancz, 1964), p.197.
11. E. Connolly, 'The State, Public Policy and Gender: Ireland in Transition, 1957–1977', (Dublin City University, Ph.D. Thesis, 1998), p.217.
12. Lovenduski, *Women and European Politics,* p.61.
13. Connolly, 'State, Public Policy and Gender', pp.226, 230.
14. A. De Clementi, 'The Feminist Movement in Italy', in Gabrielle Griffin and R. Braidotti (eds), *Thinking Differently: A Reader in European Women's Studies* (London: Zed Books, 2002), p.333.
15. M. Pugh, *Women and the Women's Movement in Britain* (London: Macmillan, 2000), p.285.
16. See B. Halsaa 'The History of the Women's Movement in Norway', in G. Griffin and B. Rosi (eds), *Thinking Differently: A Reader in European Women's Studies* (London: Zed Books, 2002); Kaplan, *Contemporary Western European Feminism*; Lovenduski, *Women and European Politics*.
17. Kaplan, *Contemporary Western European Feminism,* p.15.
18. See D. Ferriter, *The Transformation of Ireland, 1900–2000* (London: Profile, 2004), pp.388–91; R. Foster, *Modern Ireland, 1600–1972* (Harmondsworth: Penguin, 1988), pp.559–63; J.J. Lee, *Ireland, 1912–1985: Politics and Society* (Cambridge: Cambridge University Press, 1989); E. O'Halpin, *Defending Ireland* (Oxford: Oxford University Press, 1999).
19. Lee, *Ireland, 1912–1985,* p.233.
20. T. Brown, *Ireland: A Social and Cultural History, 1922–1985* (London: Fontana Press, 1985), pp.215–16.
21. O'Halpin, *Defending Ireland,* p.255.
22. F. Tobin, *The Best of Decades: Ireland in the 1960s* (Dublin: Gill & Macmillan, 1984), pp.4–5.
23. M.E. Daly, *Social and Economic History of Ireland since 1800* (Dublin: Education Company of Ireland, 1981), p.164; Lee, *Ireland, 1912–1985.*
24. Brown, *Ireland: A Social and Cultural History.*
25. Daly, *Social and Economic History of Ireland,* p.173.
26. R. Harris, *Prejudice and Tolerance in Ulster: A Study of Neighbours and 'Strangers' in a Border Community* (Manchester: Manchester University Press, 1972).

27. Connolly, 'State, Public Policy and Gender', p.220.
28. Daly, *Social and Economic History of Ireland*, p.163.
29. Ibid., p.201.
30. L. O'Dowd, 'The Church, State and Women: The Aftermath of Partition', in C. Curtin, P. Jackson and B. O'Connor (eds), *Gender in Irish Society* (Galway: Galway University Press, 1987), p.4.
31. J.H. Whyte, *Church and State in Modern Ireland* (Dublin: Gill & Macmillan, 1971), pp.159–60.
32. M. Elliott, *The Catholics of Ulster: A History* (Harmondsworth: Penguin, 2000), p.450.
33. Whyte, *Church and State*, pp.230–1.
34. For more on the IHA's support for the scheme, see H. Tweedy, *A Link in the Chain: The Story of the Irish Housewives Association* (Dublin: Attic Press, 1992), p.73.
35. For more on how religious segregation has become more pronounced since the onset of the Troubles, see David McKittrick, *Independent on Sunday*, 21 March 1993, and *Independent*, 22 March 1993.
36. J.H. Whyte, *Interpreting Northern Ireland* (Oxford: Clarendon Press, 1990), p.48.
37. Quoted in Whyte, *Church and State*, p.20.
38. T. Hennessey, *A History of Northern Ireland, 1920–1996* (London: Macmillan, 1997), p.41.
39. *Report of the Council of Education as Presented to the Minister for Education : The Curriculum of the Secondary School* (Dublin: Stationery Office, 1960).
40. Quoted in J. Beale, *Women in Ireland: Voices of Change* (Indiana: Indiana University Press, 1987), p.129.
41. M. Valiulis, 'Neither Feminist nor Flapper: The Ecclesiastical Construction of the Ideal Irish Woman', in Mary O'Dowd and S. Wichert (eds), *Chattel, Servant or Citizen? Women's Status in Church, State and Society* (Belfast: Institute of Irish Studies, Queen's University of Belfast, 1995), p.175.
42. E. Connolly, 'Durability and Change in State Gender Systems', *European Journal of Women's Studies*, 10 (2003), p.70.
43. M. MacCurtain, 'Towards an Appraisal of the Religious Image of Women', in M.P. Hederman and R. Kearney (eds), *The Crane Bag Book of Irish Studies, 1977–1981* (Dublin: Blackwater Press, 1982).
44. For an interesting exploration of this idea, see Anne Crilly (director), 'Mother Ireland' (Northern Ireland, 1988).
45. Quoted in M. McWilliams, 'The Church, the State and the Women's Movement in Northern Ireland', in A. Smyth (ed.), *Irish Women's Studies Reader* (Dublin: Attic Press, 1993).
46. Connolly, 'Durability', p.80.
47. M. Luddy, 'The Labour Movement in Ireland', in A. Bourke, S. Kilfeather, M. Luddy, M. MacCurtain, G. Meaney, M.Ní Dhonnchadha, M. O'Dowd and C. Wills (eds), *Field Day Anthology of Irish Writing: Irish Women's Writing and Traditions*, vol, 5 (Cork: Field Day, 2002), Vol. 5, pp.561–2.
48. Connolly, 'Durability', p.69.
49. Y. Galligan, *Women and Politics in Contemporary Ireland: From the Margins to the Mainstream* (London: Pinter, 1998), p.30.
50. Connolly, 'Durability', pp.74–5.
51. C. Clear, *Women of the House: Women's Household Work in Ireland: 1922–1961* (Dublin: Irish Academic Press, 2000), p.5.
52. Connolly, 'Durability', p.77.
53. Beale, *Women in Ireland*, p.39.
54. Quoted ibid., p.34.
55. Department of Industry and Commerce, *Census of the Population of Ireland* (Dublin: Stationery Office, 1956).
56. M. Hill, *Women in Ireland: A Century of Change* (Belfast: Blackstaff Press, 2003), p.132.
57. M.E. Daly, 'Women in the Irish Workforce from Pre-Industrial to Modern Times', *Saothar*, 7 (1982), p.80; See also P. Travers, 'Emigration and Gender: The Case of Ireland, 1922–60', in M. O'Dowd and S. Wichert (eds), *Chattel, Servant or Citizen? Women's Status in Church, State and Society* (Belfast: Institute of Irish Studies, Queen's University of Belfast, 1995), p.191.
58. *Report on Emigration and Other Population Problems, 1948–1954* (Dublin: Stationery Office, 1954).
59. Lee, *Ireland, 1912–1985*, p.376.

60. Department of Education to the government, 28 April 1958, Dublin, National Archives (NA), Department of the Taoiseach (DT), 56231C.
61. J. Bardon, *A History of Ulster* (Belfast: Blackstaff Press, 1992).
62. Brew: Belfast slang for social welfare, believed to be a derivative of the word 'bureau'.
63. Bardon, *History of Ulster*, p.591.
64. Daly, *Social and Economic History of Ireland*, p.217.
65. P. Bew, P. Gibbon and H. Patterson, *Northern Ireland, 1921–1996: Political Forces and Social Classes* (London: Serif, 1996).
66 Daly, *Social and Economic History of Ireland*, p.201.
67. J. Simpson, 'Economic Development: Cause or Effect in Northern Ireland', in J. Darby (ed.), *Northern Ireland: The Background to the Conflict* (Belfast: Appletree Press, 1983), p.82.
68. Ibid., p.115.
69. B. Sinclair, 'Ulster Women and the War' (1942).
70. L. McShane, 'Day Nurseries in Northern Ireland', in C. Curtin, P. Jackson and B. O'Connor (eds), *Gender in Irish Society* (Galway: Galway University Press, 1987), pp.252–5.
71. J.M. Trewsdale, 'The Role of Women in the Northern Ireland Economy', in R.J. Cormack and R.D. Osborne (eds), *Religion, Education and Employment: Aspects of Equal Opportunity in Northern Ireland* (Belfast: Appletree Press, 1983), p.115.
72. Ibid., p.100.
73. A. Finlay, 'The Cutting Edge: Derry Shirtmakers', in C. Curtin, P. Jackson and B. O'Connor (eds), *Gender in Irish Society* (Galway: Galway University Press, 1987), p.87.
74. Ibid.
75. Bardon, *History of Ulster*, pp.593–4.
76. R. Lawrence, *The Government of Northern Ireland: Public Finance and Public Services, 1921–1964* (Oxford: Clarendon Press, 1965), p.122.
77. Lee, *Ireland, 1912–1985*, p.414.
78. O'Halpin, *Defending Ireland*, p.298.
79. Sinn Féin leaflet, December 1956, Dublin, NA, Department of Foreign Affairs (DFA).
80. *Irish Independent*, 19 January 1957.
81. T.P. Coogan, *The IRA* (London: Harper Collins, 2000), p.258.
82. B. Feeney, *Sinn Féin: A Hundred Turbulent Years* (Dublin: O'Brien Press, 2002), p.215.
83. Ibid., p.218.
84. J.B. Bell, *The Secret Army: The IRA, 1916–1979* (Dublin: Poolbeg, 1990), p.306.
85. Cremin to Department of External Affairs, 29 January 1958, Dublin, NA, DFA 313/2E.
86. R. English, *Armed Struggle: The History of the IRA* (London: Macmillan, 2003), p.76.
87. J. Wallach Scott, *Gender and the Politics of History* (New York: Columbia University Press, 1999), p.27.
88. M. O'Dowd and M.G. Valiulis (eds), *Women and Irish History* (Dublin: Wolfhound Press, 1997), p.9.
89. Coogan, *IRA*, p.258.
90. M. Ward, 'Marginality and Militancy: Cumann na mBan, 1914–36', in A. Morgan and B. Purdie (eds), *Ireland: Divided Nation, Divided Class* (London: Ink Links, 1980), p.104.
91. R. Ridd, 'Powers of the Powerless', in R. Ridd and H. Calloway (eds), *Caught up in Conflict: Women's Responses to Political Strife* (London: Macmillan, 1986), p.4; M. Rosaldo, 'Women, Culture and Society: A Theoretical Overview', in M. Rosaldo and L. Lamphere (eds), *Women, Culture and Society* (Stanford, CA: Stanford University Press, 1974).
92. Ridd, 'Powers of the Powerless', p.4.
93. M.E. Neugebauer, 'Domestic Activism and Nationalist Struggle', in J. Turpin and L.A. Lorentzen (eds), *The Women and War Reader* (New York: New York University Press, 1998), p.178.
94. Interview with Dolours Price, Malahide, 7 March 2003.
95. Bell, *Secret Army*, p.282; R.W. White, *Ruairí Ó Brádaigh: The Life and Politics of an Irish Revolutionary* (Indiana: Indiana University Press, 2006), pp.83–4.
96. Personal correspondence with Noel Kavanagh, 10 July 2009.
97. Interview with Máire Ó Nualláin, Dublin, 3 December 2002; interview with Rita Whelan, Dublin, 2 April 2003.
98. Bell, *Secret Army*, p.258.
99. Coogan and Bell have slightly differing accounts: Coogan claims the name of the group was the Scelligs Players while Bell says it was the Skellig Players and Coogan sensationalizes the smuggling by claiming the women had guns 'stashed in their underwear'. See Coogan, *IRA*, p.272, and Bell, *Secret Army*, p.282.

100. Coogan, *IRA*, p.272.
101. Personal correspondence with Noel Kavanagh, 10 July 2009.
102. *United Irishman*, 11 November 1957.
103. *United Irishman*, 7 July 1957.
104. See R. Taillon, *The Women of 1916: When History Was Made* (Belfast: Beyond the Pale, 1996); M. Ward, *Unmanageable Revolutionaries: Women and Irish Nationalism* (Dingle: Brandon, 1983).
105. Interview with Máirín de Burca, Dublin, 15 March 2004.
106. *United Irishman*, 17 May 1958.
107. *Belfast Telegraph*, 19 November 1958; see Cabinet papers, Belfast, Public Records Office of Northern Ireland (PRONI), CAB/4/1074-1077.
108. Telegram of text of article, 14 July 1957, *Sunday Dispatch*, Dublin, NA, DFA 305/14/263/2D.
109. Feeney, *Sinn Féin*, p.208.
110. See de Valera to Lemass, 4 April 1962, Dublin, NA, DT 98/6/494.
111. *Irish Echo*, 7 September 1957.
112. Feeney, *Sinn Féin*, p.178.
113. G. West and R.L. Blumberg, 'Reconstructing Social Protest from a Feminist Perspective', in G. West and R.L. Blumberg (eds), *Women and Social Protest* (Oxford: Oxford University Press, 1990).
114. Lovenduski, *Women and European Politics*.
115. M. Inglehart, 'Political Interest in West European Women', *Comparative Political Studies*, 14 (1981).
116. Coogan, *IRA*, p.321.
117. 'Storming of Belfast Jail', *United Irishman*, 8 August 1958.
118. *United Irishman*, December 1958.
119. Eamonn O Murchadha, 'Róisín Dubh', 9 September 1962, *United Irishman*.
120. Though he failed to sign all of the articles, it can reasonably be assumed that he wrote them all judging from the similarity of style in each article. See *United Irishman*, 'Betsy Grey', 6 June 1959; 'The Rebel Countess', 8 August 1960; 'Mary MacSweeney', 10 October 1960; 'Annie Hutton', 11 November 1960; 'Jane Patten', 12 December 1960; 'Mary Emmet', 1 January 1961; 'Mary Jane Erwin', 3 March 1961; 'Mother Mary Aikenhead', 4 April 1961; 'Maria Steele', 5 May 1961; 'Mary Teeling', 7 July 1961; 'Ellen O'Leary', 8 August 1961; 'Jennie Mitchel', October 1961; 'Maud Gonne MacBride', 2 February 1962.
121. For more on this see C.B. Shannon, 'The Woman Writer as Historical Witness: Northern Ireland, 1968–1994. An Interdisciplinary Perspective', in Valiulis and O'Dowd (eds), *Women and Irish History*, p.251.
122. Report on Belton and Dr MacWhite's visit to the 6 Counties, 20–23 September 1955, Dublin, NA, DFA P273/1.
123. Cremin to Murphy, 1957, Dublin, NA, DFA 305/14/108bI.
124. Report on the Anti-Partition League, 1960–61, Dublin, NA, DFA 305/14/108bII.
125. London Embassy to DFA, 6 March 1958, Dublin, NA, DFA A12.
126. London Embassy to DFA, 6 March 1958, Dublin, NA, DFA A12.
127. MacCanna to DFA, 8 April 1958, Dublin, NA, DFA 313/31D.
128. MacCanna to DFA, 21 April 1958, Dublin, NA, DFA 313/31D.
129. Irish-American reaction to IRA activities, 1957, Dublin, NA, DFA A/12/2A.
130. *United Irishman*, 3 March 1957.
131. LaFreniere to State Department, 28 March 1958, College Park, Maryland, NARA, 741A.00/3-2858, XR 811.46.
132. *Irish Echo*, 1957.
133. Ronan to Department of External Affairs, 15 February 1957, Dublin, NA, DFA A12/2A.
134. Ward to State Department, 19 November 1959, College Park, Maryland, NARA 740A.00 (w)6-558.
135. Department of External Affairs to Conway, 2 February 1957, Dublin, NA, DFA 305/14/263/2.
136. *United Irishman*, 6 June 1959.
137. *Irish Echo*, 16 May 1959 and 23 May 1959.
138. L.D. Almeida, 'A Great Time to be in America: The Irish in Post-Second World War New York City', in D. Keogh, F. O'Shea and C. Quinlan (eds), *The Lost Decade: Ireland in the 1950s* (Cork: Mercier Press, 2004), p.218.

139. The Communist Party of Ireland papers are not available to the public at the time of writing.
140. Anderson to State Department, 17 January 1955, College Park, Maryland, National Archives and Record Administration (NARA), 741A.00/1-1755.
141. Anderson to the USDS, 17 January 1955, NARA, 741A.00/1-1755.
142. E. O'Connor, *Reds and the Green: Ireland, Russia and the Communist Internationals, 1919–43* (Dublin: University College Dublin Press, 2004), p.233.
143. Ibid., p.234.
144. Anderson to the USDS, 17 January 1955, College Park, Maryland, NARA, 741A.00.
145. For more on Sinclair and Stewart, see Chapter 4 below.
146. L. Edgerton, 'Interview between Lynda Edgerton and Betty Sinclair' (Belfast: Linen Hall Library Political Collection, 1980).
147. Thiel to USDS, 1 March 1962, College Park, Maryland, NARA, 741A.00.

CHAPTER TWO

'Surely women aren't inferior':[1]
A Case Study of Activism in
Dungannon, 1963–7

The twitching, nose-tapping, winking pundits had it all taped as usual, however: *she* was *after the seat*. *That* was the glittering prize, a position in the gilded halls of Stormont or Westminster! ... Who was *she* or, more properly in the then almost entirely male-dominated society of Northern Ireland, why was it *she*? ... When, in her wide-brimmed hat and striking costume, she headed a parade of homeless young mothers, their babies and prams, through Dungannon, she strode right into the conscience of a people and into the history of our times. There, indeed, all unknowing, walked the Juno, the veritable Mother of Civil Rights in Northern Ireland. (P.J. McCooey on Patricia McCluskey)[2]

For forty years the international perception of Northern Ireland has been characterized by a maelstrom of clichés regarding sectarian hatred, political violence and systemic discrimination. The clichés, not without a basis in fact, made for gripping news, suspenseful reading and electrifying viewing. And each night people around the world tuned in to the news to witness the latest spate of bombings, continually asking themselves, how did they let it get this far? This chapter explores some pivotal moments in the period immediately preceding the Troubles that contributed towards heightening the tension between the Catholic community and the Northern Irish government, dominated in large part by Protestant men.

Specifically, this chapter focuses on a small female-led public housing campaign that gave way to a larger critique of systematic government discrimination against the Catholic community. In some ways these women broke down taboos about their participation in public life and in other ways they confirmed stereotypes about the Northern Irish gender regime. The stories of these women, for the most part only mentioned on the periphery of Northern Irish history,[3] are integral to understanding not only the evolution of the civil rights movement and the Troubles, but also the evolution of women and class in the public sphere.

Daily life in Northern Ireland in the late 1950s and early 1960s was characterized by social and religious conservatism, the working classes' hunt for work, and a growing dissatisfaction among the Catholic community regarding their position within the state. The Irish state's increasingly ambivalent attitude[4] towards the Northern minority only compounded the community's dejection. A number of factors contributed to the beginning of the formation of a new consciousness among the Catholic community. Internationally the 1960s heralded new concepts of citizenship throughout the western world. Black America was pioneering the drive for civil rights and the exponential rate at which televisions made their way into homes allowed the world unprecedented access to the events of the day. As a consequence, an increasingly educated generation of Northern Irish Catholics began to rethink its role in society by applying the rhetoric of equality and social justice to its own circumstances. Towards the end of the 1960s a civil rights movement would emerge, but before it would, there was a spark that created a level of hope among the Catholic community that change was possible.[5] This chapter examines how a small protest group succeeded in creating that initial spark, which later evolved into a strong call for equality and civil rights throughout the province.

A major topic of political and social debate in Northern Ireland in this period involved development and employment. The fact that the region suffered from a higher rate of unemployment and a lower average income than the rest of the United Kingdom meant that families found themselves under great strain simply to survive. And though Northern Ireland was indeed developing, the more pronounced improvement of other regions of the United Kingdom, such as Scotland and Wales, highlighted the overall lack of economic progress in Northern Ireland.[6] To compound the issue, Catholics seemed to fare significantly worse than their Protestant counterparts in the jobs market. While other factors such as their geographic location relative to industrial centres have affected Catholic employment levels in Northern Ireland, discrimination also helped explain the rate of nearly 14 per cent of Catholic unemployment as compared to less than 6 per cent of Protestant unemployment.[7] But the most historically significant element of this phenomenon is not whether there was institutionalized discrimination in the area of employment; rather, it is that there was a growing *perception* that institutionalized discrimination against Catholics was widespread. It was this perception that began to surface in conversations about the folly of the status quo, about why Catholics had more difficulty finding employment and about what the Northern Ireland of the 1960s should become.

Another element of growing Catholic discontent with the status quo surrounded the distribution of public housing. The housing shortage that existed in the 1930s had been exacerbated by the damage sustained in the Second World War. In response, the Northern Irish government established the Northern Ireland Housing Trust in 1945. It sprang to action, achieving its goal of 100,000 new local authority houses by the early 1960s. But this significant achievement, according to Jonathan Bardon, 'set a time bomb ticking' in terms of how these houses were being distributed.[8] As outlined above in Chapter 1, the distribution of housing was controlled by local councils dominated by Unionist politicians, and because of this, allocations were closely linked to political power. Not bound to follow a points system, the district councillors could distribute homes that had been built in their own wards to whomever they believed to be most in need. The fact that the ward boundaries were gerrymandered in many areas to ensure Unionist domination of the local council led to an increasing sense of structural discrimination against the Catholic population of Northern Ireland in terms of representation and housing. Lord Cameron, in his 1969 report to the Northern Irish government, confirmed the notion that housing allocations, especially in Dungannon, Armagh and Derry, were being manipulated to maintain permanent Unionist domination of the various governing bodies.[9]

A third element that contributed to a general sense among Northern Irish Catholics that discrimination was endemic to the institutions of the state was the state's approach to law and order. Relying heavily on emergency powers instituted in the 1920s, the government was able to quash opposition with relative ease through the threat or implementation of internment without trial. The Cameron commission supported this assertion in its findings. Because the political opposition was invariably Catholic up to this point, it is not surprising Catholics felt alienated by Northern Irish security forces. No attempt was made to disguise the political nature of the security strategy in the years leading up to the late 1960s, which further exacerbated widespread perceptions that the state was willing to utilize repressive and sectarian tactics in order to guarantee its continuity.[10]

The housing policy, the perception of employment discrimination, and the state's approach to law and order combined to offer a particularly bleak backdrop to the ringing in of a new decade for Northern Irish Catholics. This feeling of malaise led an increasingly educated Catholic population to begin to articulate its sense of alienation from the machinery of the state in a small area west of the River Bann, in the unassuming town of Dungannon. Women began to seize on the newly popularized rhetoric of civil rights they had heard on the radio and saw on the television, to question the process of housing allocation in their district.

While the topic of women's activism in the Northern Irish civil rights movement has been explored in other studies,[11] it is important to broaden the analysis by more fully exploring the interactions of class and gender within this nascent movement. Through the story of Dungannon's Homeless Citizens League and Campaign for Social Justice, we can delve into how male-centred, middle-class interests emerged from an all-female working-class activist group to present an alternative to republicanism, a movement that, as discussed in Chapter 1, was in a process of reconstituting itself.

THE HOMELESS CITIZENS LEAGUE

In the early 1960s families in Dungannon, similar to their counterparts in Belfast and Derry, were benefiting from the increase in the construction of Housing Trust dwellings, but in Dungannon somehow the tenements showed no signs of emptying out. The town of roughly seven thousand had a fairly equal split of Catholics and Protestants.[12] Mostly located in sub-divided Georgian houses along Northland Row in the urban district, Dungannon's homeless, who were for the most part Catholic, lived seven or eight to a room. The overcrowding was having a significant effect on the mental and physical well-being of each family, according to the local doctor.[13] The landlords who owned these homes retained a vote for their own home, a vote for the house they let out, and, if they owned a business, they would get a vote for the business in local elections. Their tenants, on the other hand, were disenfranchised because they did not own property. Consequently, Catholics lacked significant representation to challenge the system. The government of Northern Ireland had consistently resisted British steps to democratize its electoral law between 1945 and 1948, which meant that by this period Northern Ireland stood out as a British electoral anomaly. This pluralized voting system both *perpetuated* and *was perpetuated by* a system in which Protestants controlled the council, the housing and business.

Angela McCrystal, a local factory worker, lived with her mother, an uncle, her husband and her disabled son in a two-bedroomed house in this area of Dungannon. When she began to notice that Protestant newlyweds were being issued new homes while Catholic families were waiting on housing allocation lists for up to seven years in some cases, McCrystal decided to do something: 'I asked [Ann Dunlop and Susan Dinsmore] would they go out with me and we went to find out how many people were living in accommodation who needed houses ... I just took a copybook and three of us started in Northland Row.'[14] It is important to note that some houses were being built in the Ballysaggart area for Catholics who were already living in condemned social housing, but no *new* family was eligible for these houses because of the length of the waiting lists.[15] A civil rights pamphlet published in 1969 provided convincing numbers: in Dungannon in 1963 'there were upwards of 300 families on the housing waiting list, some for as long as 12 years, and not one *new* Catholic family had been allocated a permanent house for 34 years'.[16] The young families that were living with their relatives in this condemned housing would be left homeless when their relatives were rehoused. Some of the Catholic families who were scheduled to be rehoused lived in the Fairmount Park area in old prefabricated houses that were scheduled to be torn down. That spring of 1963, as she tabulated the results of her informal survey and began to understand the extent of the housing problem, McCrystal thought about taking over the Fairmount Park prefabs. But doing so would be a flagrant move against the local council. Instead, she would simply try to highlight the issue and shame the council into action.

As racial riots broke out in Alabama on 13 May, McCrystal and sixty-six other homeless women seized on Martin Luther King's tactics and marched into the centre of town – a Protestant area. They believed two things: that women and children were unlikely to be blocked, and that women who looked respectable, like those who stood shoulder to shoulder with King in the American South, would retain the moral high ground. They marched towards the council building and staged a picket with placards that expressed similarities between the American South and their own situation in Northern Ireland. The *Dungannon Observer* reported a tense scene when women challenged local police with placards that read 'Racial discrimination in Alabama hits Dungannon' and 'If our religion is against us ship us to Little Rock', where the conflict over desegregating the local schools had necessitated the intervention of a federalized National Guard in 1957.[17] Later McCrystal explained that the parallel had been clear to her from the 1950s forwards: 'I was very impressed with Martin Luther King and also John Fitzgerald Kennedy. I always enjoyed listening to the programmes, listening to what was happening in America.'[18] The Unionist majority of councilmen tried to ignore this unusual march populated by women and babies in prams, but the tension increased in the council room as councilman Jim Corrigan, an Independent with a nationalist outlook, put pressure on the council to admit them. These women, uncharacteristic as it may have seemed at the time, had no intention of going away.

The scholarly research on the position of women in Northern Ireland is in a process of recovery, and though people such as Monica McWilliams, Eileen Evason, Lynda Edgerton, Valerie Morgan, Eilish Rooney and Rachel Ward have contributed significantly to the study of women in the contemporary period, their work has tended to focus on the period following the advent of the Troubles. This has located contemporary Northern Irish women within the context of communal violence and ethno-sectarian conflict.[19] The body of work on the status of women in Northern Ireland in the decade preceding this period, however, is relatively thin. Of the authors that have looked at these early women activists, Bob Purdie, Brian Dooley and Simon Prince discuss their protests, but their focus remains on the larger civil rights movement and not on how class and gender interacted in this fledgling movement.[20] John Nagle provides a useful contribution to the study of this early period in his analysis of how 'ban-the-bomb' and housing action in Belfast was part of a larger cross-community 'right to the city'[21] movement and a tactical precursor to the civil rights movement.[22] Similarly, however, he does not explore the core issues relevant to this book. The only focused work on these women has come from Catherine B. Shannon, who has analyzed the actions of these early civil rights activists not in the context of gender and class, but in terms of their mobilization tactics.[23] These dual systems that hierarchically organize social, cultural and political relations are pivotal to understanding the progression, successes and indeed the limitations of the early civil rights groups. Similar issues surfaced in the American South during this period and are instructive in terms of their impact on the evolution of the civil rights movement itself.

American civil rights leaders used the idea of middle-class respectability as a tactic to appeal to a wide cross section of opinion. They encouraged protesters to dress modestly and told female activists to appear dignified and ladylike in order to minimize their obvious challenge to the gender regime and to defuse this potentially explosive exposure to conservative public opinion.[24] This strategy had the desired effect in America, and now people as far away as Northern

Ireland were internalizing it and putting it to use. The Dungannon women would not conform to prevailing stereotypes about the city's homeless; they were respectable, dignified people calling for the reform of a flawed system. Their performative tactics were carefully planned to achieve results. Judith Butler discusses this phenomenon by pointing out that gender, or in this instance, womanhood, is not who these women were (their sex), but rather, how they projected who they were (through their clothing and their children).[25] Class is similarly performed. In this case, the women did so through their clothing and their comportment. The performance of respectability allowed these women – a group that sought to reconfigure the system by entering into it – to push for fundamental change in local governance. Paradoxically, while their strategy did nominally threaten those in power, it would be this very performance of respectability that would ensure that the dual power structures of patriarchy and middle-class Unionist domination would for the most part remain intact for the foreseeable future.

Sociologists Bert Useem and Mayer N. Zald identify two ways movements try to gain legitimacy: through cultivating a legitimacy of numbers or means.[26] The former is secured by mobilizing a large number of activists to challenge existing power structures. A legitimacy of means is achieved by convincing the public that the movement's strategies and tactics are the most appropriate for achieving the stated goals. While the group of women marching on Dungannon could hardly be called a 'movement', the rationale for their strategy was the same. The women's main concern was obtaining public housing, and in order to do this they took pains to establish the credibility of their cause through their measured manner and respectable outward appearance.

As part of a liberal reformist activist group, the women who began this agitation were motivated by a combination of economic and maternal concerns. Each of the participants interviewed for this chapter cited the impact of overcrowded conditions on their children and their husbands' sleeping patterns and job performance as a primary factor spurring them to action. Guida West and Rhoda Lois Blumberg, in their sociological inquiry into women's activism, confirm this reasoning: 'in fighting to survive at the grass-roots level, women have justified their political action as a struggle to feed, house and clothe their children'.[27] Those who took part in the Dungannon protest often expressed the idea that as women, securing decent housing was their familial responsibility. Monica McWilliams, co-founder of the Northern Ireland Women's Coalition in 1996, has looked at how religious institutions and the state have combined in Northern Ireland in shaping the role of women to reflect an ideology of motherhood and home-makers.[28] For Catholic women, this meant identification with the figure of Mary, whose primary identity was rooted in her status as a mother. Also, as a consequence of stagnating regional employment rates as compared to other regions in the United Kingdom,[29] the identification of womanhood with the private sphere has been born out in statistical comparisons. McWilliams points out that in 1971 'only 29 per cent of married women were economically active in Northern Ireland. This contrasts sharply with the figure of 42 per cent for Great Britain.'[30] In this period few Northern Irish women publicly questioned their domestic roles. Rather, they tended to draw strength from it by leveraging it to exert political influence regarding housing issues as evidenced in the Springtown camp housing action that took place in the 1950s in Derry.[31] The Dungannon women, seeing the housing issue as their chief responsibility, moved against their local council in a similar fashion as their Derry predecessors. What made this different from Springtown was, as Simon Prince argues, the changing global context, as well as advances in media technology.[32]

As the picket continued outside the office, Jim Corrigan continued to press council chairman Senator William Stewart to admit a deputation nominated by the protesters.[33] This group, Corrigan said, wished to read their 'Declaration of Independence'. Reluctantly Stewart admitted Angela McCrystal, Susan Dinsmore and Ann Dunlop. This 'Declaration of Independence' attempted to force a dialogue with the council by asking six questions about the idiosyncrasies of the housing allocation system:

- When these relatives are moved to the Ballysaggart Estate, where will the young people go?
- What will be the Council's policy toward those rendered homeless by slum clearance?
- Does the Council offer any definite solution to the plight of the young married people of this town, particularly of the West Ward?
- Will any future housing development be made for the sole purpose of accommodating these young people?
- Will the Council accept the suggestion that all future housing schemes include a fixed proportion of homes for young marrieds [sic]?
- When is a points system coming into operation to ensure a fair distribution of houses in this town?[34]

The council had resigned itself to listening to their questions, but was also careful not to indicate that it would take any action to alleviate the situation. The women decided to regroup in a few days.

The fact that Jim Corrigan used the term 'Declaration of Independence' is significant. He did not use the term 'proclamation', which, with its Nationalist connotations, would have exacerbated an already tense situation. However, by using this particular term, Corrigan made an obvious reference to American history. Because the declaration was made in response to oppressive British legislation by many who considered themselves Ulster-Scots, the metaphor remained just shy of an insult to the Unionists. Further, the decision to use an American event summoned images of the now daily news features on the failed American policy of segregation. Corrigan's use of this American term hinted at a worst-case scenario of what could become of this situation if it was not resolved. Considering the make-up of the group presenting the document, the use of the phrase 'Declaration of Independence', although patronizing, was apt. Their challenge to the gender regime was palpable. They were declaring their own independence from gendered discourse by bucking prevailing definitions of femininity, which, as discussed in the first chapter, emphasized domesticity and passivity. It is significant to note the apparent paradox inherent in this type of political expression in this context. At once these women empowered themselves through their decision to take on the Unionists in such a public manner and, at the same time, the mode by which they chose to empower themselves was through expressing their maternalism as respectable women aspiring to middle-class lifestyles by defending the domestic sphere.

A few weeks passed and nothing came of this attempt to engage with the council. So Angela McCrystal visited Senator William Stewart, who chaired the urban council, with a view to attending another council meeting to explain their case: 'He also had a chemist shop in Dungannon. And I remember going in to him and asking to get into the Council offices. And he said, "No. I can tell you this: you will never, ever, ever get a house in Dungannon. I will see to it that you don't."'[35] McCrystal's memory of the conversation highlights how Unionist members of the council perceived the women to be a threat. But far from intimidating McCrystal, this conversation convinced her to press on. Moreover, she had very little to lose; she had already given up her factory job to take care of her son, and she had just been told she would never be granted a home. West and Blumberg point out that 'women and men's traditionally unequal status in the world of paid and unpaid (household) work has made women more available as candidates for community organizing'.[36] The fact that some Dungannon women had the discretionary time to engage in street politics is important to understanding how this developed into a single-sex pressure group. Even more pivotal is how as unpaid household workers, women who engaged in social protest retained a degree of protection from the kinds of economic retribution their husbands might receive if they were engaged in the same protests. Though as time progressed employers would begin to target spouses of community activists, that time had not yet arrived.

On the other side of Dungannon, Patricia McCluskey, the local doctor's wife, was in her husband's surgery when she came upon some young women who were visibly upset about the inequality of housing distribution. Her husband, Dr Conn McCluskey, later wrote that 'the strain on young mothers trying to maintain order and a degree of quiet, where most facilities had to be shared, was very great. Men on night shift work found it impossible to sleep. One young mother took a drug overdose and was removed to hospital. Something had to be done.'[37] Patricia McCluskey remembered feeling that through the tax system these families had a right to a fair allocation of housing. This belief prompted her to investigate the issue further.

On 24 May the women marchers met at Dungannon's St Patrick's hall to determine their next step. Patricia McCluskey attended this meeting with the intention of helping the women draft another petition to the council. When the main speaker of the meeting failed to materialize and it looked as if the group would disband, McCluskey took the chair and called the group to order – the Homeless Citizens League (HCL) was born. Under the chairmanship of Patricia McCluskey, whose professional experience and confidence far outpaced that of the other women, the League leapt to action. Angela McCrystal, also a natural leader, remained a strong force in the group by taking up the position of secretary. However, the solidarity of the League suffered an initial setback when a few members expressed reservations to McCrystal about McCluskey's motives in taking a leadership role in the organization.[38] These reservations centred on her middle-class background: she was by no stretch one of Dungannon's homeless. In fact, she was an educated former teacher and social worker whose relative wealth could not have separated her more from those attending the meeting. McCluskey explained her motivation for leading the group by citing Christian social teaching, which emphasized charitable acts. Her position in the class structure of the town was also a factor: 'I just felt somehow or other that it was on me, as the doctor's wife, to let it be known that they weren't getting the breaks they deserved.'[39]

The first public meeting of the HCL was set for four days hence, once again, at St Patrick's Hall. The meeting was attended by 125 people, including Jim Corrigan and fellow councilmen Jimmy Donnelly and Brian Morrison, who were likely aware that the HCL's activities would spotlight their own political ineffectiveness.[40] The main discussion topic was a points system for the distribution of housing, which meant that a number of points would be allocated to homeless families for the number of children and number of years the applicant had been waiting.[41] Overall, it was designed to ensure that the most deserving would get houses. To drive home the point to the local media that the present system was failing, Patricia McCluskey compared the situation in Dungannon to her first-hand experience as a social worker with the notoriously substandard housing of the Gorbals area of Glasgow. Despite McCluskey's dramatic comparison, the politicians dominated the meeting, offering their own perspectives. Their contribution to the discussion underlined that perhaps Patricia's analogy had holes; even politicians in the Gorbals were attempting to address their housing crisis constructively. Nationalist councillor Brian Morrison defended the 'gentlemen's agreement' between members of the Council Housing Committee, which dictated that vacated Catholic homes would be filled only by Catholics and Protestant homes only by Protestants. As explained earlier in the chapter, it was this very agreement that perpetuated Unionist domination of the council and the discriminatory housing policy. But significantly, the system also benefited the Nationalists, whose complicity ensured their own political survival as leaders of the community and the only ones with the ear of the Unionist decision-makers.

As the meeting wound down, the HCL decided that they had heard the politician's point of view, and now they should encourage local business owners to present their own analysis. This attempt to attract the middle class to this working-class issue reveals the direction in which Patricia McCluskey was moving. Her drive to appeal to a wide cross section of the regional population and to garner sympathy from the voting middle class – some of whom held two or three votes in local elections – would guarantee a hearing from the local council. But the business owners were not as eager to meet with the group as Patricia had hoped. One of them wrote to the local newspaper questioning McCluskey's motives for chairing the group.[42] The tactic, however, backfired, and that particular letter actually served to

consolidate McCluskey's position on the executive by forcing the HCL
to rally to her side and issue a statement outlining her contribution to
the group.

This statement prompted McCluskey to bring the housing issue to
national newspapers such as the *Irish News* in the North, the *Irish Press*
in the South and even an unsympathetic regional paper known as the
Tyrone Courier. Until now only the *Dungannon Observer*, a local sympathetic newspaper, would take up the story. On 6 June 1963 the *Tyrone Courier* interviewed McCluskey about the League.[43] In the
interview she brought up the impending demolition of the prefabricated houses in Fairmount Park. McCluskey courted controversy by
suggesting that once those people left, the members of the HCL should
be allowed to temporarily occupy the prefabs. She concluded the bull-
ish interview by stating that every member of the League was a local
and not a stranger to the town of seven thousand, an implication that
Unionists were issuing houses to non-local Protestants rather than local
Catholics.[44] This no-name countrywoman had just issued a jolting challenge to her local government officials – in their own paper. On the
farms of Armagh and in the lanes of the Bogside the question on people's lips as more newspapers spread the word was, what next?

On 11 June the *Irish News* picked up the story, reporting that on the
previous day a group of sixty women and 200 supporters had converged on the council. Patricia McCluskey, Angela McCrystal and
Susan Dinsmore, of the eight-person organizing committee, led the
march.[45] On 15 June a picture of the HCL marches appeared in the
Dungannon Observer showing two small boys – one with his face
blackened – holding a placard that read:

> We are pals from Alabama,
> Where they say we can't agree.
> Is there really that much difference,
> When you look at him and me?[46]

The image had the desired effect of creatively contextualizing their
struggle in order to grab headlines while at the same time indicating
how superficial the inspiration taken from America was.

Throughout the summer the marches continued, as did the drumbeat
of fundamental reform. Conn McCluskey, a strong presence on the periphery of the HCL committee, later described the marches as 'sad but
impressive turnouts, the women in their Sunday best, children walking
and in prams. Stragglers were marshalled by Patricia. Here and there the
odd husband looking hangdog in his unwelcome notoriety.'[47]

Conn McCluskey's throw-away remark that the husbands were not welcomed at the marches casts the HCL in a unique light. The HCL did not go out of its way to bring men into its fold, which gave credence to the perception that the housing problem was a women's issue. Conn McCluskey later gave his interpretation of their absence: 'there were two or three men involved but [most men] hadn't the courage to tackle the issue'.[48]

One study of housing action in south-east London found that one of the reasons for women's leadership of protests involved men's demoralization at not being able to provide for their families,[49] which may explain women's roles in this protest: as discussed earlier Catholic regional unemployment rates hovered at 14 per cent, while Protestants experienced a 6 per cent average rate of unemployment.[50] Another likely reason for their absence was that the men had less freedom to rebel; the unemployed stayed away for fear that it would ruin their chances of a future job opportunity, while those men who were employed were either busy working or did not participate for fear of losing their coveted posts. The women, on the other hand, due to their numbers in the factories or if they were home, to their flexible schedules, had more agency and less fear of retaliation from employers or the Royal Ulster Constabulary. This, combined with a perception that as women they did not represent a threat to the status quo, enabled them to take a harder line in their tactics. The few middle-class women who participated in the HCL had the least amount of pressure on them; their husbands' socioeconomic stature afforded them respectability, a measure of security and, as housewives with the means to hire domestic help, flexibility in determining the extent of their activism.

As the summer drew to a close a showdown over the Fairmount Park prefabs seemed increasingly inevitable: the last of the families in Fairmount Park were being rehoused and the council was showing no sign of allowing the town's homeless into the prefabs, despite the HCL protest marches. On 23 August 1963 the council took up the gauntlet laid down by the marchers and announced its intention to give Angela McCrystal a home.[51] 'It was a complete shock,' McCrystal later said. 'I remember I went to Patricia McCluskey and said, "My God, what am I going to do?"… They were trying to divide us, which they nearly did do.'[52] That evening a few women arrived at Angela McCrystal's doorstep holding the newspaper and pointing to her name on the list of housing allocations. A few days later at a heated HCL meeting McCluskey told the members of the League that the council was trying to sow the seeds of dissent among them by issuing the house to McCrystal. McCluskey announced that even though McCrystal wanted to refuse the house, they were advising her to take it.[53] Otherwise, should the HCL's demands be met, the McCrystals would be homeless once again. Conn McCluskey later remarked: 'One of the Unionist Council ploys was that when a Catholic began to show their head what they did was, they gave them a house to keep them quiet. Angela McCrystal was given a house and this is why she's so special: she continued to fight on with the other squatters.'[54] Significantly, McCrystal was willing to destroy her chances at receiving a house in order to keep protesting with these families. In fact, that night it was she who again brought up the idea of occupying the Fairmount Park prefabs. Concerned that squatting would backfire on McCrystal, Patricia agreed to a vote on whether or not they would squat with the proviso that McCrystal would not herself squat in the prefabs.[55] McCrystal could then avoid being seen as refusing a home and eventually everyone could be housed. However, the majority of the HCL voted against the measure and McCrystal left the meeting frustrated in the belief that an opportunity was slipping from their grasp.

For the rest of the night of 27 August Angela McCrystal stewed over the HCL vote and by 11:30 she decided to take action. Aware that the prefabs were scheduled to be demolished the next morning, McCrystal wasted no time in recruiting people to squat.

> I just picked one person who I thought would probably go along with this because at the meeting I could see that [Seamus Bell] would have been anxious enough. So I went down to his house and I said, 'Seamus, would you squat?' I said, 'If you squat I give you my word that we will not leave you. We will stay with you. We will support you in every way we can. And I just feel that there is not going to be another opportunity like this again.' So he said, 'Right.' Then we went to somebody else and said, 'Well, Seamus is going. What do you think?' We tried to pick people who we knew were keen enough to go. We ended up with something like twelve families the first night.[56]

They entered the Fairmount Park prefabs at around 1 a.m. Ann Dunlop, a Protestant factory worker who had married a Catholic bricklayer, received keys to one of the prefabs from a friend who was moving out. She remembered a shared sense of self-reliance and desperation: 'If we hadn't done that, we wouldn't have gotten anything,' she later said.[57] The council had already shown its intransigence in the face of the group's previous attempts to spur reform. On balance, Dunlop and the rest of her group were justified in believing the squat to be the only way forward.

Susan Dinsmore summed up the group's frustration with HCL's decision not to take over the prefabs: 'Nobody was doing anything so we did it ourselves.'[58] Dinsmore's statement, though partially inaccurate – Patricia was making progress for the HCL in the public arena – sums up the frustration at the slow speed of progress felt by many in the group who had years of tenement life ahead of them if nothing was done. That night Dinsmore's husband squatted a prefab in place of a family that could not be there. The Dinsmores had access to Susan's parents' soon to be vacated home, so they did not squat for themselves. The eve of the protest began the women's withdrawal into the traditional domestic sphere; Susan Dinsmore remained home with her children that night, like many HCL members. Male family members generally accompanied those women who did participate in the squat. Few women, if any, squatted alone. Though male participation may seem to contradict an earlier avoidance of street action, their involvement at the late stage of the squat actually confirms a paternalist analysis of the dangers involved in the squat, which would have overridden their desire to safeguard their jobs. When the television cameras and newspaper reporters arrived in the morning, McCrystal telephoned the McCluskeys to break the news to them.

Angela McCrystal's leadership of the Fairmount Park squat rendered the HCL vote redundant. But an analysis of the vote and its aftermath is instructive; it revealed the true nature of the HCL's composition. Patricia McCluskey discouraged the squat because she was concerned about its implications for the squatters. Her opinions weighed heavily on the HCL rank and file, who were no longer suspicious of her interest in chairing the organization. Her active opposition led to a vote against moving into Fairmount Park. But many of the group were not content to let fate run its course. People remember Patricia McCluskey and the HCL because of its direct action campaign, but the HCL's tactics germinated *despite* rather than *because of* Patricia McCluskey. McCluskey seems to have gone along with McCrystal's squat in a last-ditch effort to retain control over the group. It was Angela McCrystal who first led the marches through the streets of Dungannon and the squat in Fairmount Park. In fact, the housing movement might have seen more radical campaigns without McCluskey, who encouraged moderation and constitutional agitation. Conn McCluskey later pointed out: 'You see these girls really weren't good enough for politics. They could go and support you at a demonstration but they couldn't handle the press.

So we were able to handle the press.'[59] But what he failed to recognize was that they were good enough for politics – just not the kind of politics the McCluskeys deemed legitimate.

As soon as the news of the squat reached the McCluskeys, they rushed to Fairmount Park to speak to the press. Regardless of the fact that this squat was unauthorized, Patricia decided to continue to lead the League. By remaining associated with the dissidents and indeed supporting them, McCluskey retained her position and continued to try and steer the League towards a more moderate path. In a study of power relations and street politics, Amitai Etzioni observes that during this period demonstrations carried 'a considerable amount of social stigma which explains why they [were] less "natural" means of expression for the middle and upper classes'.[60] So while Patricia appeared in the newspapers to be every bit the radical, she tried to be a moderating influence on a burgeoning protest group that resisted being tamed.

After a few days the number of squatters had grown to 120 people populating thirty-five prefabs.[61] As the publicity storm gathered, the rest of Catholic Northern Ireland simmered. Even the *Belfast Telegraph* supported the squatters.[62] In the first weeks of September the marches continued to highlight the plight of the squatters by drawing on other examples of inequality. A letter in the *Dungannon Observer* on 7 September likened Northern Ireland's Catholics to 'white Negroes' while another two weeks later compared the situation to that of South Africa or Birmingham, Alabama.[63] People in Northern Ireland were becoming more aware of the parallels to be drawn between Northern Ireland and other infamously bigoted parts of the world; and as the media kept snapping pictures, Stormont also began to take notice.

An HCL delegation was sent to see the Minister for Health and Local Government, William Morgan. Maurice Byrne, a local dentist, Christopher Mallon, a solicitor, and Conn McCluskey formed the delegation. Council chairman Senator William Stewart also met with Morgan and the delegation. Content to be part of a return to the status quo, Joseph Stewart, their titular Nationalist leader, presented the delegation to the minister. The delegation made no objection. Crucially, and in sharp contrast to the last HCL deputation that had made a formal appeal to the government, this one consisted of three middle-class men, who, while articulate, were neither members nor even organizers of the HCL. There was a two-tiered deference system at work in this situation – the working class deferred to the middle class to advocate for them and the women running the HCL ceded their jobs to men to put their case to the government. These dual power systems combined to exclude the movement's founders from the negotiations. Ann Dunlop later said of the delegation: 'We wouldn't have got anywhere. [The men in the delegation] had all the details of us all to bring to the negotiations. [The people in Stormont] wouldn't have listened to us so Dr McCluskey went.'[64] Dunlop's observation is broadly representative of the way that patriarchy and class jointly impacted on the group. Dunlop felt that a delegation of uneducated women would not have been able to negotiate successfully; she was probably correct. Susan Dinsmore confirmed this attitude and reinforced the strategic decision to ask a group of educated men to represent them: 'We wanted [the delegation] to speak for us to see if they could get houses and they did!'[65] Ronald Lawson and Stephen E. Barton suggest that as movements expand, men tend to assume the formal leadership roles: 'Not only have women been socialized to look to men for leadership, but men have (and are recognized as having) greater access to needed resources and legitimacy within patriarchal society.'[66] Sarah Evans's work on women in the American civil rights movement confirms this.[67] The parallel ends there, however. Some of the American women in the various civil rights groups she studied grew to resent the patriarchal structures under which they functioned. For the HCL women, a women-centred consciousness,[68] or a sensitivity to multiple types of oppressive hierarchies, had not formed and so the transition towards male leadership in the negotiating phase of the HCL's protest did not seem to them to be jarring, out of the ordinary or objectionable. It must be said that even today they stand by this tactic.

The class issue was closely tied to educational attainment. Christopher Mallon's experience with litigation meant that the delegation would not fall prey to legal jargon and legislative side-stepping. Conn McCluskey was armed with a dossier that detailed the housing allocation procedures and outcomes of the preceding number of years. There was no doubt among any of the squatters that these three were the best candidates to take on Stormont, and their jubilant send-off gave credence to this. Dunlop later remarked: 'We would have been no good on our own.'[69] The fact that the women of the HCL ceded control of the negotiations to these men betrays their understandable trepidation at entering into formal politics. Anthony Oberschall, in his research on social movements, makes the point that 'the upper and middle strata of society supply the substantial bulk of opposition leaders to all manner of social movements in proportions far above that of their percentage in the population at large'.[70] Enda Staunton, who erroneously refers to the HCL as a 'mainly middle-class protest group', confirms the importance we can sometimes place on leaders at the expense of acknowledging the rank and file, and indeed much of the executive.[71] In this context it is not surprising that the women of the HCL ceded control of the negotiations to these men.

Rick Wilford has done extensive work on women's participation in Northern Irish politics and their absence from traditional politics.[72] As he points out: 'The unresolved national question; the readiness to resort to violence; the doctrinal and institutional patriarchy of the Catholic Church ... together with the inclemency of both the nationalist and unionist movements to feminism – all have combined to create a formidable set of hurdles in the path of women seeking entry to the public realm.' But as discussed above, issues of class stratification have also contributed to the erection of these hurdles. In this context, it is no surprise that the HCL had more confidence in the middle-class triad led by Conn McCluskey. Moreover, their standing in the community as well as the doctor's close involvement with the League throughout the summer established their credibility.

The negotiations ended in compromise: the Ballygawley Road housing scheme was extended to cover new families. Also, the squatters would not be considered for housing until they left the prefabs, but they would not be forced out. This arrangement ensured the Unionists would maintain their majority vote by rehousing the squatters in the same ward in which they had been living.[73] When a few weeks later a newly elected Prime Minister Terence O'Neill consented not to evict the squatters until new housing was built for them, the League knew it had won the battle. But the war was about to expand to a few different fronts.

In many ways the women's protest movement and the Fairmount Park squat reinforced the traditional domesticity that prevailed in Northern Irish society. When in late September the HCL held a dinner to celebrate their victory and to honour the McCluskeys, Patricia was given a silver tea service, 'For service rendered'. She stated: 'I have been very impressed by the good housekeeping of the squatters' wives. They have made the prefabs into clean and tidy homes. They are as good cooks as they are housekeepers and the thirty-six husbands are very lucky young men.'[74] This statement would have observers believe that it was the wives who followed their husbands to the streets. McCluskey masculinized what had been a movement largely organized and populated by women, thus relegating the *bona fide* street activists back to the kitchens and elevating hangers-on to the status of community militants. The ironic gift of the silver tea service reveals the HCL's own valuation of domesticity over street politics. From their point of view, they had achieved their goal of procuring a home for themselves and now they were more than happy to retire to it, as most did. However, some, such as Angela McCrystal and Susan Dinsmore, remained active in what Pippa Norris describes as radical political activity characterized by unstructured and transitory groupings and what Vicky Randall calls *ad hoc* community action characterized by short-lived political campaigns that rely on direct action tactics.[75] McCrystal went on to help pioneer religious education programmes for those with special needs, and Dinsmore remained an important part of the tenant's association in her housing estate.

The rapid pace at which Dungannon's urban council moved to get the families rehoused proves that the League's grievances could have been easily ameliorated with some creative thinking. Significantly, it proved that while Stormont and the local government councils had the means to end the housing crisis in Northern Ireland, they would have to be publicly humiliated into doing so. More importantly, this incident showed that going over the head of local councils achieved tangible results. The campaign also highlighted the inadequacies of the Catholic population's representatives while prompting Dungannon's Nationalist representatives to give up their abstention from council politics regarding a dispute over a Gaelic Athletic Association pitch.[76]

It is worth pointing out that the tactics of the HCL were not new to the political scene in Northern Ireland. As recently as 1959 the women of Springtown Camp, Derry, had dressed in their Sunday best and marched on the guildhall in the wake of a fire to protest their substandard housing.[77] The camp had been erected during the Second World War as an American army base and was occupied shortly thereafter by hundreds of homeless families. Led by Sadie Campbell and other activists such as Molly Killen, Kathleen Porter, Mrs J. McBrearty, Mrs McCarron, Dolly Sweeny, Flory Divin and Mrs Moore, the group refused to be silenced at two consecutive Derry Corporation meetings at the guildhall.[78] They demanded to be moved from these corrugated tin huts to proper brick homes. To the great shame of the urban and rural councils (Springtown was on the city border) the situation was allowed to fester, with hundreds of families remaining until October of 1967 when the last family – the Lynches – moved out.[79]

The HCL's maternalist rhetoric was not new either; this mode of political discourse is evident throughout the twentieth century in such groups as the Ulster Women's Unionist Council, Cumann na mBan, the Suffragettes, the Irish Housewives Association, and others. This continuity of tactic and message, therefore, should have prompted little more than some raised eyebrows from the council. What made this group different was the international momentum surrounding it. At this moment in history the language of civil liberties, human rights and social justice was beginning to converge throughout the West and the media was at every sit-in, march and vigil to tell the world. Suddenly ordinary people like Angela McCrystal had access to the non-violent civil disobedience playbook that Gandhi had written and King was supplementing. The HCL took those tactics, made them their own, and benefited from an increased sensitivity to rights-based street activism.

In the end the HCL did little to undermine the gender regime and the structure of local government councils. But it must be remembered that the HCL never actually set out to do this; these women simply wanted to reconfigure Dungannon's public housing system by entering into it. In effect, however, for all their radical tactics the HCL won nothing more than an exception. Homeless families in the Bogside and along the Lower Falls would not benefit from the HCL's activism; if they sought public housing, it would be up to them to replicate the HCL in their own districts. Despite all of this, the HCL's activity should not be dismissed. Quite significantly, this protest group politicized an apathetic population by giving it hope that local and regional structures could be changed by ordinary people advocating for themselves. And even more important, the HCL reminded women across the state that they too had a vital role to play in political activism.

THE CAMPAIGN FOR SOCIAL JUSTICE

As news of the Fairmount Park victory spread, the McCluskeys began to receive letters from all over Northern Ireland asking how they had beaten the Unionist machine.[80] At this point they decided that there was a need for a steering committee to coordinate statistics from across the province in order to help others. The McCluskeys realized how effective circumventing the local administration had been, and on 17 January 1964 they launched the Campaign for Social Justice in Northern Ireland (CSJ) with the main aim being to get British and American politicians to pressure the Unionists. Ultimately the CSJ intended to bring select cases to the Commission on Human Rights at Strasbourg and the United Nations. One of the only elements they retained from the HCL's work was the tactic of setting their sights above the heads of their local government bodies. But that is the only similarity between the two groups. Unlike the HCL, the CSJ sought a comprehensive radical reform of the region's governing system in order to level the playing field between the Catholics and the Protestants. Tactically, the CSJ had no desire to involve itself in marches or sit-ins, which had been so successful for the HCL. They would not disrupt traffic or occupy buildings. Rather, they would be seen as the kind of people with whom government ministers could negotiate. It was precisely this strategy that contributed to the CSJ's success.

The original committee consisted of ten professional men and three women, another departure from the HCL. Enigmatically, Conn McCluskey is not listed in their original press release.[81] Perhaps his initial instinct was to protect his practice by keeping a low profile. Even if his practice consisted of a majority of Catholics, had he gone public he would face the possibility that pressure could have been exerted on his patients. Soon thereafter, however, as the CSJ grabbed more and more headlines, Conn's association with the group was widely recognized.

The CSJ, which grew out of the HCL, could not have been more different. Conn McCluskey explained: 'Well the Campaign for Social Justice were middle class people. Most of them professionals ... And there were a couple of councillors who had been involved in public life in some form or other and they were able to handle things.' Patricia agreed with her husband, elaborating: 'It was organized by people who knew what they were doing.'[82] This 'professionalization' of the fledgling movement precluded members of the working class while bolstering prevailing power structures within the group. In an interview with W.H. Van Voris, Patricia cited her education as being a main factor that separated her from the HCL rank and file: 'The people who were into Social Justice at the beginning were all second generation, if you like, educated ... People like my husband and myself would have been the first generation at boarding school, secondary school, university.'[83] Michael Morgan convincingly interrogates the generalization that this was the first generation of Northern Irish Catholics to enter the middle class, warning us to be careful of assuming that progress towards civil rights was a product inextricably linked to the rise of the middle class in the province.[84] Historian Simon Prince is equally sceptical.[85] But even if the McCluskeys did over-generalize about the context surrounding their rise to prominence, maintaining an outwardly middle-class group remained their objective. Both Patricia and Conn McCluskey emphasized the need for people who could articulate themselves and a need for a respectable professional group that could appeal to the political elite in Britain, Irish America and Australia. The working-class HCL women would not be able to adhere to these parameters for two reasons: their lack of education and their volatility. The programme of the CSJ demanded that its members knew how to collect and tabulate statistics, communicate through the written word, and speak on television and at international forums on human rights. Though some of their findings can be disputed – medical and law degrees hardly qualify one to supervise regional sociological studies – they were able to assemble convincing arguments to utilize for propaganda. The crucial element that turned the McCluskeys from the HCL was its members' direct action techniques. The McCluskeys may have supported the squat *after* it had been staged, but thereafter they would make sure no pressure group of theirs would engage in such radical activities. By spearheading the CSJ, the McCluskeys could control and moderate future protest activities in Dungannon.

Though Patricia became the 'chairman', as she was commonly referred to at the time, Conn was active in the CSJ's leadership. 'We wanted results. We wanted to produce our documents. And I'm afraid I was very undemocratic. I ground on, you see. I ... steamrolled the others into accepting.'[86] The CSJ's authoritarian structure and small numbers were conducive to prioritizing and generating quick figures for propaganda. The collection of this data and coordinating logistics of other projects depended on the help of a network of people such as Bríd Rodgers, who would go on to develop a long career with the Social Democratic and Labour Party, Mary Ellen O'Doherty and her family in Derry,[87] and Leon and Jill Uris,[88] among many others. Had there been a public meeting structure, projects would have taken longer to iron out. As it was, there was some dissent among the ranks of the CSJ. Personal politics and disagreement about the meeting structure became a problem reportedly forcing Olive Scott, a republican and one of the three women in the CSJ executive, to leave.[89] The other members of the CSJ rejected the notion of going public because longer meetings would infringe on their work schedules. Instead they kept the meetings to a minimum and eliminated marches with the rationale that their aim was to influence international politicians, not local ones. This insistence that large-scale reform must come from outside of the locality was a case of realpolitik on the part of the organizers, who had much to fear from the Unionist structure. With all of that education among them being so prized, it is noteworthy that the CSJ failed to see the Redmondite pattern they were replicating through their choice of tactics. And paradoxically, those who sought democracy had to cast it off in order to further the cause.

The McCluskeys are often referred to as the mother and father of the civil rights movement. If this is so, Conn sat resolutely at the head of the table, imposing patriarchal structure with a strong hand. But he could do no more than lead the private meetings. Due to the controversy the Campaign was generating, most of the group had to keep a low profile so Patricia was the only realistic candidate to chair the group. This allowed the members to distance themselves from her while helping the cause privately. In a letter to Cedric Thornberry of the National Council for Civil Liberties (NCCL) based in England, Conn confessed that Patricia signed all of the newsletters in place of the secretary of the CSJ, architect Brian Gregory, because his public involvement in the Campaign would cost him business.[90] The CSJ, therefore, ended up utilizing the perception of feminine innocuousness to safeguard their middle-class interests. Without the popular assumption that women could not succeed in politics, the CSJ would have progressed at a much slower pace than it did. Patricia's sex protected the executive from scrutiny and retaliation, while at the same time it inspired a greater degree of tolerance on the part of the Northern Irish government.

The society in which Patricia McCluskey lived valued authoritarianism and patriarchy; religious institutions and political parties supported these systems.[91] Chairing the CSJ gave her an opportunity to challenge prevailing notions of femininity even as she manipulated cliches surrounding her gender. As much as it was a protection for the group, Patricia McCluskey's leadership of the CSJ threatened traditional ideas of women's roles within Northern Ireland's fragile stability. The challenge she faced as CSJ chairman was a balancing act: she had to aggressively represent a cause advocating a radical restructuring of Northern Irish institutions, but had to do so in a way that was acceptable to her community as well as her predominantly male organization. It is not surprising, then, that she received death threats as the Campaign gained ground.[92] Nor is it surprising that she had difficulty negotiating her role as leader of the group. Simply put, there were none who shared her values before her – no Catholic female leaders of sustained media campaigns in living memory to emulate.

The marked gender differential between the HCL and the CSJ was lamentable in Patricia's eyes: 'The women didn't want to get more involved. Nobody wanted to stand out above the crowd. Women in politics give up a lot. [They must endure] terrific upheavals in family life.'[93] This sentiment touches on a crucial point regarding women's political participation and schedule flexibility; day-to-day pressures of home-making often interfered with evening meetings and political activity. Patricia commented that they 'give up', sympathetically placing the blame on them for their predicament. Her comment that 'nobody wanted to stand above the crowd', while it may be true of other women, does not bear out her own experience with the HCL. Perhaps the HCL members, having spent time on the streets and away from their families, were no longer willing to sacrifice family life, but certainly they had proved themselves more than willing to stand above the crowd. In a later interview Patricia McCluskey posited another reason for the absence of women in the CSJ, saying that the CSJ was different from the HCL because the agitation was no longer confined to housing; it now encompassed systematic discrimination in the areas of employment and public life as well as in housing.[94] Her assumption that men were more interested in the public sphere and therefore got more involved in the Campaign served to rationalize the gender differential as does more generally Conn's explanation that those who were interested just came together 'naturally'. On balance, it can hardly be deemed an accident that so few women were involved and that not one member of the Campaign executive was culled from the working classes.[95]

The CSJ began their activity by writing letters in response to British Prime Minister Alec Douglas Home's public statement of March 1964 that complaints regarding religious discrimination could be addressed through the courts. Having engaged both junior and senior counsel on the matter, the CSJ was informed that their complaints were not subject to judicial review. Further, under the terms of the Government of Ireland Act (1920) the CSJ pointed out in their second letter to Douglas Home that no provisions were made for discriminatory acts perpetuated by the local authorities. These letters set off a flurry of correspondence between the Home Office and the Prime Minister's Office recommending that their replies to the CSJ be 'as stonewalling as possible'.[96] Accordingly, Downing Street wrote that it could not infringe on Stormont's jurisdiction in this case. The CSJ responded that under section 75 of the Government of Ireland Act (1920) the British government retained responsibility for Northern Irish affairs. This correspondence with Douglas Home proved two things to members of the Campaign:

> The Parliament of the United Kingdom [had] the ultimate responsibility for discrimination in Northern Ireland, but the Prime

Minister [was] unwilling to ask Parliament to intervene.
Despite the fact that the British Prime Minister told [the Campaign] that allegations of discrimination could be dealt with by law, he [was then] either unable or unwilling to let [them] know how this [could] be done.[97]

The main message those in Northern Ireland could draw from this correspondence upon its publication by the CSJ in 1964 was that Britain was resolutely opposed to taking an interventionist postition regarding discrimination in Northern Ireland.

The CSJ was not daunted however, and continued its letter-writing campaign. The main tactic employed by the group involved using their class and social status to emphasize their own respectability. Their second major operation involved sending pamphlets on discrimination in Northern Ireland to prominent people in the United States. However, out of the 342 Irish-American organizations and dignitaries they contacted, which included Edward Kennedy, Robert Kennedy and Cardinal Richard Cushing of Boston,[98] they receive only a single half-hearted response.[99] It is difficult to determine if this failure to respond was due to a lack of interest on the part of Irish America, or if it was the result of postal tampering. In April 1964 both Philip O'Rourke, vice-president of the American Radio Association and former democratic congressional candidate, as well as Mollie Owens Callanan, a prominent socialite, complained to the San Francisco consulate-general of Ireland that CSJ pamphlets sent from Monaghan had been tampered with.[100] Though the CSJ took the precaution of posting them from the Republic, apparently it had not been enough to avoid interference. If these allegations from O'Rourke and Owens Callanan are correct, the incident reveals either an Irish or an American interest in the progress of the group.

Back in Northern Ireland, Patricia McCluskey was utilizing her local notoriety to campaign for women's participation in community life and politics. On 17 March 1964 she delivered her only public speech on women and politics at a meeting in Newcastle:

In political affairs, women too often retire and leave men to decide. Surely women aren't inferior. Women must take a more prominent place in guiding political thought ... We women are faced with our families to rear and get into jobs ... I would make a strong plea for women to assert their practical commonsense and to use their vote both in local and government elections in the best interests of themselves and their children. Do not meekly accept direction from your menfolk on who to vote for.[101]

The speech's call for women to vote conflicts with the CSJ's resigned conviction that nothing could be changed from within the state and points to an inconsistency in the rhetoric of the CSJ. Upon close inspection of McCluskey's message, one also notices that she did not want to restructure the material conditions that dictated women's domestic role and did not explicitly urge women to leave the home in favour of public life. Instead she adopted a liberal feminist stance by telling women to work towards a more reformist goal of entering into the public sphere.

But all this campaigning and talk of voting drew comment from her detractors, to whom the only logical explanation was that she must be after a parliamentary seat. In May the *Irish News* reported that Patricia McCluskey would not stand for the East Tyrone parliamentary seat despite pressure from her own camp to do so. She explained that she wanted to show people that there was someone in public life who was not after the title of Member of Parliament. In her press statement she said that members of the Campaign for Social Justice could not be politicians because they had to be seen as being above politics. Apparently ignoring their fellow CSJ member Sean McGivern's position in the Irish Republican Labour Party, McCluskey made it clear that politics was not for members of the CSJ. This elastic notion of how one participates in politics, however, allowed her to organize a primary convention to determine who the next anti-Unionist candidates would be for the Dungannon urban council election. McCluskey's approach defied the more asystematic approach that most anti-Unionist candidates pursued until this point, where generally they nominated themselves and stood unopposed.

The 600-strong May Day meeting that McCluskey organized was the first forum of its kind in the area and a triumph for local politics. For the first time residents of the West Ward took an active part in the decision-making process. Those in attendance heatedly discussed the failure of both the council and the West Ward's representatives on the council. Finally, the participants put forth nominations drawing seven names. Only one of the former council representatives, Jim Corrigan, received enough votes to go forward. Patricia McCluskey, content to label local elections as outside of 'politics', received 221 votes and Angela McCrystal and four other Social Justice candidates were put forward to contest the election.[102]

Out of the seven 'Social Justice Party' candidates that stood, four including Patricia McCluskey were elected to represent the West Ward at the Dungannon Urban District Council. Angela McCrystal, having not received enough votes to obtain a seat, bowed out of social justice activity and eventually she would shift her focus to pursue disability rights for the benefit of her son and other disabled people in the area. This election is significant because by inviting people to decide on candidates, McCluskey sparked an unprecedented popular interest in the election. Because of the primary, all three wards in Dungannon were contested for the first time in forty years.[103] Moreover, news of the first election meeting ignited political activism in other areas. Omagh was one of the towns to follow suit, with an anti-Unionist primary convention of its own.

When McCluskey was elected to the Dungannon Urban Council, the only woman among a group of men, the press fell over itself to marvel at her success. The *Universe* ran an article in July under the sensationalized headline, 'Militant housewife', detailing all that McCluskey had helped to accomplish during the run-up to the election, including the establishment of the Dungannon Credit Union, the Dungannon Housing Association and a citizens information bureau.[104] All of these organizations were designed to give the Catholic community the tools to achieve financial independence. The article mentioned that the Housing Association had already received permission to build thirteen houses on a seventeen-acre plot of land it had bought. It went on to point out that 'many of the town's professional and businessmen' were backing the CSJ's programmes, which was the main contributing factor to the initiative's success. The success of the Housing Association seemed to herald a crucial about-face for Dungannon's business community, who had been sceptical, if not hostile, to the housing demands in the years directly preceding the election. But upon closer inspection of the situation, the support of local businessmen did not represent a radical departure in thought. The Housing Association's activity remained within the gerrymandered borders of the Catholic-populated West Ward; a few new houses would not disrupt voting patterns significantly.

Other towns in Northern Ireland had a conscientious Catholic middle-class element with the economic and technical know-how to start such programmes, but what made Dungannon different was its recent HCL victory and that it had the McCluskeys. The momentum created by the HCL squat coupled with the boundless enthusiasm and charisma of the McCluskeys inspired confidence. Their use of their intellectual abilities as well as their personal connections earned them the reputation of being able to get things done. Overall, while the middle-class elements in the Campaign may have stymied the fight for a radical reconfiguration of power, they also worked tirelessly to see the Catholics blossom in their own community. The gains they helped the people of Dungannon realize raised the awareness of the effects of discriminatory policies throughout the region.

One of the objectives set out during the Campaign's initial press conference involved taking particular cases to the Commission for Human Rights in Strasbourg and to the United Nations. To this end a CSJ delegation consisting of the McCluskeys and member Tom McLaughlin visited Frank Aiken, Ireland's Minister for External Affairs, in July 1964. He and his legal advisor discouraged the Campaign from taking cases forward, explaining that their efforts would amount to nothing. Undaunted, the CSJ pursued other members of the Republic's Oireachtas, such as Brian Lenihan, George Colley and Eoin Ryan, who were all less than eager to engage with the group.[105] Though the Irish government supported their aims, one official euphemized: 'the question of any open association between the Irish authorities and the Campaign is a matter of some delicacy'.[106] Still convinced that the international judiciary remained a legitimate tool in their campaign, the CSJ put the issue to the side in favour of appealing to Britain's intellectual and political elite.[107] This correspondence seemed to yield results when Harold Wilson, the leader of the Labour Party, visited Northern Ireland in September 1964 and announced he would reform Stormont if elected prime minister. Deftly detecting a weakness in Douglas Home's programme, he electioneered accordingly. His promise renewed the CSJ's determination to press on with the campaign by endorsing Wilson.

Locally however, the Unionist establishment saw Patricia McCluskey as a muck-raking nuisance. To some she was even more than that; her calls for reform threatened the stability of the system. Stormont Minister of Home Affairs William Craig, for example, described the CSJ in a letter at that time as a 'small section of the community whose avowed intention is to overthrow the Constitution of Northern Ireland', noting that they were spreading 'scurrilous propaganda' through the pamphlets they wrote and distributed.[108] Not surprisingly, even Nationalist Council members found her presence a threat. By arguing to change the system the 'Social Justice Party' candidates threatened the Nationalists' political complacency. At one council meeting Nationalist councillor P.G. McQuaid called her 'Eva Braun, Hitler's wife' and was not expelled by chairman Senator William Stewart.[109] McCluskey's presence on the council cast doubt on the Nationalists' claim to being the only real anti-Unionist representation in Dungannon. Another reason for their hostility may have had to do with

McCluskey's challenge to the gender regime by taking her seat in the first place. Oftentimes women who entered politics did so through family connections. Patricia McCluskey's preferred manner was placid and congenial, but she could stand in her own stead in a debate as well. Bernadette Devlin, a woman who would later burst on to the political scene, remembered McCluskey as 'smarter, harder, clearer thinking than she ever let on'.[110]

In spite of all this, however, the CSJ was unable to make any tangible progress in Britain, Ireland or the United States. The Campaign's dealings with all three governments and various smaller governing bodies had come to naught, as had their appeals to Irish America. It seemed that the CSJ's only audience was the National Council of Civil Liberties in Britain. On 13 March Patricia made her first trip to London as chairman of the Campaign. There she spoke to the NCCL, sharing the platform with Betty Sinclair, secretary of the Belfast Trade Union Council, and Sheelagh Murnaghan, a Liberal MP representing Queen's University in Belfast, among others. According to Conn McCluskey, the conference was successful because it encouraged dialogue and also because it brought the issue to England. But the event went largely unreported by the British media.[111] Because of this there was little chance to garner any popular support among the British for the Campaign.

Deflated, the Campaign delegation returned to Dungannon. But by April 1965 an ally materialized on the horizon in the form of the Campaign for Democracy in Ulster (CDU). Created by three British MPs (Paul Rose, Fenner Brockway and Eric Lubbock), the CDU was a small coalition of Liberal and Labour politicians who hoped to pressure Westminster into intervening to reform Stormont. The CDU sought to include religion in the Race Relations Act and bring Northern Ireland into line with British standards of justice. Patricia McCluskey was invited to speak at the formal launch in the House of Commons in early June 1965. She accepted under the condition that she be accompanied by her husband and other members of the Campaign, explaining that she was 'only a housewife' and that the other CSJ members would be better qualified to discuss the situation in Northern Ireland.[112] This uncharacteristic timidity, when considered in the context of her recent speech in London, reflects McCluskey's discomfort with official politics as well as the kind of deference to male legitimacy articulated by Guida West and Rhonda Lois Blumberg.[113] The fact that she was anything but 'only a housewife' illustrates how deeply ingrained this deference could be. In the end, however, it was she and not her husband who successfully addressed the CDU regarding discrimination in Northern Ireland.

During her speech she criticized Labour minister Sir Frank Soskice for expressing satisfaction after a visit to Northern Ireland: 'If Sir Frank were to be told there was dry rot in the attic of his home he would surely not shrug his shoulders and say, "I have been out looking at the roof, it is perfect."' She went on to counter the obvious question about addressing the issue of discrimination through the courts by saying: 'The Unionist members of Parliament at Westminster repeatedly claim that there is no discrimination because nobody takes legal action under the 1920 Act. We have tried to take legal action. It is impossible.'[114] Simon Prince convincingly argues that CSJ failed to 'explore fully the potential of the legal process' in his analysis of their efforts,[115] though on balance, they did encounter significant hurdles to pursuing legal redress.

Using the Campaign's statistics and figures, the CDU's growing membership lobbied Westminster to drop the convention of ignoring the situation in Northern Ireland, but Wilson had gotten the election endorsement he wanted and he was no longer interested in the CSJ's concerns. His own Westminster colleagues in the CDU could not persuade him to deliver on his campaign promise. Thus, the CDU accomplished nothing more than an unsuccessful push for the creation of an ombudsman's position, which might have led to the reformation of Stormont.[116] The main significance of the CSJ/CDU link was the way in which it raised the profile of the Campaign in England. Linking up with parliamentarians gave the CSJ a measure of international legitimacy and helped involve the English public and sections of the political elite in the drive to publicize discriminatory systems in Northern Ireland.

The international letter-writing campaign also continued with pleas for money and support. Throughout this correspondence the McCluskeys developed the art of 'spin' by tailoring their letters to the intended audience. In some letters they emphasized their social class, presumably to underscore their respectability: 'We are a group of comfortably off, non political Catholic lay men and women.'[117] In other letters they underscored their commitment to achieving a classless society: 'Patricia and I are both sincere socialists.'[118] By the beginning of 1966 the CSJ was appealing to the British Home Secretary for free legal aid for a test case: 'We of the Campaign for Social Justice who, being Catholics, are all relatively underprivileged, must spend £70 of our own money to discover from Senior Counsel what we should do next.'[119] This elastic notion of their material interests functioned as a pragmatic expedient when political engineering seemed necessary. While their hard work once again came to naught, these letters reflected a new savvy that would later achieve results.

Though members of the CSJ would not have felt confident in their accomplishments, they did plant the seeds that raised the profile of the systemic inequalities inherent to the one-party system in Northern Ireland. They did this by adopting a patriarchal, undemocratic structure that focused on middle-class respectability and aspirations. Their activity was underpinned by a laudable notion of rationality prevailing over sectarianism; if Britain, the US and Ireland only knew the facts, they would work together to intervene and force a radical restructuring of the current system to do away with discrimination. While today this tack may seem naïve, it is important to remember that the emerging political climate around the world gave the group hope that significant change could be achieved. And while it did not produce results within the target governments, the research the group published provided future movements with the wherewithal to continue the fight.

OTHER STRANDS OF CIVIL RIGHTS ACTIVISM

During this period other groups within Northern Ireland began to seriously contemplate a civil rights campaign. The Communist Party of Northern Ireland had already set out its policy in a 1962 pamphlet entitled 'Ireland's Path to Socialism', which proposed that certain democratic reforms needed to be achieved in order for socialism to become a viable political philosophy in Ireland. The pamphlet discussed the consolidation of anti-Unionist groups in an effort to achieve full democratic representation. Once Northern Ireland had a 'progressive' government, the pamphlet claimed, the Communists could then begin a campaign. The year after this pamphlet was published, C. Desmond Greaves, a leading spokesman for Britain's anti-imperialist/Marxist Connolly Association, wrote a pamphlet called 'The Irish Question and the British People'. This pamphlet called for a civil rights campaign, which would encourage British voters to pressure Westminster. Anthony Coughlan and Roy Johnston, two rising stars in Irish Marxist theory, helped Greaves draft the pamphlet while they were in London. When they returned to Ireland they joined the republican debating club called the Wolfe Tone Society (WTS), which was established in 1964 as a think tank to refocus the republican movement after the IRA's failed military campaign.

In August 1966 the WTS began to discuss the establishment of a broad-based civil rights association. According to Coughlan, Northern Irish Prime Minister Terence O'Neill was now sufficiently weakened by Ian Paisley, his main opposition. Marc Mulholland's careful analysis of the pressures surrounding O'Neill during this period confirms that this was a sound observation.[120] In this politically vulnerable state O'Neill would be forced to introduce reforms if confronted by a popular civil rights movement.[121] At a meeting that month in Maghera, Derry, WTS members, the McCluskeys, IRA chief-of-staff Cathal Goulding and some Stormont MPs debated the idea of a civil rights movement. They decided to hold a seminar on 28 November at the War Memorial Building in Belfast. This meeting would involve qualified speakers and experts in law addressing a wide audience of interested people. Ciarán Mac an Ailí, a prominent Dublin lawyer with republican sympathies, discussed Special Powers legislation in both parts of Ireland and Kadar Asmal, a law lecturer and vice-president of the Irish Anti-Apartheid Movement, spoke on addressing civil rights violations through the European Convention on Human Rights.

The participants at the seminar decided to form a civil rights steering committee that would meet on 29 January to draft a constitution modelled on the NCCL's constitution. An executive was formed and on 9 April the group launched itself as the Northern Ireland Civil Rights Association (NICRA) and elected an executive. The Communist Party of Northern Ireland secured a presence on the executive and a significant number of republicans attended the meeting. Gerry Adams later wrote of the meeting that republicans 'were acting on instructions not to pack the executive; it was sufficient to have an influence. We were also instructed to vote for Communist Party nominees'.[122] Under the leadership of the McCluskeys the Campaign for Social Justice affiliated to NICRA and Conn McCluskey joined its executive. Patricia dedicated most of her time to CSJ affairs, while Conn was able to juggle his medical practice and the monthly meetings of NICRA. The CSJ would still continue its efforts at fact-finding and international propaganda, whereas NICRA would begin to address the specific problems on the ground throughout the region by advocating for people affected by specific instances of discrimination.

As the NICRA executive slowly began to grind into action and members of disparate political groups began to work together, the McCluskeys found themselves dealing with militant republicans. The fiftieth anniversary of the 1916 Rising had helped to revive national fervour and their rhetoric was beginning to set off alarm bells for moderates such as the McCluskeys. In October 1966 the CSJ wrote to British Prime Minister Wilson telling him: 'You will have noticed how the more militant rebels here, including the republicans, have been persuaded to hold their hand. At the moment they have been sold the idea that "the pen is mightier than the sword". They will not wait forever.'[123] Not receiving a response, Patricia McCluskey wrote again in March 1967 suggesting that Unionists were kicking a sleeping dog by provoking republicans. She believed that banning Republican Clubs and making arrests were adding to the gathering storm that could be defused if the Prime Minister intervened. His intervention, she told him, would be a death blow to militant republicanism.[124] She was likely wondering if the republican-engineered destruction of Nelson's Pillar in Dublin earlier that month was a prelude to another military campaign. Her appeals for British intervention fell on deaf ears, however, despite there being clear indications that the IRA was consolidating. In the Republic the Department of Justice did perceive a change in republican strategy. In late 1966 civil servants in the department composed a memorandum charting the growth of the republican movement and speculating that another campaign could be launched during the Easter commemorations.[125] While the warnings of an Easter escalation came to nothing, evidence of renewed republican effort proliferated. By 1967 they had added calls for economic and social reform on both parts of the island to their traditional republican rhetoric.

When Sheelagh Murnaghan, Queen's University's Liberal MP, failed at a third attempt to introduce human rights legislation into the House of Commons, talk of taking on Martin Luther King's tactics began to spread. At the urging of the CDU's leadership, three Labour MPs made their way to Northern Ireland in April 1967 to investigate allegations of discrimination. Though widely criticized for its one-sided anti-Unionist slant, the report they issued urged the British government to establish a Royal Commission on discrimination in Northern Ireland. Both Murnaghan and the delegation were unsuccessful in their efforts to dismantle discriminatory practices, but they did generate headlines that legitimized the widespread belief among the Catholic community that discrimination was ingrained in the basic fibre of Northern Irish society and that despite Unionist and British governmental intransigence a small minority within the government were beginning to take the issue seriously.

As tension increased on the ground and 1967 drew to a close, some members of NICRA began to rethink the role of the group. Being modelled on the British NCCL, its structure was suited to fighting individual cases. However, according to the former secretary of NICRA Edwina Stewart, 'the level of discrimination was so great [that] it wasn't just individual cases that you might have got in Britain; it was a whole system used to keep the Unionists in power'.[126] Moreover, structured in this way, NICRA appeared naïve to the sectarian structure of Northern Irish Society at this point. Speaking against a governmental ban on Republican Clubs, Chairman Betty Sinclair impotently added that this ban should also be a cause for concern for the Orange order.[127] NICRA would have to undergo a radical change if it was going to be able to begin to champion the overarching issue of institutionalized discrimination that was taking place in Northern Ireland. Despite Sinclair's best efforts, this group could never be a straight civil liberties advocacy group like the NCCL or the American Civil Liberties Union. The scales of justice were weighted too heavily to one side of the community.

CONCLUSION

The period between 1963 and 1967 saw a profound change in Northern Irish society. As education became more available and media increasingly covered international rights-based agitation movements, people began to reconsider their place within that society. Women, in particular, gained more independence due to changing social attitudes and educational opportunities. Women in the HCL began to find that they could engage in street politics, because as women they risked less retribution from employers and state forces than their husbands. These women drew direct connections between their duties as managers of the home and their activism. They brought their children to local protests and made use of their status as innocent victims of discrimination to bolster their critique of the state. Incongruously, these women both challenged the gender regime by engaging the state as equals while they also confirmed their status in the private domestic sphere by focusing exclusively on housing. Angela McCrystal's leadership of the HCL's marches culminating in the Fairmount Park squat revived street politics and captured the imagination of many Catholics in Northern Ireland. Austin Currie, who led the famous 1968 Caledon sit-in[128] that helped spark the civil rights movement, later remarked that it was McCrystal and the HCL who provided the model for people like him to emulate. His 1968 sit-in was simply a continuation of a tactic they pioneered so effectively.[129]

Patricia McCluskey's moderating influence on the HCL gave women in protest an acceptable face. Her ability to articulate the problem and engage the press allowed the HCL to exert the maximum amount of pressure on the council. Ann Dunlop explained that the HCL members were 'all too glad to have somebody in [Patricia McCluskey's] position to help [them]'.[130] McCluskey's middle-class status achieved by her own education and her husband's profession made tangible gains for the group. Ultimately however, the most crucial gains resulted from McCrystal's radical action in engineering the Fairmount Park squat. In its aftermath, Patricia McCluskey and her husband edged out a complicit working-class pressure group in an effort to harness its momentum. They remain convinced this was necessary in order to bring the movement forward, and it would be difficult to dispute that. Their lobbying efforts did eventually lay the groundwork and supply the wherewithal to emerging political heavyweights such as Austin Currie to challenge Unionist political domination of the province. Their leadership of the CSJ was essential to the formation of the Northern Ireland Civil Rights Movement. In fact, forty years later they were honoured as the key activists that got the movement under way at the 'McCluskey Summer School' conference to commemorate the civil rights victories won in those years.

The women of the HCL did not remain in the McCluskey group after it became the CSJ; their main goal of securing a house was fulfilled and they could now busy themselves in making it a home. These women never claimed to be feminists, nor radicals, despite their radical tactics. In fact their entire reformist campaign centred on procuring homes so they could take what they saw as their rightful place in the family structure and ultimately, the state. Judging from the relative youth of their children at the time, their domestic lives were rich with competing priorities.

The Dungannon protest groups are the only groups in this study without any significant republican crossover membership. The one woman in the CSJ who had republican sympathies left the group because of its moderate posture, according to Conn McCluskey. The most likely explanation for the republican movement's lack of organized interest in these groups is timing. The HCL sprang up and quickly disintegrated the year following the formalized declaration of the border campaign's failure in 1962. At the time the tattered remnants of the ailing organizations that made up the republican movement lacked the ability and the interest to try to infiltrate the groups. Moreover, it was only during the time of the CSJ's campaign that the republican movement even began to consider social agitation as a legitimate form of republican expression. The McCluskeys' iron-clad grip on the CSJ meant that the group would remain firmly on the path of constitutional activism and its small numbers rendered it difficult, if not impossible to infiltrate even if republicans had been ready to do so. This demonstrates that extraparliamentary campaigns within the nationalist community could make some progress, even in Northern Ireland, when the republican movement was in abeyance.

Though Stormont, Leinster House and Westminster were well aware of both groups, the records available indicate that in the case of the HCL Stormont tried to short-circuit a potentially threatening group by quickly acceding to their request. But this led to the formation of the CSJ, which expanded its rhetoric to include province-wide discrimination, and all three governments ignored the group. Westminster ignored it because it would force it to intervene in Northern Ireland, Leinster House ignored it because it could upset diplomatic relations with Britain and Northern Ireland, and Stormont ignored it because it would lead to an investigation into how the Unionist Party maintained its dominance in the province. It is likely that the HCL's short-lived campaign escaped significant comment due to its rapid disintegration and its female-based membership. The CSJ garnered a more comprehensive analysis, probably because of its middle-class connections, its professionalism and its ability to propagandize on an international scale. Though the Dublin government failed to publicly support the group, officials saw the CSJ as a group of moderates that did 'useful work' in the propaganda war against the Stormont government.[131] Overall, each government's lack of responsiveness to the CSJ provided a downtrodden Catholic population with the requisite political alienation and rhetorical ammunition necessary to take the cause to the streets in the future.

The importance of Angela McCrystal and Patricia McCluskey can be measured by the number and diversity of civil rights groups that took up the cause. The gendered context of their contribution to the movement is often overlooked. Their sex was both an obstacle and an advantage; at times they were patronized and at times the mere fact they were women earned them publicity. Generally the novelty value of women taking part in public debate allowed them more latitude in challenging institutionalized discrimination in Northern Ireland. In spite of their activism, and in direct contrast to West and Blumberg's theory of women in social protest,[132] however, both groups failed to develop a new political consciousness regarding their place within the gender regime. Though some of the HCL women remained active in political groupings, they did not come to challenge their role as housewives. We may be able to attribute this to the fact that the civil rights movement and a subsequent rapid increase in political violence interrupted the emergence of a second-wave of feminism in Northern Ireland for a time. That civil rights movement, conceived of and inspired by a broad coalition of radical and moderate activists, would supply many women in Ireland with a mode of political expression, which built on the HCL and CSJ's tactics. This, in itself, helped many women to challenge prevailing gender regimes by continuing to develop their public profile as activists. How that came about in the absence of a second wave of feminism is what will be explored in Chapter 4.

NOTES

1. Patricia McCluskey quoted in *Dungannon Observer*, 18 March 1964.
2. P.J. McCooey about Patricia McCluskey in C. McCluskey, *Up off their Knees: A Commentary on the Civil Rights Movement in Northern Ireland* (Ireland: Conn McCluskey and Associates, 1989), pp.2–3.
3. The following histories fail to offer significant analysis of women at the root of the civil rights movement in Northern Ireland: E. Staunton, *The Nationalists of Northern Ireland, 1918–1973* (Dublin: Columba Press, 2001); J.J. Lee, *Ireland, 1912–1985: Politics and Society* (Cambridge: Cambridge University Press, 1989); D. Ferriter, *The Transformation of Ireland, 1900–2000* (London: Profile, 2004); P. Bew, P. Gibbon, and H. Patterson, *Northern Ireland, 1921–1996: Political Forces and Social Classes*, revised and updated edn (London: Serif, 1996); V. Feeney, 'The Civil Rights Movement in Northern Ireland', *Éire-Ireland* (summer 1974); R. Foster, *Modern Ireland, 1600–1972* (Harmondsworth: Penguin, 1989); D. McKittrick and D. McVea, *Making Sense of the Troubles* (Harmondsworth: Penguin, 2001); K. Christie, *Political Protest in Northern Ireland, Continuity and Change* (Reading: Link, 1992).
4. S. Prince, *Northern Ireland's '68: Civil Rights, Global Revolt and the Origins of the Troubles* (Dublin: Irish Academic Press, 2007).
5. For theoretical approaches to 'trigger events' and transformative potential see B. Moyer et al., *Doing Democracy: The Map Model for Organizing Social Movements* (Gabriola Island, BC: New Society, 2001); D. Hess and B. Marin, 'Repression, Backfire and the Theory of Transformative Events', *Mobilization: An International Journal*, 11, 2 (2006).
6. J. Simpson, 'Economic Development: Cause or Effect in Northern Ireland', in J. Darby (ed.), *Northern Ireland: The Background to the Conflict* (Belfast: Appletree Press, 1983), p.81.
7. Figures taken from the 1971 census. See ibid., p.101.
8. J. Bardon, *A History of Ulster* (Belfast: Blackstaff Press, 1992), p.593.
9. *Disturbances in Northern Ireland: Report of the Commission Appointed by the Governor of Northern Ireland (the Cameron Report)* (Belfast: Her Majesty's Stationery Office, 1969).
10. P. Hillyard, 'Law and Order', in Darby (ed.), *Northern Ireland: The Background*, p.35.
11. C.B. Shannon, 'Women in Northern Ireland', in Mary O'Dowd and S. Wichert (eds), *Chattel, Servant or Citizen? Women's Status in Church, State and Society* (Belfast: Institute of Irish Studies, Queen's University, 1995), pp.238–53; B. Dooley, *Black and Green: The Fight for Civil Rights in Northern Ireland and Black America* (London: Pluto Press, 1998); Prince, *Northern Ireland's '68*.
12. Bardon, *History of Ulster*, p.637.
13. McCluskey, *Up off their Knees*, p.10.
14. Interview with Angela McCrystal, Dungannon, 31 March 2003.
15. *Disturbances in Northern Ireland: Report*, ch. 12; R. Rose, *Governing without Consensus: An Irish Perspective* (London: Faber, 1971), pp.294–5.
16. Campaign for Social Justice in Northern Ireland, 'Northern Ireland: The Plain Truth' (Dungannon: 1969, revised 1972); italics the author.
17. *Dungannon Observer*, 18 May 1963.
18. Interview with McCrystal, Dungannon, 31 March 2003.
19. V. Morgan, 'Women and the Conflict in Northern Ireland', in A. O'Day (ed.), *Terrorism's Laboratory – the Case of Northern Ireland* (Aldershot: Dartmouth, 1995); E. Evason, *Against the Grain: The Contemporary Women's Movement in Northern Ireland* (Dublin: Attic Press, 1991); R. Ward, *Women, Unionism and Loyalism in Northern Ireland* (Dublin: Irish Academic Press, 2006); E. Rooney, 'Transitional Intersections: Gender, Sect and Class in Northern Ireland', in Emily Grabham, *et al.* (eds), *Intersectionality and Beyond: Law, Power and*

the Politics of Location (London: Routledge Cavendish, 2008); L. Edgerton, 'Public Protest, Domestic Acquiescence: Women in Northern Ireland', in R. Ridd and H. Calloway (eds), *Caught up in Conflict: Women's Responses to Political Strife* (Basingstoke: Macmillan Education in association with Oxford University Women's Studies Committee, 1986).

20. B. Purdie, *Politics in the Streets: The Origins of the Civil Rights Movement in Northern Ireland* (Belfast: Blackstaff Press, 1990); Dooley, *Black and Green*; Prince, *Northern Ireland's '68*.
21. H. Lefebvre, 'The Right to the City', in *Writing on the Cities*, ed. E. Kofman and E. Lebas (1968; Oxford: Blackwell, 1996).
22. John Nagle, 'From "Ban-the-Bomb" to "Ban-the-Increase": 1960s Street Politics in Pre-Civil Rights Belfast', *Irish Political Studies*, 23, 1 (2008).
23. Shannon, 'Women in Northern Ireland'.
24. M. Chappell, J. Hutchinson and B. Ward, '"Dress modestly, neatly... as if you were going to church": Respectability, Class and Gender in the Montgomery Bus Boycott and the Early Civil Rights Movement', in P.J. Ling and S. Monteith (eds), *Gender in the Civil Rights Movement* (London: Garland, 1999), p.77.
25. J. Butler, *Gender Trouble: Feminism and the Subversion of Identity* (New York: Routledge, 1990), p.25.
26. B. Useem and M.N. Zald, 'From Pressure Group to Social Movement: Organizational Dilemmas of the Effort to Promote Nuclear Power', *Social Problems*, 30 (1982), pp.144–56.
27. G. West and R.L. Blumberg, 'Reconstructing Social Protest from a Feminist Perspective', in G. West and R.L. Blumberg (eds), *Women and Social Protest* (Oxford: Oxford University Press, 1990), p.22.
28. M. McWilliams, 'The Church, the State and the Women's Movement in Northern Ireland', in A. Smyth (ed.), *Irish Women's Studies Reader* (Dublin: Attic Press, 1993), p.79.
29. Simpson, 'Economic Development', pp.81–2.
30. McWilliams citing *Regional Trends* (1992).
31. See www.springtowncamp.com for more on this squat and the sit in at Derry's Guildhall.
32. Prince, *Northern Ireland's '68*.
33. *Dungannon Observer*, 18 May 1963.
34. Ibid.
35. Interview with McCrystal, Dungannon, 31 March 2003.
36. West and Blumberg 'Reconstructing Social Protest from a Feminist Perspective', p.25.
37. McCluskey *Up off their Knees*, p.10.
38. Interview with McCrystal, Dungannon, 31 March 2003.
39. Interview with Conn and Patricia McCluskey, Foxrock, 5 March 2003.
40. Staunton, *Nationalists of Northern Ireland, 1918–1973*, p.235.
41. *Dungannon Observer*, 1 June 1963.
42. Interview with Ann Dunlop, Dungannon, 23 November 2003.
43. *Tyrone Courier*, 6 June 1963.
44. Ibid.
45. *Irish News*, 11 June 1963.
46. *Dungannon Observer*, 15 June 1963.
47. McCluskey *Up off their Knees*, p.11.
48. Interview with the McCluskeys, Foxrock, 5 March 2003.
49. A. Gallagher, 'Women and Community Work', in M. Mayo (ed.), *Women in the Community* (London: Routledge & Kegan Paul, 1977), pp.121–41.
50. Simpson, 'Economic Development', p.101.
51. *Dungannon Observer*, 24 August 1963.
52. Interview with McCrystal, Dungannon, 31 March 2003.
53. Ibid.
54. Interview with the McCluskeys, Foxrock, 5 March 2003.
55. Interview with Dunlop, Dungannon, 23 November 2003.
56. Interview with McCrystal, Dungannon, 31 March 2003.
57. Interview with Dunlop, Dungannon, 23 November 2003.
58. Interview with Susan Dinsmore, Dungannon, 25 November 2003.
59. Interview with the McCluskeys, Foxrock, 5 March 2003.
60. A. Etzioni, *Demonstration Democracy: A Policy Paper Prepared for the Task Force on Demonstrations, Protests and Group Violence of the President's National Commission on the Causes and Prevention of Violence* (New York: Gordon & Breach, 1970), pp.19–22.

61. McCluskey, *Up off their Knees*, p.12.
62. Bardon, *History of Ulster*, pp.636–7.
63. *Dungannon Observer*, 7 and 21 September 1963, respectively.
64. Interview with Dunlop, Dungannon, 23 November 2003.
65. Interview with Dinsmore, Dungannon, 25 November 2003.
66. R. Lawson and S.E. Barton, 'Sex Roles in Social Movements: A Case Study of the Tenant Movement in New York City', in West and Blumberg (eds), *Women and Social Protest*; West and Blumberg, 'Reconstructing Social Protest from a Feminist Perspective', p.24.
67. S. Evans, *Personal Politics: The Roots of Women's Liberation in the Civil Rights Movement and the New Left* (New York: Vintage, 1979).
68. West and Blumberg, 'Reconstructing Social Protest from a Feminist Perspective'.
69. Interview with Dunlop, Dungannon, 23 November 2003.
70. A. Oberschall, *Social Conflict and Social Movements* (Englewood Cliffs, NJ: Prentice-Hall, 1973), p.155.
71. Staunton, *Nationalists of Northern Ireland, 1918–1973*, p.235.
72. R. Wilford, 'Women and Politics in Northern Ireland', in J. Lovenduski and P. Norris (eds), *Women and Politics* (Oxford: Oxford University Press, 1996), p.46.
73. Purdie, *Politics in the Streets*, p.89.
74. *Dungannon Observer*, 28 September 1963.
75. V. Randall, *Women and Politics: An International Perspective* (Basingstoke: Macmillan, 1991), p.58; P. Norris, 'Gender Differences in Political Participation in Britain: Traditional, Radical and Revisionist Models', *Government and Opposition*, 26, 1 (1991).
76. Purdie, *Politics in the Streets*, p.90.
77. *Dungannon Observer*, 27 November 1959.
78. 'Women in Civil Rights Conference', http://www.springtowncamp .com/files/news/2008/ may/ 03.html (29 June 2009).
79. 'Springtown Camp and Civil Rights' Women', http://www.nicivilrights.org/?p=30 (29 June 2009).
80. Interview with the McCluskeys, Foxrock, 5 March 2003.
81. Press release, 17 January 1964, Belfast, PRONI, Campaign for Social Justice (CSJ) Papers D/299/1.
82. Interview with the McCluskeys, Foxrock, 5 March 2003.
83. Quoted in W.H. Van Voris, *Violence in Ulster* (Amherst: University of Massachusetts Press, 1975), p.50.
84. M. Morgan, 'The Catholic Middle Class: Myth or Reality', *L'Irlande Revue Politique et Sociale*, 1, 3 (1987), pp.95–114.
85. S. Prince, 'The Northern Irish Civil Rights Movement in Context', lecture, Queens University Belfast, October 2008, p.11
86. Interview with the McCluskeys, Foxrock, 5 March 2003.
87. See Mary Ellen O'Doherty Appreciation, http://www.springtowncamp. com/files/news/ 2008/may/02.html (29 June 2009).
88. McCluskey, *Up off their Knees*, p.27.
89. Ibid., p.55.
90. McCluskey to Thornberry, 12 November 1967, Belfast, PRONI, CSJ Papers, D/2993/1.
91. McWilliams, 'Church, the State and the Women's Movement in Northern Ireland', p.44.
92. McCluskey to Thornberry, 12 November 1967, Belfast, PRONI, CSJ Papers, D/2993/1.
93. Quoted in M. Bolster, 'Women on the March: Women in the Civil Rights Movement in Northern Ireland in the 1960s' (MA thesis, University College Dublin, 1991), p.19.
94. Interview with the McCluskeys, Foxrock, 5 March 2003.
95. Sean McGivern was probably as close as the CSJ got to having a working-class member; he was the Secretary of the Irish Republican Labour Party and had spent six years on the Belfast Corporation.
96. A.I. Langdon to Prime Minister's Office, 28 August 1964, Belfast, PRONI, HO/5/185.
97. Campaign for Social Justice in Northern Ireland, 'Northern Ireland: Why Justice Cannot Be Done – the Douglas Home Correspondence' (1964).
98. Patricia McCluskey to Cushing, 22 August 1965, Belfast, PRONI, D/2993/1.
99. Patricia McCluskey quoted in Van Voris, *Violence*, pp.53–4.
100. Whelan to External Affairs, 22 April 1964, Dublin, NA, DFA, 2001/43/1304.
101. *Dungannon Observer*, 18 March 1964.

102. *Dungannon Observer,* 2 May 1964.
103. *Dungannon Observer,* 9 May 1964.
104. *Universe,* 13 July 1964.
105. McCluskey, *Up off their Knees,* p.22.
106. R. Nic Aongusa to Taoiseach, 3 February 1967, Dublin, NA, DFA, 2001/43/1304.
107. Correspondence, 13 July 1964, Belfast, PRONI, CSJ Papers, D/2993/1.
108. McCluskey, *Up off their Knees,* p.20.
109. Undated document on discrimination in employment, Belfast, PRONI, CSJ Papers, D/2993/1.
110. Quoted in Bolster, 'Women on the March', p.21.
111. McCluskey, *Up off their Knees,* p.26.
112. McCluskey to Paul Rose, 23 April 1965, Belfast, PRONI, CSJ Papers, D/2993/1.
113. West and Blumberg, 'Reconstructing Social Protest from a Feminist Perspective', p.24.
114. McCluskey, *Up off their Knees,* p.27.
115. Prince, *Northern Ireland's '68,* p.79.
116. V. Feeney, 'Westminster and the Early Civil Rights Struggle', *Éire-Ireland* (1976), p.10.
117. CSJ to Cardinal Richard Cushing of Boston, 22 August 1965, Belfast, PRONI, CSJ Papers, D/2993/1.
118. Conn McCluskey to Paul Rose, 6 December 1965, Belfast, PRONI, CSJ Papers, D/2993/1.
119. CSJ to Home Secretary Roy Jenkins, 25 January 1966, Belfast, PRONI, CSJ Papers, D/2993/1.
120. M. Mulholland, *Northern Ireland at the Crossroads: Ulster Unionism in the O'Neill Years, 1960–9* (Basingstoke: Macmillan, 2000).
121. A. Coughlan, 'Our Ideas', *Tuairisc – Newsletter of the Wolfe Tone Society* (31 August 1966), pp.7–10.
122. G. Adams, 'A Republican in the Civil Rights Movement', in M. Farrell (ed.), *Twenty Years On* (Dingle: Brandon, 1988), p.43.
123. CSJ to Wilson, 5 October 1966, Belfast, PRONI, CSJ Papers, D/2993/1.
124. Patricia McCluskey to Wilson, 23 March 1967, Belfast, PRONI, CSJ Papers, D/2993/1.
125. Secretary to Minister of Department of Justice, 24 November 1966, Dublin, NA, DT, 98/6/495.
126. Interview with Edwina Stewart, Belfast, 1 July 2003.
127. M. Milotte, *Communism in Modern Ireland: The Pursuit of the Workers' Republic since 1916* (Dublin: Gill & Macmillan, 1984), p.257.
128. A. Currie, *All Hell Will Break Loose* (Dublin: O'Brien, 2004), pp.89–98.
129. Interview with Austin Currie, Lucan, 1 September 2003.
130. Interview with Dunlop, Dungannon, 23 November 2003.
131. Memorandum to Nolan, 11 April 1967, NA, DFA, 2001/43/1304.
132. West and Blumberg, 'Reconstructing Social Protest from a Feminist Perspective', p.17.

CHAPTER THREE

Putting Themselves in Every Story: New Visions of Womanhood and Republicanism in the Irish Republic, 1967–9

When Gay Byrne planned a Mr-and-Mrs-style quiz for his 1966 Valentine's Day instalment of the 'Late Late Show' he could not have anticipated the furore that would erupt over a seemingly innocent game. In response to a question on the colour of the nightdress she wore on the night of her wedding, a woman confessed she was uncertain whether or not she had worn one. Thomas Ryan, Bishop of Clonfert, immediately condemned the show as pornography and a media frenzy was born. Denunciations of the show rang out from pulpits and weaved themselves through the lines of news editorials and letters. Educational meetings and sports authorities went on record in support of the bishop. In response Byrne offered the requisite *mea culpa* the following day. The story finally died down after a few weeks and the 'Late Late Show' seemed poised for a return to the status quo. Enter Brian Trevaskis, a Trinity College student. The discussion on the Catholic Church erupted when Trevaskis accused Michael Brown, Bishop of Galway, of being a moron for spending so much on a new cathedral rather than on feeding the poor. Accusing the bishop of not knowing the meaning of the word *Christianity*, Trevaskis brought up the Church's leading role in the mistreatment of unwed mothers in Ireland. Gay Byrne must have thought his short career in television was over, but the nation continued to watch, mouths agape and stuck to their seats. What could possibly be next?

Eamon de Valera's admonitions five years earlier at the 1961 launch of Irish television, which likened the power of the medium to atomic energy, now seemed more clairvoyant than cautionary: 'Never before was there in the hands of men an instrument so powerful to influence the thoughts and actions of the multitude.' Television and a growing variety of print media were combining to initiate new discussions about Irish society, the role of women, and Catholicism. These new discussions challenged hegemonic standards of propriety and broadened popular challenges to the status quo. This chapter explores how public discourse in the Republic of Ireland combined with international influences and modernizing forces to lead to the emergence of a women-centred consciousness among activists who would emerge in the early 1970s.

RADICAL DISCOURSE OUTSIDE OF IRELAND

If we define radical activism loosely as an attempt to effect fundamental change to the dominant political regime, we must concede that the term *radical* represents a sliding scale; contemporary hegemonic standards define what it means to be radical at any given point. Chapter 1 established how prevailing notions of postwar stability combined with industrial expansion to create a socially conservative aesthetic in western society and ultimately Irish society, even among anti-state activists. The prevailing sociopolitical climate in the Republic at that point opposed all brands of radicalism, including the home-grown traditional variant that republicanism had been at that period. Somehow radicalism rebounded from this contraction and abeyance period and grew to encompass a broad cross-section of causes by the early 1970s. One significant factor that contributed to this phenomenon was the emergence of new discourses outside of Ireland.

Contributing to these new discourses was a surge in education throughout the West. Hobsbawm citing Unesco statistics points out that 'between 1960 and 1980, to stick to well-schooled Europe, the number of students tripled or quadrupled in the most typical country, except where it multiplied by four to five, as in Federal Germany, Ireland and Greece; by five to seven, as in Finland, Iceland, Sweden and Italy; and seven to nine-fold, as in Spain and Norway'.[1] In record numbers young adults entered into third-level education and women occupied an exponentially increasing proportion of these record numbers. Another feature of this period is the revolution of culture that was beginning to take place in terms of increased social permissiveness, the breakdown in the nuclear family structure, increasing secularization and the ascendancy of youth culture.

The revolution of the late 1960s that took place throughout the western world can trace much of its ancestry to developments in the United States. Though America had phased out much of its sex-based discriminatory industrial practice due to economic pressure for women to take a more complete part in the workforce, women still struggled to achieve social and material equality with men. In 1963 Betty Friedan illuminated this problem in her seminal work, *The Feminine Mystique*, and later wrote that the book

> was a relief more important to women than I had ever dreamed, to have [their] questions put into words ... And they wrote me personal, impassioned letters, expressing their relief. They also wrote me of the insuperable problems they now had to face trying to move in society not just as 'my husband's wife, my children's mother, but as myself'.[2]

Through her work Friedan empowered her contemporaries to utilize this new language of women's oppression to question their own circumstances. At the same time debates surrounding the Vietnam issue, student politics and civil rights combined to articulate a new vision of the prevailing political structure. On occasion these movements overlapped and at other times members of these movements saw few connections. When Stokely Carmichael, a leader of the American civil rights movement, jokingly commented that the only position for women was prone, a new feminist consciousness was already beginning to take root.[3] Though he made the comment at a dinner to a mixed-sex group of insiders who admittedly laughed along with him, the sentiment he expressed, even in jest, provoked debate throughout the movement; while most women found their civil rights work empowering, others began to identify sex and gender hierarchies. At times these women faced resistance from their respective civil rights organizations; when women in Students for a Democratic Society moved to address the issue in 1965 and 1966, they received disdainful responses. Similarly, at the National Conference for a New Politics in Chicago, Jo Freeman and Shulamith Firestone could find no platform to discuss women's concerns, which prompted them to organize their own feminist groups that would raise awareness about the issue. This resistance to acknowledging the gender regime, even among self-proclaimed radicals, hastened the articulation of a women's rights agenda both inside and outside these movements.

The end of the 1960s became a golden age for the proliferation of women's groups throughout the United States, as they developed practical networks and a theoretical framework to analyze the gender regime at work in America. As the networks proliferated, American feminism experienced a hiving off into three categories of focus, which occasionally combined forces on specific issues: radical or separatist, liberal or equal rights, and socialist feminism. Liberal feminists claimed the most numbers in this period; their moderate message of reform instead of revolution appealed to the largest cross section of American women. Betty Friedan led this camp by helping to establish the most powerful of the liberal groups in 1966, the National Organization of Women (NOW). Their main goal can best be understood through an article in their bill of rights published at their second national conference. They believed women's equality could be achieved by the removal of 'legal and economic barriers to women's progress in a competitive world'.[4] Their lobbying and campaigning victories had far-reaching effects, which culminated in President Johnson signing Executive Orders 11375 and 11246 prohibiting sex discrimination in government employment. Radical feminists focused on patriarchal oppression of women and challenging the structures which support male oppression of women. They devised imaginative media campaigns to highlight their message. Their most famous, a protest outside the Miss America competition where they threw cosmetics and high-heeled shoes into a trash bin (a journalist later superimposed fire rising from the bin), pushed the feminist agenda to the forefront of media coverage. The success of the radical feminists in garnering media coverage and the liberal feminists in achieving concrete legislative change provided the world with a touchstone against which it could measure its own social attitudes. These new social movements of the period experienced similar trajectories and splits, gaining legislative reforms and producing extremists, leftists and moderate groups.

The British experience also helped influence international second-wave feminism. Throughout this period the dominant radical forces in Britain – the New Left, members of the trade union movement, peace activists and students – embraced socialism as the prime liberating ideology. Similar to the female members of the American civil rights movement during this period, women in the British New Left began to articulate their dissatisfaction with the prevailing power structures within the movement. The 1967 Dialectics of Liberation conference, which failed to mention women, confirmed Juliet Mitchell's 1966 observation that the subordination of women had become a 'subsidiary, if not an invisible element in the preoccupations of socialists'.[5] Some British women, who had cut their teeth in the peace movement and the

Campaign for Nuclear Disarmament, began to wrestle with a widespread prejudice against feminism among a significant portion of their fellow activists. Many in the New Left spoke out against feminism as being divisive; feminist goals, they argued, could be met through the class struggle. Similar to the American experience, these women formed feminist groups to address their feelings of alienation from their own political organizations. One difference between the American and the British experience of radicalism was Britain's focus on socialist goals and rhetoric, even within the budding feminist movement. In light of this dual-natured activism in Britain, the ideal issues around which to rally came up in 1968 when Liz Bilocca set up a committee to improve the safety conditions on the Hull fishing trawlers and when women sewing-machinists at Ford motor factories in Essex and Lancashire went on strike for equal pay. British women of the New Left immediately began to organize around these working-class issues to raise awareness about women's position in British society as workers and wives of workers.

The British trade union movement was integral to the success of such campaigns. On 4 September 1968 the British Trade Union Congress voted to support those undertaking industrial action for equal pay for women. This resolution did not go far enough for delegate Joan O'Connell, who called for sympathetic strikes, saying: 'for too long we have been fobbed off with promises and cosy cups of tea in the House of Commons. Barbara Castle has equal pay for equal work – why should not the rest of her sex have it.'[6] Barbara Castle, the Secretary of State for Employment and Productivity, eventually introduced an equality bill, but she was viewed by many socialist feminists to be an exception to the prevailing gender regime rather than the rule. Socialist concerns characterized much of British feminist agitation in the late 1960s and helped women gain a series of victories in the labour market in terms of equal pay campaigns and consciousness raising.

Elsewhere in Europe the main radical issues were women's liberation and student politics. Students seized educational institutions to demand changes to curricula, faculty and the administration. Their rhetoric centred on a deep distrust of adults, authorities and the system that perpetuated economic and social inequalities. Through their actions they engineered a revolution in education, politics and social awareness. Feminism grew out of these movements and influenced them as well. Though the issue of equal pay had been addressed in Italy in the early 1960s, there were still problems of job classification and segregation. Italian feminists looked towards a British analysis of workers' rights to further the second wave in their own country. Other European countries experienced women's liberation through small campaigns and singular thinkers and writers. Switzerland's Iris von Roten wrote *Women in Playpens*, which sparked off protests as early as the 1950s, but surprisingly the major issue of women's suffrage remained unsettled for many years due to regional direct democracy. Therefore, Swiss feminist activism had more in common with America and Britain's first wave of feminism than with their respective second wave. Conversely, the Dutch women's movement concentrated on sexuality, love, marriage and homosexuality, as pioneered by Joke Kool-Smit's article, 'The Discontent Amongst Women'.

France, whose Simone de Beauvior seemed to have already taken feminism as far as it could go in her 1949 tour de force, *The Second Sex*, found they had cause to celebrate when the Napoleonic codes were repealed in 1965. After that French feminist theory flourished. Spain's Lidia Falcón published *Los Derechos Laborales de la Mujer* in 1962 and *Los Derechos Civiles de la Mujer* in 1964, which helped articulate the position of women in Franco's Spain. Norway's experience of the women's movement corresponded with the student movement; in 1967 an investigative committee was formed to articulate strategies for getting women more involved in Norwegian politics. Finland's New Left counter-culture allowed women to play a big role in its organization. In Iceland the Redstocking movement, a namesake of an American liberation group, was formed by socialist feminist teachers. In Germany, as in Norway, women found their niche in a radical student movement.[7]

Overall, there are very few generalizations one can make, other than that throughout Europe the late 1960s was a period that underwent comprehensive social change due to a combination of international influence and home-grown initiatives. Small groups of intellectuals and singular writers dominated radical politics – each country producing a basic theoretical framework using the ideas and observations of its own thinkers and writers as well as ideas taken from theorists in other western countries. Ireland shared a similar experience.

CHANGES FOR WOMEN IN IRELAND

When Evelyn Owens and Helen Burke sat down to read the *Irish Times* at the end of August 1967 they came across an article that somehow encapsulated everything they had been fighting against. The interview, conducted by Ida Grehan for the women's page of the *Irish Times*, asked Taoiseach Jack Lynch what he thought of women's roles in public life. Lynch's answers – which blamed women for their own lack of representation, denied that women faced any institutional roadblocks, and admitted that pay discrimination was an archaic practice – exposed a government struggling to come to terms with rapid changes in the gender regime. Lynch concluded the interview by saying:

> I don't regard Irish women as being in a Celtic twilight that was imposed on them, but I think the women can emerge from their Celtic twilight by their own actions rather than by anybody else facilitating the women in doing this. If we had a bolder approach to public life, a bolder approach to matters that women regard as being the peculiar domain of men, women themselves can break out of this twilight.[8]

Evelyn Owens and Helen Burke of the Associations of Women Citizens of Ireland[9] responded immediately by writing a critical letter to the *Irish Times*:

> Please, Mr Lynch, forgive us for sounding cynical. We know now that the Treaty of Rome will not help Irish women out of the Celtic twilight. Back to your dishes, women. If your place isn't in the home it doesn't appear to be any place else either. But wait, a gleam of hope – study French and you may yet earn your place in the sun.[10]

Both the opinions of Lynch and of Owens and Burke exemplify a revitalized debate regarding women and citizenship that emerged during the late 1960s. The discussion that began around citizenship rights in the first part of the century was slowly coming alive again as a combination of modernizing forces, legislative reform and radical discourse contributed towards redefining Ireland.

The Ireland of the late 1960s was a far different place than it had been a decade earlier. T.K. Whitaker's *First Programme for Economic Expansion*, which had been adopted to boost productivity, open up Ireland's markets, shrink unemployment and stem emigration, was beginning to bear fruit; between 1959 and 1964 investment increased by 35 per cent.[11] In November 1968 the *Irish Times* observed that the success of the *First Programme* could be measured by the emigration rate, and by the mid-1960s the rate seemed to lay testament to Whitaker's vision by falling from 14.8 per thousand to 5.7 per thousand between 1961 and 1966.[12] The only major stumbling block for the *First*

Programme was its lack of provision for social housing. Between 1955 and 1959 the number of state-funded new homes built in the Republic had plummeted from 10,490 to 4,894.[13] This programme, then, with its neglect of the housing issue, placed a great deal of pressure on already under-resourced housing authorities. The demographic shift towards urban centres and the ebbing tide of emigration meant that the housing problem, if not quickly addressed, threatened to grow into a crisis.

Other issues, however, temporarily distracted the public from the dismal housing issue. One element that was ripe for significant progress was education, with increasing numbers of students staying in school for longer periods. A committee commissioned by the government to investigate Irish schooling reported in 1967 the need for comprehensive reform of the educational system.[14] Minister for Education Patrick Hillery responded by initiating plans to build comprehensive schools and technical colleges. Hillery's successor, Donogh O'Malley, continued the drive for reform by introducing free secondary education in 1967. These measures helped to cultivate a more highly educated cohort of school-leavers. Overall, the increasing involvement of the state in welfare legislation, social spending and economic reorganization contributed to a revolution in the relationship between the individual and the Irish state. But in order to sustain this new momentum, Connolly observes, the Irish government would have to re-evaluate and restructure the gender regime.[15]

One of the most profound changes of the 1960s involved the mechanization of housework tasks. Catriona Clear observes that the introduction of household technologies eliminated much of the physical labour associated with keeping a house in post-Independence Ireland, even though these technologies often introduced new household tasks to the daily routine.[16] During the 1960s urban homes that lacked basic toilet facilities rapidly acquired indoor plumbing and time-saving appliances such as washing machines. For the first time the Republic underwent a widespread consumer drive that was reinforced by mass media such as television and women's magazines. Also, as people moved closer to the cities, the types of jobs they sought necessarily transformed from farm work to skilled manual work and white-collar positions.[17] This new consumer culture, coupled with rapid urbanization, paved the way for a fortified class structure to assert itself with vigour. Convenience items like the washing machine, marketed to free housewives for more important things, only succeeded in expanding their housework load by encouraging a competition of cleanliness. The myth of the blissful middle-class housewife, as sold to Irish women through this new consumer culture, became a common aspiration among all classes of women.

NEW DEBATES IN THE IRISH MEDIA

One of the main mediums for proselytizing the consumer aesthetic was television. John Horgan makes the point that by the late 1950s British broadcasting was available to approximately 40 per cent of the Irish population.[18] The Irish government established its own television service on 1 January 1961 to provide 'an antidote to the type of paganism which is being propagated by foreign television', according to one TD.[19] One of the main objectives set for Radio Telefís Éireann was to develop programmes based on an Irish concept of marriage and motherhood, with suitably feminine female characters who would appeal to young girls.[20] Even with this remit the Catholic bishops were vociferously sceptical about this new mode of communication and the moral dangers it presented. The hierarchical concern about public morality was fuelled by Minister for Justice Brian Lenihan's introduction of reforms to the notoriously strict censorship laws in 1964 and 1968. Reflecting the tenor of the time, Lenihan packed the Censorship Board with more moderate members, established limited viewing certificates and introduced a bill to limit the terms of banned material.

The relaxation of the censorship laws contributed to the proliferation of the nascent radical press in Ireland, which represented a new departure in Irish media history. Though never as revolutionary as its continental counterparts, the Irish radical press sought to push the boundaries of journalism by courting controversy around issues of public morality, left-wing activism and feminism. John D.H. Downing's loose definition of 'Radical media' refers to media that is generally small-scale, that assumes different forms and that expresses 'an alternative vision to hegemonic policies, priorities, and perspectives'.[21] Publications such as *United Irishman, Nusight*, Irish women's magazines and the *Irish Times* all saw themselves as providing an alternative to mainstream newspapers such as the *Irish Independent* or the *Irish Press*.

During this period the editorial staff of the *Irish Times* prided itself on addressing issues from a left-of-centre perspective. Not nearly as popular as the other dailies,[22] the *Irish Times* was effective in spurring other newspapers towards journalistic innovation and hard-hitting investigation. Probably two of the most ground-breaking reporters, Michael Viney and Mary Maher, consistently led the call to eradicate social neglect by coming to terms with the unspoken. Maher, a native of Chicago, helped to introduce 'women's issues' to the *Irish Times* readership as early as 1967. In the late 1960s equal pay became a significant debate in the media, reflecting the changing attitude towards women in the workplace, a move towards Europeanization and an increasingly sophisticated public. Maher's challenge to the status quo can be seen in an early article about women's third-level education, where she wrote: 'The viewpoints put forward on the page should hopefully begin the dialogue on what might be done to educate Irish girls for the future ... to what extent can the system, with a conscious effort change the society?'[23]

Minister for Education Donogh O'Malley attempted to answer this last question; his ambivalence underscored the government's reluctance to tackle the issue of gender relations: 'What part can the schools play? This is something that in all its aspects will have to be considered in connection with our application to join the EEC. I feel that it would be out of place for me to comment on it now.'[24] While today equal pay debates may seem reformist in nature, it was a controversial topic for a country that identified the female sex with domesticity through much of its constitutional and social values.

With the establishment of the *Irish Times* 'Women First' page in 1967, Maher and her colleagues' consistent coverage of issues like equal pay presented a new kind of reporting – a personalized feminist socialist perspective. Their work built on the crusading social journalism of Dorothy Macardle and the early *Irish Press*[25] by bringing back a conscientious voice that spoke of possibility and social change. Elgy Gillespie later wrote about the *Irish Times* of the 1960s: 'the most exciting change came in the form of the Women First page, and the women writers who filled it; led by Mary Maher and Maeve Binchy, they penned the ripping reads of the day – first-person entertainments exposing shame, scandal, fear, misery, and abuse. The New Journalism had arrived, and we put ourselves in every story.'[26] Mary Maher confirms this sense of pioneering spirit so demonstrative of the enthusiasm of the 1960s:

> It was a beginning. Contraception, unmarried mothers, deserted wives, family law, children's courts, prison conditions – all the issues that didn't exist out loud in 1967 – were to follow, faster than we perhaps imagined ... The other national dailies followed suit within months of the inauguration of Women First with their own pages.[27]

The issue of equal pay that led the media crusade for a redefinition of

Leabharlanna Fhine Gall

women in Irish society, did not find unqualified support among the trade union movement,[28] though Mary E. Daly makes the point that this was changing due to women's increasing participation within the movement.[29] Rosemary Cullen Owens cautions us not to forget the role of abeyance groups in paving the way for women in the late 1960s to engage new debates regarding women's position in Irish society through their lobbying and letter-writing efforts: 'While the major developments in the field of employment and equality were not debated realistically in the public arena until the late 1960s, the seeds for subsequent change were nurtured by the groundwork of organizations ten-fifteen years earlier.'[30]

Another debate that followed on from the equal pay debate involved an articulation of dissatisfaction over women's perceived political apathy. Throughout this period the *Irish Woman's Journal* engaged in a full-scale assault on this political apathy with articles such as 'Will she *ever* learn – and fight back?', 'Alternatives to Duds' and 'Women's place in modern Ireland', which concluded with the line: 'Irish women should stop complaining and start campaigning.' Many groups did just that. Probably the most famous of these groups is the *ad hoc* committee of women's groups that formed in the wake of the 1967 meeting of the International Alliance of Women with the objective of establishing a commission to inquire into the status of women. Diarmaid Ferriter points out that Charles Haughey, Minister for Finance, publicly welcomed the establishment of such a reform commission, but that he privately admitted that doing so would allow the government to delay the introduction of equal pay, citing the commission's on-going investigation.[31] Despite this political engineering, the commission made significant gains for women in this period through their preferred method of activism: intra-governmental lobbying.[32]

A main drive for journalists such as Mary Maher and *Woman's Way* resident feminist Monica McEnroy was to level the professional playing field. One article taught women to write a cover letter and curriculum vitae,[33] while another article encouraged women's participation in trade unions.[34] One article pushed for equal pension rights,[35] while another embraced Betty Friedan's mother-and-career woman argument advanced in the *Feminine Mystique*.[36] The records available indicate that the government only seriously began to contemplate women in the workforce in 1969, when it published its *Third Programme for Economic and Social Development*.

Until now there was very little talk about women's roles on the farm. Though portrayed in the media as a lifestyle rather than a job, 4.2 per cent of adult women classified themselves as agricultural workers in the 1961 census.[37] Debates surrounding women's position within the farmhouse were coloured by economic considerations that often dictated a tractor be bought before a water tap could be installed. Daly reminds us that in comparison to rural electrification, the provision of running water to rural households was relatively slow in part due to the resistance of farming organizations, which prioritized technology associated with male work habits over that of female work habits.[38] Living under isolating conditions, the only outlets for countrywomen to engage in public life and the only representation these women enjoyed came from the ICA.[39] Though the radical media could provide little for these women, their coverage of the issue of aquification as well as the issue of women's isolation was instructive for many urban dwellers in educating them about rural social problems and tracking the collapse of the rural demographic system.

Another area of public interest involved women's roles within the home. Catherine Rose echoed Betty Friedan's *Feminine Mystique* when she wrote that the Irish woman was 'easy prey' for manufacturers whose function was to make her buy 'things to fill the house, things to clean the things that fill the house, things in which to store the things she buys to clean things …'[40] Increasingly, articles and books such as Dorine Rohan's *Marriage: Irish Style* and Michael Viney's *The Broken Marriage: A Study in Depth of a Growing Irish Social Problem* brought the subject of unhappy marriage into public discourse and forced readers to contemplate women's position in Irish society in the context of current legislation and interpersonal relationships.[41] There was less popular agreement about the adoption of divorce legislation than of equal pay, yet the all-party Dáil committee on the constitution established at Lemass's prompting in 1966 recommended the adoption of divorce legislation in 1967, despite the vocal opposition of the Church.[42] The board justified the recommendation by pointing to the issue of discrimination against religious minorities whose religion permitted divorce. They pointed out this would help with North/South relations.[43] This recommendation, one that would take a further thirty years to achieve, did demonstrate a new level of pragmatism among the political elite in terms of confronting social issues. Yet, one wonders if the decision to take on the Church on this particular issue was more of a stalling tactic in light of other, more easily enacted family law reforms that came to the fore in this period. Regardless, family breakdown did capture the imagination like no other family law issue.

The numbers of deserted wives in the Republic during the late 1960s is not known; their 'invisibility stemmed from the refusal of the state to undermine the authority position of husbands, and also from the social disgrace of marriage breakdown'.[44] Though there were numerous articles expressing sympathy for deserted wives, Father Brendan M. Maguire, who wrote for the *Irish Woman's Journal*, revealed the great public suspicion with which these women were viewed when he asked: 'Is it possible the wife herself may bear a share of the blame for her husband's desertion?'[45] Listing reasons including women's sexual frigidity, their difficulties with budgeting money and their ineffective methods of dealing with alcoholic husbands, he answered the question in the affirmative.

Debate on family breakdown led to discussion of more topics regarding the Irish family, which had been previously addressed. Unmarried mothers were by far the most scorned during this period. Diarmaid Ferriter estimates that up to 30,000 unmarried mothers and other young girls believed to be 'simple-minded, assertive, pretty or even having suffered rape and talked about it' were sent to Magdalen laundries (homes for 'wayward women' run by nuns) until 1996, when the last one closed.[46] Labelled as 'home wreckers' and 'loose women' in Letters to the Editor sections of newspapers, during this period the radical media began to chronicle their plight. Despite this they remained without an advocacy group of their own.

One group of women whose success can likely be traced to the sympathy they were able to garner did take on the establishment and win significant reforms. The National Association of Widows in Ireland (NAWI) worked to draw attention to their vulnerable status within the welfare state in terms of pension and taxation rights. It helped that unlike deserted wives and unmarried mothers, the prevailing perception was that their morality was beyond reproach. By manipulating the state-sponsored concept of women's economic dependence, they demanded increases in welfare provisions in order to protect their position within the class structure.[47] Their tactics relied heavily on political lobbying, and as members of the *ad hoc* committee that would soon establish the Commission for the Status of Women, their strategy was primarily parliamentary in focus.[48] Though they grabbed media attention and sympathy, overall they were 'socially conservative and not radical in their demands' for comprehensive financial support from the state, nor did they make their objectives part of a wider discourse on equal citizenship rights.[49] In the early 1970s NAWI would occasionally resort to street politics in order to achieve their demands, but because their activism was primarily located in the arena of political lobbying and not street politics, a detailed analysis of their work lies outside the scope of this study.

By far the most gripping of controversies in the late 1960s in terms of women and the family was the debate over fertility control. Though people throughout the world struggled with the morality of utilizing contraceptive devices, Ireland's Catholic hegemony, combined with its strict laws banning the importation of contraceptives for sale, rendered procuring such things difficult, if not impossible. The Church's response to this increased public discourse on birth control was to institute marriage guidance centres that promoted the 'rhythm method'. But their efforts could not stem the tide; more and more women were looking to contraceptives to control conception. Myrtle Hill points out that by 1967 approximately 12,000 Irish women were reported to be taking birth control pills and the number was rising.[50] One pharmaceutical company reported that 75 per cent of Irish women taking birth control pills were using them for 'social reasons'.[51] These numbers, combined with a public policy hostile to family planning, paved the way for public debate on the morality of contraceptive devices and medication.

When it was published on 25 July 1968, Pope Paul VI's *Humanae Vitae* provoked heated reaction throughout the world. In the encyclical the Pope admitted that population growth and the changing role of women brought up a number of concerns, but held that 'any action which either before, at the moment of, or after sexual intercourse, is specifically intended to prevent procreation' was contrary to natural law and therefore must be prohibited. This prompted *Irish Woman's Journal* editor Sean O'Sullivan to fire back a strongly worded column, which is worth quoting at length.

> The reality of *Humanae Vitae* is this: perpetuated misery and dissatisfaction of both husband and wife in marriage and more broken marriages; the perpetuation of illegitimate children by husbands with other women; the seeking of release from frustrations and repression by husbands who in reality have far less belief in the strictures of Catholicism and the pious acceptance of papal announcements by wives who couldn't care less, after their fourth or fifth child, if intercourse was abolished altogether … *Humanae Vitae* like no other papal pronouncement, is unacceptable to thinking, discerning people. We can accept the assumption of the Blessed Virgin Mary, we can take it that there is no hope of understanding, but we cannot take it that God is a sadist, that He endows us with certain physical properties or qualities and

then denies us the use of them except in circumstances that are ideal, but which life negates and cancels out.[52]

O'Sullivan's reaction, though particularly vitriolic, reflected the growing popular dissatisfaction with the encyclical and, by extension, a large part of Catholic teaching. Mary Kenny, who would soon become the de facto leader of the Irish Women's Liberation Movement in the early 1970s, wrote an open letter in the *Irish Times*, following on from O'Sullivan: 'If you are against population control by contraception then you must also be against population control by penicillin. Anything else is cheating.'[53] This astute point, and others like it, found its way into the press and began to convince people there might be a higher law than the directives of the Pope – a concept of social justice. Ironically it was, in fact, the concept of social justice that Pope Paul VI had outlined in *Populorum Progressio*, issued just over a year earlier, that would capture the imagination of Catholic dissidents.

Protests abounded throughout the world, especially from the medical community.[54] The furore created by *Humanae Vitae* dominated public discourse on women's roles in the late 1960s, signalling two things. First it revealed a liberalizing tendency towards religion itself and religious dissent. Second, it helped bring to a culmination an emergent feminist consciousness that had been quietly fomenting since the middle of the decade. The newly popularized language of rights and social justice was now broadening to include reproductive control. This second wave of feminist thought that was bubbling to the surface of popular discourse became uniquely Irish through the reception of *Humanae Vitae*; the uniformity of acceptance (begrudging though it sometimes was) among the political, hierarchical and medical elite combined with strict legislation on the issue ensured a new and distinctive response from the growing community of progressives in Ireland. A distant drumbeat of discontent could be heard as Monica McEnroy, a nurse and journalist, bitterly pointed out:

> Very soon we will have to get out and march for some basic human rights. It is apparently not possible to shame Irish political and medical prejudice and the fat chaps from the unions who attend [International Labour Organization] conferences in Geneva and disappear to the boys' powder room to spend innumerable imaginary pennies when the vote on equal pay comes up.[55]

REPUBLICANISM REDEFINES ITSELF

By the middle of the 1960s the republican movement was engaged in a re-evaluation of its tactics in the wake of the failed 'border campaign'. Morale had significantly fallen and it looked like the republican movement had two choices: to restructure or to fold. Cathal Goulding, IRA chief-of-staff, later made the point that the circulation of *United Irishman* had fallen from the hundred-thousand bracket of 1957–9 to a mere fourteen thousand in 1967.[56] The leadership's 1965 Easter statement emphasized that the republican movement had decided to restructure and it was looking to revitalize its tactics: 'The past year has seen a steady and real consolidation of our strength based, not on false expansion of membership nor a stream of unreal activity, but on an internal examination of our movement in all its branches, a re-education of our people in the necessities of today and on an open-minded scrutiny of our present situation.'[57] Through their writing and their participation in debates among the republican leadership, the two leading lights of the republican shift to the left, Roy Johnston and Anthony Coughlan, had been encouraging a more political approach.[58] Their main argument was that the 'border campaign' had proved the redundancy of a military campaign without a complementary political programme. Instead they argued for republicans to abandon their historic singularity of purpose and explore the possibility of entering into the kind of political activist alliances that had been cropping up throughout Europe in the mid-1960s. They grounded this strategy in a left-wing analysis of the national question in the hope that the New Left could succeed where traditional republicanism had failed. Cathal Goulding, as IRA chief of staff, and Tomás MacGiolla, as Sinn Féin president, believed that this new focus on political action would appeal to a wider cross section of Irish society, which could be called on in an effort to destabilize the governments on both sides of the border.

The Irish government was aware that the IRA had been increasing its numbers since the end of the border campaign,[59] at the same time Goulding had begun to de-emphasize military training in favour of political education. Richard English reminds us, however, that the military arm of republicanism was far from dead in this period,[60] and Henry Patterson points out that Goulding had to acquiesce to a degree of military training to retain recruits and traditionalists as he attempted to nudge the movement towards socialism.[61]

Also during this period the *United Irishman* moved towards a left-wing analysis by focusing on working-class politics and a range of activist issues, including anti-Apartheid action and agitating for fishing rights on privately owned land in Ireland. An example of this shift towards social action is the republican movement's role in spurring the formation of the National Water Restoration League, a tactic meant to appeal to a wider cross section of people by opposing the privatization of waterways. The *United Irishman* covered its 1966 launch in Galway, reporting that Roy Johnston was the main speaker at the event,[62] but overall this initiative, and others like it, had little initial impact in growing the organization and creating broad coalitions. Moreover, in spite of all the talk of uniting across national boundaries, some of their coverage reflected a suspicion of foreign investment that at times bordered on the xenophobic.[63]

Under the headline 'Radicals must unite – republican exclusiveness must end', the *United Irishman* reported that Cathal Goulding's 1967 Bodenstown speech opposed the establishment of a Free Trade Area and stressed unity between republicans and radicals. Admonishing the movement for failing to fully connect with social issues, Goulding spelled out the new strategy of broadening the republican base.[64] Also that year, Sinn Féin leader Tomás MacGiolla spoke at the party's Ard Fheis, indicating another possible direction in republican social activism: housing. He told delegates that Sinn Féin should take a militant stand on property speculation, ground rents and 'the general exploitation of the people's need for housing'.[65] The best strategy, MacGiolla advised delegates, was to diversify their political activism. This strategy was not news to the Department of Justice, who had seized a detailed policy document on 7 September 1966 during the arrest of senior republican Sean Garland.[66] The department's 1966 review of the movement indicates they were in possession of comprehensive intelligence about the new strategy even before the seizure of the Garland documents. Their report details how the Political Education Programme was spearheading 'the organization's agitational, economic, social and political policy' through its participation in a host of action groups, including the Wolfe Tone Society, the Dublin Housing Action Committee, the Economic Independence Committee, civil rights groups and various Republican Clubs.[67]

In 1967 and 1968 this new policy began to gain ground and the *United Irishman* added coverage of Dublin's housing crisis,[68] the student movement,[69] the Irish Anti-Apartheid Association[70] and protests against the Vietnam war[71] to its coverage of the National Water Restoration League[72] and civil rights action in the North.[73] Occasionally the newspaper dabbled in women's rights with discussion on the Irish government's failure to ratify the European Social Charter:

> Article Four stipulates the right to a fair remuneration and this article was not acceptable because a section of it required equal pay for men and women for work of equal value ... Article Eight which recognized the right of women to protection could not be accepted by our humanitarian rulers because they could not agree with the clause making dismissal during absence on maternity leave unlawful. Neither could they agree with another clause providing nursing mothers with sufficient time off for the care of their infants.[74]

This article, however, reads more as a swipe at the Dublin government than an endorsement of any women's agenda.

Overall, during this period of re-evaluation the *United Irishman* seems to have struggled with integrating a radical action agenda into its reportage. J. Bowyer Bell characterizes the *United Irishman* as becoming during this period a 'first rate monthly agitating against the appalling housing, investigating ownership of Dublin ground rents, exposing hypocrisy and attracting new reviewers and correspondence',[75] but a review of the paper yields a different interpretation. The *United Irishman's* radical tokenism – dedicating only one or two articles to each social cause over a period of four years (1965–8) – indicates a failure to construct a comprehensive left-wing agenda that accounts for the interweaving of single issues into a greater cause. Though towards the end of this period the paper was finding its feet as a radical publication concerned with social issues, its development in this direction was uneven and piecemeal during the period. Its editors, Tony Meade and then Seamus O'Tuithail, may have been committed Gouldingites, but a 'first-rate' left-wing monthly, the *United Irishman* was not. Its failure to make connections and to engage with *Humanae Vitae* on any level betrayed an underlying republican conservatism on women's issues and an overall discomfort with this new drive towards social action. Leslie Joseph Burnett of Belfast disapprovingly outlined this tension in a letter to the editor:

> The glossing over of the Pope's Encyclical on birth control by the paper would seemingly show the United Irishman to be at least pandering to readers with Catholic convictions if not indeed being positively pro-Catholic. Surely foreign interference with the lives of people is every bit as repugnant when it is foisted upon us by Rome as it is when it comes from London or anywhere

else. There seems to be a close parallel between the Unionist link with London and the Catholic hierarchy link with Rome. Our Church leaders whether Catholic or Protestant should be subject to God, not foreign interference.[76]

In this period the *United Irishman* never became the radical publication Goulding, Coughlan and Johnston would have hoped for, because it had to maintain an appeal to its traditional base during this new development phase of Marxist thought. Burnett, as a Belfast native, was acutely aware of the importance of appealing to the Protestant working class as a means to achieving a broad support base and restyling the movement. In pointing out that the publication had shown its true colours by failing to engage with this papal encyclical, she anticipated the ideological dichotomy between what its leaders wanted it to be and what its constituents actually were – a dichotomy that would eventually tear the movement asunder.

REPUBLICANISM AND SOCIAL ACTION

The most important unifying issue of the late 1960s, about which many members of disparate political constituencies could agree, was the housing crisis in Dublin. In May and September 1967 Mary Maher published comprehensive articles exposing the housing conditions of those who lived in the overcrowded slums of Mountjoy Square.[77] It was the pictures included that transformed the story from a hard-hitting piece of muck-raking journalism into a story that had the capacity to galvanize its readers. By utilizing the government's own statistics, Maher exposed the extent of the problem: public housing was distributed on the basis of family size and the Dublin Corporation only catered for families of three and up. Maher pointed out that though approximately 12,000 families had applied for housing, only 5,347 were recommended for an allocation.

A few days after Maher's first article appeared in the *Irish Times* Labour TD Michael O'Leary pressed Minister for Local Government Kevin Boland to explain the land speculation that was taking place in Mountjoy Square.[78] During the same month the Dublin Housing Action Committee (DHAC) was formed.[79] Inspired by Sinn Féin activists looking to forge links with other radical groups, the DHAC maintained an ostensibly independent structure. The main personalities in the group were Máirín de Burca, a young socialist and former member of Cumann na mBan, who had returned to Sinn Féin after it had shown signs of contemplating social action, and Prionsias de Rossa, another young republican socialist and future parliamentary politician. As allegations against the government about housing grew louder, the government defended itself by arguing that it had built 2,871 more houses in the 1967/8 period than it had in the 1963/4 period, and that few other European countries had done as much to house its citizens.[80] The DHAC maintained that the most acute crisis lay in overcrowded, substandard housing and that instead of focusing on repairing existing housing, the government was selling off the land to corporate speculators, who were intent on converting the property to office space.

Though the DHAC was fighting for housing for the same type of population as the Homeless Citizens League of Dungannon, there were fundamental differences between the groups. First, the HCL was started and run by the homeless themselves; though the DHAC had homeless members and organizers, it was set up and organized by people with homes who possessed a broad political philosophy and agenda. Second, the HCL suffered homelessness and political domination due to a sectarian systemic structure. In the 1960s Dublin was beginning to show signs of greater prosperity; the uneven levels of government investment had drawn into sharp relief the intolerable conditions of Dublin's marginalized, which prompted the formation of the DHAC. Sectarianism and the property franchise were not the critical issues here. Third, the DHAC represented a coalition of left-wing activists, humanitarians and political parties, while the HCL remained independent of such influences. And fourth, the HCL was dominated by women. In the first few years of the DHAC's existence, its rhetoric centred more on overcrowding and expanding family size than on specifically acknowledging that housing was linked to women's issues, an argument it would later articulate. The records available indicate that the DHAC made surprisingly little of the potential connections between overcrowding, motherhood and fertility control. Upon analysis, it seems that the two groups had nothing more than tactics in common.

The DHAC adroitly grabbed headlines by picketing City Hall and staging sit-ins at homes scheduled for demolition, like their Dungannon counterparts. Oftentimes the gardaí were used to disperse the group and, on occasion, to arrest leading figures. By January 1968 the DHAC had brought together members of the Communist Party, the Labour Party, Sinn Féin, the Citizens Advice Bureau, Maoists, Trotskyites, members of the Salvation Army, members of the St Vincent de Paul Society, members of the Irish Student Movement, students in Trinity College and University College Dublin Republican Clubs, a member of the Catholic clergy, and Hilary Boyle, an eccentric heiress.[81]

The arrest of many activists, including Prionsias de Rossa, Máirín de Burca and Máire MacGiolla, wife of president of Sinn Féin Tomás Mac-Giolla, during a sit-in allowed the DHAC to publicize their activism even more comprehensively. In June 1968 the *Irish Times* ran an article complete with pictures of those who had been arrested. The story published the DHAC's five demands:

- Declaration of a housing emergency and adoption of emergency measures to provide adequate temporary family accommodation, but making all vacant accommodation available as living accommodation.
- Introduction of bye-laws to prohibit the demolition and conversion to other uses of sound living accommodation.
- The repair of dwellings by Dublin Corporation where landlords refuse to do so.
- An immediate halt to the building of prestige office blocks and the redirection of the capital and labour involved to the construction of family accommodation.
- House loans of 100 per cent to low income citizens at low interest rates.[82]

The government was aware of the overlap in membership between the republican movement and the DHAC, though there is surprisingly little other than press cuttings to indicate this in the relevant files.[83] Records of the Dáil debates have been more forthcoming in revealing official perception of the group. During one debate the Minister for Local Government, Kevin Boland, described two of the organizers as 'members of an illegal organisation', a reference to the IRA.[84] One TD seeking to spur a red scare described the protesters as a group of 'fellow travellers', while another said that they were led by a 'gullible priest who does not know anything about anything'.[85] These allegations touched on popular fears that the IRA was using innocents to further their cause. Máirín de Burca responded by saying: 'It is necessary for us to be agitators, but the government misconstrues our objectives. We agitate solely for the implementation of our five-point plan.'[86] On one level, however, IRA membership was beside the point. Regardless of who was on the streets carrying the placards, the issue of the housing crisis remained valid. As much as the government sought to discredit the group, the pictures in Mary Maher's articles and on television's 'Outlook' programme did not lie. Though few would clamour to join what was very probably a republican front organization, they would instead express their growing sympathy for Dublin's indigent by writing to the Letters section of the newspapers urging a re-evaluation of existing legislation.

Another group set up by Sinn Féin, which followed on from the DHAC, was the Citizens Advice Bureau. This group endeavoured to collect statistics on the extent of the housing problem and advise those struggling to find adequate housing on how to contact solicitors, barristers and architects for professional advice. More openly linked with Sinn Féin, the Bureau was a leading presence at all of the DHAC rallies, protests and major evictions. This group connected the republican movement with housing agitation with dizzying permutations. Sean Dunne, for example, was the chairman of the Citizen's Advice Bureau and a member of the DHAC. Seamus O'Toole was a member of the DHAC and a *United Irishman* writer.[87]

Though the DHAC never achieved its five-point plan, it was significant for other reasons. First, it raised awareness of radical politics in an Irish context. Second, it allowed women such as Máirín de Burca and Máire MacGiolla a platform to engage in street politics in leadership roles. Third, bringing the housing issue to the fore, the DHAC and the Citizen's Advice Bureau – and by extension Sinn Féin – made room for radical politics in public discourse. It brought together different political groups for a unified purpose; this had the effect of spurring mainstream parties into action. Máirín de Burca remembered this period as a process of convergence where these different groups came together on specific issues: 'There was the Housing Action Committee, the Irish Voice on Vietnam, there was the Anti-Apartheid Movement and the Irish Women's Liberation Movement. One led into another, they all became part of the whole.' But a study of the *United Irishman* indicates that left-wing agitation was not necessarily an organic phenomenon and a natural outgrowth of republicanism. During this period *United Irishman* did not present a coherent narrative of republicanism and social action, and for many traditionalists these causes did not become 'part of a whole'. For some such as de Burca, what may have started as a tactic to destabilize the government quickly turned into a coherent and encompassing socialism, but for others the gulf between liberating Ireland and liberating women was difficult to bridge.

Probably the most important link to radical agitation devised by the leadership of the republican movement at this time was its relationship with the budding civil rights movement in Northern Ireland. The most comprehensive governmental intelligence on this new direction was compiled by the Irish Department of Justice, which indicated that the general goal of the movement was threefold: social and radical economic action, political action, and military action.[88] In an interview in 1970, Cathal Goulding explained the thinking behind getting involved with civil rights in Northern Ireland:

> When we decided on the agitation campaign, we first of all decided that we would become engaged in things I've referred to: housing, land, fisheries, trade union agitation and so on. We realized that in the Six Counties, however, before launching these activities, we would first have to work for the establishment of basic civil rights in order to establish democracy and abolish discrimination. This would also give us the political maneuverability to establish the Republican movement openly.[89]

Bearing striking similarities to the strategy of the Communist Party of Northern Ireland at the time,[90] this interview found the two groups coming into closer collaboration. Though some have called their joint action a conspiracy, Bob Purdie argues that it was more of a convergence of interests.[91] This convergence of interests as well as other relevant civil rights topics are explored in greater detail in the next chapter.

This period also saw a proliferation of radical student activism throughout Ireland. With the student population in Ireland rising at exponential rates and the international drive towards student activism, it was only a matter of time before Irish students began to rethink their role within society. What prompted student activism, however, was not simply a response to international momentum; it was a response to specific conditions within Ireland. The debate surrounding Catholics attending Trinity College and the later debate on the amalgamation of Trinity and University College Dublin helped politicize many students.[92] In December 1967 Cork students held a national teach-in to give students the opportunity to voice their concerns about their role in Irish society, among other things. Though the teach-in did not herald an Irish 'hot summer', it signalled an emerging consciousness among students. One might assume the republican movement would take the opportunity to forge connections with students, but generally it did not. A handful of students joined the DHAC during their rallies, but overall any radical and republican activity remained confined to a small minority of students.

The one radical voice to show serious potential for galvanizing the Irish student body was a newspaper called *Nusight*, which aimed to explore radical issues and student concerns: 'We readily admit that we will advocate radical and fundamental change, where we feel it to be necessary, in a way never before seen in this country. Further, we will do so with all the power and vehemence of our monstrous little voice', the May 1968 editorial boasted. While this newspaper demonstrated a penchant for hyperbole and the shocking cover photograph, its articles were simplistic analyses of mainstream issues. Yet its very existence demonstrated that students were looking to new sources for new ideas that more clearly reflected their interests. Howard Kinlay and Ciaran McKeown, both senior figures in the Union of Students in Ireland and future journalists, McKeown also a future founder of the Peace People, underscored this feeling in their June 1968 *Nusight* editorial: 'Of course Connolly's ideas are there, and they may still inspire. But we need someone with vigour and energy and an ideal, showing us how and telling us why. We want inspiration to set to and tackle the problems of our society.'

In 1968 the Union of Students in Ireland led 3,500 students in a march to broaden the university grants scheme, but they received very little popular support and chose not to continue with another march.[93] McKeown later wrote: 'Southern students were only too happy to get up and attack Northern politicians and police, and cry for a thirty-two-county socialist republic – so long as they did not have to make one iota of sacrifice to open up educational opportunity in the South.'[94] According to his assessment of this short-lived campaign, the only people who canvassed with him to encourage agitation for free third-level schooling was a group of Northern Irish students, who would not be affected by the reform in question. Their canvassing was not well received; as Northerners they were seen to be meddling in affairs that did not concern them. This episode ironically demonstrated that some issues could draw cross-border support and could conceivably unite activists outside of the republican paradigm, but it also illustrated how problematic the cultivation of cross-border activism was. Other forms of student protest would come to the Republic in the early 1970s, when a group of students took over the UCD administration building and the National College of Art and Design to protest conditions, but for now students were just beginning to develop a consciousness about street politics and radical protest. The Irish government did not demonstrate significant concern about the potential for student unrest during this period, though it was taking steps to build the Belfield campus in such a way as to limit the opportunity for mass protest.[95]

This period is well known as the time the West began to contemplate the second wave of feminism, and certainly pockets of women in the Irish state were beginning to redefine women's roles in Irish society. As demonstrated in the letter Leslie Joseph Burnett wrote to the *United Irishman* discussed above, the republican movement was slow to seize on this trend. Cumann na mBan, in particular, failed to engage with feminism, or indeed with any aspect of the republican rethink to the same level as the IRA and Sinn Féin. Their activities, to the extent that they were recounted in *United Irishman*, continued without change. They organized dances, sold the odd newspaper, learned first aid and acted as couriers. The Irish government's intelligence on the group indicated that in 1966 Cumann na mBan took the decision to cooperate more closely with the IRA, but their activities and role actually changed little during this period.[96] In March 1966 the IRA sent a directive to its own members and members of Cumann na mBan detailing these supporting activities and emphasizing that Cumann na mBan members should be well schooled in the history of the republican movement, 'in particular'.[97] This emphasis on Cumann na mBan members learning history is typical of women's roles in nationalist conflict, as Monica E. Neugebauer's research on domestic activism in Palestinian homes indicates. Above all, the perception of women's main role is to produce soldiers for the cause and to instil a nationalist identity to her children.[98] Learning republican history and Irish, the two main subjects the IRA emphasized in this directive, helped Cumann na mBan members easily fulfil auxiliary roles in the movement.

Was their secondary status inevitable? Studies of women in armed conflict note that typically women play supportive roles as auxiliaries to the male solider.[99] In this sense the formation of Cumann na mBan is a characteristic response to a rise in militant activity. But by acquiescing to this role and by remaining in a segregated group, republican women failed to fundamentally critique the gender regime within the republican movement; this would require criticizing the tradition and history of Cumann na mBan, itself. Any criticism of Cumann na mBan could expose individual women to charges of disloyalty to the present movement and crucially, to the memory of past campaigns. The available documentation on women's activities within the republican movement suggests that republican women have rarely, if ever, publicly criticized Cumann na mBan for any reason. In the late 1960s, therefore, though some women such as Máirín de Burca might have resigned from Cumann na mBan and later joined Sinn Féin, the republican movement's gender regime remained intact. The advancing median age of members of Cumann na mBan and their domestic commitments helped reinforce the gender regime. Thus, Cumann na mBan continued to recruit, as the IRA had strongly encouraged in their 1966 directive, and to play a role in fundraising, newspaper sales and publicity.

The fact that the group did not engage in a significant re-evaluation of itself while the IRA and Sinn Féin were boldly seeking to redefine themselves as radicals and social progressives, sealed the fate of this group on the periphery of the movement. Engagement with social issues would have forced the group to come to terms with its policy on birth control and feminism, in general. That the women of this group did not engage with such issues contributed towards maintaining the status quo, maintaining the patriarchal structure and maintaining new generations of young republicans in the old traditions. Had these women come to terms with feminism, they might have demanded to play more of a central role in the movement, they might have demanded that the movement take a stance on birth control, indeed they might have taken steps to control their own fertility, which could ultimately impact on the production of the movement's most critical resource: its young. So in this sense Cumann na mBan's failure to innovate and engage in the rethink might have suited those in the republican leadership who were less willing to compromise regarding policy and who were anxious to maintain continuity in the movement.

It was the IRA leadership and not Cumann na mBan that created the conditions for a modest contemplation of a limited feminist discourse to emerge from the republican movement in the next few years by endorsing Máirín de Burca's candidacy for co-secretary of Sinn Féin. Soon after she rejoined Sinn Féin she was elected to the secretariat, she later remembered, to keep a traditionalist – most likely Margaret Buckley – from membership of the Ard Comhairle. 'The person they didn't want was one of the old guard. She wouldn't have been interested in agitation or social problems of any kind ... They wanted someone who was with them on the issues of the left.'[100] According to de Burca, her name appeared in a list the IRA had circulated prior to the vote, which saw her become co-secretary of Sinn Féin. As a dedicated socialist and someone who consistently drew connections between working-class politics and republicanism, de Burca encapsulated this new direction in her rhetoric and her visible commitment to a variety of left-wing causes. As a fairly new face, her ascendancy to the Ard Comhairle of Sinn Féin was a bold move – she would be the highest ranking woman in the movement. De Burca later explained: 'Obviously we couldn't become members of the IRA ... [However,] there was nothing to stop a woman from doing anything in the party but [achieving a top position in the Ard Comhairle] was unlikely. But you could be the secretary because traditionally that was what women did.' This statement calls into question the career of Margaret Buckley, who seems to have been an exception to the rule of the gender regime within the movement. It also reflects an unspoken tension between what was generally possible and what was probable.

In terms of women's participation within the radical activist milieu, Máirín de Burca led the charge. During this period she became involved with Sinn Féin, housing action, anti-Vietnam war action and Anti-Apartheid protests. Her high rank within Sinn Féin seems to have influenced the media to cover her participation in other movements more thoroughly, but she was not the only female campaigner. Women such as Hillary Boyle and Máire MacGiolla became vocal campaigners for the DHAC. Female students began to agitate to be included in all-male societies at Trinity. Máire Woods, pacifist, budding feminist and (paradoxically) future partner of IRA Chief-of-Staff Cathal Goulding, became a significant contributor to the Irish Voice on Vietnam. These were the years that Irish women became active in radical politics. Though they had no feminist agenda, their simple assumption that they were equal to their male counterparts contributed to their success. This handful of women opened doors for others by providing an example to younger women anxious to enter into the 1960s social revolution. This would soon lead to a cohesive feminist rhetoric, which would emerge in the next few years (see Chapter 5).

IRISH AMERICA'S RESPONSE TO THE NEW DIRECTION IN REPUBLICANISM

Predictably the new direction in republicanism in Ireland did not translate to Irish America. America's traditional antipathy to socialism forestalled any meaningful push towards left-wing politics in Irish America, and the fractured IRA support group, Clann na Gael, did what it could to discourage this move but had little impact on the republican leadership in Ireland. The records available indicate that Irish America maintained a traditional view of republicanism throughout this period. The emerging conflict in Northern Ireland (see Chapter 4) quickly eclipsed any other news of the new direction in Irish republicanism. It was only when the Irish republican movement split in 1969/70 that Irish America as a whole began to define its support for republicanism in opposition to Goulding's new direction.

Probably the most significant group that emerged from Irish America during the late 1960s was a small group known as the American Congress for Irish Freedom (ACIF), run by virulently anti-communist James Heaney, a lawyer based in Buffalo, New York. Though the unfolding situation in Northern Ireland dominated the small organization, it was originally conceived of as a nationalist pressure group rather than a civil rights group. Niall Ó Dochartaigh points out that the ACIF 'briefly enjoyed a high public profile as the only existing focus for Irish-American activism' at the beginning of the Northern Irish civil rights movement in 1968.[101] The ACIF cultivated links to Dungannon's Campaign for Social Justice and offered the group legal services, funds and advice throughout this period and until its demise in 1970.[102]

Generally, Irish-American politics remained traditional in its ideology and Catholic in its religious identity. We should not assume, though, that this means Irish America was suspended in Independence-era politics unaware of modern developments in Ireland. Niall Ó Dochartaigh's study of Boston republicans contradicts this cliché; most of the active members of the Irish-American political scene were Irish-born or first generation during this period.[103] But like other immigrant groups they clung to traditionalism as a cultural marker in order to maintain a sense of identity. This traditionalism was characterized by a nationalist and, in some cases, republican outlook.[104]

Though Irish Americans might have engaged with left-wing issues and feminism on an individual basis, as a group Irish America avoided controversy by clearly demarcating itself from Black civil rights (despite obvious parallels), the Anti-Vietnam protests, the student movement and feminism. As reflected in the *Irish Echo* and other Irish-American publications of the period, the main area of interest was narrowly confined to Irish affairs, networking, socializing and cultural affairs.

In terms of government documents, very little is available covering this period. Irish diplomats in America had very little to report back to the Department of External Affairs in terms of Irish-American radicalism. This is supported by the fact that internally, the department of justice was only prepared to consider the newly formed London-based IRA front group, Clann na hEireann, to be worthy of mentioning in a security review and yet had nothing to say on militant republicanism in America.[105] Clann na hEireann spent this time trying to establish itself as an umbrella group for the Irish community in Britain,[106] which meant that it could offer the Irish republican movement little in the way of practical support. Overall, the Irish in Britain, like their counterparts in America, had little cohesion, and the government records reflect this; the British government and the Northern Irish government had little of note in terms of support of the republican movement among emigrant communities. These years represent the end of an insular period in the Irish emigrant community, where the goings-on of cultural groups superseded nationalist and republican politics in daily conversation and coverage in the local media.

CONCLUSION

Throughout this chapter we have seen how both international and local factors combined to influence radical activism in the Republic of Ireland throughout the late 1960s. Certainly media coverage of world-wide student politics, the New Left, feminism, the American civil rights movement and anti-Vietnam war protests created a sense of momentum, but much of the radical activism in the Republic sprung from an Irish context. During this period public debate around the issue of women in Irish society took centre stage as the state began to engage in a reluctant re-evaluation of their place in Irish society. Through establishing its own television station the state sought to define itself against the cultural hegemony of Britain, but the advent of television brought with it its own cultural significance outside the control of the state. Television and a budding radical press began to push boundaries by courting controversy, challenging the status quo and provoking debate.

Publications such as the *Irish Times, United Irishman, Nusight, Hibernia, Woman's Way* and *Irish Woman's Journal* began to widen the discussion of social issues, presenting a left-wing, or in the case of the women's magazines, an occasional socially progressive, voice to their readership. Dealing with issues such as equal pay, housing, women's changing lifestyles and contraception, these publications brought these social issues to an ever-widening readership and forced mainstream newspapers such as the *Irish Independent* and the *Irish Press* to follow suit.

Republicanism was a pivotal element to the transformation of public debates in Irish society because of its move towards social action and its interaction with many of the other movements that emerged during this period. Brian Feeney makes the point that during this period there was hardly a demonstration, North or South, which was not attended, organized or policed in part by the republican movement, and that 'there was hardly a tenants' or residents' association that did not count a republican or two among its committee members'.[107] In redefining itself as a radical political force, the republican movement sought to avoid past mistakes by appealing to a larger cross section of Irish society. Critically, it failed to appeal to traditional militants, whose suspicion of socialism and attachment to abstentionism was difficult to overcome. The *United Irishman* was caught in the middle of this factional tension as it struggled to present itself as a first-rate left-wing publication aimed at unifying the working class and covering social issues.

Most glaringly, the *United Irishman* failed to engage with an emerging feminist discourse that surrounded the issues of equal pay and contraception – a subject well covered by *Irish Woman's Journal*, the *Irish Times* and even *Woman's Way*. With the omission of this story the *United Irishman* missed a major opportunity to appeal to portions of the Protestant community and truly become the radical alternative it aspired to be. Its silence on women's issues cannot be attributed to a lack of awareness of women's secondary status; it had used the issue of the Irish government's prevarication on equal pay to attack the government in April 1965. The most logical explanation for its silence on women's issues and indeed Cumann na mBan's inertia during a period of significant re-evaluation of republicanism involved maintaining the status quo. Cumann na mBan had been founded on traditional sex roles. To argue for the redefinition of women's roles within the movement would be to challenge history and to challenge the future; Cumann na mBan was the auxiliary force that guaranteed the cause would continue through having children and teaching them republican history. As a group that has historically focused on continuity, seeking to redefine its role would have proved difficult, if not impossible, for its own members as well as for the rest of the movement.

In some ways women such as Máirín de Burca did not threaten the status quo. By not adhering to the traditional woman-as-mother mould, her lack of domestic commitments set her apart from the majority of republican women, which pre-empted criticism that her activism forced her to shirk her home duties. However de Burca did begin to redefine women's roles in radical activism during this period. Her simple presence in the Ard Comhairle and the media coverage surrounding her broad-based activism broke down barriers for those who came after her. De Burca, with the help of a handful of other journalists and activists, opened doors for a new type of female activist that would emerge in the early 1970s. The Irish state was aware of de Burca's work and had been taking its own steps to re-evaluate the gender regime, but it failed to connect social activism and feminism in a way that might have anticipated the manifestation of the second wave of Irish feminism that was to come.

During this period Irish America, disorganized as it was, demonstrated less interest in the republican rethink than in local politics, dances and events. What it heard of this new turn towards socialism it rejected, preferring to cling to traditional Catholicism and republicanism. The Irish government was rightfully unconcerned by the Irish emigrant community's perfunctory attempts at supporting what remained of traditional Irish republicanism. In terms of governmental awareness of this new turn in Irish activism, the Irish, British, Northern Irish and American governments were aware of New Left forces within republicanism, but attached relatively little significance to this new strategy, probably because republicanism was a significantly weakened force by this time.

Generally during this period, the Republic of Ireland experienced a germination of radical activism that opened new debates on women's place in society and social issues. This germination was a gradual process that opened doors for women to redefine their roles as activists and community leaders. The republican movement's progression towards the left was also a gradual process, which seems to have left the Irish government mildly concerned but no more than that. The rise in public debates around the role of women coincided with the beginning of the government's re-evaluation of the gender regime, uneven though it was. Its approach to the kind of policy reform required to redefine women's roles in Irish society was gradual. A women-centred consciousness began to emerge through a non-republican radical press that brought international ideas and causes into Ireland from abroad, but also tailored them to fit an Irish paradigm. By the end of this period women in the Republic were poised to take part in a dramatic shift in their social, economic and political roles. Could this shift in the gender regime have happened without this 1967–9 germination period? The next chapter explores just that.

NOTES

1. E. Hobsbawm, *The Age of Extremes: The Short Twentieth Century, 1914–1991* (London: Abacus, 1994), p.296.
2. B. Friedan, *'It Changed My Life': Writings on the Women's Movement* (Cambridge, MA: Harvard University Press, 1977), p.18.
3. S. Evans, *Personal Politics: The Roots of Women's Liberation in the Civil Rights Movement and the New Left* (New York: Vintage, 1979), p.239.

4. D. Bouchier, *The Feminist Challenge: The Movement for Women's Liberation in Britain and the USA* (London: Macmillan, 1983), p.47.
5. J. Mitchell, 'Women: The Longest Revolution', *New Left Review*, 40 (1966), p.12.
6. *Irish Times*, 4 September 1968.
7. For details on the development of each state's experience of feminism, see G. Kaplan, *Contemporary Western European Feminism* (London: UCL Press, 1992).
8. *Irish Times*, 29 and 30 August 1967.
9. Not to be confused with the suffragette group called the Irish Women Citizens Association.
10. *Irish Times*, 5 September 1967.
11. J. Meenan, *The Irish Economy since 1922* (Liverpool: Liverpool University Press, 1970), pp.260–1.
12. Central Statistics Office, *Statistical Abstract of Ireland* (Dublin: CSO, 1970–1), p.27; E. Delaney, *Irish Emigration since 1921* (Dublin: Economic and Social History Society of Ireland, 2002), p.26.
13. Central Statistics Office, *Statistical Abstract of Ireland* (Dublin: CSO, 1960), p.2.
14. *Investment in Education. Report of a Survey Team Appointed by the Minister for Education in Conjunction with the OECD* (Dublin: Stationery Office, 1967).
15. E. Connolly, 'The State, Public Policy and Gender: Ireland in Transition, 1957–1977' (Ph.D. thesis, Dublin City University, 1998), p.101.
16. C. Clear, *Women of the House: Women's Household Work in Ireland: 1922–1961* (Dublin: Irish Academic Press, 2000), p.170.
17. D.B. Rottman and P.J. O'Connell, 'The Changing Social Administration', in F. Litton (ed.), *Unequal Achievement: The Irish Experience, 1957–1982* (Dublin: Institute of Public Administration, 1982), p.71.
18. J. Horgan, *Irish Media: A Critical History since 1922* (London: Routledge, 2001), p.80.
19. Pádraig Ó Fachtna, Dail Debates, Vol. 180, c. 594, 16 March 1960.
20. M. Hill, *Women in Ireland: A Century of Change* (Belfast: Blackstaff Press, 2003), pp.143–4.
21. J.D.H. Downing, *Radical Media: Rebellious Communication and Social Movements* (London: Sage, 2001), p.v.
22. D. Ferriter, *The Transformation of Ireland, 1900–2000* (London: Profile, 2004), p.528.
23. *Irish Times*, 2 November 1967.
24. Ibid.
25. See for example, Dorothy Macardle, 'Some Irish mothers and their children', *Irish Press*, 14 September 1931.
26. E. Gillespie (ed.), *Changing the Times: Irish Women Journalists, 1969–1981* (Dublin: Liliput Press, 2003), p.9.
27. Mary Maher in ibid., p.12.
28. Irish Congress of Trade Unions, *Twelfth Annual Report* (Dublin: ICTU, 1970), p.355.
29. M.E. Daly, 'Women in Irish Trade Unions', in D. Nevin (ed.), *Trade Union Century* (Cork: Mercier Press in association with Irish Congress of Trade Unions and Radio Telefís Éireann, 1994), p.112.
30. R.C. Owens, *A Social History of Women in Ireland: 1870–1970* (Dublin: Gill & Macmillan, 2005), p.303.
31. Ferriter, *Transformation of Ireland*, p.575.
32. For a more comprehensive account of their activities see L. Connolly, *The Irish Women's Movement: From Revolution to Devolution* (New York: Lilliput Press, 2002); H. Tweedy, *A Link in the Chain: The Story of the Irish Housewives Association* (Dublin: Attic Press, 1992).
33. *Irish Times*, 7 and 8 June 1968.
34. *Irish Woman's Journal* (February 1968).
35. *Woman's Way*, 10 May 1968.
36. H. Murphy, 'Woman's Place ... Again', *Irish Woman's Journal* (January 1968), p.5.
37. Census of 1961 cited in C. Clear, '"Too fond of going": Female Emigration and Change for Women in Ireland, 1946–1961', in D. Keogh, F. O'Shea and C. Quinlan (eds), *Ireland in the 1950s: The Lost Decade* (Dublin: Mercier Press, 2004), p.137.
38. M.E. Daly, '"Turn on the tap": The State, Irish Women and Running Water', in M. Gialanella Valiulis and M. O'Dowd (eds), *Women and Irish History* (Dublin: Wolfhound Press, 1997), p.218.
39. For more on the role of the ICA, see D. Ferriter, 'Mothers, Maidens and Myths: A History of the Irish Countrywomen's Association' (Dublin: ICA, 1995).

40. C. Rose, *The Female Experience: The Story of the Woman Movement in Ireland* (Galway: Arlen House, 1975), p.34.
41. D. Rohan, *Marriage: Irish Style* (Dublin: Mercier Press, 1969); M. Viney, *The Broken Marriage: A Study in Depth of a Growing Irish Social Problem* (Dublin: Irish Times, 1970).
42. See for example *Irish Times*, 15 December 1967.
43. J.H. Whyte, *Church and State in Modern Ireland* (Dublin: Gill & Macmillan, 1971), p.346.
44. Connolly, 'State, Public Policy and Gender', p.114.
45. F.B. Maguire, 'Women against the World', *Irish Woman's Journal* (August 1967), p.39.
46. Ferriter, *Transformation of Ireland*, p.538.
47. Connolly, 'State, Public Policy and Gender', p.112.
48. Connolly, *Irish Women's Movement*, p.108.
49. Connolly, 'State, Public Policy and Gender', p.112.
50. Hill, *Women in Ireland*, p.145.
51. *Irish Times*, 14 March 1968.
52. S. O'Sullivan, 'Sex Segregation?', *Irish Woman's Journal* (September 1968), p.6.
53. *Irish Times*, 1 August 1968.
54. *Irish Times*, 14 March 1968.
55. M. McEnroy, 'Failure of a Revolution', *Woman's Way* (7 June 1968), p.42.
56. J. Dowling, 'Interview with Cathal Goulding, Chief of Staff of the IRA', *New Left Review* (November/December 1970), p.55.
57. *United Irishman* (May 1965).
58. A. Coughlan, 'Our Ideas', *Tuairisc – Newsletter of the Wolfe Tone Society* (31 August 1966).
59. Review of unlawful and allied organizations, 24 November 1965, Dublin, NA, DT, 98/6/495.
60. R. English, *Armed Struggle: The History of the IRA* (London: Macmillan, 2003), p.84.
61. H. Patterson, *The Politics of Illusion: A Political History of the IRA* (London: Serif, 1997), p.107.
62. *United Irishman* (May 1966).
63. *United Irishman* (1965).
64. *United Irishman* (July 1967).
65. *Irish Times*, 20 November 1967.
66. Secretary of Department of Justice to Minister of Justice, Review of unlawful and allied organizations, December 1, 1964–November 21, 1966, 24 November 1966, NA, DT, 98/6/495.
67. Secretary of Department of Justice to Minister of Justice, Review of unlawful and allied organizations, December 1, 1964–November 21, 1966, 24 November 1966, NA, DT, 98/6/495.
68. *United Irishman* (January 1968).
69. *United Irishman* (June 1968).
70. *United Irishman* (July 1967, 1968).
71. *United Irishman* (July 1967).
72. *United Irishman* (series, 1968).
73. *United Irishman* (September 1968).
74. *United Irishman* (April 1965).
75. J.B. Bell, *The Secret Army: The IRA, 1916–1979* (Dublin: Poolbeg, 1990), p.346.
76. *United Irishman* (November 1968).
77. *Irish Times*, 5 May 1967.
78. Dáil debates, Vol. 228, c. 895, 16 May 1967.
79. *United Irishman* (May 1967).
80. Dublin Housing Action Committee, Dublin, NA, DT 2000/6/423.
81. *Irish Times*, 20 January 1968; Joseph Dowling and Charles Haughey, Dáil debates, Vol. 234, c. 779, 2 May 1968; *Hibernia*, 10 October 1969
82. *Irish Times*, 17 June 1968.
83. Dublin Housing Action Committee, Dublin, NA, DT 2000/6/423.
84. Dáil debates, Vol. 234, c. 1096, 8 May 1968.
85. Joseph Dowling and Charles Haughey, respectively, Dáil debates, Vol. 234, c. 779, 2 May 1968.
86. *Irish Times*, 17 June 1968.
87. *Irish Times*, 16 January 1968.
88. Secretary of Department of Justice to Minister of Justice, Review of unlawful and allied organizations, December 1, 1964–November 21, 1966, 24 November 1966, NA, DT, 98/6/495.
89. Dowling, 'Interview with Cathal Goulding, Chief of Staff of the IRA', p.55.
90. Communist Party of Northern Ireland, 'Ireland's Path to Socialism' (programme adopted 1962; published 1963).

91. B. Purdie, 'Was the Civil Rights Movement a Republican or Communist Conspiracy?', *Irish Political Studies*, 3 (1998).
92. Whyte, *Church and State*, pp.305–7.
93. *Irish Times*, 20 November 1968; C. McKeown, *The Passion of Peace* (Belfast: Blackstaff Press, 1984), pp.41–2.
94. Ibid., p.55.
95. Union of Students in Ireland, 1967–1968, Dublin, NA, DT 99/1/343.
96. Secretary of Department of Justice to Minister of Justice, Review of unlawful and allied organizations, December 1, 1964–November 21, 1966, 24 November 1966, NA, DT, 98/6/495.
97. Secretary of Department of Justice to Minister of Justice, Review of unlawful and allied organizations, December 1, 1964–November 21, 1966, 24 November 1966, NA, DT, 98/6/495.
98. M.E. Neugebauer, 'Domestic Activism and Nationalist Struggle', in J. Turpin and L.A. Lorentzen (eds), *The Women and War Reader* (New York: New York University Press, 1998), p.178.
99. See L. Dowler '"And they think I'm just a nice old lady": Women and War in Belfast, Northern Ireland', *Gender, Place and Culture*, 5 (1998); J.B. Elshtain, *Women and War* (Chicago, IL: University of Chicago Press, 1987); Neugebauer, 'Domestic Activism and Nationalist Struggle'; R. Ridd, 'Powers of the Powerless', in R. Ridd and H. Calloway (eds), *Caught up in Conflict: Women's Responses to Political Strife* (London: Macmillan, 1986).
100. Interview with de Burca, Dublin, 15 March 2004.
101. N. Ó Dochartaigh, '"Sure, it's hard to keep up with the splits here": Irish-American Responses to the Outbreak of Conflict in Northern Ireland 1968–1974', *Irish Political Studies* (1995), p.139.
102. Campaign for Social Justice Papers, Belfast, PRONI, D/2003/1.
103. Ó Dochartaigh, 'Irish-American Responses to Conflict in Northern Ireland', pp.156–7.
104. For more on the phenomenon see M.A. Jones, *American Immigration* (Cambridge: Cambridge University Press, 1960).
105. Secretary of Department of Justice to Minister of Justice, Review of unlawful and allied organizations, December 1, 1964–November 21, 1966, 24 November 1966, NA, DT, 98/6/495.
106. T.P. Coogan, *The IRA* (London: Harper Collins, 2000), p.331.
107. B. Feeney, *Sinn Féin: A Hundred Turbulent Years* (Dublin: O'Brien Press, 2002), p.229.

CHAPTER FOUR

[Sic]:
Women and Civil Rights
in Northern Ireland, 1968/9

You should find from the rest of this platform the least dishonest person and put him [*sic*] in. (Bernadette Devlin on selecting an anti-Unionist candidate for the Mid-Ulster election of 1969)

One man [*sic*], one vote! (Civil Rights demand and rallying cry)

The end of the 1960s was as tumultuous a period for Northern Ireland as it was for many countries and regions throughout the western world. Characterized by discontent and street politics, this moment in time saw the rapid emergence of a rights-based consciousness among the Catholic population of Northern Ireland. Student unrest mirrored continental movements, but an underlying sectarianism informed this new consciousness and informed the society in which the civic and student protests began to take root. Two major civil rights groups emerged out of this new political consciousness: the Northern Ireland Civil Rights Association (NICRA) and the student-based People's Democracy (PD). This chapter explores how broad civil rights alliances formed and quickly fractured due to emerging republican and loyalist violence. By tracing women's involvement in Northern Irish street politics, this chapter establishes how new paradigms of political involvement welcomed women's active participation. Irish women's history is still in a process of recovery where well-intentioned writers are attempting to document the basic story of women's activity, but they have done so without significant attention to gender regimes.[1] This makes it necessary to first help document some strands of their experiences as street activists in order to analyse the complexities of the prevailing gender regimes within these movements.

THE BEGINNING OF CIVIL RIGHTS ACTIVISM

The turbulence of 1968 crashed through the Western consciousness as a new generation asserted itself and attempted to redefine national and international notions of citizenship. News from America detailed a simmering crisis between blacks and whites, students and university administrations and anti-war activists and state forces. As discussed above in Chapter 2, accounts of the American experience coupled with an emerging political consciousness among Northern Irish Catholics contributed towards a growing awareness of institutionalized sectarian inequalities that permeated Northern Irish society. The nature of political expression was in flux and some Northern Catholics began to question the usefulness of traditional politics and letter-writing campaigns. Even moderates such as Conn McCluskey of the Campaign for Social Justice began to contemplate a new strategy: 'It began to dawn on me that if the Northern Ireland Catholics had been waiting for our reasoned arguments and carefully collected statistics to influence events, they might have waited for a further fifty years.'[2] The Northern Ireland Civil Rights Association had not become what its founders hoped it would be; its ineffectual executive and single-issue structure could not begin to address the kind of inequalities faced by its constituents.[3]

At this moment throughout Europe and the United States, localized events began to spark surges of political expression in the form of social movements. Many of the sparks came when students began to articulate demands regarding their education. Their sky-rocketing numbers gave them a new confidence. Hobsbawm observes that 'not until the 1960s was it undeniable that students had become, both socially and politically, a far more important force than ever before'.[4]Anti-authoritarian leaders emerged from the ranks of the student masses that had flooded into unprepared and under-resourced third-level institutions, and Northern Ireland was no different. They first got the opportunity to flex their muscles when some students from Queen's University established a Republican Club despite a ban by the Minister for Home Affairs, William Craig. When pressed to disband, the students refused. Though very little came of the stand-off, and it was not the spark that ignited the call for civil rights, the incident signalled a new confidence among Northern Irish students. When asked for a statement, Betty Sinclair, representative of NICRA, secretary from the Belfast District Trades Union Council and lifelong member of the Communist Party, told the newspaper that the students' actions signalled that Craig's ban on Republican Clubs would backfire on him.[5]

The spark prompting a surge in civil rights action did not come from Belfast, though. It came from Derry. The most pronounced of the economically disadvantaged regions of Northern Ireland, Derry cried out for investment. Jonathan Bardon makes the point that 'In March 1966, 5.9 per cent in the province were unemployed but in Derry 23.3 per cent of males and 4.8 per cent of females were out of work.'[6] Government-directed development as well as multinational investment consistently located new industry close to Belfast for logistical reasons, which further exacerbated the resentment felt among the Derry unemployed. The decision to locate a university in Coleraine and then a Michelin factory in Ballymena – regardless of the genuine rationale – fuelled the prevailing belief among Derry Catholics that the Northern Irish administration was not interested in investing west of the River Bann, where Catholics predominated. Nationalist politician Eddie McAteer once observed: 'I never cease to marvel at the wonderful patience of the sorely tried people of Derry. The fuse, however, is burning dangerously low.'[7]

Probably what is most interesting about Derry was an emerging militancy among a small group of people. They began to look at the unemployment situation, the manipulation of voting boundaries and the problem of inequitable housing distribution as three strands of a Unionist noose that was strangling the Catholic parts of the city. Agitation groups proliferated throughout the early to mid 1960s: the Derry Unemployed Action Committee, the Derry Young Republicans Association, the Northern Branch of the Credit Union and the Derry Housing Association all formed with the aim of helping the Catholic community to help itself.

But by the late 1960s self-help had only a limited impact on Derry's Catholics, and now they began to look to another small group of community activists for answers. Led by Eamonn McCann and Eamon Melaugh, this group of New Left radicals shared overlapping membership in a rapidly radicalizing Derry Labour Party and a new organization designed to pick up where the Derry Housing Association had left off. It would be called the Derry Housing Action Committee. In 1967 seven corporation houses were built in Derry and the year after that the city received four more.[8] The Housing Action Committee sprang on to the streets in 1968, picketing and interrupting council meetings, and their imaginative tactics garnered press attention and raised awareness about Derry's housing crisis. On 22 June 1968 the group manhandled the caravan of a homeless family to block a road running through the Bogside area for twenty-four hours. McCann believes that while this demonstration was not as daring as others, it was a turning point for Derry:

> It seemed a very radical thing to do but actually had we been the slightest bit radical we would have brought it into the city centre. We didn't. We blocked the main street through our own area. It was really very timid. That certainly was the first time that the conservative Nationalists of Derry realized that there was another force emerging. So it was crucial in that respect.[9]

Afterwards the leaders of the demonstration were bound over for two years and some were fined. Janet Wilcox, a left-wing activist from England and one of the organizers of the action, issued a statement in which she threatened that if nothing were done about the housing problem, Derry would deteriorate into violence.[10] This statement, though dramatic, reveals an increasing sense of desperation as well as an increasing militancy among the Derry activist milieu and, indeed, some of its female constituents.

From the beginning women had a strong presence on the Housing Action Committee in Derry. Women such as Bridget Bond, Nellie Gorman, Cathy Harkin, Janet Wilcox, Mary Nelis and Pam Murphy fully participated in housing demonstrations and related activity, which built on the tactics of the prolonged Springtown squat that began in 1946 and lasted until 1967 as well as on the actions of Dungannon's Homeless Citizens League. Wilcox was even able to mesh street politics and traditional politics by agreeing to stand as the Derry Labour Party candidate in the local election of 1967. For the most part, however, these women were Derry street activists. The main differences between Derry housing action and what happened in Dungannon were the former's revolutionary rhetoric, developed political consciousness and mixed-sex membership. Largely influenced by a left-wing analysis of the Derry's housing situation, women like Janet Wilcox joined the group not to reform the system but to revolutionize it, and their significant contributions to the work of this burgeoning group is a key area of emerging research on history of the civil rights movement in Northern Ireland.

Probably the most prominent of the female housing activists was Bridget Bond, whose commitment to families in need was so strong she reportedly pored over local editions of the *Belfast Telegraph*'s obituaries section to find recently vacated accommodation. Known for her leadership of squats in homes, and even in Derry's guildhall mayoral chamber, Bond demonstrated how dedication and radical activism could achieve tangible results.[11] Mary Nelis, who later would become a prominent republican politician, explained that housing action grew out of safety concerns, space issues and concern for children. After the novelty wore off of being allocated a home in the new, isolated Creggan estate of Derry City, women in her area began to organize themselves:

> Contraceptives and birth control weren't in our vocabulary so you had something like 300 wains in fifty-two houses ... Most of us were in the unhappy position where most of our husbands or partners had no work or were in England. We were all one-parent families before the phrase was even coined. Most of us relied on families and if my mother could she'd trip up and down to Creggan with my sisters. It was the issue of children, the roads not being finished, the lack of space, etc., that was the cause that after a year or two we organized ourselves to try and organize this to be a proper place to live, with proper roads and proper lighting and schools.[12]

Nelis's statement bears out the anecdotal stories that the men of Derry did not maintain a strong presence in the civic life of the city either due to unemployment or absence. This observation supports the employment figures cited above, suggesting a rationale for the strong presence of women in Derry's activist milieu.

Ann Gallagher, in a study of housing agitation in London during the same period, noted that men tended to lead community groups within well-off housing estates, while women became more visible in working-class estates. She observed that women activists proposed a similar explanation for the motivation behind women's activism: women 'bore the brunt' of inadequate conditions. Gallagher also proposed other possible reasons for women's activism on housing issues in working-class neighbourhoods:

- As the traditional breadwinner a man might feel more demoralized by inadequate living conditions and might be reluctant to draw attention to his perceived failure to provide for his family.
- Woman's undervalued 'borrowed status' within the community could free her from social constraints against militant action.
- A precipitating event could spur a woman to rethink her position within the community and may free her to rebel against perceived unjust conditions.
- Oftentimes more women than men populate the poorer estates due to single-parent systems and migrant work systems.[13]

Anecdotal accounts of women's activism in Northern Ireland during this period tend to dovetail with a combination of these motivating factors, as does Mary Nelis's account of her own motivation for taking part.

Eamonn McCann explained that 'Women in Ireland, Catholic Ireland in particular, were seen as homemakers so if you had a housing thing to do … women's role was to make a home for the family and therefore to fight for homes for their families.'[14] If Catholic women were beginning to vocalize dissatisfaction with the public housing system, why then, were so few working-class Protestant women objecting as well? Though this subject requires further research and analysis, anecdotal evidence suggests that working-class Protestants were less willing to criticize local government out of a concern for being identified as disloyal. Also, working-class Protestants tended to occupy a somewhat higher level of employment status than their Catholic counterparts, which may have imposed more constraints on those who did want to express housing grievances to their local governing bodies.[15]Moreover, because a significant strain of the housing argument involved a criticism of gerrymandered borders originally established to perpetuate a Unionist majority, complaining about housing allocation could be seen as running counter to the interests of the Protestant community. The inequitable method of housing distribution also meant that Protestants had less to complain about – their concerns simply were not that acute.

Derry's housing action continued in the summer of 1968 with the proliferation of squatting as a direct action tactic. Coinciding with the 'caravan incident' in Derry, Austin Currie, a Nationalist MP and more of a moderate figure than the Derry activists, squatted in a house in Caledon to protest the fact that it had been allocated to Emily Beattie, a single woman with connections to the Unionist party. She had been selected over 269 other applicants who had been on the Dungannon Rural District Council's waiting list, in some instances for years.[16] As the Cameron Commission later reported: 'In concentrated form the situation expressed the objections felt by many non-Unionists to the prevailing system of house allocation in Dungannon Rural District Council. By no stretch of the imagination could Miss Beattie be regarded as a priority tenant.'[17] Where the caravan incident had raised awareness throughout Derry, the spectacle of an MP being forcibly removed from a house outside of Dungannon raised awareness throughout Ireland and the United Kingdom.

This prompted Currie to contact the Northern Ireland Civil Rights Association about organizing a march. As stated above, the NICRA executive had already been rethinking its role as a legal advocacy group in the province. A march would allow it to address pervasive inequalities in Northern Irish Society in a public forum. The 24 August march from Coalisland to Dungannon marshalled a crowd of 2,500.[18] Upon arrival in Dungannon the marchers were met with approximately 400 police with dogs barring them from the centre of town due to a counter-demonstration.[19] Deciding to throw together a rally on the spot, Betty Sinclair, now the chairman of NICRA, addressed the crowd: 'What we have done today will go down in history and in this way we will be more effective in showing the world that we are a peaceful people asking for our civil rights in an orderly manner.'[20]

Betty Sinclair, a veteran of street politics, seemed to be the ideal chairman (the term 'chairperson' or 'chairwoman' was not yet in vogue): her Protestant background gave lie to the idea that NICRA was simply a 'Catholic rights' organization, her position on the Belfast and District Trades Union Council maintained a tie with the labour movement, and her long-standing membership in the Communist Party seemed to ensure that Stormont could not dismiss NICRA as being a republican plot, though this soon would become a contention. But in the long term Sinclair's ascendance to the helm of the association would prove a double-edged sword: the very element that got her elected – her political credentials – informed her analysis of the situation. In *What Is To Be Done?* Lenin encouraged revolutionary socialists to take leadership positions in the struggle for democracy as a stepping stone to revolution.[21] Having attended the Lenin School in 1934–5, Sinclair was dedicated to a rigid interpretation of revolutionary theory, which dictated that the leaders of democratic movements must achieve the broadest base possible before revolution could occur. New Left tactics such as street confrontation were de-emphasized in favour of coalition-building. Thus, Betty Sinclair's leadership of the march, and the action to come, would reflect a growing gap between the generations and their political outlooks.

Sinclair's ascendance to the chairmanship can be interpreted as a Pyrrhic victory for women in street politics. Her political philosophy, which prioritized the class struggle over any other, rejected the need for feminism. So while her presence as a female leader may have broken some traditional social conventions, her philosophy barred her from acknowledging its significance. To Sinclair, feminism was a middle-class point of view that distracted from the more important goal of achieving a classless society. Later she explained:

> I wasn't going to take second seat to any man ... For me the question of women is the question of class ... Then you came up against the difficulty that many women had things to do at home. Even in socialist societies women don't have these facilities. Who is going to watch the children? Lenin put it plainly that in order to give women complete equality we must be able to give her the economic conditions to express this equality ... It can only be solved on the basis of class struggle. I don't like feminism ... that the men are all wrong and the women are all right ... Feminism is not a working class outlook.[22]

That Sinclair was a woman meant very little to her and to others in the movement in terms of feminism and political representation. Moreover, her lack of domestic commitments at this point in time allowed her to assume the chairmanship without reference to traditional women's concerns, and her activist credentials ensured that none could question her motivation for doing so.

The Dungannon march spurred a surge in interest in Northern Ireland's inequalities. Sinclair later noted: 'We had been looking for a spark for years. At Dungannon we realized that we had found it.'[23] But a crucial problem arose in terms of what kind of spark it was and how it would impact Northern Irish society. Eamonn McCann represented a youth-driven emergent radical activism that interpreted the obstruction of the Dungannon march as a signal to raise the stakes: 'By this time our conscious, if unspoken strategy was to provoke the police into over-reaction and thus spark off mass reaction against the authorities.'[24] Sinclair – a reluctant protester – sought to consolidate support off the streets. This fundamental disagreement over tactics can be looked at in the context of burgeoning social movements throughout the western world. The American civil rights movement had experienced similar tensions where Black Power radicals increasingly questioned Martin Luther King's tactics. In many cases it boiled down to age divisions and to a fear that the momentum would be lost.

Jo Freeman, a prominent organizer within American feminism and a theoretician of the movement, articulates four essential elements involved in the formation of a social movement:

- The growth of a pre-existing communications network.
- The network must be cooptable to the ideas of a new movement.
- A series of crises that galvanize into action people involved in a cooptable network.

- A subsequent organizing effort to weld the spontaneous groups together into a movement.[25]

If the Dungannon march was the spark and NICRA was the cooptable network, then the burgeoning street protests were well on their way to coalescing into a social movement, regardless of Sinclair's level of comfort with such tactics.

Two groups began to emerge within the movement: on the one hand there were radicals such as Eamonn McCann, and on the other people such as Betty Sinclair and the members of the Campaign for Social Justice who, despite being unlikely bedfellows, eschewed street activism for a variety of reasons discussed earlier. Though Sinclair maintained her revolutionary socialist outlook, in this instance she sided with middle-class moderates, because they agreed on tactics, and for the sake of maintaining unity between otherwise disparate groups. From the beginning the radical street activists and more moderate members of the movement had different interpretations of the objectives of the movement, which can best be underscored by Derry radical Eamon Melaugh's comment to McCann on his way into the subsequent NICRA meeting after the march: 'Remember, our main purpose here is to keep our grubby proletarian grip on this jamboree.'[26]

The next march, scheduled to take place in Derry, saw both factions within the nascent movement square off. In a letter to Michael Farrell, leader of a radical coalition called the Young Socialist Alliance, McCann described meeting with the NICRA executive. McCann voiced his concern that if Minister for Home Affairs William Craig were to ban the march NICRA would comply: 'I think one would have to push for a "we are marching and that's that" position. The [Derry Housing Action Committee] and the Republican Clubs will push for that but I can't see anyone else.'[27] After much back and forth in the planning stages, the Derry activists eventually did strong-arm the NICRA executive into holding the march despite the ban.

At an organizational meeting McCann tried to assert his authority over the march by bringing up the question of carrying flags.

> Sinclair finally stated that no red flags or 'unauthorized' slogans will be permitted. I said, to push the point, that having talked to some of the [Young Socialists] ... I had no doubt that there would be a YS contingent with a red flag and that I would 'react physically' to any attempt to remove it. Sinclair steered the discussion away into safer waters, but not before herself and [John] McAnerney had agreed that 'the Young Socialists were the biggest problem'.[28]

When the radicals attended the march with placards that read 'Class war, not creed war' and 'Working class unite and fight!', the NICRA executive could do little more than register their irritation. This incident revealed to all of the organizers that Betty Sinclair had little hold on a movement that was expanding so rapidly. When the march was rerouted, Sinclair aped Sisyphus by telling the crowd: 'There may be people here who think you have to spill blood for this. That would mean you are playing Mr Craig's game.'[29] McCann took a different tack: 'I don't advise anyone to charge that barricade. I also want to make it clear that as a private individual that I can do nothing to stop them.'[30] The crowd predictably convulsed into violence immediately following McCann's remarks, and the television cameras captured images of what looked to many like indiscriminate police violence.[31]

Soon after the march Derry moderates held a meeting ostensibly to coordinate civil rights agitation, but also to consolidate their position. When McCann realized Gerry Fitt and John Hume of the moderate Derry Citizens' Action Committee had outmanoeuvred him and packed the meeting, he stormed out saying: 'This meeting tonight was middle-class, middle-aged and middle-of-the-road and it could give the kiss of death to the developing radical movement in Derry. I believe the thing to do is continue with open militant demonstrations.'[32] Betty Sinclair's statement of a few weeks later underlines the divisions within the movement: 'I think it would be incorrect to put [the civil rights movement] down as revolutionary ... There is nothing revolutionary about asking for civil rights.'[33]

Eamonn McCann's wrangles with the NICRA executive and Betty Sinclair, in particular, are instructive. They demonstrate that the leadership of the civil rights movement was already a weakened movement, even at its inception. Older activists and moderates discounted the Derry radicals in the same way the radicals wanted to discount the moderates. Betty Sinclair tried to keep the movement together without taking time to recognize the new force that was emerging within Northern Irish street politics. Her disdain for Trotskyite thinking and, as Hazel Morrissey points out, her inexperience in facing criticism from within the ranks of the Left made it difficult for her to recognize the potential divisiveness of New Left radicals within the movement.[34] The moderate line, as characterized by Sinclair's leadership of NICRA, would not be able to withstand the development of student street politics that emerged in the wake of the 5 October Derry march.

1. Republican women and men at Bodenstown in 1954. Photo courtesy of Noel Kavanagh.

2. Homeless Citizens League in Dungannon, c. 1963. *Left to right*: Bernie Hill, Jean Mohan, Patricia McCluskey, Angela McCrystal, Margaret McArdle, Ann Dunlop and son, Maureen Fearon, Susan Dinsmore and son. Photo courtesy of Ann Dunlop and Susan Dinsmore.

3. Recent photo of Angela McCrystal. Photo by Tara Keenan-Thomson.

4. Women march in Derry against Internment without trial, 18 August 1971. Photo courtesy of Edwina Stewart for NICRA.

5. Betty Sinclair addressing demonstration outside Mulhouse Street RUC/army barracks in Belfast, 21 September 1974. Photo courtesy of Edwina Stewart for NICRA.

6. Newry march, 6 February 1972, one week after Bloody Sunday. *Left to right*: Ann Hope, NICRA treasurer (bearing wounds she received in the Derry march now known as Bloody Sunday), Jimmy Doris, past Chairman of NICRA, Madge Davison, assistant organizer for NICRA, Hugh Lough, then NICRA member, Margo Collins, and Paddy O'Hanlon, Stormont MP. Photo courtesy of Edwina Stewart for NICRA.

7. Bernadette Devlin mural also depicting women sounding the alarm by bashing bin lids and children taking part in the Battle of the Bogside. Mural painted by the Bogside Artists, Derry, in 1996. Photo: Martin Melaugh, CAIN (cain.ulster.ac.uk)©.

8. Brandywell women marching against internment without trial c. 1971. Photo: Eamon Melaugh, CAIN (Cain.ulster.ac.uk/melaugh) ©.

9. Cumann na mBan mural in West Belfast. Photo: Martin Melaugh, CAIN (Cain.ulster.ac.uk/melaugh) ©.

10. Cumann na mBan poster, n.d., courtesy of *An Phoblacht*.

11. Female members of the Official IRA, Derry, c. 1972. Photo: Eamon Melaugh CAIN
(Cain.ulster.ac.uk/melaugh) ©.

12. Maura Drumm speaking on the internment of women in 1971. Photo courtesy of *An Phoblacht*.

FREE LIZ McKEE
END
Sectarian
Murders
and

13. Picket in Belfast, 1971. *Right to left*: Maura Drumm and Marie Moore in combat jackets. The pickets were organized to protest against the arrest of men similarly clad. Photo courtesy of *An Phoblacht*.

14. Protest against the searching of children, Derry, c. 1972. Photo: Eamon Melaugh, CAIN (cain.ulster.ac.uk/melaugh) ©

BRITISH ARMY BEWARE
YOU'RE TREADING ON THIN AIR
THE MOTHERS OF DERRY ARE UNITED
OUR CHILDREN WILL NO MORE BE SLIGHTED

15. Máirín de Burca addressing a Sinn Féin meeting on 27 July 1970. Photograph courtesy of the *Irish Times*.

16. Mary Kenny of the Irish Women's Liberation Movement. Courtesy of *This Week* magazine, 26 March 1971.

17. Irish Women's Liberation Movement's contraceptive train, Dublin, 22 May 1971. Image courtesy of Attic Press Collection, UCC Library Archives Service. Photo by Roisin Conroy.

18. Fownes Street Journal, September 1973. Courtesy of Attic Press Collection, UCC Boole Library Archives.

19. *Irish Times* women journalists, from left: Mary Maher, Geraldine Kennedy, Patsey Murphy, Ranagh Holohan and Christina Murphy on 6 March 1980. Photograph: Pat Langan, courtesy of the *Irish Times*.

THE PEOPLE'S DEMOCRACY

All over Europe in 1968 a growing body of students began to consolidate their power and articulate demands: Italians took over their universities and at the Sorbonne students attempted to plan a new future for France. Buckman points out that this year 'saw the baptism of new radicals, now isolated from the Old Left by their revolutionary actions and the theory which had grown from them'.[35] Crouch concurs by noting that student activism sometimes seemed 'more concerned to prove a point to a past generation of left-wingers' than to achieve a particular objective.[36] Another common element among student protests throughout the world was its emphasis on participative, egalitarian and unrestrained 'direct action at the grass roots'.[37] This emphasis on mass participation paved the way for women to engage in street politics with increasing numbers.

Political and historical context informs the construction and development of social movements, which means we cannot begin to analyse the development of a radical student movement in Northern Ireland without considering sectarianism. Fergal Keane observes that in Northern Ireland there are 'essentially two separate societies with little or no crossover. Each has their own schools, pubs, newspapers, sports – own everything – with only the common language of shopping ever bringing them into contact with each other.'[38] One cannot simply look at the protest march planned by Queen's University students to follow the Derry march in terms of student politics alone. Rather, it must be contextualized in terms of entrenched tribalism and political and social sectarianism.

When 3,000 students (including twenty members of the academic staff) who had met at Queen's on 9 October to march to Belfast's city hall were told their march had been re-routed, they staged a sit-in.[39] The sectarian context of Northern Irish student politics emerged in the context of the re-routing decision; to march from Queen's to City Hall would have taken the marchers through loyalist territory, which would threaten their safety. After a three-hour stand-off the group retreated and held a meeting to articulate their demands: one man, one vote, fair election boundaries, houses on need, jobs on merit, free speech and a repeal of the Special Powers Act, which had been adopted in 1922 and continually renewed to combat militant republican activity. These demands were broadly reformist in nature and spoke more to the issue of sectarianism than to New Left student politics. At that meeting a coordinating committee of ten was elected, three of whom were women (Bernadette Devlin, Pádrigín Drinan and Ann McBurney).

The students, like the Derry radicals and the NICRA moderates, had taken to the streets to draw attention to civil rights abuses on the part of the government. If we apply Amitai Etzioni's observation that radicals take to the streets when they perceive that the current regime is demonstrating a 'lack of responsiveness', which is endemic to the system,[40] the Queen's protesters were not yet radicals. A statement by Bernadette Devlin, one of the committee members, confirms how very reformist this 'non-political' group was: 'If we can get civil rights established we can return to our books and studies with the satisfying knowledge that we have achieved something in the interests of the community.'[41]

This new group, now called the People's Democracy (PD), initiated a turn away from traditional political concerns for the idealistic Northern Irish youth. One member, Eilis McDermott, told Mary Maher of the *Irish Times*: 'I think civil rights is the most important issue now ... no one thinks the Border is important now.'[42] This statement is broadly reflective of a tentative move towards social agitation and away from traditional republicanism among sections of Northern Ireland's Catholic youth. Ann Hope, a trade unionist and Wolfe Tone Society member, later connected this new fervour to international waves of protest: 'People were looking for a different way. The whole struggle in the States, the non-violence, the stuff that Martin Luther King [was] doing, seemed to be the way forward.'[43] Some, having lived through the failure of the border campaign, were looking to the success of other countries in terms of social action and protest politics. Dolours Price, who came from a long line of republicans and who went on later to become one of the first female members of the Irish Republican Army, remembered: 'There would have been a moment in time when I thought that there was a possibility that the conversion of the Protestant working class to revolution could happen and I would have had stand up rows with my father. I'd say, "Hey, look at the IRA. You tried that and you lost! You failed ... There *is* another way".'[44] The formation of the People's Democracy epitomized this new optimism and at that brief moment in late 1968 it seemed that social action had the capacity to overtake traditional republicanism as the leading force in Northern Irish radical politics. In the autumn of 1968 Bernadette Devlin told the *Irish Times*: 'Everywhere you go people are talking about civil rights and People's Democracy, even if they're attacking it. I don't think Queen's can ever be the same again. We've had such a rude awakening.'[45] This new group, with its emphasis on participatory democracy, helped to create space for women to express themselves politically and learn how to lead and organize.

One PD member, Patricia Beresford, said: 'I didn't know what the issues were and they didn't affect me: my father has a vote, I'm not discriminated against. Then I went to this meeting and I saw things differently for the first time.'[46] Beresford was taking her first shaky steps in the discourse of civil rights and equality. Significantly, she had failed to appreciate that her father having a vote did not make her or her mother any more equal. This statement reveals the entrenchment of the prevailing gender regime, which was not part of civil rights discourse, as evidenced by the call for 'one man, one vote'. In the United States notions of women's liberation within the civil rights movement were being mooted as early as 1964 and 1965, but they had not penetrated Northern Ireland.[47] A reason for this could be that by 1964/5 American civil rights activists had already been agitating for a significant amount of time; their consciousness around gender regimes had been given time to develop. Another reason could be the simple presence of a women's liberation movement in the United States that had begun in 1963 with Betty Friedan's *The Feminine Mystique*.

As the year 1968 came to a close more marches were scheduled and banned. The PD's open-air meetings began to disintegrate into scuffles between PD members and followers of a virulently anti-Catholic cleric, Ian Paisley. As the province fomented and branches of NICRA began to spring up outside of the two main cities, Prime Minister Terence O'Neill, Minister for Home Affairs William Craig and Minister of Commerce Brian Faulkner were summoned to Downing Street by Prime Minister Harold Wilson, who obliged the men to answer the civil rights grievances with a reform package.[48] On 22 November O'Neill announced a five-point plan, including a points system for housing allocation and the repeal of sections of the Special Powers Act. This failed to quell the demonstrations, prompting O'Neill to deliver an impassioned plea for calm, asking activists on 9 December: 'What kind of Ulster do you want?' After the speech he sacked William Craig and NICRA responded by imposing a moratorium on demonstrations to give O'Neill time to implement the changes.

The PD, with the impetuousness that became characteristic of student politics, responded by planning an ambitious march that would be modelled on the American Selma–Montgomery march. The PD had been moving leftward at a rapid rate and its direct democracy structure meant that those who had the loudest voice and those who had their ear were able to wield a considerable amount of influence. Jo Freeman and later Vicky Randall, in their studies of women in politics, look at the tyranny of structurelessness. When there are no formal structures a core group can, according to Randall, 'devise and manipulate tacit rules to ensure their *de facto* control and to exclude fringe members'.[49] Eamonn McCann also brings this up in his assessment of the group:

> There was … a deep distaste of leadership and actually this was a delusion because actually what it meant was the people who were self-confident, articulate and clearest emerged as leaders without ever being elected … Far from it being a democracy it meant that there was a lack of accountability. Decisions could be taken one week and different people could get together the following week and by sheer force of element or argument or a different group of people, a different decision would occur. So the democratic basis of the People's Democracy was far from clear.[50]

The march would have brought the group through loyalist constituencies, which would expose it to violent counter-demonstrations. After a debate, the majority of the PD decided against the march. Another meeting was called nearer to the end of term, where Michael Farrell announced that even if the PD did not march, his Young Socialist Alliance would go it alone. The fraction of the PD that attended the meeting reversed the earlier decision and decided to march. Eighty people began the march and more joined in along the way.

The group was violently assaulted by a well-coordinated group of loyalists laying in wait with rocks and cudgels at Burntollet Bridge. According to the *Sunday Times* Insight Team, members of the Royal Ulster Constabulary colluded with the group of loyalists in the ambush.[51] When the battered and beaten group of students arrived in Derry, the Bogside erupted into violence. Regardless of the fact that many of the NICRA moderates had not supported the march, after the ambush sympathy flooded in. Patricia McCluskey wrote to the PD: 'Your heroism and your bearing have added a new dimension to our considerable estimate of your qualities. I can tell you that we older people regard you with more admiration and respect than perhaps you think us capable of. We are all at one with your endeavours.'[52] This short-lived support reflected a groundswell of emotion and not a significant change of allegiance on the part of the moderates of the civil rights movement.

If the acknowledged strategy of the main architects of the march was to provoke physical confrontation in order to weaken the moderate base of civil rights, as the Cameron Report observes, the organizers did achieve their goal.[53] It was media coverage of the ambush that prompted Dodie McGuinness, a nurse from Derry, to get involved in civil rights activism. She remembered: 'Burntollet opened my eyes. I was fairly open-minded then … but I saw those beaten, bloody students being brought into the hospital and it changed my attitude … I began to get involved.'[54] The fact that those beaten young people were articulate students who represented the brightest minds in the province added to the shock value of the ambush. The violence visited on these representatives of tomorrow's economic and academic elite contributed towards radicalizing a significant element within a heretofore moderate segment of Catholics in Northern Ireland, who saw the ambush as a Pasileyite intimidation tactic. It also reinforced sectarianism among people from both traditions. Dolours Price remembered the ambush: 'When I was beaten into the river in Burntollet, when I looked into their eyes and I saw nothing, I thought, "Uh-uh, that is not going to work" – the conversion of the Protestant working class … So I suppose that was the beginning of my return [to republicanism].'[55]

In addition to polarizing the civil rights movement, the march had the effect of radicalizing the PD itself. The moderate students, who were left in the group, some alienated by what they believed to be a denial of their democratic vote against the march, fell away. Devlin later commented on the decision to march: 'Personally, I hadn't a clue … and was there because I'd signed for a demonstration that nobody else would sign for and I'd done that really because I was pissed off with these serious-minded revolutionaries who still had one eye on their degrees and their middle-class parents.'[56] Those who had been on the march formed a central core, which remained impenetrable to those on the outside. This new left-wing rhetoric being used by the more vocal members of the PD meant that the group would not be able to retain its broad student base. Instead it would appeal to the most militant activists, who were eager to continue its unspoken policy of 'calculated martyrdom'.[57] During this period Bernadette Devlin aptly observed the weakness of the PD, saying that it was 'totally unorganized and totally without any form of discipline within ourselves. I'd say that there are hardly two of us who really agree … we are all madly tearing off – nowhere'.[58]

The formation of the PD and the Burntollet ambush were pivotal developments in the civil rights era. In terms of the prevailing gender regime, the formation of the PD opened up the field to young women who otherwise might not have had the opportunity to express themselves through traditional politics. Its structurelessness, though more generally a significant bar to democracy for reasons explained above, actually allowed for the possibility that articulate women and men could rise in prominence without being elected. The aftermath of Burntollet enabled them to sharpen their political rhetoric while giving them a sympathetic platform from which to speak. Burntollet also polarized the activist community, forcing many to commit to more militant action than perhaps they might otherwise have taken. Burntollet, despite its negative consequences, spurred a period of consciousness-raising throughout the province, which allowed for an increased rate of non-traditional political participation among ordinary citizens.

THE ELECTION OF BERNADETTE DEVLIN

The death of Unionist MP for Westminster George Forrest in 1969 prompted a by-election in the mid-Ulster region. Many anti-Unionists feared that their vote would be split if republican Kevin Agnew and Nationalist Austin Currie stood, so Patricia McCluskey decided to tear a page from her days chairing the Homeless Citizens League and organize a 'unity' convention to select a candidate agreeable to all shades of anti-unionism. When Bernadette Devlin's name surfaced as a possibility, she declined immediately, telling the meeting:

> I am not a candidate in this election because I don't believe we will get the kind of unity I want – which is unity of the working class, Catholic and Protestant. The unity being talked about here is Catholic unity. I think politics is basically a dirty job. I am not expert enough to play the dirty job clean, and I am not prepared to play the dirty job dirty. My suggestion is that you should find from the rest of the platform the least dishonest person and put him in.[59]

However, after a long debate she was convinced to stand for the Mid-Ulster seat. Nationalists, republicans and various members of the civil rights movement had all acquiesced to support her candidacy largely because this fresh new face did not appear to be a stayer in politics.[60] Patricia McCluskey later commented:

> I was the one who first sponsored all Bernadette's meetings in Mid-Ulster. Somebody had to do it … [The other anti-Unionists] respected me as a mother figure. I could say things that even my husband couldn't say to even the extremist republicans. I was

telling them that they hadn't succeeded the way they were doing and they must try a new approach, just to let us have our tea party on the lawn, nothing more.[61]

Rosemary Ridd makes the point that there were certain conditions under which women would be allowed a level of leeway in political activity: 'Where women do assert themselves in some political role as women, they must be well received, even honoured.' But they are only received well 'if they are seen to hold steadfast to their conventional domestic roles'.[62] This blanket generalization problematizes the role of women such as Bernadette Devlin and Betty Sinclair, who expressly lacked a 'conventional domestic role'. However, it also may hold true for someone such as Patricia McCluskey, who was able to successfully trivialize her accusation of political ineffectuality by manipulating traditional gender/class notions of political expression in order to obtain her goal of displacing traditional candidates.

A period of fierce electioneering ensued, with Devlin visiting sixteen places in ten days.[63] Her opponent was Anna Forrest, the widow of Unionist George Forrest, who had held the seat before his death. At their only brief meeting the two agreed that it was time two women were contesting a seat. Forrest added: 'The men have had it their own way too long.'[64] This off-handed comment, while it was meant to be mildly amusing, signalled a changing view of women's roles. Though a handful of women had been elected to Stormont and Westminster in Northern Ireland over the years, to have two women contesting a seat was certainly a new phenomenon. Robert Lee Miller and colleagues make the point that women's participation in traditional politics has had a difficult history. Citing an historic willingness of all political traditions to employ coercion, they observe that women of both religious traditions in Northern Ireland have found the climate particularly inhospitable to their entry into formal politics.[65] This study hypothesizes that the civil rights movement might have sparked more of an interest in politics for members of the Catholic community,[66] which was certainly the experience of Bernadette Devlin, who had been a psychology student before the movement began.

During the campaign members of the People's Democracy, while demonstratively uncomfortable with this foray into traditional politics, spoke on Devlin's behalf at rallies. However, her candidacy did represent the thin edge of a wedge between Devlin and the PD leadership.[67] After a rapid election campaign, Devlin emerged victorious on 17 April 1969 by a margin of 4,211 votes. The successful campaign highlighted the emergence of a revitalized anti-Unionist coalition regardless of Devlin's adamant statements decrying pan-Catholicism at the expense of working-class unity. For Catholics in Northern Ireland, Devlin's 'unity' election engendered a feeling of solidarity, the kind to which a downtrodden population could cling. This was a strong demonstration of the strength a united front could muster, and it was not lost on the Unionists. At this stage republicans greeted Devlin's candidacy with bemused quips on both sides of the border. She was considered to be wildly naïve in terms of her rhetoric and so politically inexperienced that she was viewed as nothing more than a placeholder for the anti-Unionist vote. The media encouraged this portrayal of her.

Annabelle Sreberny-Mohammadi and Karen Ross, in their study of media coverage of female MPs, observe that 'the media help to establish the parameters which structure public thinking about the social world' and that this involves 'gatekeeping public access to information, with a judicious editing decision here, the selection of a particular image there'.[68] The publicity around Bernadette Devlin's election concentrated on her novelty value and her appearance at the expense of her message. She later wrote that on the day after the election

> Reporters and photographers steeled around the house like swarming bees, demanding idiotic, phoney photographs of the MP sitting on a rug, surrounded by all her little cousins. They all took a fancy to the garden swing: everybody had to have photographs of the 'swinging MP' ... The press were interested only in the gimmick publicity of the twenty-one-year-old female who makes it to be a member of Parliament.[69]

Most of the female MPs Sreberny-Mohammadi and Ross interviewed confirmed that media accounts of them focused on their age, looks and domestic and family circumstances, which is broadly similar to the coverage Devlin received during the election. The *Irish Echo* printed a strongly laudatory profile of Devlin, mentioning that she was 'by no means beautiful – and she makes no attempt to hide that fact' and that 'her story has all the elements of heroism' because she was 'orphaned when she was a child'. Instead of looking at her controversial politics, the reporter focused on what she would wear to her maiden speech in the Commons: She thought she might wear jeans and smiled 'making no attempt to hide the gap in her teeth'.[70] These accounts of the 'militant in a miniskirt' are crucial to this study of the transformation of women in politics because it emphasizes the incongruity of two interacting factors: patriarchy and feminism.

One can observe through this reportage how both the reporters and Devlin, herself, indulged in a patriarchal portrayal of her political mode of expression. However, it must also be noted that Devlin, who is described as making no attempt to hide her unattractiveness, consistently calls into question a more traditional press coverage style that emphasized women's difference from men. Later Devlin would unconsciously underscore her role in redefining sex and gender roles, ironically utilizing sexualized imagery: 'I became their Gipsy Rose Lee, fortune-teller of Northern Ireland. A sort of harem of journalists, British and foreign, trotted about two feet behind me.'[71] But it is difficult to measure just how much Devlin contributed towards the introduction of a feminist agenda, considering the fact that she, herself, had not developed a women-centred consciousness and was almost as suspicious of feminism as Betty Sinclair had been. She only later articulated feminist goals on her second trip to the United States,[72] and even then she made it clear that feminism took second seat to social revolution. But overall it is difficult to deny that her very presence on the political scene presented Catholic women with a new benchmark for gauging political expression. Yet however influential she was to reinvigorating political discourse by providing a role model to emulate, she could not represent all shades of political activists in Northern Ireland.

NICRA SPLITS

The year 1969 began with tensions between radical activists and a more moderate executive. The Burntollet Bridge ambush had polarized an increasing amount of moderates and more and more people began to criticize NICRA for imposing a moratorium on marches. At the 1969 annual general meeting in early February, the fragile coalition splintered. The PD, frustrated with NICRA's moderation, contemplated packing the meeting in order to elect a more radical executive, but Frank Gogarty, who functioned as a link between the groups, later explained that he dissuaded them from this course of action.[73] Gogarty's sympathies lay with the PD; he had a particular antipathy for Betty Sinclair, who he described in markedly sexist terms as 'one great reactionary bitch who is holding up the revolution'.[74] As it turned out the PD would not have had to pack the meeting, because, according to Gogarty, the republicans had decided to do the same:

The 'boys' came to the rescue ... They made sure they had

enough to 'pack' the meeting to ensure that <u>not one</u> of Austin Currie's pets got back onto the committee ... I will only add one comment and it is this: we have now a <u>more militant</u> committee in CRA. We meet next Wed. [*sic*] to elect our officers ... Chairman will not be Betty Sinclair.[75]

Gogarty was eventually voted in as chairman; Sinclair remained on the executive but, as predicted, she lost her seat at the head of the table. A few weeks later Bernadette Devlin announced a joint NICRA/PD march from Belfast through a loyalist neighbourhood to Stormont without the permission of the NICRA executive. At a 14 March debate on the issue three different votes ended up being split seven to seven, with Gogarty casting his deciding vote for the march to go ahead.[76] Sinclair, John McAnerney, the secretary, Fred Heatley, the treasurer, and Raymond Shearer walked out in protest. McAnerney later commented:

All we needed was time ... a lull in which to see if Captain O'Neill was going to carry out the further reforms he had promised. But PD would not give us time and their political views are infringing on the non-political aims of the NICRA ... We have been taken over by people preaching the most extreme form of revolutionary socialism, the sort of politics that have been causing trouble in France, Germany, Japan and many other parts of the world.[77]

The movement had officially descended into recrimination, with each side publicly attacking the other.

The four vacancies created by the walkout were filled with Belfast-based people and meetings began to run later into the night, which forced older members with family commitments or those who lived in the country to leave NICRA meetings early. Conn McCluskey later pointed out that this paved the way for younger, Belfast-based executive members to take an increasingly active role in the decision-making process.[78] The changes in the executive allowed more women to rise to positions of power within the group. Edwina Stewart believes she was brought on to the executive as secretary at this point because she was Protestant and because, as a woman, there was a perception she could be easily manipulated.[79] It was probably a combination of these factors, in addition to her activism in the Communist Party, her ability to take shorthand and her willingness to fill in for the previous secretary that made her a logical choice. Ann Hope had been involved with the group since the first meetings in 1967. Her organizational skills and willingness to deliver international lectures about NICRA made her an invaluable treasurer and emissary. Madge Davison, also a member of the Communist Party, was originally hired to do secretarial work but rose to the rank of organizer as she took on more of the logistical work.

The ascendancy of more women into leadership positions was related to their sex but also correlated with their activist careers as well. All of them had backgrounds that made them ideal candidates to maintain the appearance of a balance of political power. There is only a relatively thin body of evidence to suggest that any of these women were easily manipulated, as their voting records bear out a philosophy consistent with their main political allegiances. On analysis, their sex seems to have been less of a factor in their ascension to the executive than their politics. Ann Hope explained:

> Women were always accepted for their skills. Women weren't seen as a threat to the men ... You didn't just look at those who came on by saying, 'Oh great, there's another woman' or 'Great, there's another man'. You were saying, 'I hope that's not another PD' or something like that because it was about particular politics, who best could bring this forward.[80]

Edwina Stewart explained why she believed NICRA women did not confront similar issues as their American and British counterparts: '[Men] were at an earlier stage of respect for women as your mother ... I think it's an older attitude, if you know what I mean.'[81] This observation implies that traditionalism in terms of sex and gender relations contributed towards masking tensions and even eliminated the kinds of tensions that had surfaced elsewhere in American and British activist groups during the period. If Stewart's analysis is true, it may help to explain why a second wave of feminism failed to take root in Northern Ireland in this period. But as women came to the fore within the leadership of the civil rights movement their street activism also became crucial to the changing face of political expression in Northern Ireland, as evidenced by Bernadette Devlin's actions in the summer of 1969.

12 AUGUST 1969

Communal tensions were running high on the eve of the traditional Apprentice Boys march, which commemorated the Protestant victory over the Catholics during the Siege of Derry in 1689. Both communities and the police anticipated trouble and readied themselves for the worst. Catholics in the Bogside were beginning to collect materials for the construction of barricades and five Landrovers were stationed at anticipated flashpoint areas.[82] Riots soon began to engulf the Bogside and by the next day violent confrontations and rioting in Belfast ensued. The Scarman Report later noted that 'neither the IRA nor any Protestant organization nor anybody else planned a campaign of riots. They were communal disturbances arising from a complex political, social and economic situation.'[83] These communal disturbances evolved into street warfare in the two main cities of Northern Ireland. Bogsiders in Derry threw up barricades and began hurling petrol bombs to repel what they believed to be rioting police and aggressive Protestant mobs.

Bernadette Devlin found a megaphone and quickly assumed control of part of the defence effort, though some considered her an outsider and seemed to ignore her.[84] Television footage from the day reveals a composed Devlin directing Bogsiders to gather bin lids to give to the men and boys on the barricades. As the street fighting wore on, television footage shows how Devlin tried to use her new-found political clout to negotiate with Robert Porter, Minister for Home Affairs. Her efforts did not meet with any measurable success. Even though the press eagerly ran pictures of Devlin, alone, hoisting a large rock over her head, other women contributed in leadership roles during the rioting. Eileen Doherty managed the Citizens' Action Committee from her home,[85] Cathy Harkin and Mary Holland helped write and produce the Barricade Bulletins,[86] and Sarah Wilson, with the help of the neighbourhood's children, used her silkscreen to make up notices and posters of meetings and schedules.[87]

On the ground most of the front-line action was left to local men and boys, but there were women who remained on the front lines as well. Nell McCafferty remembered taking an active part in throwing petrol bombs along with other women from the Bogside.[88] This experience is supported by a notice printed in some of the Bogside's Barricade Bulletins: 'In the absence of sufficient male volunteers, the Defence Association will ask women to come forward to fill the gaps.'[89] Another notice appeared a few days later thanking Bogside women for joining the men on the barricades.[90] There are accounts that leaders of the defence committee viewed women's activism as secondary to their own efforts and that some female activists such as Bernadette Devlin, Nell McCafferty and Cathy Harkin were barred from meetings specifically because they were women.[91] These contradictions suggest that necessity more than anything else contributed to carving out a role for women in the effort and that women's activism in Catholic Derry, where women occupied a strong role in community life, faced similar obstacles to egalitarianism as the rest of the province.

Though later the Scarman Report largely exonerated the police, in both cities the Royal Ulster Constabulary and the 'B Specials' were perceived by Catholics to be collaborating with Protestant mobs. The experience of this period contributed to a re-evaluation of women's roles in terms of the communal effort to 'defend' the area.[92] As noted above, women participated in many aspects of the effort in Catholic areas, though not so much in Protestant areas because the rioting was generally confined to Catholic neighbourhoods. Predictably, there were fewer women in leadership roles and more women in catering and supply-chain management, but overall the rioting of August 1969 politicized those remaining who had not already formed opinions about the unfolding events, and it drew both sexes into direct action in significant numbers.

Anthony Oberschall makes the point that popular disturbances do not break out without a preparatory period 'filled with numerous incidents that signal the existence of widespread grievances', which can help us understand the rioting in a broader context of popular confrontation.[93] In this case, the Apprentice Boys' march was simply a precipitating incident. The Scarman Report supports this in its finding that the rioting that took place in Derry and Belfast happened during the summer marching season for Protestants, which followed massively publicized events between August 1968 to April 1969.[94] One could argue that women only participated en masse in the street fighting due to their maternalist motivation for protecting their communities and more, specifically, their own homes.[95] Others could make the case that women joined the effort simply as a reaction to the escalating violence and the introduction of CS gas. The truth most likely lies where these arguments meet.

August 1969 was a consolidation period for women's increasing involvement in community and street politics in urban Northern Ireland. Nell McCafferty, a Derry native, described how women entered into public discourse:

> The movement liberated Catholic women, albeit unintentionally. They burst out of their homes ... and spent their Sundays marching around the city, demanding freedom, just like the men and children. They joined in the chant for votes, houses and jobs, carried

banners, sat down defiantly in the roadway when the Royal Ulster Constabulary blocked the route, helped build barricades, inhaled tear gas, broke the law for the first time in their adult lives and agreed that there was no time to go home to make the supper.[96]

The experience of Chrissie McAuley, the daughter of a Catholic mother and a Protestant father, supports McCafferty's recollection. When her home in Belfast was attacked during this period, she and her family fled to another neighbourhood and returned later:

> I can remember the smell of burnt out homes was still heavy in the air. This was the beginning of my awakening process. I began to ask the serious questions about why this area was attacked and about why the British army was now on the streets. You're not supposed to need the army on the streets to protect you.[97]

Perhaps due to the scope of her study of women in Ireland, Myrtle Hill regretfully fails to document this shift into the public political sphere.[98] An analysis of how women reacted to the politicizing events of August 1969 is imperative to understanding the surge in political activity among women in the Catholic community that followed the incidents.

The fighting finally tapered off when the British army was called to duty. A summary of the casualties cannot paint the picture; to properly contextualize it, it must be noted:

> The violence of July and August had resulted in ten deaths in the region; 154 people suffering gunshot wounds; 745 injured in other ways; around 300 treated at first-aid posts for the effects of CS gas; 16 factories gutted by fire; 179 homes destroyed and another 417 damaged; 60 Catholic-owned public houses attacked and 24 of them left in ruins; and in Derry one dairy alone losing 43,000 milk bottles during the three-day battle in the Bogside. Catholic-owned or occupied premises accounted for 83.5 per cent of the damage.[99]

Richard English articulates the most significant lesson that both Catholics and Protestants learned from the summer of 1969: all their fears had been justified.[100] While the IRA had not materialized on the levels that William Craig had been predicting, a significant portion of the Protestant population now viewed the Catholic community to be just as subversive. Mary Kenny went to Belfast in the aftermath of the riots and asked women who were organizing a refugee centre what

Dublin could do for them. One said: 'A man from Dublin came along and gave us a lot of medical kits which was very helpful. But tell them in Dublin, all we want from them is guns.'[101] The mother of a 9-year-old boy who was shot from outside his home while hiding inside added: 'I would like to get a gun myself and use it. If I could join the IRA now, I would. I wish Mr Lynch would send people in to help us because we will be massacred if it goes on like this.'[102] Though these quotations represent a knee-jerk reaction in the heat of the moment, they can be looked at in terms of how rapidly unfolding events politicized the women of the area. It is likely that many of the Falls Road residents came from republican families, but the IRA in the lead-up to the summer was largely a spent force, militarily. The women who spoke of arming themselves were responding to their experiences of their own communal vulnerability by articulating a revitalized mode of political engagement not seen since the civil war.

In the aftermath of the battle of the Bogside, Bernadette Devlin was sent to New York. Paddy Devlin (no relation), a campaigner from Derry, had told her in no uncertain terms that it was time for her to leave the area.[103] From his point of view, her unwillingness to accept the arrival of the army, coupled with her strong revolutionary rhetoric, meant that she would be a liability to constructive efforts to rebuild and negotiate with the armed forces. Kevin Boyle, a member of the PD, took a different view of why she went: 'People worried after '69 that she would be killed. There was a new type of violence emerging ... I subsequently found out the republicans advised her to go ... Of course she was a dramatic figure to send to America, to concentrate attention.'[104] The hastily thrown together trip had all the earmarks of official cooperation. Bernadette Devlin later explained: 'The [Irish] Free State[105] army or government or somebody [arranged it] ... I did not have a passport never mind a friggin' visa.'[106]

Hosted by a newly formed National Association for Irish Justice (NAIJ), Devlin arrived in New York and announced her intention to raise one million dollars for the relief of the victims of the summer's disturbances. Irish America welcomed her with open arms. Seán Cronin, a senior IRA figure in the 1950s and prime architect of the border campaign who by then lived in the United States, summarized reaction to Devlin in America for the *Irish Times* using the kind of well-trodden patriarchal compliments that characterized all of her coverage from the moment she was voted into Parliament:

Without a doubt, Bernadette is the best envoy Ireland ever sent to

America. She has taken over the city and her cry for justice has come across loud and clear. Not even Eamon de Valera in 1920 commanded the audiences she has. She is young and articulate and her mini skirts help too. All consider her to be the brightest, the freshest, and of course the prettiest Irish politician to come to these parts in living memory.[107]

She was invited to take part in 'Meet the Press' and 'The Johnny Carson Show'. She received the key to the city of New York from Mayor Lindsay, she met with U Thant of the United Nations, and she was showered with cash all the while.

But as she made her way out of New York, she began to notice disparities between what Irish America thought of Northern Irish Catholics and what it thought of American blacks. Marvelling at how Irish Americans could have black servants,[108] Devlin later wrote that she began to pick up distinctly orange tones in the green rhetoric of local Irish-American leaders when they discussed American civil rights.[109] In Philadelphia, when she invited a black tenor to sing 'We shall overcome' after dancing with him on stage, she outraged hundreds. She shamed the audience into standing and later noted that even though many did voluntarily get to their feet, those who did not were the dignitaries, priests and members of the Ancient Order of Hibernians occupying the front rows.[110] When she visited a manufacturing venture for black Americans called Operation Bootstrap in California, to some, she had begun to step over the line.

On her way back to the east coast Devlin stopped in Detroit, where news of her support of the American civil rights struggle had spread. At one speaking engagement she refused to speak until the venue admitted the crowd of black people who were waiting to see her outside.[111] While she was in Detroit, Chicago activists decided to make clear their position on Devlin's calls for racial equality. They left messages with the NAIJ organizers that if she visited Jesse Jackson's project for the economic advancement of black people in Chicago, Operation Breadbasket, she would face consequences.[112] The final wedge between Irish America and Devlin during this tour occurred when she arrived in Chicago, where her very public row with the widely popular Mayor Richard Daley came to a head. Devlin called the mayor corrupt and compared his police force to the RUC in Northern Ireland; he responded by cancelling a reception for her.[113] This exchange, coupled with her vociferous support for black America, sounded the death knell for Devlin's short-lived relationship with Irish America.

Her unsuccessful attempts to address this issue publicly caused tension between her and some of the organizers, but the main problem that emerged between them was the issue of how the money would be spent – on relief or armaments.[114] This profound disagreement about the destination of the money mirrored a bigger confusion in Irish America, which surfaced in an *Irish Echo* editorial. The largest Irish-American newspaper in the New York metropolitan area, it urged its readers to support the tour 'for social justice for all in Ireland and for a united 31 [*sic*] county Irish Republic'.[115] The American media, by electing to simplify her avowed aim of establishing a 'socialist workers' republic' to a more traditional-sounding 'united republic' muddled the issue further. Pete Sweeney, a building foreman who attended one of the New York rallies, said of her: 'I think she's not half as much a revolutionary as she should be. The only way unification will come in Ireland is by force.'[116] Sweeney's statement is broadly representative of the failure among the Irish-American population to come to terms with the incongruity of Devlin's revolutionary socialism and their own traditional Irish republicanism. Though Devlin repeatedly articulated her position, the watered-down analysis of her speeches in the media perpetuated this fundamental misunderstanding between Devlin and her audience.

What brought the tension between Devlin and the tour organizers to a head was an overheard telephone conversation where one organizer said: 'Never mind, play her along. We've got the money and that's all that matters.'[117] When she realized she was being duped, Devlin abandoned the tour and boarded the next flight to Ireland. When she arrived home Eamonn McCann confronted her over her acceptance of the key to New York from Mayor Lindsay. As a result, Devlin asked McCann to return the key during his speaking tour of the United States, which was scheduled for a few months hence. McCann travelled to New York in March of 1970 and set to the task. The *New York Times* reported that he was presenting the key to the Black Panthers, 'as a gesture of solidarity with the black liberation and revolutionary socialist movements in America'. McCann read out Devlin's message, which sympathized with those living in America's slums: 'To all these people, to whom this city and this country belong, I return what is rightfully theirs, this symbol of the freedom of New York.'[118] This 'gesture of solidarity' did more to alienate Devlin's American supporters than anything else she could have done, and contrary to what she may have hoped, it did very little to shore up her credibility among her colleagues in the People's Democracy. In fact, the only person it seemed to satisfy was McCann himself. Those who knew where this had come from could not have mitigated the damage to international relations if they tried. If Irish America had been suspicious of her attempts to address American racism, now they were convinced she had betrayed them.

To all who knew her, this wildly dramatic publicity stunt smacked of McCann's influence in its novelty and its impetuousness. McCann later remarked: 'I knew it would alienate some but I certainly had a very naïve view about the Irish-American community. I remember Jimmy Breslin said to me, "That was really ... stupid, McCann. It was a great idea but you should have done it on the *last* day!"' Immediately following the presentation the rest of McCann's speaking engagements in the US were abruptly cancelled.[119] Notably, the British government was not concerned with Devlin's visit or the key incident. In fact, these two episodes did not even make it into diplomatic reports. The Republic was markedly more concerned. Charles Whelan, Consulate-General in New York, sent a memorandum to Eamonn Gallagher of the Department of External Affairs in Dublin explaining: 'the fact that Bernadette Devlin is personally associated with this gesture ... will make it far more difficult for any civil rights supporter from the Six Counties to obtain assistance, financial or otherwise'.[120]

This was an understatement. Irish America, already more than irritated by Devlin's tour, placed its wallet firmly back in its pocket and chose instead to set up home-grown fundraising groups that would ensure funds would find their way to the traditionalist republican movement in Northern Ireland. A few days later, when Devlin wrote to New York's Saint Patrick's Day parade committee with the ludicrous offer to march under certain conditions, the *Daily News* reported that Devlin would not be welcomed under any circumstances.[121] Not only was she refused; some members of the community used the key affair to attack the entire civil rights movement, including its US affiliate, the NAIJ. Charles Whelan reported to External Affairs that such prominent leaders as Judge James Comerford and Father Donal O'Callaghan destroyed the Civil Rights Association's credibility by claiming that the Left had infiltrated it and that those who conceived of it were no longer in control. Whelan also claimed that at an Ancient Order of Hibernians meeting attacks on Devlin were greeted with loud cheers. In an effort to downplay the impact of such poor judgement to other civil rights activists, Devlin allegedly confided in Ivan Cooper, 'Och! Sure that was just a joke!'[122] But the damage was done and Irish America was not laughing.

It is impossible to measure just how much the key incident damaged Irish-American donations for relief, considering the period that preceded it. One member of an Irish-American group later reflected: 'It's very hard now to get money after Bernadette giving the key to the Black Panthers. This was such a crime that it has dried up support out there. I think only Paisley could have thought this one up.'[123] And if Ian Paisley, the rising star of militant loyalism, had, it would have been a stroke of genius. After this, the traditionalists in Irish America would find it very difficult to trust another civil rights leader. In their eyes, it was the second time they had tangled with radicals, who, they felt, were more concerned with political credibility than moving towards Irish unification.

But how significant was that credibility that they so steadfastly worked to maintain? The links with the Black Panthers never amounted to more than a passing news brief. In fact, when Devlin had visited Operation Bootstrap, Eleanor Childs, the young education director, had commented: 'Her cause is probably cool, but we have other things to do.'[124] Eilis MacDermott, another PD member who had visited the Black Panthers and later wrote their praises, naïvely assumed that the Black Panthers had 'more to offer to our movement in terms of advice and support than have many of the sentimental traditionalist Irish-American populations';[125] the Panthers offered Northern Ireland nothing at all, not even verbal support. The relationship between Irish radicals and black radicals was a one-sided one, and romantic in its own way. Bernadette Devlin would continue this attempt at solidarity by visiting Angela Davis in jail a year and a half later. But overall, neither the black activists nor the Irish activists had anything significant to offer each other, and there is no evidence of any attempt by either group to do more than hold preliminary meetings.

Soon after Bernadette Devlin arrived home, she was served with a summons to appear in court to answer for her part in the battle of the Bogside, which provoked a groundswell of anger. Immediately Nationalist politician Eddie McAteer contacted the British government asking why the Northern Irish administration would engage in the lunacy of issuing writs against Devlin just as things were beginning to settle down. McAteer conceded that Devlin was a 'bloody menace', but said that she should be forgotten, not brought to prominence.[126] The British representative in Northern Ireland claimed he was not apprised of the RUC's intention to arrest Devlin, and that had he been consulted he would have advised against it. Many others in the Republic were flabbergasted at what appeared to be the combative posture of the authorities. *Hibernia* looked at the consequences of arresting Devlin: 'Anti-Unionists will regard her as a sacrificial lamb offered up to appease the wrath of the Shankill gods. Her imprisonment would muzzle the whispering campaign of criticism amongst a certain section of her former support and ensure that there would be a thunderous outcry ... that the law was different for a woman, a member of Parliament or a Fenian.'[127] This is exactly what happened when, towards the end of 1969, Devlin stood trial and was convicted. An issue of the PD's *Free Citizen* from the period summed up the feeling on the ground: 'When Bernadette Devlin was convicted of riotous behaviour and incitement to riot, the whole of the Bogside was convicted with her.'[128]

But though the PD supported her upon her arrest, the group's newsletter confirmed *Hibernia*'s observations that a whispering campaign was indeed afoot by pointing out in the same supportive article that it was uncomfortable with Devlin's popularity. Tension had been growing since her election campaign, and can be observed in the transcript of a PD strategy session that took place a few days after the election, when Devlin squared up with some of her colleagues, such as Eamonn McCann, Michael Farrell and Cyril Toman. She told them: 'Despite the fact that all of you supported me in getting into the bourgeois Parliament, very few of you remained for the final scene of my crucifixion, when all the pan-Catholics turned up to celebrate. It was really too much for the good socialists.'[129] McCann supported her by saying: 'It is necessary to go to Westminster to demand the solution to these problems to show that Westminster is a farce, and that we will have to do it ourselves.' Toman agreed, saying that it was important to show that the minority had 'got up off their knees'. But her tone resonated with Farrell, prompting him to clarify his position:

> I am worried about two aspects of the electoral campaign in Mid-Ulster. The first is that Nationalist MPs did speak on Bernadette's election platform, which clearly was an embarrassment. These people are Green Tories, they are capitalists and they are Catholic sectarians and even their so-called left-wingers are as much our enemy as the Unionist party ... Secondly, the platform should have been a clearly socialist one and not one which emphasized unity in terms, which could only mean of all classes within one creed rather than the unity of one class regardless of creed.[130]

By declaring his apprehension about the election of Devlin, Farrell brought a budding personality clash into the open. As a strategic thinker and strong leader, Farrell had emerged as the main Trotskyite force driving the PD. By January 1970 the PD's newsletter, the *Free Citizen*, was accusing Devlin of indulging in a 'cult of personality' while maintaining that her politics were 'confused'. This sudden about-face on Bernadette Devlin as a politician is typical of the leader–follower interaction discussed by Anthony Oberschall in his study of social movements: 'If [the leaders] are successful, they may be the subject of adulation and a cult of personality, surrounded by syco-phants and hangers-on … Often their best friends and early associates later turn against them over questions of strategy and ideology.'[131]

The media had also begun to rethink its relationship with Bernadette Devlin. Anne Chisholm wrote: 'One thing is instantly plain: the jour-nalistic raptures that greeted her election and arrival in Westminster were remarkably short-lived.'[132] According to Chisholm, Devlin was a metaphor for the entire Irish problem: the minor irritation had grown into a dangerous presence that the English just hoped would go away. She was full of contradictions: on one hand her rhetorical prowess and meteoric rise to fame suggested she was a truly capable politician. On the other hand, her close relationship with other radical leaders appeared to influence her actions.[133] A note from the Irish ambassador to London, Donal O'Sullivan, summed up perceptions of her that pervaded officialdom: 'The extremist political leaders on the Left are Eamonn McCann, Michael Farrell, and Cyril Toman and Bernadette is their victim – willing no doubt but nonetheless a victim.'[134] Erskine Holmes had campaigned for her during her first election, but soon withdrew his support. He discussed his rationale for doing so in an interview a few years later:

> You could almost tell from her speeches who was influencing her. She fell into the hands of a fellow called Gerry Lawless at one stage – he's in one of these Trotskyite fringe organizations in London – and you could see his line coming through. Then Eamonn McCann got her back onto his tack again, and you could spot *it* coming through. Then you could see Bowes Egan's parlia-mentary questions being asked … Her favourite phrases were 'the people' and 'our rights, our fundamental rights' … When she's stuck for an answer, she'll go back to talking about 'our rights'. 'We're not asking for concessions, we're asking for our rights.' That's another of her simple points. There's no content there, there's no intellect there, really just a good, sharp little mind.[135]

Bernadette Devlin was a product of her time. Though people such as

Farrell and McCann had left university only a few years earlier, they had used that time to flesh out their socialism. Farrell taught and McCann spent time in London writing for the radical press. Devlin, however, was a psychology student when the protests began, and by her own admission her introduction to socialism happened on the fly at the meetings. She could never have been the political icon she was initially held up to be by the media; her rhetorical prowess masked her lack of experience and undeveloped philosophy.

One might question whether Devlin's sex was a factor in fostering the perception of her political pliability. Probably the most significant question for this study is how she was perceived by the population at large. For one thing, she catapulted herself into the limelight by engaging in traditionally male-dominated activities: formal politics and street leadership. In this sense she challenged normative perceptions of gender and sex roles. But, during the period, the issue of sex discrimination did not pass her lips during countless speeches in Northern Ireland about systemic inequality. And while she cannot be singled out for failing to countenance this – women's rights simply was not a significant part of the agenda during this period – neither can she be lauded as an unproblematic role model for women. Eamonn McCann later remarked on Devlin's role in the battle of the Bogside: 'Gender did have something to do with it because she wasn't sorry and *that* shocked people.'[136] Without women like Bernadette Devlin subverting gender relations by pointing out the narrow-mindedness of journalists or refusing to apologize for her part in the battle of the Bogside, it is hard to predict whether anything would have breached the unspoken conventions that defined the public and private spheres in Northern Ireland. Though not a feminist, the example set by Devlin as a politician and orator contributed towards opening a door for other women to engage the state in a dialogue both on the streets and in parliament.

CONCLUSION

In 1968 and 1969, as CS gas blanketed the Bogside, refugee centres were hastily thrown up in Belfast and the civil rights association split, a pragmatic restructuring of the gender regime took place. Women's political activism was becoming a necessary part of daily life now that politics had been moved out of Stormont and on to the streets. The concept of feminism, however, would not find a strong foothold in the North because of the advent of the Troubles. Some men and women involved in civil rights protests and community defence considered feminism to be a distraction from civil rights and community activism, if they engaged with it at all. The faint echoes of feminism among Derry labour activists[137] and equal pay resolutions at NICRA meetings[138] were drowned out by the mounting drumbeat of sectarian violence. This might have been the time to consider gender inequality as people debated other forms of bias, but most interviewees indicated that introducing feminist concerns to community meetings held the danger of over-complicating a mounting crisis situation. Moreover, they said, it just was not on the radar of political discourse at the time. These factors, combined with sectarian community divisions and structural patriarchy, proved to be too hostile an environment for the second wave to take root at this time. The PD had made some noises about the ban on contraceptives in the Republic,[139] but that read more like a tactic to attract Northern Protestants to their cause and did not appear to be a sincere move to adopt a feminist outlook. Eamonn McCann later reflected back on the statement 'one man, one vote': 'At the time it didn't occur to anybody as grating, strange or inappropriate. And indeed, it has to be said that I remember thousands of women chanting "one man, one vote".'[140]

Working-class Catholic women benefited from women's increasing contribution to street politics, albeit without developing the women-centred consciousness that might find fault with that chant. But the picture of women's engagement did not end there; middle-class women such as Patricia McCluskey, and those who gravitated towards formal political action such as Bríd Rodgers, belonged to a constituency that rejected street protest but none the less benefited from women's increased politicization. Altogether, the increasing numbers of women on the streets and in leadership positions built on itself and helped to begin a restructuring of the gender regime, but without the significant concomitant dialogue on sex roles in Northern Irish society that has happened elsewhere under different circumstances.

Groups such as NICRA, local action committees and the PD emerged in this period and made a strong case for a re-evaluation of citizenship legislation and public policy. They injected a new voice into Northern Irish political debate and vied with the fracturing republican movement to be the representative voice of the downtrodden nationalist community, though they consistently sought to recruit a cross-community constituency. The success of these groups was due to concise and coherent demands, which dovetailed with notions of social justice that surfaced internationally at this time. Their success, combined with increasing sectarian violence, precipitated a crisis

within the republican movement that would soon result in the movement splitting along socialist /physical force lines. Ironically, the very
civil rights movement that left-wing republicans helped to establish
threatened for a brief moment to displace it as the strongest critic of
the Northern Irish government in the region.

Also during this period Bernadette Devlin emerged as a problematic
political icon. Her very presence on the floor of Westminster was
testament to a surge in Catholic political expression. Her explosive rhetoric and tenacious politicking grabbed the headlines and focused the
world on Northern Ireland. The rapturous manner in which she was
initially greeted owed much to watered-down, ageist and patriarchal
media portrayals typical of the treatment many women have encountered when entering the traditional political sphere. Her antagonism of
Irish America in an attempt to shore up her local credibility must be
understood in the context of her rapid rise to prominence without the
benefit of having formulated a coherent political philosophy. Probably
the most significant effect of Devlin's experience with Irish America
was that it forced Irish America to define itself more clearly in relation
to Northern Ireland and to black America. After her, Irish America
would work with traditionalist republicans of its own choosing. In
terms of feminism, the phenomenon of Bernadette Devlin's ascendance
to prominence is even more difficult to evaluate. Though she became
a crucial figure to Northern Irish politics, Devlin was defined by those
politics, by the ethno-sectarian conflict that produced her. She could
never hold a place among the emergent international second-wave
feminist leaders of the period because she was limited by her politics
to working for change within the traditional male-oriented framework
of Northern Irish political expression. Yet she provided a crucial link
between social/political conservatism and the tentative articulation of
feminist goals that would emerge in the groups that proliferated after
this germination period, such as the Northern Ireland Women's Rights
Movement, Relatives Action Committee, the Socialist Women's Group,
Women Against Imperialism, the Sinn Féin Women's Department and
even the Northern Ireland Women's Coalition.

Various scholars have argued that women who have participated in
gender-integrated movements have developed a women-centred political consciousness and that 'in fighting for any cause, women become
sensitized to the multiple types of oppression experienced by members
of their sex'.[141] But this argument is too simplistic an analysis for this
study. Wilson points out that 'a highly active woman in a tenants'
organization may limit her militancy to this single issue; it may never

lead her to a more political understanding of the economic system that creates housing problems any more than it may lead her to an understanding of her own oppression as a woman'.[142] It cannot be assumed simply that more women agitating on the streets and standing for seats in elections effects an automatic surge in the development of a feminist consciousness. In this time frame, a large-scale feminist consciousness certainly did not develop, nor did individual women express a significant interest in seeking out feminist connections. Indeed, in such a divided society, there was little or no room for a feminist agenda to develop in the 1960s and 1970s. What becomes clear here is a perceptible increase in Catholic women's political expression that can be connected to a rise in international student politics and civil rights. This increased political expression would lay the groundwork for a more comprehensive re-evaluation of the gender regime and ultimately for the creation of a feminist consciousness a few years later.

NOTES

1. For examples of this see B. Purdie, *Politics in the Streets: The Origins of the Civil Rights Movement in Northern Ireland* (Belfast: Blackstaff Press, 1990); P. Arthur, *The People's Democracy, 1968–73* (Belfast: Blackstaff Press, 1974); C. McCluskey, *Up off their Knees: A Commentary on the Civil Rights Movement in Northern Ireland* (Ireland: Conn McCluskey and Associates, 1989); E. McCann, *War and an Irish Town*, updated edn (London: Pluto Press, 1993).
2. McCluskey, *Up off their Knees*, p.111; Arthur, *People's Democracy*.
3. For more on discrimination see J. Bardon, *A History of Ulster* (Belfast: Blackstaff Press, 1992), pp.648–53; *Disturbances in Northern Ireland: Report of the Commission Appointed by the Governor of Northern Ireland (the Cameron Report)* (Belfast: Her Majesty's Stationery Office, 1969).
4. E. Hobsbawm, *The Age of Extremes: The Short Twentieth Century, 1914–1991* (London: Abacus, 1994), p.296.
5. *Irish Times*, 8 March 1967.
6. Bardon, *History of Ulster*, p.647.
7. *Irish News*, 19 January 1968.
8. Purdie, *Politics in the Streets*, p.175.
9. Interview with Eamonn McCann, Derry, 8 February 2003.
10. *Derry Journal*, 5 July 1968.
11. N. McCafferty, *Nell* (Dublin: Penguin, 2004), pp.128, 146.
12. 'From a Diary of Derry' (www.irelandsown.net/wire.htm, 7 May 2005).
13. A. Gallagher, 'Women and Community Work', in M. Mayo (ed.), *Women in the Community* (London: Routledge & Kegan Paul, 1977), pp.131–3.
14. Interview with McCann, Derry, 8 February 2003.
15. For more on this see E.A. Aunger, 'Religion and Class: An Analysis of 1971 Census Data', in R.J. Cormack and R.D. Osborne (eds), *Religion, Education and Employment: Aspects of Equal Opportunity in Northern Ireland* (Belfast: Appletree Press, 1983), pp.40–1.
16. 'Caledon Was About Forcing British to Address Injustices in the North' (http://www.nicivilrights.org/?p=64, 14 July 2009).
17. *Cameron Report*.
18. Bardon, *History of Ulster*, p.652; Sunday Times Insight Team, *Ulster* (Harmondsworth: Penguin, 1972), p.45 (estimates 4,000 marchers).
19. Bardon, *History of Ulster*, p.652.
20. *Irish News*, 26 August 1968.

21. V.I. Lenin, *Collected Works* (London: Lawrence & Wishart, 1960), Vol. 5, p.425.
22. L. Edgerton, 'Interview between Lynda Edgerton and Betty Sinclair' (Belfast: Linen Hall Library Political Collection, 1980).
23. Quoted in Sunday Times Insight Team, *Ulster*, p.46.
24. McCann, *War and an Irish Town*, p.91.
25. J. Freeman (ed.), *Social Movements of the Sixties and Seventies* (New York: Longman, 1983), pp.21–2.
26. McCann, *War and an Irish Town*, p.93.
27. McCann to Farrell, cited in Purdie, *Politics in the Streets*, p.139.
28. McCann to Farrell, cited in ibid., p.153.
29. Quoted in 'Derry: The Walls Come Tumbling Down', *Fortnight*, 7 October 1988, pp.7–8.
30. Quoted in Ibid.
31. *Cameron Report.*
32. *Irish Times*, 10 October 1968.
33. *Irish Times*, 29 October 1968.
34. H. Morrissey, 'Betty Sinclair: A Woman's Fight for Socialism', *Saothar* 9 (1983), p.130.
35. P. Buckman, *The Limits of Protest* (London: Little Hampton Book Services, 1970), pp.50–1.
36. C. Crouch, *The Student Revolt* (London: Bodley Head, 1970), p.17.
37. Ibid., p.31.
38. *Village*, 6–12 May 2005.
39. Arthur, *People's Democracy*, p.29.
40. A. Etzioni, *Demonstration Democracy: A Policy Paper Prepared for the Task Force on Demonstrations, Protests and Group Violence of the President's National Commission on the Causes and Prevention of Violence* (New York: Gordon & Breach, 1970), p.49.
41. *Irish News*, 21 October 1968.
42. *Irish Times*, 27 November 1968.
43. Interview with Ann Hope, Belfast, 30 June 2003.
44. Interview with Dolours Price, Malahide, 7 March 2003.
45. *Irish Times*, 27 November 1968.
46. *Irish Times*, 27 November 1968.
47. See S. Evans, *Personal Politics: The Roots of Women's Liberation in the Civil Rights Movement and the New Left* (New York: Vintage, 1979).
48. Bardon, *History of Ulster*, p.656.
49. J. Freeman, 'Political Organization in the Feminist Movement', *Acta Sociologica*, 18 (1975). V. Randall, *Women and Politics: An International Perspective* (Basingstoke: Macmillan Education, 1991), p.255.
50. Interview with McCann, Derry, 8 February 2003.
51. Sunday Times Insight Team, *Ulster*, p.66.
52. CSJ to PD, January 1969, Belfast, Public Record Office of Northern Ireland (PRONI), Kevin Boyle Papers, D/3297.
53. *Cameron Report.*
54. Quoted in E. Shannon, *I Am of Ireland: Women of the North Speak Out* (London: Little, Brown, 1989), p.49.
55. Interview with Price, Malahide, 7 March 2003.
56. Quoted in B. Dooley, *Black and Green: The Fight for Civil Rights in Northern Ireland and Black America* (London: Pluto Press, 1998), p.55.
57. *Cameron Report.*
58. L. Baxter et al., 'The People's Democracy: A Discussion on Strategy', *New Left Review*, 55 (1969), p.13.
59. B. Devlin, *The Price of My Soul* (London: Andre Deutsch, 1969), p.164.
60. J.B. Bell, *The Secret Army: The IRA, 1916–1979* (Dublin: Poolbeg, 1990), p.360.
61. Quoted in W.H. Van Voris, *Violence in Ulster* (Amherst, MA: University of Massachusetts Press, 1975), p.114.
62. R. Ridd, 'Powers of the Powerless', in R. Ridd and H. Calloway (eds), *Caught up in Conflict: Women's Responses to Political Strife* (London: Macmillan, 1986), p.4.
63. Arthur, *People's Democracy*, p.62.
64. *Irish Echo*, 19 April 1969.
65. R.L. Miller, R. Wilford and F. Donoghue, *Women and Political Participation in Northern Ireland* (Aldershot: Avebury, 1996), p.15.

66. Ibid., p.22.
67. Arthur, *People's Democracy*, p.58.
68. A. Sreberny-Mohammadi and K. Ross, 'Women MPs and the Media: Representing the Body Politic', in J. Lovenduski and P. Norris (eds), *Women in Politics* (Oxford: Oxford University Press, 1996), p.114.
69. Devlin, *Price of My Soul*, p.171.
70. *Irish Echo*, 3 May 1969.
71. Devlin, *Price of My Soul*, pp.184–5.
72. See *Washington Post, Times Herald*, 10 February 1971 for an example of Devlin explicitly addressing feminist concerns.
73. Gogarty to George, 18 February 1969, Belfast, PRONI, Frank Gogarty papers, D/3253/1.
74. Ibid.
75. Ibid.
76. Northern Ireland Civil Rights Association, '"We shall overcome": A History of the Struggle for Civil Rights in Northern Ireland, 1968–1978' (Belfast: NICRA, 1978), p.19.
77. Arthur, *People's Democracy*, p.61.
78. McCluskey, *Up off their Knees*, p.132.
79. Interview with Stewart, Belfast, 1 July 2003.
80. Interview with Hope, Belfast, 30 June 2003.
81. Interview with Stewart, Belfast, 1 July 2003.
82. R. Stetler, *The Battle of the Bogside* (London: Sheed & Ward, 1970), p.71.
83. *Violence and Civil Disturbances in Northern Ireland in 1969 (the Scarman Report)* (Belfast: Her Majesty's Stationery Office, 1972).
84. Bardon, *History of Ulster*, p.668.
85. Shannon, *I am of Ireland: Women of the North Speak Out*, pp.46–7.
86. Interview with McCann, Derry, 8 February 2003.
87. McCann, *War and an Irish Town*, p.122.
88. Quoted in J. Levine, *Sisters: The Personal Story of an Irish Feminist* (Dublin: Ward River Press, 1982), p.214.
89. Barricade Bulletin 5, 21 August 1969, Microfilm Collection, Linen Hall Library.
90. Barricade Bulletin 13, 29 August 1969, Microfilm Collection, Linen Hall Library.
91. McCafferty, *Nell*, p.169.
92. Inverted commas are used to denote popular perceptions of the street confrontation from the Catholic point of view. See 'The Protestant invasion theory' in *Scarman Report*.
93. A. Oberschall, *Social Conflict and Social Movements* (Englewood Cliffs, NJ: Prentice-Hall, 1973), p.295.
94. *Scarman Report*.
95. For more on maternalism see G. West and R.L. Blumberg, 'Reconstructing Social Protest from a Feminist Perspective', in G. West and R.L. Blumberg (eds), *Women and Social Protest* (Oxford: Oxford University Press, 1990), p.22.
96. N. McCafferty, *Peggy Deery: A Derry Family at War* (Dublin: Attic Press, 1988), p.10.
97. Interview with Chrissie McAuley, Belfast, 25 June 2003.
98. M. Hill, *Women in Ireland: A Century of Change* (Belfast: Blackstaff Press, 2003), Ch.4.
99. Bardon, *History of Ulster*, p. 671.
100. R. English, *Armed Struggle: The History of the IRA* (London: Macmillan, 2003), p.103.
101. *Irish Press*, 18 August 1969.
102. Ibid.
103. Quoted in Van Voris, *Violence*, p.164.
104. Quoted in ibid., p.166.
105. The title of 'Free State' was discarded in favour of 'Éire' in 1937 and then the Republic of Ireland in 1948, though the 'Free State' moniker still survives in republican vernacular today.
106. Quoted in Dooley, *Black and Green*, p.83.
107. *Irish Times*, 1 September 1969.
108. Dooley, *Black and Green*, p.87.
109. B. McAliskey, 'A Peasant in the Halls of the Great', in Michael Farrell (ed.), *Twenty Years On* (Kerry: Brandon, 1988), p.87.
110. Dooley, *Black and Green*, p.88.
111. S. Davidson, 'Bernadette Devlin: An Irish Revolutionary in Irish America', *Harper's Magazine* (January 1970), pp.78–87.

112. Ibid., p.85.
113. Dooley, *Black and Green*, pp.89–90.
114. Davidson, 'Bernadette Devlin', pp.78–87.
115. *Irish Echo*, 30 August 1969.
116. Quoted in Davidson, 'Bernadette Devlin', p.78.
117. Ibid., p.83.
118. *New York Times*, 3 March 1970.
119. Interview with McCann, Derry, 8 February 2003.
120. Whelan to Gallagher, March 1970, Dublin, NA DFA 2000/5/42.
121. *Daily News*, 9 March 1970.
122. Whelan to Ronan, 14 March 1970, Dublin, NA, DFA, 2000/5/42.
123. Enright to CSJ, CSJ papers, Belfast, PRONI, D/2993.
124. Davidson, 'Bernadette Devlin', p.83.
125. E. McDermott, 'American Militants', *Free Citizen*, 9 (1969), Linen Hall Library Microfilm Collection, Linen Hall Library.
126. Oliver Wright to British representative in Belfast, 24 September 1969, London, National Archives (NA), CJ 3/18.
127. *Hibernia*, 4 November 1969.
128. *Free Citizen*, 13 (n.d.), Belfast, Microfilm Collection, Linen Hall Library.
129. Baxter *et al.*, 'People's Democracy', pp.11–13.
130. Ibid.
131. Oberschall, *Social Conflict and Social Movements*, p.148.
132. *New Statesman*, 24 April 1970.
133. Though this assessment of Devlin may seem to be a patriarchal one, an overwhelming body of evidence suggests that Devlin's political inexperience contributed to a degree of pliability in the early part of her political career.
134. Donal O'Sullivan to H.J. McCann, 4 March 1970, Dublin, NA, DFA, 2001/43/1407.
135. Quoted in Van Voris, *Violence*, p.117.
136. Interview with McCann, Derry, 8 February 2003.
137. C. Harkin, 'Come Back Mrs Pankhurst, We Have not yet Overcome', *Ramparts*, Derry Labour Newssheet (January 1969)
138. Resolutions, 14/15 February 1970, Belfast, Linen Hall Library, Political collection, NICRA papers.
139. *Irish Times*, 2 November 1968.
140. Interview with McCann, Derry, 8 February 2003.
141. West and Blumberg, 'Reconstructing Social Protest from a Feminist Perspective', p.20; Evans, *Personal Politics*.
142. E. Wilson, 'Women in the Community', in Mayo (ed.), *Women in the Community*, p.6.

CHAPTER FIVE

'The Sinn Féin demand': Feminism and Republicanism in the Irish Republic, 1968–73

In January 1976 the political journal *Hibernia* reflected back on popular opinion towards contraceptives between 1971 and 1974 in the Irish Republic. Its first opinion poll in 1971 asked women of childbearing age if the sale of contraceptives should be allowed by law. Forty-one per cent agreed and 55 per cent disagreed (4 per cent had no opinion). Their 1973 poll revealed that 69 per cent of married women between the ages of 16 and 44 wished for a change in the law. In 1974 *Hibernia* replicated the 1971 poll, which resulted in 68.7 per cent of women of childbearing age indicating their support for the legalisation of contraceptives.[1] The Irish government and judiciary, anxious to avoid a confrontation with the Church on this issue, summoned a growing number of family planning clinicians operating openly in Dublin to the courts for selling contraceptives and distributing literature on fertility control. But by 1974 the government could no longer stem the tide of shifting popular opinion; that year the Supreme Court ruled that the use of contraceptives was a matter of marital privacy.

The Family Planning Bill of 1974, and the debate surrounding its introduction, underlined how out of touch many leaders in the Dáil remained. Failing to even hint at how this bill could protect women's rights, debate focused on morality, Catholic teaching and the bill's implications for North–South relations. After much alarmist discussion about it being an effort to 'smash the family',[2] it was defeated 75 to 47, with the Taoiseach, Liam Cosgrave, voting against his own government's bill along with Minister for Education Dick Burke and five Fine Gael backbenchers. Brendan Corish, who wore three hats as Leader of Labour, Tánaiste and Minister for Health, was absent from the Dáil that day. But the government's reluctance to tackle the issue had been obvious long before the 1974 vote. As far back as 1971 Senators Mary Robinson, John Horgan and Trevor West's effort to introduce a bill failed when they were denied a first reading.[3] In fact, it took Irish law makers until 1979 to secure its passage. Even then, the bill that was finally passed focused more on practical restrictions than on rights of autonomy and privacy. This hard-won battle finally gained traction due to the organizing efforts and hard work of the Irish Contraception Action Programme, a coalition of women's groups, trade union interests and family planning organizations.

How did Irish society move from its meek attempts to break social taboos regarding fertility control, deserted wives and equal pay in 1967, to so vocally taking on the Church and Irish patriarchy in 1979? It took a decade of action to broaden social attitudes and mainstream discourse in the Republic through media coverage of street agitation. The establishment of women's pages, first in the *Irish Times* and then in other national newspapers, heralded an increasingly popular acceptance of both second-wave feminism and left-wing activism. It was this connection between women's issues, journalism and activism that created space for the emergence of second-wave feminism in the Republic of Ireland.

CONTEXTUALIZING THE SECOND WAVE

International media coverage of feminist street action originating in America and spreading throughout Europe was an important factor in determining the shape and trajectory of Irish second-wave feminism. Characterized by a multipronged approach, the second wave focused on the development of theory as well as protest tactics in order to make feminist advances into public discourse and eventually into legislation. Hobsbawm cites as a crucial component to the social revolution that took place in the second part of the twentieth century, the 'significant, even revolutionary, changes in women's expectations about themselves and the world's expectations about their place in society'.[4] Specifically in the western world women, aided and educated by a rapidly expanding media, responded to modernizing forces, entered the jobs market, took part in radical politics and engaged in public discourse with increasing numbers.

In November 1969 American feminists, already a diversifying pool of constituent groups, had decided to make a push towards unification. The Congress to Unite Women called on America's 500-odd groups of women's liberationists to articulate their demands. But the Congress did little to unite the groups, and instead it underlined differences between liberal, radical and socialist feminists even more forcefully.[5] Then the National Organization of Women (NOW) called a strike for equality and 50,000 women attended the New York march. In spite of this short-lived unity, factions sprang up throughout the country: the League for Women's Rights argued for marriage and divorce law reform, the National Women's Political Caucus campaigned for the election of women; Native American women, Black women, lesbians and abortion rights activists formed their own groups.

The difficulty the movement encountered regarding the unification of such disparate groups came from how it was originally conceived and launched. American feminism had emerged out of the civil rights and student/anti-war movements and initially it was characterized by its focus on a white/middle-class analysis of the gender regime. It pioneered both liberal feminist theory, which focused on law reform, and radical theory, which while equally rights-based, focused on separatism and sexual oppression. Its emphasis on consciousness-raising, or shared testimonials, and street activism widened the scope of those who were willing to participate, but significant minority groups such as African Americans, Native Americans and lesbians worked towards forging their own paths outside of the mainstream movement. Most famous for its rapid legal gains, the American feminist movement also grabbed headlines with its imaginative street theatre tactics. Overall, the success of the second wave in the United States, as elsewhere, lies in the movement's multilayered approach; where the radical strand broke taboos to get an issue on to the agenda, the liberal strand worked towards legislative re-evaluation of the issue. Likewise, where African-American feminists could forge links with civil rights communities in order to push an issue within a particular community, the white and liberal feminists could play an 'inside game' to get the issue on the radar of the political establishment. Feminism was also able to dovetail with other popular campaigns at the time for many activists – the rights-based groups and the peace movement could all claim a core of feminist constituents. One constituency that had little crossover membership with the feminist movement, however, was comprised of republicans in Irish America.

The available evidence seems to suggest that Irish America, unsurprisingly, steered clear of the feminist movement as a whole. The *Irish Echo* refrained from tackling the issue in any meaningful way, most likely for the same underlying reason it avoided the civil rights movement in America. Generally speaking, members of the Irish-American community were focused on their own integration into America while they worked towards achieving a middle-class aesthetic,[6] which valued conservatism and patriarchy, to the exclusion of feminism and civil rights activism. Most of the group's lobbying and activist power was reserved for Irish-American concerns and for activities that promoted Irish nationalism during this period. Moreover, the gains being made by British feminists at the time rarely extended past the Irish Sea, which eliminated the only other possible area of concern to Irish America – Northern Ireland. This single-minded focus on nationalism served to insulate Irish America from even the mildest interaction with feminism. Its challenge to patriarchy and Catholic doctrine rendered a public acceptance of feminist principles out of the question. Anecdotal accounts, however, suggest that privately Irish-American women were beginning to embrace some aspects of feminism, such as fertility control and career development.

In Britain the 1967 Abortion Act and the 1967 Family Planning Act had widened the scope of women's reproductive rights,[7] the 1969 Divorce Reform Act came into force, Barbara Castle steered her equal pay bill through the Commons in 1970, and Oxford's Ruskin College hosted the first national gathering of the women's movement. The 600-strong conference, careful to avoid the pitfalls of the American experience, defined itself as operating outside of the system, thereby bypassing parliamentary politics and the kind of pressure group tactics in which NOW engaged.[8] Women marched in London and Liverpool for four demands: equal pay, equal education and job opportunities, free contraception and abortion on demand, and free 24-hour nurseries.[9] A major characteristic that differentiated the British women's movement from the American movement is that the former evolved out of the Campaign for Nuclear Disarmament, trade unionism and New Left politics. Consequently, the British movement focused on socialist feminism and class politics in a much more comprehensive way than did most American groups. While some campaigns captured headlines, such as the 1970 Miss World protest, the more comprehensive campaigns centred on working-class women's activism, such as the night cleaners' drive to unionize and the proliferation of women's strikes and industrial disputes. One frustrating element of the progression of feminism in Britain is that public policy victories did not automatically transfer to Northern Ireland. While equal pay legislation was adopted in both London and Belfast in 1970, it took a year of organizing and activism to extend Britain's Sex Discrimination Act to Northern Ireland in 1976. On balance, however, the feminist movement in

Britain during this period accomplished significant gains in both public policy and raising consciousness regarding the gender regime.

The rest of Europe experienced a broadening awareness of feminism in a similar manner. In the early 1970s, having emerged from student politics and anti-war activity, some French feminist groups such as Psych et Po increased their international profile and developed new theoretical frameworks for looking at the gender regime amid a flurry of international acclaim and – indeed it must be noted – a high degree of hostility from other strands of the French feminist movement.[10] When the essay 'Fight for the Liberation of Women' was published, it quickly became the manifesto of a women's movement that was gaining ground. Probably the most memorable actions were the laying of a wreath for the wife of the Unknown Soldier, and the 'I have aborted' campaign, where prominent women signed their names to a newspaper advertisement stating they had procured the illegal procedure.

The Netherlands, Norway, Denmark and Iceland underwent a period of general feminist activity characterized by the proliferation of feminist literature and the formation of groups inspired by the American feminist movement. The women of Denmark and Iceland borrowed the 'Redstocking Movement' title from a New York collective to form their own socialist/feminist groupings, and the women of Norway took a similar course of action.[11] Much of the radical activity in West Germany manifested itself as a challenge to a generation that was perceived to have colluded in Second World War atrocities. Evolving out of the student movement, the most memorable actions were an 'I have aborted' campaign and the 'tomato-throwing incident' where female members of Sozialisticher Deutscher Studentenbund (German Student Union) threw tomatoes at male members who refused to listen to a female delegate's speech.[12] In some southern parts of Europe feminism took more time to develop. Portugal, Spain and Greece were emerging from dictatorial regimes that made it extremely difficult for women's movements to find their feet, though they eventually did.

What we can draw from the European experience is a lesson in relativity. As Lovenduski finds in her study of the development of European feminism, each country's experience of feminism is defined by its particular circumstances:

> In each country in which a woman's emancipation movement appeared, it soon adopted forms and sets of preoccupations and practices which reflected national political life. Patterns of class stratification, religious allegiance, legal arrangements and political

divisions combined to produce a variety of forms and types of women's emancipation movement. International in some of its concerns and universal in some of its demands, the first wave of feminism was, like its 1970s successor, also culturally specific.[13]

One overarching commonality was the second wave's focus on oppositional and extra-parliamentary activity, as Kaplan points out.[14] Many took part in consciousness-raising activities, street theatre and protest marches and rallies precisely because they were outside traditional modes of political expression. Drawn from other anti-authoritarian political movements such as civil rights in the United States, peace action in Britain and republicanism in Ireland, and hearkening back to the first wave, these feminist groups throughout the western world can be characterized by their rapid proliferation and subsequent hiving off into constituent parts. This gave the second wave of the women's movement a multifaceted approach that sought to use street activism to draw attention to prevailing inequalities, to secure legislative reform and, in some cases, to demand radical change.

Linda Connolly argues that Irish historians tend to invest too much in 'modernization theory' in order to explain the second wave of Irish feminism. From her point of view, 'The women's movement is considered an unintended consequence and accidental outcome of the wider phenomenon of new social movements of the 1960s.'[15] She points to first-wave feminism in Ireland and the long history of women's activism as evidenced by groups such as the Irish Housewives Association (IHA) or the Irish Women Citizens Association, to show that women were not 'easily oppressed' or 'exceptionally impressionable'.[16] For her, the modernization theory is an 'insufficient view' due to its disregard for a wider historical context.[17] Though this theory does help explain some aspects of the trajectory of feminism in this period, her objections to it are well founded. Locating this study in a chronological time frame is critical to grasping the full nature and provenance of this type of activism and its demands. Equally as important is setting Irish feminism in its geopolitical context, internationally and island-wide.

POLICY CHANGE IN IRELAND

One significant feature of Irish life in the early 1970s was the rapid integration of a women's equality agenda in public policy circles. Probably one of the more memorable representations of the changing face of policy debate is the arrival in 1969 of a young Mary Burke (soon to become Robinson), who was elected to the Seanad as an Independent. One of her aims was to promote secularism among state institutions with the goal of easing North–South tension. A dynamic figure pushing for the reformation of women's legislation and family issues, her arrival on the political scene marked the emergence of a feminist voice in Irish parliamentary politics in this period.

Another important development in the move towards the promotion of women's equality was Fianna Fáil's acquiescence to pressure from the women's ad hoc group established to lobby for the creation of a Commission on the Status of Women (CSW). In 1970 Taoiseach Jack Lynch formally established this commission to look into the implementation of an equal pay policy. He was primarily responding to growing pressure from the European Economic Community (EEC) to fall into line with the equal pay provision of the Treaty of Rome.[18] Predictably, during equal pay discussions, the Department of Finance emphasized the expense of the adoption of such a policy.[19] But the EEC directive was unequivocal and increasingly the Irish government realized that by failing to act, it would open itself up to litigation and industrial disputes with trade unions and other groups, which could become just as costly, if not more so.[20] The trade union movement, however, had not yet shaken itself into contemplation of a new EEC gender regime. At the 1969 Trade Union Congress (TUC) several women's groups within the movement argued unsuccessfully for equal pay and equal increases in the annual wage round. At that point they were still only earning approximately 56 per cent of what their male counterparts earned.[21] This is unsurprising in light of the fact that shortly thereafter the Commission on the Status of Women reported only seven female full-time officials were engaged in negotiating wages and conditions of employment out of a total of 230 officials.[22]

In early 1970 Thekla Beere, chairman of the Commission on the Status of Women, set out on a fact-finding mission to establish the position of women in the workforce throughout Europe.[23] Of the countries surveyed, Germany and France seemed to be approaching the highest level of equal pay. In both cases equal pay legislation had been instituted and women were free to go through labour courts to enforce it. A June 1970 report by the European Commission supported the Commission on the Status of Women's survey by indicating that 'on the whole, the gaps between the average hourly earnings of men and women [were] gradually diminishing, but [were] still considerable in all the countries'.[24]

Though there was much hand-wringing within the Department of

Finance and within the government in general over the introduction of equal pay measures, it was becoming politically untenable to continue to skirt the issue. Eileen Connolly makes the point that because Fianna Fáil had softened their opposition to equal pay in the run-up to the 1969 general election, thereafter Foreign Affairs Minister, Patrick Hillery, would find it increasingly difficult to back-pedal in the Dáil.[25] In fact, by November 1969 Charles Haughey, Minister of Finance, declared in the Dáil that the introduction of equal pay was of 'fundamental importance for the economy generally'.[26] During negotiations with the EEC, Hillery would still express difficulty with an immediate implementation, but the message was unmistakable, equal pay was on its way: 'My government are prepared to accept the principle of equal pay for the same work as between men and women but we wish to discuss in the course of negotiations the question of suitable transitional measures.'[27]

In 1971 the Commission on the Status of Women submitted an interim report on the adoption of equal pay for work of equal value. The report recommended the implementation of equal pay legislation and it gave suggestions on how the government could enforce equal pay laws. The CSW suggested that equal pay could be achieved by phasing in the policy over a five-year period. Their final report in 1972 recommended the removal of the marriage bar and the introduction of various pieces of legislation that would tackle sex discrimination in employment. The main victory of the report was that it called into question discriminatory legislation that had been progressively enacted for more than fifty years and crucially, it addressed grievances regarding equal opportunity that had been voiced by different women's groups for just as long. After the publication of the report, the CSW recommended the establishment of a more permanent body, the Council for the Status of Women, which would monitor the implementation of the recommendations. The government's acquiescence to this request indicated that it did not see the advancement of a women's equality agenda ending with the disbandment of the Commission.

The changes in government policy in attempting to come to terms with women in the workforce and the introduction of social welfare legislation, such as allowances for deserted wives, prisoners' wives and unmarried mothers, which also came through during this period, allowed the state to be seen as being responsive to grievances. But the adoption of equal pay was by far the government's biggest challenge in this area. That it successfully met this challenge and followed it up by laying the groundwork for a women's status monitoring body helped to short circuit much of the emerging liberal feminist discourse. Though some legislation, such as divorce, was still a long way off, much was gained in terms of public policy for the second wave during this period. But another force that was not as satisfied with reformism began to coalesce within the radical political scene. Catherine MacAonghusa was one of the first in Ireland to record the emergence of this new force and to try to articulate why some women were drawn to it in an Irish context:

> In recent months our television screens have repeatedly shown pictures of marchers and demonstrations for civil rights, for housing improvement, for American withdrawal from Vietnam, for student power ... And in all these demonstrations a goodly proportion of these participants have belonged to what used to be called the weaker sex ... I frankly cannot explain why it should be that women play such a prominent part in revolutionary politics yet remain in a sort of background 'purdah' in our political parties ... When women are young and at the height of their capabilities many of them have young children and find it difficult to get out ... Where the demonstrations and marches succeed in attracting women so much more than do the political parties may well be in the fact that their objectives are clearer, seemingly simpler, and often nearer to the day-to-day life of women.[28]

MacAonghusa's observation gets to the heart of this study by calling attention to the incongruence of women's willingness to engage the government outside of government buildings in radical protest politics and their low numbers in parliamentary politics. Many interviewees for this study build on MacAonghusa's point by adding that scheduling considerations were also critical in determining their own level of political activity. They observed that attending a march or two was much easier to schedule around family commitments than taking on a full-time career in the traditional political arena. The one hopeful note in MacAonghusa's letter is when she points out that the surge in women's participation has contributed towards their repositioning in society ('what used to be called the weaker sex').

RADICAL POLITICS

Increasing women's roles in the Dáil, however critical to repositioning women in Irish society, did not capture the political imagination in the same way as elements of radical politics did. While much of the attention of republicans and left-wing radicals was focused on the unfolding situation in the North, there were some instances of radical action in Dublin. Probably one of the more far-reaching movements was what is now known as the 'Gentle Revolution' at University College Dublin (UCD) and the National College of Art and Design. In the late 1960s student demands, particularly in France and Italy, had an impact on Irish notions of educational opportunities. At UCD, Ireland's most populous university, students protested for a reform of the curriculum, the facilities and the administration of the institution by taking over administration offices, which prompted the provost to issue a reform package almost immediately.[29] Unsurprisingly, Trinity students were less fervent; the few radicals in the university banded together to form a Maoist collective, which eventually purged itself into oblivion, having accomplished little other than a modest academic reform of the assessment system.

On a much smaller scale than other radical political groupings, student activism in Dublin engaged women in a similar way as did the events in Northern Ireland in 1969, but because the UCD administration short-circuited demands by quickly announcing a reform plan, student protest would never approach the kind of engagement the PD could draw due its interaction with the emerging sectarian conflict. Goulding's republican movement did try to connect with the few student radicals in Dublin, but this link was tenuous at best. The only issue around which students rallied with republicans in any numbers was housing – an issue upon which a significant proportion of Dubliners could agree. The republican movement's failure to attract students is most likely the result of the disorganization produced by a power struggle within republicanism and events in the North.

Responses to the rapidly unravelling situation in the North were fast and furious among republican traditionalists, who blamed themselves for failing to protect an exposed Catholic community throughout the summer's disturbances. During the autumn two distinct camps emerged within the movement: the pro-Goulding 'Officials' and the more traditionalist 'Provisionals'. The Gouldingites, who sought to maintain the left-wing alliances and broad-based agitation, proposed an abandonment of political abstentionism. Those who followed Ruarí Ó Brádaigh and Seán MacStiofáin and who called themselves Provisional Sinn Féin and the Provisional IRA were suspicious of left-wing political agitation, unwilling to end the policy of abstention and were more focused on the armed wing of the movement. The December 1969 General Army Convention of the IRA and the January 1970 Sinn

Féin Ard Fheis confirmed the split and set each group on a recruitment drive.

Throughout this period the Officials and people associated with the Officials cultivated their presence in various organizations in order to gain an increased activist profile and to boost recruitment.[30] Máirín de Burca emerged in the late 1960s as a strong force within Official Sinn Féin policy formulation. As discussed in Chapter 3, her rapid ascent to the secretaryship of the Ard Comhairle reflected the left-wing aspirations of the Official movement. De Burca later remarked that her non-membership in the IRA also rendered her the safest spokesperson for the group.[31] In addition to her work with Official Sinn Féin, she was active in the Irish Voice on Vietnam, the Anti-Apartheid movement and the Dublin Housing Action Committee. Frances Gardiner points out that for Irish women political activism was often at variance with the traditional role of women-as-homemaker as outlined by the constitution, because it was seen as a distraction from home duties.[32] De Burca's devotion to political activism took precedence over any domestic goals she may have had, and her lack of home-based commitments became an advantage.

Through her public speeches and letters to the media she consistently emphasized working-class unification and broad-based left-wing action. Her high visibility and strong oratory gave her perhaps a more respected voice in shaping Official republican day-to-day policy in terms of left-wing politics. Reflecting predictable left-wing scepticism of Ireland's entry into the EEC, Official Sinn Féin sought to combat a free trade area by forging links with radicals throughout Europe.[33] De Burca looked to forming links beyond the EU as well: on 25 September 1970 *Hibernia* reported that she had recently been to Amman to meet with a group of Arab revolutionaries and that the Officials had written to the members of the American Black Panther Party. A study of the available government records indicates that the Irish and British governments were not particularly concerned about de Burca or her efforts at forging international links for the Officials. In a few years de Burca would see her efforts at forging those kinds of links culminate in a speaking tour of the United States, at which point the American government would become increasingly more interested in her activities.[34] But overall, the links de Burca helped to foster for the Officials earned the occasional bit of press coverage and little else for two main reasons: these movements had little in terms of resources to share; and often they agreed or at least could express solidarity on theoretical issues, but little else.

A cornerstone of de Burca's activism lay in her opposition to American foreign policy; it allowed her to make connections with other left-wing activists outside of the republican movement, which in turn gave her the opportunity to take part in working for an issue that had more mainstream acceptance than Official republicanism enjoyed. De Burca's association with people such as pacifist Máire Woods, who would soon embark on what seemed to be an incongruous twenty-year relationship with Cathal Goulding, initially expanded de Burca's audience to include a significant number of Irish people who rejected American intervention in Vietnam but equally rejected paramilitarism. In this period de Burca engaged in two lively swipes at American foreign policy. When President Nixon visited Ireland in November 1970 she was arrested with some other protesters for throwing eggs at his motorcade. She was found guilty and fined £2 for throwing a missile. The sympathetic judge made sarcastic remarks about the term 'motorcade' and acknowledged their right to protest. That and the lenient sentence prompted an American embassy official to write back to the US State Department: 'These extraordinarily lenient sentences typify not only permissiveness with which dangerous left-wing agitators in Ireland are being encouraged but also toleration of hostile acts against US in this country which the embassy badly needs the means to combat.'[35] The second protest was a bit more forceful and was not treated with the same leniency. In April 1971 de Burca led ten people to the American embassy with placards that read 'Get out of Indo-China'. When they arrived at the door of the closed embassy, they hurled cow's blood on to the steps, lowered the flag and set it on fire. De Burca and fellow activist Marie McMahon received three-month jail sentences for their roles in the protest.

Probably what de Burca is most well-known for is her leadership along with others of the Dublin Housing Action Committee. By the early 1970s the group was reaching its peak in terms of publicity, both through in-house *United Irishman* coverage of the protests and through mainstream media attention. Its group squats and scuffles with police consistently drew headlines and provoked debates about the housing situation in Dublin. Taking a cue from housing campaigns in Britain, the DHAC began to rely less on street protest and more on direct action squatting, as indicated by their leadership of an extended squat in a Hume Street building that was to be demolished and sold to business developers. Though it sustained criticism from former members for eschewing its radical roots in favour of providing social services for the city's homeless, it got an injection of support with the arrival of the Prohibition of Forcible Entry Bill in 1971, which allowed for the arrest of squatters and groups facilitating squatting. In August of that year Máirín de Burca was sent to jail for refusing to name squatters in a house on Gardiner Street and also that year she and Mary Anderson were arrested while protesting the bill in front of the Dáil. This was probably one of the most far-reaching and significant of de Burca and Anderson's protests; Mary Robinson successfully argued on their behalf that the Juries Act of 1927 was unconstitutional because any all-male, property-owning jury selected for their trial would not constitute a jury of their peers. Though this case ground on for a few years, eventually it succeeded in striking a far-reaching blow for equality legislation by finding for de Burca and Anderson.

Women's activism was beginning to make inroads, but not without difficulty. Another housing campaigner, Hilary Boyle, remarked on the difficulty women activists faced in this period by writing that in Ireland there was a 'deeply entrenched notion among almost all men, and a great many women too that any woman who fights for human rights promptly ceases to be a Helen and becomes a harpy'.[36] Boyle, an unlikely street activist, used her prominence as an heiress to raise funds for the DHAC and raise awareness of the issue through her indefatigable letter-writing skills. By calling attention to women's sometimes unwelcome notoriety in the activist scene, Boyle was able to challenge the gender regime, which was only now beginning to be affected by women's equal participation and leadership of street campaigns.

Frances Gardiner points to 1969 as a year when political interest among Irish women began to increase.[37] This could be due to a variety of reasons, including increasing educational achievement, increasing numbers of women entering the workforce, the unfolding situation in Northern Ireland and an increased visibility of female political activists throughout the world. Gardiner concludes her study of Irish women's political interest by observing that 'much of women's political participation has been through pressure group activity ... and not mainstream powerful interest organizations'.[38] This statement supports Catherine MacAonghusa's contemporary observations and much of the research into women's interest in informal, ad hoc and radical politics conducted by Randall[39] and Lovenduski.[40] The pressure group activity fed into an emergent women-centred consciousness. As Irish women began to take part in this kind of street action, a new equality agenda emerged.

IRISH WOMEN'S LIBERATION MOVEMENT

If progress was being made for women by liberal feminists who concentrated on agitating for equality legislation by lobbying and letter-writing, why then, did there need to be a women's liberation movement in Ireland? The simple answer is age and education. Young women who began to think about women's liberation as a logical extension of radical politics saw the older group of CSW women as being useful to the advancement of a women's agenda, but unable to achieve a widespread programme of fundamental changes. The way the CSW had gone about achieving change – lobbying, persuading, letter-writing, cajoling – seemed too collaborationist or reformist for women of the younger generation. Mary Maher, one of the founder members of the Irish Women's Liberation Movement, later explained: 'Where we were at, we needed a dramatic gesture. I think we automatically understood that we were not the previous generation ... and we had to draw attention ... We were not content to be a [group like the] Widows Association. We wanted to make a big splash to say "Terrible things are happening and we wish them not to happen".'[41] Ailbhe Smyth observed the same thing. From her point of view the CSW was made up of women who were active in public life, 'but certainly not noted for their radicalism'. The women's liberation movement, on the other hand, was 'specifically – and self-consciously – radical and leftist, and thus distinguished itself carefully from the reformist "Women's Rights" feminism of the earlier group'.[42]

The idea for forming a women's liberation group arose over a cup of tea at Bewley's. The original group of women, who were generally connected to left-wing political action and/or republicanism – Mary Maher, Máirín de Burca, Margaret Gaj, Máirín Johnston, Máire Woods – decided to meet with some American women de Burca knew to further explore the issue. The group held their first meeting on 13 October 1970[43] at Maher's home because, according to another women's liberation activist – June Levine – Maher could not secure adequate childcare.[44] Trivial as it may sound, this observation underscores the reality of women's activism. A prime factor that deterred women from political activism was the inescapability of domestic commitments associated with womanhood, as many of the interviewees for this study indicate. Those who did participate fell into three categories: either they had resources to divert to childcare, as did Brigid Hogan O'Higgins, TD; they were past their childbearing years, as many within the CSW leadership were; or they had few domestic commitments, as did Máirín de Burca. Few accounts of the Irish women's movement adequately address the problem of child-rearing and activism most likely because a significant portion of the leadership of the movement, with notable exceptions like Maher and Levine, lacked children. But the very fact that the first meeting took place in Maher's home is telling in terms of the aims and nature of this nascent group – its fluid boundaries and changeable meeting sites meant that it could adapt to the complexities of women's lives.

It was this first meeting that underscored for some activists the need for a women's liberation group in Ireland; the hugely divergent circumstances in which American and Irish women found themselves startled some of the participants.[45] Some in the founders group observed that women in America already had access to contraception and were now demanding abortion rights, which went far beyond what the Irish activists knew they could feasibly work towards. In their minds contraception was the main issue.[46] Generally, however, access to an international perspective helped to mould and inform the structure and goals of the group. Mary Maher had come to Ireland from Chicago in 1965. Having developed an awareness of social justice during the early part of the American civil rights movement, Maher found integrating into Irish life to be a profound learning process. In America she was up on all of the latest feminist theory. But Betty Friedan, Sheila Rowbotham and Gloria Steinem did not prepare her for the complexity of women's roles in Ireland. She explained:

> There would have been bars that didn't allow women. Then another part of [the situation] was that women were taking part in society [through] the IHA ... they were an incredibly vociferous organization about prices and things like that ... These women weren't afraid to speak out but they did have to get through the 'marriage state' before they were able to [get organized] ... I suppose in most ways I would have found it more oppressive but I was often surprised at the way women in middle age were quite forthright.[47]

Another journalist who was emerging as a leading light of the women's liberation group was Mary Kenny. When she came back to Ireland from working at London's *Evening Standard* in 1969 she found women's position to be 'less developed' than their position in other European countries.[48] Kenny explained what she saw as the major contributing factor to this type of gender regime: 'Neutrality in WWII greatly held women back from modernization. Many social changes which had occurred in the UK were directly because of the war.'[49] Other factors such as religion, economics and demography, which Kenny covers in greater detail in her book *Goodbye to Catholic Ireland*, also had a profound impact on the retention of such institutionalized inequalities.

Table 1 Founders of the Irish Women's Liberation Movement with occupation
and/or political identification*

Attendees of the meeting at Bewley's, Westmoreland Street, Dublin in 1970	
Máirín De Burca	Joint secretary of Official Sinn Féin, Dublin Housing Action Committee, later a journalist
Margaret Gaj	Scottish restaurateur
Máirín Johnston	Labour party member
Mary Maher	Women's page editor of the *Irish Times*
Máire Woods	Doctor, anti-Vietnam activist, later instrumental in the Sexual Assault Treatment Unit at Dublin's Rotunda Hospital

Members who joined soon thereafter to help form the Founders' Group	
Mary Anderson	*Irish Independent* reporter
Eavan Boland	Poet
Hilary Boyle	Journalist, broadcaster, oldest member in her late 60s, Dublin Housing Action Committee
Mary Earls	Owner of a Kilkenny bookshop
Nuala Fennell	Freelance journalist, later helped found AIM and later Fine Gael Minister of State for Women's Affairs and Family Law
Rosemary Humphries (sister of Bernadette Quinn)	Nurse
Mary Kenny	Women's page editor of the *Irish Press*
June Levine	Editor of the *Irish Women's Journal* and later a researcher for RTÉ
Nell McCafferty	*Irish Times* reporter from Derry
Mary McCutcheon	Women's page editor of the *Irish Independent*
Marie McMahon	Owner of a typesetting business
Fionnuala O'Connor	Teacher from Lisburn, later a journalist
Eimer Philbin Bowman	Psychologist
Bernadette Quinn (sister of Rosemary Humphries)	Pharmacist and writer, later helped found AIM
Mary Sheerin	Secretary and short story writer
Inez Sweetman (Sister of Rosita Sweetman)	
Rosita Sweetman (Sister of Inez Sweetman)	Writer

* Information sourced from J. Levine, 'The Women's Movement in the Republic of Ireland: 1968–1980: Introduction', in A. Bourke, S. Kilfeather, M. Luddy, M. MacCurtain, G. Meaney, M. Ní Dhonnchadha, M. O'Dowd and C. Wills (eds), *The Field Day Anthology of Irish Writing: Irish Women's Writing and Traditions*, vol.5 (Cork: Field Day, 2002) pp.179–80.

The fact that many of the group's founders were socialists and journalists is important in explaining the birth of this international trend
in Ireland.[50] Their profession and experiences as activists trained them
to track social and political developments throughout the world, to

relate them to the situation in Ireland, and to organize around those issues. In terms of party affiliation, most of the founders considered themselves independent socialists, communists, Official republicans or members of the Labour Party. The tiny group of communists based in Dublin was suspicious of feminism but had little power to restrict the activities of its handful of members, while the Officials were slowly warming to the idea of feminism due to de Burca's support for both causes. The development of women's pages in the national press further enabled these women to combine their journalism with an articulation of a women's agenda. What was also critical to their development was that the group could cover or commission coverage on their own events. Jo Freeman points out that many of the founder members of the National Organization for Women in America were also journalists or had worked with the media. This connection, Freeman writes, initially allowed the group to give the impression that it was larger than its actual size.[51] The relationship between the newspapers and Irish feminists has been described as 'almost collusion ... all we had to do was pick up the phone and we got publicity'.[52] Smyth makes the point that despite Irish conservatism and parochialism, the Irish women's liberation group was able to 'develop a public profile more rapidly and effectively than in many other European countries'.[53]

Some of the increased awareness came from outside of the group and took the form of letters to the editor of different newspapers and magazines. A Mrs E. Quinn of Westport wrote a letter to *Woman's Way*, a heretofore socially conservative magazine that began to dedicate an increasing amount of space to covering the growth of the second wave of feminism. Unwittingly Quinn predicted the formation of an Irish women's movement just as it was getting underway in Dublin:

> American housewives have flaunted the conventions and set themselves up as feminists. They are certainly hollering now and when Americans holler they can be heard even on this side of the Atlantic. Instead of women measuring up to a man, man must now measure up to women. The war of the sexes is on and instead of wondering what they can do for their country, American men will now have to start wondering what they can do to keep the love and respect of their wives who don't intend to vegetate, even in luxury. How long will it be until the rest of the world follows suit? This could be contagious.[54]

But not all of Ireland was ready for a women's movement. Some of the letters, like the above, that appeared with increasing frequency provoked irritated responses from those who were content with their role in Irish society.[55] The link with American feminism was very much part of the Irish experience, despite the very different gender regimes of each country. One activist remarked that because Mary Kenny and Mary Anderson had been 'very much backwards and forwards to the States', they were able to suggest American consciousness-raising exercises and bring other ideas of organizing back with them.[56] Mary Maher recalled how the American feminists at the first meeting approached the group with a clearly thought-out plan of how to establish a movement in Ireland.[57] Their plan was not so easily transferable, however. According to de Burca: 'We had to follow our own path because we couldn't go the total American way' by embracing issues like abortion rights.[58]

Curiously there were few links if any with British feminists. De Burca and Maher could not explain why so few connections were made between the Irish and British groups. Maher put it down to an 'odd disjointedness' between the groups, and explained that very early on the British groups turned towards radical separatist feminism, which did not surface in Ireland until later in the movement.[59] Mary Kenny hinted at a more overarching reluctance to associate with British feminists: 'There was always an odd hostility towards Britain.' Given that most of the founders group came from a leftist political tradition and that much of the British movement was based in socialist politics, one might expect the relationship to be closer. Most likely, the 'odd disjointedness' between the Irish and British movements reflected an historic distrust, if not a more pronounced association with Irish republicanism among some within the leadership.

After the initial meetings with the American feminists, the group began to investigate women's legal status in the Republic of Ireland. Over the next few months they held more meetings, invited more women and discussed their research. Their findings shocked them: legally, deserted wives had to admit their husbands to the home upon his return, whereas a woman who left the home had no rights; husbands could legally determine the amount of money to give to their wives each week; a husband had the right to choose how his child was educated; and he had the right to register a child on his passport – the mother had no such right. They discussed at their meetings the issue of equal pay when one of the women found that for every 26p a woman made at her job, a man made 47p and that less than 1 per cent of women workers in Ireland were in the higher professions.[60] By early 1971 the group decided to publish its research in a pamphlet called

Chains or Change? The civil wrongs of Irish women. Marie McMahon
was able to publish the pamphlet from her typesetting business in Baggot
Street. The pamphlet also articulated six demands:

One family, one house
Equal rights in law
Equal pay, removal of the marriage bar
Justice for widows, deserted wives and unmarried mothers
Equal education opportunities
Contraception[61]

While these demands might seem tame by today's standards, at the
time they were considered 'radical, challenging and deeply subversive
of the status quo'.[62] Also, they reflected the specific Irish context out
of which they grew. Even though demands for equal pay, equal treatment under the law, equal education opportunities and contraception
shared common threads with the European and American demands,[63] demands for the removal of the marriage bar, for 'one family,
one house', and for justice for widows, deserted wives and unmarried
mothers were unique. These 'Irish' demands reflected the by now
anomalous constitutional aspiration of the woman-as-homemaker as
well as the housing crisis in Dublin. The 7,000 copies of the pamphlet
they distributed did not cause an immediate sensation; its effect was
a slow burn.[64] It must be said that some people were critical of its
demands on the grounds of morality as well as the inclusion of what
was seen to be a Sinn Féin demand of 'one family, one house', considering Sinn Féin's work with the Dublin Housing Action Committee.

The 'one family, one house' demand had been difficult to get into
the demand list from the beginning, according to de Burca.[65] It was
Marry Kenny and Nuala Fennell, a woman who later went on to
become a Fine Gael TD and junior minister, who articulated strong
opposition to the demand, arguing that its inclusion would put
conservative women off the movement. From their point of view the
best strategy was to keep the aims as broad-based as possible in order
to keep as many women together as possible. De Burca, Maher and
others countered with a persuasive argument that equality would mean
very little to women if they had no home and since they were still very
much tied to the home, bad housing affected them more.[66] Maher knew
the issue was explosive but was determined to address what she saw as
the biggest issue of the day.[67] In the end their arguments swayed the
group and the pamphlets went out with the 'Sinn Féin demand' as part
of the list. But the resentment generated by the debate surrounding it

would remain beneath the surface of relations among the group of founders.

On 6 March 1971 some of the group were invited to take part in Gay Byrne's 'Late Late Show'. Before they actually stopped to think through their long-term strategy they had jumped at a chance of launching the movement in a nationwide forum. On the night of the broadcast the founders' group took seats in the audience armed with facts and prepared questions. The panel they chose consisted of Mary Robinson, who while not a member of the group, pointed out the inequalities women faced in the judicial system; Mary Cullen, who as an historian discussed working mothers; Lelia Doolan, who as one of the only female television producers in the Irish Republic talked about women's education and social conditions; Máirín Johnston, who dealt with discrimination in the workplace; and Nell McCafferty, who spoke about deserted wives, single mothers and widows (lesbianism was still completely off the charts of Irish discourse at this point).[68] This savvy manipulation of the media by packing the audience with members who could ask leading questions underscores the group's sophistication and experience with the media. The show went according to schedule, with the prearranged questions being asked at the proper intervals. But regardless of how well planned the show might have been, Garret FitzGerald, a Fine Gael TD, disrupted it by appearing on the stage halfway through in an attempt to enter into the debate. The show then degenerated into a free-for-all.

This incident bears out the saying that even bad press is good press. After the show *Chains or Change?* was taken up and reviewed by the national press and the Irish Women's Liberation Movement was catapulted into the limelight. The founders' group was thrilled but totally unprepared. Levine later wrote: 'Like it or not, and some did not, we *were* women's liberation.'[69] A few years after this Catherine Rose interviewed some of the founder members about the night. Mary Maher said that because of the show the movement got 'too big, too fast'; Mary Anderson thought they might have been able to keep things together if they had more structure; and Máirín de Burca thought they should have waited to go public until they had decided what kind of movement they wanted.[70] An indication of just how fast the group grew is attendance figures for the first general meeting in Dublin's Mansion House on 14 April 1971. Most expected 300, but when 1,500 people came the organizers were shocked.[71] The meeting was cathartic for some of the participants, who for the first time felt that their inferior status within the gender regime was being addressed.[72] But Maher,

Anderson and de Burca were all correct; the founders' group had gone public too fast to control the group's development.

At the meeting twenty-eight branches were established in Dublin alone and some of the founders' group went to local branch meetings to help organize them. One of these women remembered the challenges this posed:

> We were all sent out to all the new branches to get them to accept the six point plan. This was quite difficult ... for example, the notion of one family, one house. I remember having a very difficult time in Donnybrook trying to get this through because they weren't into the social aspect of it, they didn't want to get into left-wing politics. They just wanted contraceptives and equal rights. But we got it through in the end – I don't think there was any branch that did not accept the six point programme.[73]

It was at the early meetings of the founders' group that the 'one family, one house' demand became a sticking point that divided participants into different camps according to class consciousness. Many who opposed the demand felt that it would push them into the service of existing groups such as Official Sinn Féin and the Dublin Housing Action Committee. But the socialists and republicans saw a necessary interaction between women's liberation and left-wing politics, and the more the demand was opposed, the more committed they became. Women's identification with the home in the constitution made it nearly impossible to oppose those who supported the demand in debate. De Burca and her supporters argued that there were dual systems of oppression that fed off each other and collaborated to keep a middle-class patriarchy in power. This early application of dual systems theory, as pioneered by Zillah Eisenstein in 1981 and developed by others including Sylvia Walby in 1990, highlights the kind of a fusion of left-wing politics and women's politics that many socialist feminists were just beginning to employ at this time.[74] This fusion of the two political outlooks can best be illustrated through an exchange between two of the founder members, where June Levine told Máirín de Burca that there were accusations that pressing for the 'one family, one home' demand was involving the group in 'politics and revolution'. De Burca told Levine: 'We are involved in politics. We're trying to change the things that affect people's lives. That's as political and revolutionary as you can get. What else do you think we're at?'[75] This exchange reveals that some founder members did not consider women's liberation to be political, nor did some see the same clear links between socialism and feminism that de Burca saw. At the heart of this exchange is a fundamental lack of consensus about politics, power and oppression, which would soon prove to be the downfall of the budding Dublin-based movement.

Dublin, however, was not the only city that experienced the women's movement in the Republic of Ireland in this period. The Markievicz Women's Movement, based out of University College Cork, included Judy Barry, Ann Madigan, Margaret Dillon, Fionnuala Lee, Mary Shaw, Katy O'Connor and Nuala O'Donovan. Named after Constance Markievicz, a senior figure in James Connolly's left-wing Citizen Army during the Easter Rising of 1916, this small group focused on debate and discussion documents. They covered sex-based discrimination in Cork, the evolution of the family unit, divorce and Church doctrine in their newsletters.[76] With its republican and socialist connotations, the name of this group further illustrates how important historical context can be to developing movements. The Markievicz Women's Movement held seminars about women's rights, started study groups, protested the Miss University College Cork contest and wrote to the Pope deploring his refusal to accept Elizabeth Müller as a diplomat because of her sex.[77]

This group is interesting as an example of second-wave feminism that had no overt links to other strains of radical politics, but which evoked such links through its name. Why, then, have so few heard about it? Its focused campaigns, its position outside of Dublin and its lack of contacts within the media ensured that it would remain in obscurity. Moreover, student-based movements tend to suffer at the hands of yearly commencement ceremonies and have difficulty sustaining drawn-out campaigns, which was the case with the Markievicz Women's Movement. Perhaps the most convincing reason why the group did not make more of an historical impression was that it failed to adequately address what many in the Dublin group saw as the main issue: contraception. What the Dublin group was more able to do, as a group of political activists and journalists, was to track international trends, apply them to the Irish situation and publicize their conclusions. This research by the Dublin group led them to the conclusion that the American movement's call for an equal rights amendment and the British movement's call for women's workplace rights were unifying campaigns upon which most women could agree. In Ireland the right to contraception could be that campaign. By failing to tackle contraceptives and publicize themselves effectively, the Cork group lost an opportunity to launch itself as a broader movement and became redundant in the face of such a dynamic movement coming out of Dublin.

By the early 1970s various camps, including conservative groups, were arguing for legislation on the topic of contraception. The Fianna Fáil government's reluctance to open debate on the issue had served to alienate both nascent pro- and anti-contraceptive rights camps. Moreover, the loosening of international laws regarding the procurement of contraceptives combined with international activism around women's independence and family law reform highlighted the Republic's increasingly anomalous stance on contraceptives in northern Europe. Though other strongly Catholic states such as Spain and Portugal shared similar prohibitions to the availability of contraceptive devices, their history of anti-democratic legislation tends to offset them as suitable comparisons. Eileen Connolly points out:

> Ireland's unique political history, which included a nineteenth century experience of colonialism and religious repression, resulted in an identification of Catholicism being embedded in its macro political culture as part of its definition of Irishness. This has given adherence to Catholic teaching a strong and more central role in the definition of the state than is the case for other European Catholic states.[78]

As explained in Chapter 3, the Pope's 1967 encyclical *Humanae Vitae* prompted an international wave of debate about the relevance of Church teaching to modern life. These debates, coupled with estimates of increasing contraceptive use in Ireland, revealed a country at odds with itself regarding the role of religion, culture, the law and the gender regime.

The opening of Máire Mullarney's Dublin-based family planning clinic in 1969, which circumvented the law regarding the sale of contraceptives by asking for donations, underlined a growing demand for such services. Much of the debate in the Republic of Ireland came to a head in 1971, when Mary Robinson's first attempt at moving a bill to legalize the importation of contraceptives through the Seanad failed. Robinson argued that this bill was necessary now that there were two family clinics in Dublin claiming to have seen 30,000 clients in 1971 alone.[79] Though this initial attempt was defeated, it signalled a growing movement against the prevailing legislation. Also at that time, despite his party's failure to countenance such an argument in the Dáil itself, Taoiseach Jack Lynch indicated that changes in the law regarding contraception were being considered. But it was not a response to the changing position of women in the state, or Robinson's activities in the Seanad, rather it was a gesture to Northern Protestants. The legalization of contraceptives 'would go a long way towards helping the reunification of Ireland', Lynch told a New York audience on his annual Saint Patrick's Day trip.[80] This provoked bitter protests from Dublin's Archbishop McQuaid, who fired back in a 28 March pastoral that 'Any contraceptive act is always wrong in itself. To speak, then, in this context, of a right to contraception, on the part of the individual, be he Christian or atheist, or on the part of a minority or of a majority, is to speak of a right that cannot even exist.'[81] It is telling that even in this context the archbishop chose male pronouns.

This response from McQuaid could have been anticipated judging from his public statements on the papal encyclical regarding this issue. In fact, the archbishop's response was the primary concern of the Fianna Fáil government. During this period, in spring 1971 Justice Minister Des O'Malley requested that the Irish diplomatic corps submit reports on the status of contraceptive laws in their respective countries and the Church's reaction to the laws.

The information in Table 2 reveals that the Minister for Justice was interested in how the introduction of contraceptives impacted on Church–state relations. A supplementary note attached to the memorandum confirms this concern: 'The Catholic Bishops are not known to have opposed either the state of the law or the laxity in enforcement in any of these countries.'[82] Judging from McQuaid's March pastoral, the hierarchy's reactions to any change in the importation laws would not be as placid as had been the case in the countries listed above, and the Irish government knew this.

The priorities of many in Ireland, however, were already moving towards the acceptance of contraceptive devices. *Hibernia* ran a March editorial arguing that the place for this debate was in the mind of each citizen. A few days later *This Week* dedicated its cover story to the changing perception of the issue of contraception. The Labour Party supported a secularization of the legislation by deciding to vote in favour of legalizing contraceptives at its Galway Conference.[83] By June only 63 per cent of the people polled by *This Week* supported keeping the legislation as it was, which meant that a significant amount of the country was warming to the possibility of a change in the legislation.[84] Debate raged on in the media, with both sides well represented, and in

Table 2
Information on contraceptives gathered by Minister for Justice from Irish Embassies, 1971*

Country	Per cent Catholic	Availability	Hierarchal Response
Canada	4	Before 1968/69 sale and advertising banned but importation not banned. Now relatively easy to obtain from doctors or pharmacies.	Bishops said in 1966 that a ban on information about contraception would be wrong.
Australia And New Zealand	Less than 20	No legislative ban, it is a matter for each state. Only pharmacists can sell contraceptives. But they may not advertise or display contraceptives. The pill available on prescription.	Bishops have not taken a position.
Italy	Predominantly Catholic	Most devices available. The pill available on prescription.	Information on attitude of Catholic Church unavailable.
Spain	Predominantly Catholic	Pill only available on prescription for health reasons. Everything else prohibited but tolerated.	Catholic Church thinks it is a matter for the individual.
France	Mostly Catholic	Contraceptives sold at pharmacies. Adults can purchase. Minors need permission of parents. Advertising only allowed in professional journals.	The bishops have taken no position.
Netherlands	82	Contraceptives freely available to all at any age. Very liberal attitude.	The bishops have taken no position.
Switzerland	45	Contraceptives freely available. Advertising is not allowed.	The bishops have taken no position.
Federal Republic of Germany	47	Pill available on prescription. Tasteful advertising permitted. Slot machines widely available.	—
Portugal	Mostly Catholic	Most have prescriptions for contraceptive devices, but the sale to those without prescription done widely but not openly.	—

* Information taken from Report compiled by Minister for Justice from Irish embassies, 26 April 1971, Dublin, NA, DFA 2004/7/2681.

September the Irish Family Planning Rights Association launched an appeal for funds to support a constitutional test case against the ban on the importation of contraceptives. *Hibernia* observed that the most surprising thing about this appeal for funds was that it had not been taken up earlier. Mary Kenny later reflected back on that period and the debate surrounding the issue:

> The birth control dispute made young women more hostile to the Church. The idea had taken hold that women were entitled to plan their lives and fulfil their hopes without having to submit to endless pregnancies. The Pill did more than control fertility: it sowed sedition; it evangelized for autonomy. It gave women the idea that they could be just as free as men, since never again need the fear of pregnancy hold them back.[85]

The power of the contraceptive pill was in the attitudes and actions it allowed people to embrace, not simply what it allowed people to avoid.

United Irishman was the only element of the radical press that steered its editorial columns to safer waters, and the Officials refrained from including the issue in Ard Comhairle meetings. Though the movement had Máirín de Burca, who was by this time actively seeking an official policy on contraceptives from the republican leadership, like the Provisional republicans, it still managed to remain aloof due to the unfolding situation in the North.

Overall, in spite of republican avoidance, records on public discourse at the time indicate that the ground was fertile for the emergence of a radical movement that would prioritize the issue of contraception in an effort to speed up the popular acceptance necessary to spur legislative reform. Mary Maher later explained: 'The thinking behind it was that we knew that this was the biggest issue. We knew the numbers of people. We knew the huge birth statistics, and we knew that most women were willing to consider this, whatever their class.'[86] Their strategy would be to draw publicity to bring the issue further into the open. According to Maher:

> that was the point of radical politics – about the unspoken ... We were going to name the fact that other women in other countries got to use [contraceptives] ... And then a more 'respectable' element would take the cause up and establish the case in the high court, which is right. Then the word is in the paper all the time. Then you can't ignore it anymore.[87]

Oberschall notes that this is a typical tactic of weaker groups when attempting to engage a more powerful group: 'Since these groups lack positive inducements that they can exchange for the demands and reforms they seek, they resort to protest, the use of negative inducements.'[88]

After a meeting held on 16 May in the North Star hotel near Connolly station, it was decided that a group would go to Belfast to purchase birth control pills and contraceptive devices and upon their return declare them to Dublin's customs officials. Mary Maher, in an ironic twist, was heavily pregnant and unable to make the trip. She remembered a debate over whether the press should have been informed. She recalled making the point that the press should have been alerted only after a dignified confrontation upon the group's arrival from Belfast. This kind of act of civil disobedience, Oberschall writes,

> heightens interaction between the opponents, compels a response by the target group, and provides for an occasion to reconsider relations between the dominant and the subordinate groups. Civil disobedience is a tactic for forcing such a reconsideration of dominance relations in the full light of publicity under circumstances more favourable to the protest group than to the authorities or target group. Civil disobedience is a moral weapon.[89]

The group hoped that this moral weapon would galvanize the public and ultimately spur the government into action.

On 22 May 1971, World Communications Day, forty-seven women went to Belfast to buy contraceptives. They were instructed that upon arrival in Dublin they should declare that they possessed the pill and swallow it in front of the customs officers.[90] Nuala Fennell disassociated herself from the operation, citing its counterproductivity. Maher was in hospital having her baby and Margaret Gaj stayed home to nurse a sick husband. Later Máirín de Burca explained that she remained in Dublin because she believed that the best strategy was to confine the operation to married women.[91] These notable absences underscore the entrenched gender regime that organized Irish society and often barred women from participating in politics. Traditional expectations of women's roles in terms of their inability to control their fertility, their domestic commitments and their domestic status permeated to the very top of even the most radical group of feminists. The train trip back from Dublin adopted a carnival atmosphere even before the train arrived at the station. De Burca may have remained in Dublin, but she coordinated a press reception in the station to record the inevitable spectacle of the women's confrontation with customs officials. Colette O'Neill, an unknown from the Sutton branch, read a statement drafted by Nell McCafferty, articulating the group's demands.[92] That night Kenny and O'Neill appeared on the 'Late Late Show'. But Maher's strategy of conducting a dignified protest and only informing the press after the fact had been rejected in favour of the more conspicuous tactic. The next day the newspapers were awash with pictures of Mary Kenny leading a group of exuberant young women in song as they provoked and shocked customs officers with their contraband. The Irish Federation of Women's Clubs registered a feeling that many observers shared: 'If one is concerned for the mental and physical health of married women, family planning and the availability of contraceptives should be looked into. However, it should be looked into in a serious way by responsible people, not by people wanting to encourage permissiveness in Ireland, bringing the country to the level of many European countries.[93] Lelia Doolan agreed but asked: 'Does this also mean that [the movement's] action, as an element of public argument, is to be ignored?'[94] The way in which the ensuing debate unfolded reflects the observations of Amitai Etzioni, who writes that often the point of demonstrations such as this gets lost: 'Rather than paying attention to the needs communicated by the demonstrations, the majority of the citizenry on the sidelines focuses its attention on the communicative acts themselves, and condemns both them and their participants.'[95]

Many on the sidelines blamed Mary Kenny for this descent into the undignified. Jo Freeman points out that because movements like this generally have no spokesperson, the press tends to focus on the most articulate. Inevitably, Freeman writes, these 'media stars' find themselves being denounced as publicity seekers even as they take pains to cast off this unwelcome notoriety.[96] Kenny had emerged as the un-elected leader of the movement due to the combination of her position as women's page editor at the *Irish Press* and her media-friendly charisma. Whether she courted this distinction or not remains a matter of debate. Later she would explain that she looked at the demonstration as a piece of street theatre, citing Abbie Hoffman's 'show don't tell' philosophy as her main inspiration.[97] She also admitted to being embarrassed by their affair: 'I knew the whole display had been vulgar and crude. Yet I also knew that gesture politics worked.'[98] Nuala Fennell and Mavis Arnold later wrote that the plan had backfired; 'an ideal opportunity to demonstrate the idiocy of the contraceptive laws was lost.' This action, they wrote, alienated a great many of the moderates in the movement.[99] While the operation polarized an embattled group, it achieved its goal by forcefully bringing the issue out of the Seanad and into the open. In fact, everything went according to Maher's overall plan. Two years later the issue was taken up by what Maher had called in a strategy discussion 'more respectable' elements who would bring the issue through the judicial system in the McGee case. It may have pushed people away, but due to prior disagreements regarding the six-point programme, many of these women had already been unhappy with the direction in which the movement was going.

Branches of the women's liberation group performed their own actions as well. These actions, while including the founders' group as well, reflected the diversity of the movement. Probably the most memorable of the branch activities was the Sutton group's demonstration outside the Dáil to coincide with debate over Mary Robinson's bill. As Mary Kenny sang 'We shall not conceive', Hilary Orpen, an RTÉ presenter, Máirín de Burca and Fionnuala O'Connor climbed through a window in the Dáil to invade the debating chamber and were quickly escorted out. The Sutton group also produced a journal called *Succubus*, they picketed the Eurovision song contest regarding contraception, they picketed the homes of priests to draw attention to the housing crisis and they met with the Ballymun group to learn about how substandard urban planning was affecting women on the estate.[100] The Clonskeagh group engaged in what Naomi Klein describes as 'ad busting' or 'culture jamming' by 'hijacking billboards in order to drastically alter their messages'.[101] In placing stickers over sexist advertisements they were participating in a kind of street politics that surged in international popularity during the second wave of feminism.[102] The Ballymun group, in a manner similar to their counterparts in inner-city Britain, protested issues such as the lack of local amenities and the remote location of the development.[103] What is notable about these branches is that their relative autonomy allowed them the freedom to pursue their own priorities. This type of structurelessness was typical of most of the international second-wave groups that sprang up during the period. Lack of structure was a central and powerful component of the second wave in that it allowed for a flurry of uncoordinated activity but, as pointed out in Chapter 4, it also sowed the seeds of its own destruction in terms of the emergence of elites and the manipulation of decisions. The only other campaign that a significant number of the Women's Liberation branches participated in in significant numbers was the August 1971 Dáil protest against the Prohibition of Forcible Entry Bill, a bill that was designed to prevent squatting. Three hundred women rallied in front of the Dáil resulting in the arrest of Máirín de Burca and Mary Anderson. It was this protest that would ultimately tear the fragile movement asunder.

THE CLASH BETWEEN WOMEN'S LIBERATION AND REPUBLICANISM

After the Dáil protest the Sutton group demanded a meeting to concentrate on 'women's issues'.[104] At the meeting on 15 September 1971 disagreement raged about how republican and left-wing political affiliations were having an undue influence on the group. Most of the criticism was directed at founder members such as Máirín de Burca, whose membership in the Ard Comhairle of Official Sinn Féin proved to be a constant irritant to a large segment of the women's movement. At this meeting Máirín de Burca resigned from the group in response to allegations that she was using the movement as a 'Rentacrowd' for her own political purposes.[105] Jo Freeman explains that this is a common phenomenon within structureless groups, particularly between the years 1969 and 1971. She argues that because there was no formal structure or control, groups left themselves open to manipulation. Consequently, strong leaders were often forced to withdraw after being denounced for using the movement for their own purposes, even when no manipulation had occurred.[106]

Some might argue that de Burca used the women's movement to further Sinn Féin policies. Certainly broad-based radical agitation had been an acknowledged tactical policy of Official Sinn Féin in the period leading up to the formation of the Irish Women's Liberation Movement. However, all records indicate that the Officials were only beginning to warm to the idea of feminism (at the urging of de Burca) in this period. Moreover, this simplistic analysis ignores a more subtle understanding of Máirín de Burca as a political leader and radical activist. It was de Burca who introduced second-wave feminism to a tentative, if not reluctant, Official Sinn Féin leadership, not the other way around. A resolution on social affairs, which demanded full employment, equal pay for women, the legalization of contraceptives and divorce and provision for unmarried mothers was passed at the October 1971 Ard Fheis due to her influence.[107] She later remarked that though the Ard Comhairle did not enthusiastically welcome her activism on women's issues, they never tried to curtail her action in this arena: 'It was there and it was a fact. And a lot of women came with me, obviously. They were members as well so it was something they couldn't ignore whereas the [Provisional republicans] didn't really have that connection.'[108] Had de Burca been simply following a directive to broaden the base of Official involvement in radical activism, and had she simply been using the feminists to advance republicanism, it is unlikely she would have had to push for the resolution.

De Burca's resignation came too late for moderate Nuala Fennell, who alerted the press to her own resignation. She wrote: 'if you are not anti-American, anti-clergy, anti-government, anti-ICA, anti-police, anti-men, then sisters, there is no place for you [in the movement]'.[109] Letter upon letter appeared in the press from members of the group defending their position on the Prohibition of Forcible Entry Bill and pointing out that originally Fennell, herself, had voted for the housing demand. Oddly enough, Hilary Boyle also resigned at this time citing the exact opposite reason as Fennell: not enough emphasis was being put on housing and other working-class issues, according to Boyle.

Mary Kenny was spared from resigning over the 'one family, one house' issue when she was offered a job at the *Evening Standard* in London. At the October seminar in 1971, before Kenny left and Fennell resigned, she had implored people not to identify too closely with political causes such as housing because those issues were the bread and butter of other political groups such as the Dublin Housing Action Committee and the Officials. Though Kenny had agreed with the housing issue, she anticipated a split due to an overemphasis on the housing issue, which 'could be suicide for us', she told the group.[110] Mary Hobbs, a British feminist responsible for unionizing the night cleaners in London, and one of the only British connections the Irish group established in this period, picked up on this message when she spoke at the seminar: 'Get the women in, particularly the working class women. Most of them won't go for things like abortion and contraception. They think it's against God and all that toffee so you get them into the workshops on things they can agree with like equal pay. Then you can start working on them for other things.'[111] But the sombre mood of the meeting was a telling sign that there was hardly anything on which the women could now concur. Mary Kenny, de facto leader of the movement, wrote a final letter to the press on the housing issue and its divisive nature, which deserves to be quoted at length.

> I should like to go on the record as being most vigorously opposed to the Forcible Entry Bill ... It should be opposed at every opportunity and I have done what I could, I think, in adding my voice to those who have and are opposing it. However, I feel that while a women's liberation movement should give solidarity to any groups which formed an opposition to this disagreeable Bill – just as, in the United States, women's liberation has consistently and on every occasion opposed the dreadful war in Vietnam – none the less, one should not lose sight of the

primary women's liberation aims: to free women from unjust laws pertaining especially to them, to liberate them from male oppression, exploitation, conditioning and the feudal kind of capitalism which at present keeps us down. Housework is also a burning political issue.[112]

One of the most lucid arguments against incorporating the housing issue into women's liberation came approximately one year too late. Without its unelected charismatic leader and some of its main organizers the movement stagnated, leading others to move on to evolving feminist concerns such as domestic violence and single-parent families.

An element of the demise of the group, which is often referred to but rarely analysed, is the women's movement's relationship with the unfolding events in Northern Ireland. Ailbhe Smyth later reflected that 'underlying [the debate that led to the resignation of Máirín de Burca] and other disagreements, one senses the shadow of republicanism – always present, but rarely allowed to surface directly and explicitly'.[113] Divisions over the housing issue reflected larger debates over the extent to which the group should support what was commonly seen as an Official Sinn Féin demand, and the extent to which by supporting the housing demand Women's Liberation could be linked to republicanism and/or left-wing politics. We must also keep in mind that Máirín de Burca was not the only founder member to engage in Northern politics. Had this been a case of one person versus the whole group, de Burca would have been eliminated earlier. Her outspoken ideas and her public persona drew attention, but what led to the serious factional tension was her ability to marshal support. Maher agreed with the housing issue from a socialist point of view. Nell McCafferty, a Derry native, may not have supported all that de Burca stood for but none the less demonstrated through her writing that there was a place for Northern politics in Southern life. Marie McMahon, a member of the Labour Party, was also a strong force in the People's Democracy, editing its newsletter.[114] Like Maher, her approach had less to do with republicanism and more to do with left-wing rights-based activism. Thus, even if the founders' group was not entirely republican, the tensions between them and the liberal feminists that soon joined the movement can be easily understood. A majority of the founders' group were developing a socialist feminist analysis of women's roles in Irish society, North and South. Further, as many of them embraced radical politics, a significant portion of them became outspoken and confident in their political opinions. While their media savvy certainly helped the group publicize itself, it also contributed to their demise. Debate on tactics was carried out in the open, inviting the readers of all the major newspapers to take sides.

It is no coincidence that one founder named Donnybrook as the area that presented the biggest challenge to passing the housing demand. As a predominantly middle-class group, the Donnybrook women (similar to a significant portion of women in other branches) were resistant to supporting the housing issue because of its class-based foundation and because of its association with the Dublin Housing Action Committee and Official Sinn Féin. Their apprehension at being identified with the republican movement must be viewed in light of the violence that was erupting in Northern Ireland. Though the Official movement would ultimately change their rhetoric to eschew the gun in favour of the ballot, at this stage they were still a 'serious potential force' committing a rash of political violence in 1972 alone.[115] In an effort to consolidate policy the Irish Women's Liberation Movement took a stand on militancy by passing a resolution on 22 February of that year supporting non-violence in pursuit of its aims.[116] But the resolution did little to shore up the leadership of the non-party-political wing of the movement, increasingly called the Fownes Street group in reference to their meeting location and journal title. Women such as Maureen and Cathie Killeavey, Marge Lenahan, Ann Fitzgibbon, Joan Forsythe and Lunia Ryan edited the *Fownes Street Journal* by steering clear of North/South politics and embracing the language of non-violence. Increasingly noisy meetings of the volatile movement ground on through the months, but by November many members had given up on achieving consensus. The founders–Fownes Street split was solidified after the *Irish Times* reported that a founder had proposed a resolution on the withdrawal of British troops from Northern Ireland at a conference for feminists in Britain.[117] A correspondence followed in which the Fownes Street group repudiated the motion and underscored the point that the majority of Women's Liberation members rejected violence as a mode of political expression.

The founders' group of Irish Women's Liberation constituted an elite within radical activism in general and also within the women's liberation movement; the fact that these high-profile women 'knew how to organize radical politics'[118] hastened a process of what Max Weber and Robert Michels called 'oligarchization', where a bureaucratic structure emerges.[119] They go on to argue that this produces a process of 'conservatization', where the movement begins to accommodate itself to the society in which it operates. In Irish Women's Liberation, this second process was not given time to manifest itself before the group lost its momentum. The process of oligarchization, which in the Irish context began at the Mansion House meeting, produced what Jo Freeman calls a 'star system' where the founders' group, because of their organizational skills, connections to the media and high-profile status, emerged as an elite oligarchy that insisted on branch acquiescence to its programme.[120] Mary Flynn's analysis of the Irish Women's Liberation Movement concurs with this process. She identifies the founders as self-proclaimed 'spiritual directors' of the movement, who, according to some, 'acted more as the inquisition'.[121]

An analysis of the short-lived Women's Liberation Movement reveals that it had successfully raised social consciousness about women's inequality in Ireland despite its volatile history, and it succeeded in influencing public policy and the policies of radical political groups such as the Officials. Mary Maher explained her reaction to its demise:

> At the time I was very outraged and upset but you do what you do and you keep going on and saying 'this is outrageous' and 'we must all stay together', and I gradually realized that this was history and this is the way things happen. It served its historical purpose and it's bound to be diverse ... But that's what you have to work through in any political movement.[122]

Marin Lockwood Carden makes the point that throughout the second-wave movement women responded to conflict within the movement by contributing to a process of proliferation.[123] Freeman, who observed this process during the American Congress to Unite Women, does not see proliferation as a necessarily negative component of the movement's development. Instead, she notes, conference organizers began to realize that a diverse movement might be better than a united one.[124] In the case of the movement in Ireland, this proliferation process allowed women to pursue focused issues in an effort to address social problems and skirt divisive topics such as the Northern question or left-wing politics.

The early 1970s can be characterized by the formation of a myriad of women's social projects, such as AIM (founded by Nuala Fennell, Deidre McDevitt, Bernadette Quinn, Ann McAllister and focusing on marital breakdown), Women's Aid (for battered women), the Women's Political Association, the Fownes Street group and Irishwomen United (which focused on similar issues as the IWLM but added self-determined sexuality to the mix). In addition to the proliferation of constituent groups, other structural changes to Irish society paved the way for a redefinition of the gender regime. In 1972 the Church supported a referendum on the removal of the reference in the Irish Constitution to it occupying a special position in Irish society. In 1973 the first test case regarding the importation of contraceptives (the McGee case) was brought before the justice system and eventually won on appeal. Also in that year the Commission on the Status of Women submitted its final report, which argued for a repeal of the marriage bar and a dismantling of structural barriers to women entering the workforce.

CONCLUSION

A combination of circumstances created the conditions for the rise of second-wave feminism in Ireland. Publicity generated throughout the western world about student politics, left-wing politics, civil rights in America and Northern Ireland, women's liberation and radical activism contributed to a politicization of a new generation of activists that was more educated and more willing to publicly question the status quo than had the previous generation. In the Republic of Ireland a combination of reformism and government-led policy change succeeded in creating the space for a debate on women's roles within the Irish gender regime. The far-reaching and comprehensive gains made by liberal feminists through their work in the CSW were crucial in laying the groundwork for the success of the younger, more radical branch of the second wave and should not be underestimated.

The early 1970s saw the praxis of the kind of radical rhetoric that had emerged in the late 1960s in women's magazines and left-leaning newspapers. The subject of street politics began to dominate public discourse, and whether it was reaction to external events such as the civil rights activity in America or an increase in sectarian violence in Northern Ireland, the rapid proliferation of street groups brought into the public a revitalized form of alternative political expression. The Official republican movement was endeavouring to broaden its base by engaging in a diverse range of left-wing agitation centred on housing action and class politics. The Provisionals, more focused on unfolding events in the North, left the field open for the Officials to dominate the radical scene in Dublin. Through street activism women began to rise in the ranks of radical political groups at an unprecedented rate. The developing situation in Northern Ireland, as well as political developments throughout the western world, drew more and more women into activism and widened the field of their political expression.

Probably the most significant female leader that emerged from this period within the Southern radical political milieu was Máirín de Burca, whose activism ranged from participating in the Dublin Housing Action Committee to being elected co-secretary of Official Sinn Féin's Ard Comhairle and ultimately to founding the Women's Liberation group. Her feminist activism forced the Officials to pass resolutions on restructuring the gender regime in the early 1970s, though it would still be a few years before the Officials earnestly addressed the issues by forming a women's committee.[125] The Irish Women's Liberation Movement was prematurely launched and consequently its sky-rocketing membership overwhelmed the founders' group, forcing the movement into a de facto structurelessness that allowed the founders' group to impose a provisional control over the newly forming branches. This structurelessness ultimately led to the demise of the group when the perceived 'Sinn Féin demand' against the Prohibition of Forcible Entry Bill came to the fore; unelected leaders that had emerged bickered over the correct definition of 'women's issues', leading to splits and resignations.

Characterized by a few imaginative protests and street actions, the Irish women's liberation group made use of its media savvy to draw attention to itself and to boost recruitment. The fact that many of these women were political organizers and journalists contributed to their popular success. The contraceptive train is generally viewed as a demonstration that backfired because it alienated so many of its possible supporters. This simplistic view ignores how the media coverage of the train broke down taboos and introduced the flaws of customs' legislation into public discourse in a forceful way. Indeed, years later Nuala Fennell would admit that coverage of the event did provide 'the jolt that was necessary' to effect significant change in women's lives.[126]

The development and demise of the group followed similar trajectories as other international second-wave movements, but it remained a uniquely Irish process in response to the Northern question and because leftist republican politics was becoming increasingly explosive. Linda Connolly and Tina O'Toole underscore this point: 'the Irish case therefore demonstrates that there is never a neutral relationship between nationalism and feminism in any given context and that nationalism is a key context of *difference* in the women's movement'.[127] The proliferation of women's groups that arose because of these splits helped to focus second-wave feminism and probably accomplished more than the founders' group had originally thought possible. Upon reflection, de Burca expressed regret at failing to appeal to working-class women as well as to rural women: 'The fault that it did not develop that way as I see it, was with myself and some others who were too dogmatically left-wing political and the trendies, who were impatient with the pace the movement would have to take if it were to appeal to the mass of Irish-women.'[128] Women's liberation was not going to solve the housing issue, just as American feminism was not going to solve the war in Vietnam. The fact that it split could have been predicted from its inception; what is more interesting is how it helped break taboos in public discourse in order to introduce a women-centred consciousness to Irish society.

It is difficult to analyse the women's movement in Ireland as solely a component of a larger second wave of feminism, though it does bear parallels to second-wave feminist groups throughout the western world. The fact that republican politics and the unfolding events in the North remained an ever-present but barely acknowledged threat to group unity, and the fact that its demands briefly unified otherwise disparate groups of women while simultaneously tackling Catholic social teaching – an intrinsic element to Irish identity at that point – supports the idea that second-wave feminism in Ireland was inextricably linked to Ireland's political development as much as international influences.

This period represents a turning point for women and radical politics in the Irish Republic. Official republicanism dominated the radical political environment and maintained links with disparate activist groups spanning the spectrum of extraparliamentary politics. The Official movement had difficulty embracing second-wave feminism in its earliest stages; *United Irishman* barely recognized it and the movement's leadership (barring Máirín de Burca) made little of the issues of equal pay and contraceptives during this period. Máirín de Burca's vociferous support for feminism eventually demanded that a reluctant Official republican movement articulate its relationship to feminism. Insofar as housing was a woman's issue, the Officials' work with housing did speak to feminist concerns, but not because it was, in and of itself, feminist, but rather because it could appeal to the working classes. The period 1971–3 saw the integration of feminist concerns into Official republican philosophy, which still represents faster integration rates than those of the other existent parties of the period. Chapter 6 looks at women activists in Northern Ireland in the early 1970s and focuses on women in Provisional republican politics, in order to see how another strand of republicanism interacted with the changing roles of women in radical politics.

NOTES

1. *Hibernia*, 16 January 1976, p.17.
2. Oliver J. Flanagan, Dáil debates, Vol. 274, c. 926, 11 July 1974.
3. Noel Browne and John O'Connell introduced an identically worded bill the following year in the Dáil. As with the Seanad bill, it was refused a first reading.

4. E. Hobsbawm, *The Age of Extremes: The Short Twentieth Century, 1914–1991* (London: Abacus, 1994), p.313.
5. D. Bouchier, *The Feminist Challenge: The Movement for Women's Liberation in Britain and the USA* (London: Macmillan, 1983), p.55.
6. For more on this phenomenon see N. Ignatiev, *How the Irish Became White* (London, 1995); D.R. Roediger, *The Wages of Whiteness: Race and the Making of the American Working Class* (London, 1991).
7. For an interesting assessment of this act see 'Abortion Act 1967' held 10 July 2001 (Institute of Contemporary British History, 2002, http://www.icbh.ac.uk/downloads/abortion.pdf), pp.1–62.
8. M. Pugh, *Women and the Women's Movement in Britain* (London: Macmillan, 2000), p.317.
9. A. Coote and B. Campbell, *Sweet Freedom: The Struggle for Women's Liberation* (Oxford: Basil Blackwell, 1987), p.15.
10. S. De Beauvoir, 'France: Feminism – Alive, Well and in Constant Danger', in R. Morgan (ed.), *Sisterhood is Global* (New York: Anchor, 1984), pp.234–5; G. Kaplan, *Contemporary Western European Feminism* (London: UCL Press, 1992), p.165.
11. D. Dhalerup, 'Three Waves of Feminism in Denmark', in G. Griffin and R. Braidotti (eds), *Thinking Differently: A Reader in European Women's Studies* (London: Zed Books, 2002), p.346; Kaplan, *Contemporary Western European Feminism*, pp.78, 87.
12. U. Gerhard 'The Women's Movement in Germany', in Griffin and Braidotti (eds), *Thinking Differently*, p.327.
13. J. Lovenduski, *Women and European Politics: Contemporary Feminism and Public Policy* (Brighton: Wheatsheaf, 1986), p.6.
14. Kaplan, *Contemporary Western European Feminism*, p.42.
15. L. Connolly, *The Irish Women's Movement: From Revolution to Devolution* (New York: Lilliput Press, 2002), p.72.
16. Ibid., p.10.
17. Ibid., p.11.
18. Memorandum on equal pay, NA, DFA 2003/1/244.
19. Connolly to Neligan, 9 January 1970, NA, DFA, 2003/1/244.
20. Memorandum from the Mission of Ireland at the European Union, 26 January 1970, NA, DFA 2003/1/244.
21. J. Beale, *Women in Ireland: Voices of Change* (Indiana: Indiana University Press, 1987), pp.145–6.
22. Progress Report on Implementation of the Recommendations on the Report of the Commission on the Status of Women, December 1976, Cork, Boole Library Archives, Attic Press Collection 6.2.2/1165, p.34.
23. Report on visit by chairman and secretary of the Commission on the Status of Women to Brussels, early 1970, NA, DFA 2003/1/244.
24. European Commission's report on equal wages for men and women, 22 June 1970, NA, DFA 2003/1/244.
25. E. Connolly, 'The State, Public Policy and Gender: Ireland in Transition, 1957–1977' (Ph.D. thesis, Dublin City University, 1998), p.135.
26. Dáil debates, Vol. 242, c. 2126, 27 November 1969.
27. Hillery to EEC, 21 September 1970, NA, DFA, 2003/1/244.
28. *Irishwoman's Journal* (May 1969).
29. *Irish Independent*, 27 February 1969, *Irishwoman's Journal* (July 1969); see also N. O'Faolain, *Are You Somebody? The Life and Times of Nuala O'Faolain* (Dublin: New Island, 1996), pp.105–6.
30. See *Hibernia*, 17 April 1970 and Blatherwick to Thorpe, 21 January 1971, London, NA, FCO 33/1593.
31. Interview with de Burca, Dublin, 15 March 2004.
32. F. Gardiner, 'Political Interest and Participation of Irish Women, 1922–1992: The Unfinished Revolution', *Canadian Journal of Irish Studies*, 18 (1992), p.20.
33. See *United Irishman* (November 1971 and May 1972).
34. See Moore to State Department, November 1970, Maryland, NARA, XR POL 23-8 IRE, POL 7-US-Nixon; Máirín de Burca's tour of USA, 1976, Kay Boyle Papers, Morris Library, University of Delaware, F29.
35. Moore to Department, November 1970, Maryland, NARA, XR POL23-8 IRE, POL 7 US/Nixon.

36. *Hibernia*, 10 October 1969.
37. Gardiner, 'Political Interest and Participation of Irish Women, 1922–1992', p.20.
38. Ibid., p.37.
39. V. Randall, *Women and Politics: An International Perspective* (Basingstoke: Macmillan Education, 1991), p.58.
40. Lovenduski, *Women and European Politics*, p.126.
41. Interview with Maher, Dublin, 24 May 2004.
42. A. Smyth, 'The Contemporary Women's Movement in the Republic of Ireland', *Women's Studies International Forum*, 11 (1988), p.332.
43. Mary Flynn, *Feminism vs. Nationalism: Women's Liberation Ireland 1971–3*, Cork, Boole Library Archives, Attic Press Collection, 6.1.4/1138.
44. J. Levine, *Sisters: The Personal Story of an Irish Feminist* (Dublin: Ward River Press, 1982), p.136.
45. Ibid., p.138.
46. Ibid., interview with De Burca, Dublin, 15 March 2004
47. Interview with Maher, Dublin, 24 May 2004.
48. Correspondence with Mary Kenny, 12 May 2004.
49. Correspondence with Kenny, 12 May 2004.
50. See Máirín de Burca's letter, *Irish People*, 31 May 1974 and Mary Maher's letter, *Irish People*, 14 June 1974.
51. J. Freeman (ed.), *Social Movements of the Sixties and Seventies* (New York: Longman, 1983), p.19.
52. Anonymous activist quoted in Connolly, *Irish Women's Movement*, p.124.
53. Smyth, 'Contemporary Women's Movement', p.334.
54. *Woman's Way*, 16 October 1970.
55. *Irishwoman's Journal* (February 1969).
56. Quoted in Connolly, *Irish Women's Movement*, p.115.
57. Interview with Maher, Dublin, 24 May 2004.
58. Interview with De Burca, Dublin, 15 March 2004.
59. Ibid.
60. R. Sweetman, *On Our Knees* (London: Pan Books, 1972), p.41.
61. Smyth, 'Contemporary Women's Movement', p.334.
62. Ibid.
63. See Bouchier, *Feminist Challenge*, pp.46, 94; Kaplan, *Contemporary Western European Feminism*.
64. R. Ó Glaisne, *Saoirse Na mBan* (Dublin: Cló Grianréime, 1973), p.33.
65. Interview with de Burca, Dublin, 15 March 2004.
66. Levine, *Sisters*, p.155.
67. Interview with Maher, Dublin, 24 May 2004.
68. L. Connolly, 'The Women's Movement in Ireland, 1970–1995: A Social Movement Analysis', *Irish Journal of Feminist Studies*, 1 (1996), p.56.
69. Levine, *Sisters*, p.170.
70. C. Rose, *The Female Experience: The Story of the Woman Movement in Ireland* (Galway: Arlen House, 1975), pp.82–3.
71. Ó Glaisne, *Saoirse*, p.34.
72. June Levine, address to WERRC Conference, May 1995, cited in Connolly, *Irish Women's Movement*, pp.119–20.
73. Anonymous activist quoted in ibid., p.119.
74. Z. Eisenstein, *The Radical Future of Liberal Feminism* (New York: Longman, 1981); S. Walby, *Theorizing Patriarchy* (Oxford: Basil Blackwell, 1990).
75. Levine, *Sisters*, p.183.
76. *Markievicz Women's Movement*, no. 2 (9 March 1971), Cork, Boole Library Archives, Attic Press Collection 6.1.4/1139.
77. Ó Glaisne, *Saoirse* p.27.
78. Connolly, 'State, Public Policy and Gender', p.230.
79. F. Kennedy, *Cottage to Crèche: Family Change in Ireland* (Dublin: Institute of Public Administration, 2001), p.230.
80. *Woman's Way*, 21 May 1971.
81. Quoted in J.H. Whyte, *Church and State in Modern Ireland* (Dublin: Gill & Macmillan, 1971), p.405.

82. Report compiled by Minister for Justice from Irish embassies, 26 April 1971, Dublin, NA, DFA 2004/7/2681.
83. *This Week*, 26 March 1971.
84. *This Week*, 25 June 1971.
85. M. Kenny, *Goodbye to Catholic Ireland* (Dublin: New Island, 2000), p.242.
86. Interview with Maher, Dublin, 24 May 2004.
87. Ibid.
88. A. Oberschall, *Social Conflict and Social Movements* (Englewood Cliffs, NJ: Prentice-Hall, 1973), p.308.
89. Ibid., pp.322–3.
90. Levine, *Sisters*, p.174.
91. Interview with de Burca, Dublin, 15 March 2004.
92. N. McCafferty, *Nell* (Dublin: Penguin, 2004), p.266.
93. Quoted in Ó Glaisne, *Saoirse* p.38.
94. Quoted in Ibid.
95. A. Etzioni, *Demonstration Democracy: A Policy Paper Prepared for the Task Force on Demonstrations, Protests and Group Violence of the President's National Commission on the Causes and Prevention of Violence* (New York: Gordon & Breach, 1970), p.9.
96. J. Freeman, 'Political Organization in the Feminist Movement', *Acta Sociologica*, 18 (1975), p.227.
97. Correspondence with Mary Kenny, 12 May 04.
98. Kenny, *Goodbye to Catholic Ireland*, p.239.
99. Cited in Connolly, *Irish Women's Movement*, p.120.
100. *Succubus*, Cork, Boole Library Archives, Attic Press Collection, 6.1/1110.
101. N. Klein, *No Logo* (London: Flamingo, 2000), p.280.
102. See S.J. Douglas, *Where the Girls Are* (New York: Times Books, 1994), p.227.
103. See M. Mayo (ed.), *Women in the Community* (London: Routledge & Kegan Paul, 1977).
104. Smyth, 'Contemporary Women's Movement', p.336.
105. Mary Flynn, 'Feminism vs. Nationalism: Women's Liberation Ireland 1971–3', Cork, Boole Library Archives, Attic Press Collection, 6.1.4/1138.
106. Freeman, 'Political Organization in the Feminist Movement', p.237.
107. Blatherwick to Thorpe, 2 November 1971, London, NA, FCO 33/1594.
108. Interview with de Burca, Dublin,15 March 2004.
109. Levine, *Sisters*, p.230.
110. Ibid., p.122.
111. *Hibernia*, 8 October 1971.
112. *Hibernia*, 16 July 1971.
113. Smyth, 'Contemporary Women's Movement', p.336.
114. L. Connolly and T. O'Toole, *Documenting Irish Feminisms* (Dublin: Woodfield Press, 2005), p.41.
115. R. English, *Armed Struggle: The History of the IRA* (London: Macmillan, 2003), pp.175–6.
116. Flynn, 'Feminism vs. Nationalism'.
117. *Irish Times*, 14 November 1972.
118. Connolly, *Irish Women's Movement*, p.121.
119. H.J. Gerth and C.W. Mills (eds), *From Max Weber: Essays in Sociology* (New York: Oxford University Press, 1946); R. Michels *Political Parties* (Glencoe, IL: Free Press, 1949).
120. Freeman, 'Political Organization in the Feminist Movement', p.238.
121. Flynn, 'Feminism vs. Nationalism'.
122. Interview with Maher, Dublin, 24 May 2004.
123. M.L. Carden, 'The Proliferation of a Social Movement Ideology and Individual Incentives in the Contemporary Feminist Movement', in K. Louis (ed.), *Research in Social Movements, Conflicts and Change: An Annual Compilation of Research 1* (Greenwich, CT: JAI Press, 1978), p.187.
124. Freeman, 'Political Organization in the Feminist Movement', p.230.
125. For more on this see 'Women's Rights in Ireland', pamphlet by the Women's Committee of (Official) Sinn Feín (1975), Kay Boyle Papers, Morris Library, University of Delaware, F57.
126. N. Fennell, 'Irish Women: Agenda for Practical Action' (Dublin: Stationery Office,1985).
127. Connolly and O'Toole, *Documenting Irish Feminisms*, p.148; italics the authors.
128. Quoted in Rose, *Female Experience*, p.83.

CHAPTER SIX

'Not *burning bras but rattling bin lids'*:[1] *Women and Militant Republicanism in Northern Ireland, 1970–3*

What is remarkable, given that there was something like 20,000 people there and only one woman was injured, I think they targeted who they shot. It wasn't random shooting. They targeted men. (Ann Hope recounting the events of Bloody Sunday)[2]

Women were becoming more involved and fronting more operations. They were no longer just carrying guns but they were also pulling the trigger and that made a difference. (Angela Nelson, interned without trial in May 1973 at age 17)[3]

When Dolours Price and her mother, Chrissie, rounded a West Belfast corner in 1971, they were shocked to discover a checkpoint had been hastily thrown up. The Northern Irish government had adopted the policy of internment without trial for men, which prompted Dolours to join the IRA, but for her it was this moment that crystallized the fact that a new chapter had begun in the emerging conflict. The soldiers were now in her neighbourhood, checking people as they walked by without individualized suspicion. A few men stood spread eagle against armoured cars, or 'pigs' as many in the region called them. Their eyes darted down the street in search of any friendly face. While still far enough away Dolours' mother slowed down and asked if she was carrying anything. Dolours denied she was, twice. Her mother gave her a stern look and Dolours produced a handgun. 'They're making the young ones take their coats off,' her mother said as she stuffed it under her jacket and into the back of her waistband. At the checkpoint the soldiers asked Dolours to take off her jacket. As a matter of practice women were subject to less scrutiny than men; she knew she was not in danger of being put up against the vehicles. All bets were off with mothers though. Chrissie was waved through, the gun securely under her buttoned coat. When they got home, Chrissie buried the gun in the garden, but not before she meticulously cleaned and treated it, putting to use her Cumman na mBan training from the border campaign. When the IRA quartermaster arrived later to retrieve the weapon and unwrapped the gun from its cocoon of socks and plastic, he quipped that she, too, should join the IRA – they could use her talent.[4]

Between 1970 and 1973 women's roles grew to encompass new elements of political activism in nationalist Northern Ireland. Their domestic responsibilities afforded them a central role within the community, which eventually allowed them to cultivate a new social role in street politics. Earlier events of 1968/9 had helped lay the groundwork for a change in the structure of the gender regime by allowing women the space to enter into political discourse. Women such as Bernadette Devlin, Edwina Stewart and Ann Hope had quickly risen to become political figures and role models for this new type of expression, but a feminist consciousness did not surface during this period due to a variety of factors, including the intensity of unfolding sectarian warfare and an ensuing sense of tribalism. As the pot simmered women's roles changed within the nationalist community. Events such as the Falls Road curfew and the introduction of internment for men forced the republican movement to rethink its prevailing gender regime. That day at the checkpoint Dolours learned something important: mothers remained safe, but for young women things would not be the same.

THE ROLE OF WOMEN IN CATHOLIC NORTHERN IRELAND

Within Northern Ireland Catholic women's roles had been evolving along their own trajectory since Partition. Chapter 2 has traced how women in Northern Ireland attempted to transcend their minority status by asserting their rights within the Northern Irish system. An analysis of how Catholicism informed that minority status is instructive. Margaret MacCurtain has argued that Marian Catholicism acquired a special intensity in Ireland after the Great Famine, seeing church attendance rise by 50 per cent in the decades following it.[5] During the late nineteenth century images of Mother Ireland began to appear in ballads, which built on the iconography of Marian Catholicism to define Nationalist politics.[6] Pearse, O'Casey and Yeats all transposed Mother Ireland and the Sean-Bhean Bhoct, the poor old woman, over the suffering of the Blessed Mother. And by the late 1960s Marian Catholicism had been popularly interwoven with a nationalist identity for more than half a century and was firmly entrenched in prevailing notions of Catholic Irishness. Catherine Shannon points out that 'in its Irish manifestation the Marian cult often strongly emphasizes a positive role for the Virgin Mother as intercessor to secure salvation'.[7] This belief system 'symbolizes motherhood as sacrifice and suffering in the greatest of its causes', according to Hugh Brody.[8] Monica McWilliams argues that the Church and state forces have combined to shape the role of Catholic women in order to ensure that their primary role was that of homemaker and mother. This supports the idea that by the beginning of the 1970s women's identities revolved around their domestic commitments.[9] Catholic ideology, combined with Northern Ireland's non-representative, discriminatory modes of welfare distribution, especially in the area of housing, gave credence to Catholic women's identification with Mary's eternal sorrow, even in the face of her 'positive role'.

Lynda Edgerton makes the point that women in Catholic Northern Ireland had limited choices when it came to their future. According to prevailing social expectations of Catholic womanhood, the two most viable options for adult women became motherhood or perpetual virginity.[10] In terms of employment, the conventional ban on married women remaining in the civil service and in banking combined with a trend of Catholics not being as widely employed in as many sectors as Protestants to further limit women's options.[11] As discussed earlier, even in a factory town like Derry, women's employment rates were not as reliable as popular anecdotes would indicate. In a province as economically depressed as Northern Ireland, this meant that women were primarily identified with the home in urban areas and for obvious reasons, rural areas as well. In 1971 only 29 per cent of Northern Ireland's married women identified themselves for the census as 'economically active', which contrasts sharply with the figure of 42 per cent for Great Britain in that same year.[12] Overall, the position of Catholic women in the period leading up to the 1970s made believing in the nobility of the mother in her domestic role more than a trope of cultural and religious life, it was a psychological expedient that helped women endure the status quo.

Though other countries underwent a surge in feminist activity in the early 1970s, Northern Irish women in the nationalist community were more focused on rising communal tensions and street activism. Women's concerns spanned community divisions and, like trade unionism, had the capacity to unite both Catholic and Protestant traditions, but they failed to do so in the confusion of the moment and the mounting communal tension. Though small feminist groups such as the Lower Ormeau Women's Group and Queen's University Women's Liberation Group were beginning to articulate feminist concerns in the 1972–3 period,[13] the tribalism produced by the Troubles ensured that this kind of unity would not gain ground at the same rate as it did in the Republic. Somehow during this period, though, women became more central to street politics and they were able to take on powerful roles in both the civil rights administration and the republican movement. A new gender regime was emerging in these early years of the 1970s within two movements, and it was one without an overt feminist agenda.

THE FALLS ROAD CURFEW

The violence in Derry in October 1968, the Burntollet march, the loyalist attacks on public utilities and finally the battle of the Bogside of August 1969 had put the entire province on edge. Particularly in Belfast, sectarian tensions that had been simmering since 1968 were beginning to boil over, exacerbated by the close proximity of ghettoized neighbourhoods organized along ethno-sectarian lines. The government decision to bring in the British army during the battle of the Bogside proved to be fateful; though it temporarily stemmed the violence, it introduced a new element of military weaponry. This would eventually lead to a contest of one-upmanship between the army and the Provisional Irish Republican Army, which was emerging as the more militant of the two republican factions. At the end of June 1970, Bernadette Devlin's arrest for her part in the battle of the Bogside and strife after a contentious loyalist march led to rioting across the province. In Belfast five men were killed outside St Mathew's Church and the British army was blamed by both sides for failing to take decisive action. This spurred further rioting, resulting in the death of twelve people. On 3 July the members of the Royal Ulster Constabulary (RUC) and the British army moved into Balkan Street to confiscate weapons and further rioting ensued. This prompted Lieutenant-General Sir Ian Freeland, the General Officer Commanding, to institute what he called a 'movement restriction',[14] or what most people in the area referred to as the 'Falls Road curfew'. The area in the Lower Falls covered approximately fifty streets and a house-to-house search during the 34-hour curfew yielded 100 firearms, 100 homemade bombs, 250 lbs of explosives, 21,000 rounds of ammunition and 8 two-way radio sets.[15]

The material damage and alleged looting perpetrated by the soldiers during the search gave many, particularly women, cause to object, according to the *Irish Times*.[16] Though in-depth searches necessarily result in damage to floorboards and other potential storage areas, the gravest complaints involved allegations of the deliberate destruction of religious decorations, unnecessary and excessive structural damage, and theft. Chrissie McAuley, who went on to become a Sinn Féin councillor and advisor on equality and human rights, was a young girl during the curfew. For her the curfew was a turning point in her political awareness: 'When the British army came in to raid my home I watched my mother watching her few possessions being destroyed. I knew then that you either stood with the community or against it.'[17] This statement is broadly characteristic of the conclusions drawn by the residents of the Lower Falls, who at this point began to feel that the police and now the army had taken sides against them. It is difficult to properly contextualize this statement in terms of measuring property damage, because so few residents lodged formal complains out of fear of retribution. However, anecdotal evidence and accounts by the many contemporary newspapers support the notion that the curfew was particularly difficult for the women of the area; the most powerful image in these accounts drew on the Marian aesthetic by portraying mothers who were powerless to defend their homes during the curfew.

The gendered context of the house-to-house searches during the Falls Road curfew emerges quite clearly in the vernacular as 'the rape of the Falls'. The invasion of the domestic sphere by units of armed men was seen as a violation on a par with the sort of transgression that stereotype would dictate only happens to women. Claudia Card, in her work on martial rape, writes: 'If there is one set of fundamental functions of rape, civilian or martial, it is to display, communicate, and produce or maintain *dominance* ... Of many forms of martial terrorism, rape in a patriarchal culture has a special potential to drive a wedge between family members and to carry the expression of the perpetrator's dominance into future generations.'[18] While Card's analysis centres on bodily rape, the motives behind a metaphorical rape would remain the same in the mind of the survivor. At the time many drew parallels with rape because of the assertion of dominance and perceived destruction of women's domestic spheres. One woman later remarked on the sense of violation that came with house searches: 'I think it's worse in the home because your home has been violated. Everything, all your personal belongings have been interfered with.'[19] The experience of the destruction of religious symbols and looting suggested to the residents of the Falls Road that the army fostered a culture of intimidation and harassment.

The imposition of a curfew meant that families were confined to their homes. Because food delivery vans did not get through the cordon, milk and bread were in short supply. At this time typical shopping habits involved daily trips to a local shop, because not many people had refrigerators or storage space for more than one day's supply of food. This meant that few households had the supplies to sustain themselves with. A main concern involved the supply of milk for young children and medicine for those suffering from respiratory difficulties due to the CS gas used by the military. Begoña Aretxaga makes the point that milk was 'both a metonymic representation of food and a symbol of emotional nurture. The inability of women to provide milk during the curfew encapsulated the enforced impossibility of providing for the physical and psychological well-being of family members'.[20] According to Aretxaga, interfering with the supply of milk became for these women the 'height of British depravity'.[21] It was this, she believes, that prompted women to adopt new methods of political expression.

In London, the newly elected conservative prime minister, Edward Heath, received a brief detailing the military's perception of the manoeuvre. The report explained that the overall feeling among the soldiers who were participating in the action was that it had been 'very successful in administering a shock to the extremists and in boosting morale among the troops and the moderates'.[22] This statement raises questions about motives behind the imposition of the curfew and reveals a fundamental lack of insight into policing in a divided community. According to the available records the prevailing analysis among government officials was that the rioting was led and encouraged by republican extremists. Oberschall points out that it is a common response for authorities in such a situation to search for and prosecute ringleaders who they see as the 'lawless, restless, rootless, violence-prone bottom layer of the population'.[23] The curfew can be seen as an effort by the security forces to assert itself against the 'violence-prone' Lower Falls after its earlier indecisive action at the end of June. Though it was not designed to be a search and arrest operation, it can be read as a clear message to the fledgling republican factions and their ringleaders. Following the curfew Home Secretary Reginald Maudling declared that the British forces were now in a state of 'open war' with the IRA.[24] The desired response to the curfew had not gone according to plan; instead of breaking a fledgling movement, the shock of the action succeeded in consolidating nationalist opinion against the security forces throughout the province. The *Sunday Times* Insight Team aptly pointed out that the curfew converted 'what was perhaps only an increasingly sullen Catholic acceptance of the Army into outright communal hostility'.[25] Bell supports this observation saying that after the curfew IRA recruitment soared.[26]

Many accounts of the curfew written on 3 and 4 July draw special attention to the anger felt by the Lower Falls women. By the evening of 4 July the women of the Upper Falls, similarly enraged at what they regarded as unnecessarily oppressive tactics by the security forces, planned marches. The first march on 5 July attracted more than 3,000 women and began at approximately 12:24 p.m.; the second march of more than 1,000 women took place at about 5:30 p.m. Organized by Dolly Monaghan and Máire Drumm, a prominent member of Provisional Sinn Féin and wife of a leading republican and former IRA prisoner, among others, they began at St Paul's church in Cavendish Street and made their way to the Lower Falls via Leeson Street. Lily Fitzsimons, another woman who would become a prominent member of Provisional Sinn Féin, participated in the march and later commented: 'It was one of the greatest days of solidarity that I can remember ... The soldiers didn't know what had hit them, they were literally overwhelmed by a sea of determined women.'[27] A legion of women marched through the line singing provocative songs such as the civil rights anthem 'We shall overcome' and the republican rebel song 'A soldier's song' and waving a tricolour flag. They were armed with as much bread and milk as their prams could hold and they made their way to a distribution centre in Raglan Street.

The women who organized the march, ostensibly to relieve those within the cordon, found a way to assert themselves without posing the kind of threat that might have spurred retribution from the security forces. Outwardly, it was a humanitarian effort but on another level it was an indication that the army would encounter resistance if it persisted in such tactics – a kind of resistance they were not trained to handle. The *Newsletter* aptly pointed out the next day that the march 'was as much a demonstration as a relief measure'.[28] One marcher later remarked that the humanitarian effort was secondary to the ultimate goal of breaking the curfew: 'Bringing the milk and bread, that was a necessity but the main thing was breaking the curfew.'[29] Once the curfew had been broken there would be no need for relief, she reasoned. Dolly Monaghan's statement reported the next day confirms this thinking: 'We said we would break the curfew if it was not lifted ... They couldn't mow us down, could they? And they couldn't trap us all in jail. There wouldn't be room.'[30] Though these comments seem naïve in light of the events that followed the curfew, they reflect the normative expectations of state security policy.

What made the march possible was a popular tacit acceptance of a social convention that implied that women, in and of themselves, posed little threat to security. Parita Mukta, in her study of Hindu women activists, discusses a 'myth of innocence' that allowed women to mask their activism.[31] In Northern Ireland a similar 'myth of innocence' informed this tacit acceptance of social conventions regarding women, which allowed their activism to adopt a unique role in street politics as it had during the Irish Revolution. In a society characterized by its ideological polarization, this tacit agreement of women's innocuous nature was probably one of the only subjects on which all sides of the brewing conflict could agree. The marchers later gave the impression that they knew they were not going to be stopped by the security forces, but when pressed were unable to articulate a reason why they were not stopped. Though the march was empowering to these women, *as women*, it did not mark the emergence of a women-centred consciousness. The acknowledgement that women experienced multiple layers of oppression within the nationalist community had yet to surface, most likely due to their unique position in that society. This march allowed them to leverage that position to demonstrate their power – a power incongruously derived from their secondary status and the perception that they were incapable of committing political violence.

Keeping in mind that this was a time when street violence was generally confined to more primitive technology and when the IRA was estimated at numbering fewer than one hundred activists, it is necessary to interrogate the reason why soldiers respected a code of gentility and refrained from stopping them. One soldier told a reporter: 'Well, we are human. Everybody just seems to think that we are ogres.'[32] Lorraine Dowler builds on Mukta's concept of the 'myth of innocence' by arguing that it was an assumption of innocence that allowed women to bend rules and breach borders men simply could not:

> In West Belfast women's identities have been relegated to the home, however, as a result women have enjoyed a spatial freedom not shared by most of the men of this area. Because of their presumed political 'innocence' women could *transcend* the boundaries of West Belfast ... It is not surprising ... that they do not pose the same kind of threat as men do in a public space.[33]

Mukta cites a report on Indian women activists that claims that women can be manipulated into neutralizing security forces and they can also manipulate societal attitudes about their innocence. But in the march to break the curfew, who was manipulating who? Was this a republican plot?

There is no evidence to suggest that people other than those mentioned above planned the march, and on balance it seems unlikely either the Official or the Provisional IRA was sophisticated or organized enough to orchestrate the march amid the confusion of the moment; the Officials were still trying to regroup in Dublin, and the Provisionals had only begun to engage the army a few days prior to the curfew. Moreover, had either republican group chosen to move against the army, they certainly would have done so through guerrilla fighting, not through local women. The march, while organized by republican women, was so effective precisely because it was an unplanned civilian action by women. Cynthia Cockburn, who wrote on women and community action in Britain in 1977, makes the point that 'women's action till now has been relatively weak. But it has one great power – unexpectedness. Women's action is revolutionary because its nature is to cut cross all the fossilized expectations'.[34] The presumption of their innocence, aided by bottles of milk and loaves of bread, created a space for shocked soldiers to respect a code of gentility and a space for the women to cultivate a fusion of public and private roles in their flamboyant act of defiance.

One interesting component of the march was the 'greening' of it. That they sang the traditional republican anthem, 'A soldier's song', and waved a tricolour speaks more to the development of tribalism in West Belfast than to the idea that it was a republican plot. In the context of the kind of enforced political hegemony that outlawed republican flags and emblems, these acts should not be viewed as preplanned measures, even if some of the organizers and many of the marchers were republicans. It is likely that the 'greening' of the march evolved spontaneously out of a combination of frustration at the imposition of the curfew and communal solidarity. Critically, the soldiers did not respond to the provocation. The lessons local republicans gleaned from the march were critical to the development of the paramilitary campaign on which they were beginning to embark. First, British soldiers were hesitant about moving against women, which demonstrated to the republican movement the usefulness of the 'myth of innocence'. Second, the propaganda to be generated by unarmed women engaging in such provocations was immeasurable. So, though the republican movement most likely did not organize the action, it had much to gain by the circulation of images of the march. In fact, this march remained a potent symbol that would inspire republican activism for years to come.[35]

People's contemporaneous responses to the breaking of the Falls curfew is best characterized by a letter to the *Irish News* written by an unnamed veteran of the Second World War:

> In sincere humility I pay tribute to the women of the Falls for their wonderful gesture of humanity and kindness towards their sisters of the Lower Falls on Sunday. Their courage in defying massive fire-power to feed the hungry and succor the children was an example to us all of applied Christianity. Should their deeper protective instincts be aroused I tremble for the troops, etc.[36]

This man's self-identification as a veteran may suggest that the humanitarian appearance of this march appealed to a wider community than members of the republican movement. The characterization of the march as 'applied Christianity' once again underscores parallels drawn between the role of nationalist women in Northern Ireland and the Virgin Mary. His last sentence speaks to the issue of women's agency; it was an articulation of what many had only vaguely registered, that the power women could marshal collectively was a threat to state security. Dowler believes that women in this society only enter the public arena when 'there is imminent danger of violation of the domestic sanctuary'.[37] Though this phenomenon has somewhat changed in the more recent past, at this point in the emerging conflict, women were still embarking on political action, as Dowler describes, in response to a threat to their domestic identities.

The breaking of the curfew brought women's roles in militarism and street politics to the fore in much the same way that it had during the First and Second World Wars. As militarism began to increase, women's agency in both spheres grew in significance. Advertisements, which appeared in Northern Ireland's newspapers directly after the event, called on women to use their influence to discourage militancy: 'Trust the mothers to show sense!'[38] Other appeals joined these advertisements: on 10 July the women of the Ulster Unionist Council appealed for restraint to all the women in Northern Ireland,[39] and a few days later Maureen Lynch, wife of the Republic's Taoiseach, Jack Lynch, called for women's unity in the North.[40] The advertisements and calls for women's unity reveal the perception of women's unique position in managing the emerging conflict. By appealing to the wisdom of women as mothers and potential widows, the advertisements highlight the valuation of motherhood so common to nationalist contexts. V. Spike Peterson points out that it is mothers who are responsible for the ideological reproduction of nationalist ideology, as we have seen with Cumann na mBan: 'They are largely responsible for inculcating beliefs, behaviours, and loyalties that are culturally appropriate and ensure intergenerational continuity.'[41] And if, as Cynthia Enloe points out, 'cultural constructions of masculinity in many societies have been dependent on... elevating women as mothers-of-soldiering-sons, valuing women chiefly for their maternal sacrifices for the nation', appealing to mothers would have a strong resonance with both women within the domestic sphere and their husbands and sons, who would form the majority of those engaging in street violence.[42]

In Stormont, Northern Irish Prime Minister James Chichester-Clark attended a Joint Security Committee meeting with some of his cabinet and senior members of the security committee. Sir Ian Freeland began the meeting by saying that the curfew mission had been completed satisfactorily and that the 'invasion of the women of Andersonstown' had only caused minor problems for the soldiers.[43] The Chief Constable indicated that he would be in a position to prosecute some of the women if the committee deemed it appropriate, but there was no enthusiasm for this idea. One official even went as far as to scrawl 'Let's hope he doesn't' in the margin of the meeting notes.[44]

The issue of arresting Northern Irish women for politically motivated actions had always been a thorny one for Stormont. At times the Northern Irish police forces had moved against republican women, but the instances of this were so rare that they proved the rule. The fact that no women were arrested for defying the curfew suggests that Stormont decided to continue its unspoken policy of skirting the issue of women's militancy, according to the long-established tacit acceptance of women's special status in Northern Irish society. As the meeting wound down a chief inspector of the special branch warned that the Civil Rights Association would label the curfew an atrocity and the Minister for Home Affairs, Robert Porter, suggested that Freeland look into the legalities of imposing another curfew in the future. In fact, the dubious legality of the confinement operation would do more to fuel republican propaganda than Freeland had anticipated. Overall, the relatively small cache of arms culled by the army during the curfew was hardly worth the hostility the action had provoked among the Falls Road residents. And if the intention was to shock people into submission, then it certainly had the opposite effect.

The day after the curfew ended a third women's march was held in the Falls Road area. This time there was no pretext at relief. A few hundred women marched to the Springfield Road complaint centre with crudely lettered placards that read 'Fix my slates', 'Six counties, English shame' and 'What happened to British justice?'[45] The wording of their placards is significant; some called attention to the material damage to their homes while others set their sights on political reform. By appealing to English notions of justice, these placards aimed to shame the army. Where these women had a few days earlier waved bread and bottles, now they clutched placards and signs. Aretxaga suggests that the marches 'achieved the quality of a myth of origin, the starting point of women's popular resistance'.[46] Chrissie McAuley, who was inside the cordon, later remembered the euphoria as the women came through. Her description of the marches is emblematic of the folk memory that grew out of that period. She believed that the women who marched 'knew they were going into the lion's den but they saw that they needed to break the stranglehold and they rose to the challenge. That went down as the benchmark of resistance'.[47] Women's marches had happened before, but this one was different in light of the scale of weaponry the soldiers possessed, the scale of violence leading to the imposition of the curfew, the sheer unexpectedness of a unified women's street action, and its political objectives. Nationalist women had marched before this, and as discussed in Chapter 2, there had been cases where their objectives were indeed political. The significance in this series of marches lay in its context; the nationalist community at large was beginning to see itself as a unified collective getting 'off its knees', as the popular saying went, to assert itself. To the rest of the community, the women with their placards in-hand were becoming symbols of resistance and role models to emulate.

Bardon calls the imposition of the curfew a 'political blunder' while Desmond Hamill, historian of the army's presence in Northern Ireland during the period, heartily agrees.[48] The tension was not confined to Belfast either; the curfew represented a turning point in community relations between the Catholic population and the security forces throughout the province. A public relations disaster for the security forces and the government, the curfew set the tone for the events that followed within government circles and on the ground. While it demonstrated to Catholics that the British forces could be as heavy-handed as the local police, it clearly signalled to the loyalist community a potential allegiance. The fact that no Protestant homes were searched when, by all accounts, they held the preponderance of weaponry, was received as a victory for loyalists in the area. Militarily, the Falls Road curfew achieved very little; it demonstrated decisive action at the expense of one of the Catholic population's neighbourhoods and most of the Catholic population's patience. Through this episode Catholics became aware of their own vulnerability and a group of Lower Falls women demonstrated an awareness of their potential power as street activists. From this moment forward many began to articulate that they should look to themselves to maintain their security against old enemies, the Royal Ulster Constabulary, the loyalists and now the British army.

INTERNMENT

Between the summers of 1970 and 1971 street violence became the order of the day. Unable to successfully defuse the situation, Chichester-Clark resigned, making way for Unionist hardliner Brian Faulkner to assume the position of Prime Minister of Northern Ireland in March. By August internment without trial was introduced throughout the province. On the first night of internment, 9 August 1971, 342 men were arrested – almost all of them Catholic.[49] In the first six months of internment, 2,357 men had been arrested – again that number was disproportionately Catholic.[50] Almost immediately it became clear that the outdated intelligence on which the army had been relying was yielding very few of the top IRA leaders. Instead, septuagenarians who had been added to police watch lists during the War of Independence and then the Irish Civil War in the 1920s, pacifists active in the civil rights movement, and communists who sold the odd newsletter, found themselves arrested and quickly released in large numbers – a testament to the army's hastened and haphazard preparation. O'Malley framed the feeling that took root in the nationalist community: 'The horrifying circumstances of that morning were never to be forgotten. Whole areas were sealed off, paratroopers smashing down doors and literally dragging men from their homes in front of hysterical wives and terrified children, the brutal knock in the middle of the night ... The army, "the Brits", had become the enemy.'[51] The two major effects of internment on the ground called into question the wisdom of such large-scale security operations. First, it solidified resentment of the security forces among many parts of the Catholic community. Second, the mortality rate sky-rocketed and people, increasingly alienated, looked to paramilitaries for protection.[52] That so many were released proved to even the most moderate of nationalists that they were not exempt from harassment or even internment. Many Catholics began to see the introduction of internment as a method for breaking the nationalist community through deep interrogation, brutality and, some alleged, even torture.[53]

At this time NICRA began to lose male members due to internment or fear of internment. It increasingly fell to women such as Edwina Stewart, Ann Hope and Madge Davison to maintain the momentum of the civil rights movement. Some men left the association to pursue militant activity, others were either interned or intimidated out of participating in the movement. The gendered nature of internment – the fact that women escaped internment for a full seventeen months after the first group of interned men – is one element of the Troubles that has not been sufficiently explored and deserves further investigation. Lynda Edgerton touches on it when she points out that it was in the immediate aftermath of internment that many women entered into organizing positions within the association: 'When NICRA adopted the strategy of setting up local branches and committees, these were composed mainly of women ... eventually a number of women were co-opted onto the executive committee.'[54] Margo Collins, for example, began as a regional organizer for Newry and was brought on to the executive to fill gaps in flagging male participation.[55] Bríd Ruddy, who was also co-opted to the executive as a member of the PD described the process:

> When internment happened one of the consequences of it was a complete deficit of men. The first time I spoke publicly at a meeting was at a rally on the New Lodge Road I think the night after internment was introduced ... My profile was immediately raised and linked with anti-internment ... It was at that stage I was 'spotted' by NICRA and co-opted ... Co-option onto the executive was a way of creating new leaders after the other leaders had gone as a result of internment. Ivan Barr, the chairman and Kevin McCorry, the organizer and Dessie O'Hagan, an executive member had been interned, Malachy McGurren and Liam McMillan had stopped attending meetings, Aidan Corrigan and Kevin Agnew had resigned so at least six leaders had gone and replacements were needed urgently. So from then on I was part of both organizations, PD and NICRA.[56]

Another strand of this experience was its effect on the domestic sphere. The strain that internment exerted on family members of interned men and those 'on the run' has passed into folk memory; stories of loneliness, depression, and prescription sleeping tablets characterize many discussions about women's experience of the period. As the local NICRA leader, Bridget Bond interviewed fourteen Derry women about the effects of internment on their families.[57] These interviews suggest that the wives of interned men faced not only a sense of loneliness and familial tension, but also a certain amount of discrimination from doctors, educators and local government officials. This experience quickly politicized women and encouraged them to increase their participation in street activism and network formation.

Also essential to women's increased activity in groups perceived to be subversive was what Francine D'Amico and Laurie Weinstein in their study of the history of women in the US military call 'gender camouflage', which dictated that women were not equal participants in militant activities. Similar to Mukta's 'myth of innocence', under this principle women might work *with* those who argued to smash Stormont by force, but in the Northern Ireland of 1971 there was a widespread convention that they did not work *in* these groups.[58] Regardless of whether the security forces or the political administration believed that women could possibly have reason to be interned (and judging from the arrest of Bernadette Devlin, they must have known women's engagement in what they perceived to be subversive activity could be possible), a prevailing notion of their innocence, as Mukta describes, meant that women possessed a higher degree of leeway or 'gender camouflage' in terms of public political activism than did their male counterparts.

Gendered groups such as the Political Hostage Action Committee (a precursor to the Relatives Action Committees that sprang up later in the decade) and Women Against Internment began to organize to protest the policy of interning men without trial.[59] They made use of both street action and lobbying to protest the internment of their male relatives, friends and neighbours. They were able to form street protests and hold rallies precisely because they were not initially perceived to be a security threat. One woman remembered that by necessity these groups had to be populated by women: 'It wasn't safe to have a man in a group of any sort.'[60] The women tried to put their message across using any avenue open to them, and their activities ranged from visiting with Taoiseach Jack Lynch and Stormont MPs to going house to house in order to raise awareness and ask for support. When the political climate allowed for more assertiveness, such as after Bloody Sunday when thirteen men were killed by paratroopers in Derry, these women used their political clout and visibility to negotiate for visits with their interned husbands, brothers and fathers – their major threat being that they would bring a significant portion of Northern Irish women on to the streets.[61] Though this threat was never acted upon in the period of this study, it was used as a negotiating tactic that empowered women to push for tangible results.

WOMEN WITHIN THE REPUBLICAN MOVEMENT

Women were just beginning to be permitted to join both the Provisional IRA and the Official IRA as full members at the introduction of internment, though they would not materialize as full-scale activists for another few months. Up until the summer of 1971 they could join Cumann na mBan and act as auxiliaries for IRA operations. In general, though, this organization was viewed as a relic of an earlier period; their function within the movement had not undergone any significant structural changes since before the border campaign, if not earlier. There were, however, some staunch Cumann na mBan supporters in the republican movement who continued the tradition. It was an attractive option for some republican women for a variety of reasons. First, the group's historical development dates back to April 1914; in some cases mothers, grandmothers and aunts had been members, which provided the women of the 1970s with a strong measure of continuity. Second, as the violence escalated, the group did perform essential tasks such as providing cover and first aid for volunteers. Third, joining a female-oriented group allowed women an amount of flexibility with their commitments within the movement and within their homes. Their training was less rigorous and flexible schedules allowed women to maintain their domestic commitments. Finally, a young republican family could protect their domestic arena by allowing the male to take a role in the IRA while the female could join a group that demanded less in terms of time commitment and which was publicly seen to be less of a threat to public order than the IRA. Though its importance was beginning to wane, an organization such as Cumann na mBan still made sense under the traditional gender regime that organized Northern Irish society.

With the move towards the egalitarian goal of women's full participation in militant activism, one could argue that women's position within the republican movement was changing. But there is evidence that a significant proportion of republican women cleaved to traditional roles and modes of expression during this period, perhaps as a reflection of traditional ideology or as a backlash to changing sex roles within society at large. The fact that, according to one prominent Sinn

Féin councillor, Cumann na mBan has not officially disbanded, supports this.[62] During this period the Dublin-oriented Official republican movement began to lose ground in the North to the more avowedly militant Belfast-oriented Provisionals. Where the Officials could dominate the Republic's radical political scene, it had less success with attracting socialists in the North. The Communist Party of Northern Ireland, with its small but forceful membership, diluted the Official movement's recruiting power by addressing similar left-wing issues. Therefore, though the Officials would have been marginally more amenable to women's issues, increasing numbers of women joined the Provisionals. They were drawn to a movement that looked set to eclipse the Officials as the superior paramilitary force.[63]

The recruitment of female IRA members coincided with the escalation of violence and ironically a new emphasis on some aspects of traditional gender roles and nationalism. At this time some female Provisional republicans launched a spate of tar-and-feather attacks on women seen to be consorting with soldiers.[64] The general public greeted this tactic of policing women's sexuality with revulsion. But, women in both the Provisional and Official wings of the movement saw it as a necessary tool to discourage informing.[65] Tarring and feathering also functioned as a warning to those women whose husbands were interned in some cases that infidelity was a community concern. Though this practice was discouraged after the negative popular reaction, some intimidation tactics intended to police women's personal life remained part of women's roles in the republican movement.

Despite these sharp reminders that traditional attitudes remained strong within the movement, the bulk of the evidence suggests that women's roles were in a state of flux as they began to play more central parts within the movement. This period was a liminal phase where women were still able to play on a perception of their innocuous role in street politics while asserting themselves in new ways. Máire Drumm is an example of a woman who made a career out of pushing the limits of the tacit acceptance of women's special status. A lifelong republican and wife of a senior figure in the movement, Drumm entered early on to this path with her women's march on Crumlin Road jail in 1958, which stormed the gates to protest a ban on prison visits.[66] Though unsuccessful, the march had raised morale for the men interned and the women outside. Drumm was able to apply the experiences of the first march to organizing the successful Falls Road curfew march.

The year 1971 was Drumm's most active year, which correlates with the introduction of internment. In January she was elected Vice

President of Provisional Sinn Féin, probably because of an assumption that her sex would allow her to escape internment, though her political stature also qualified her for the position.[67] By this time women were beginning to dominate the ranks of Sinn Féin as more men joined the IRA.[68] In February 1971 Drumm led what became known as the 'combat jacket pickets' through the streets of Belfast to protest the arrest of men in paramilitary dress at funerals. Also at that time she gave a speech in Derry saying, 'It is a waste of time shouting "Up the IRA", the important thing is to join.'[69] She was finally jailed for the last two incidents, receiving a sentence of six months for each offence. What is significant about Máire Drumm, as a case study of the de-composition of the myth of innocence, is her singularity of tactic and her willingness to taunt the security forces, each time surrounded by a legion of like-minded women. Initially her tactics raised morale by playing on stereotypes of acceptable women's behaviour and indeed, what seemed to be British military impotence. The poem printed in Chapter 1 regarding the storming of the Crumlin Road jail demon-strates how her marches were received within her community and how, by standing the prevailing gender regime on its head, she could emerge victorious regardless of the actual outcomes of the march. Her fiery rhetoric had a profound impact on young women who saw her speak. After the 'up the IRA' speech, for example, Bridie McMahon joined the IRA and later cited Drumm's speech as a primary motivating factor.[70] Significantly, out of the hundreds of speeches and demonstrations in which Drumm participated in Northern Ireland, it was only when she assumed a male persona by donning a combat jacket and beret or by openly recruiting for the Provisional IRA, the male-dominated organi-zation, that she was arrested in this period. At times Drumm has been classed alongside Bernadette Devlin as a strong female figure who emerged out of the Northern Irish conflict – both were defined by the troubles that brought them to prominence – but Drumm stands out in this period because of the specificity of her rhetoric. Where Devlin during this period generalized about the coming socialist revolution, Drumm spoke about taking specific actions, such as joining the IRA to effect revolution by force.

At this time most women were still developing their political con-sciousnesses by taking part in the civil disobedience campaign orches-trated by civil rights groups as a response to internment. According to Lynda Edgerton, the idea to withhold rent and rates (including gas and electricity) was tabled at a meeting in Armagh composed mainly of women.[71] Women, still so strongly identified with the domestic sphere, ensured the success of the strike and took part in other forms of civil disobedience, such as stopping traffic and forming endless queues at post offices and other government offices. Those who could be more outspoken in their protest and those who subscribed to republican ideologies followed the example of Máire Drumm. Building on her demonstrations that women in groups were less vulnerable to retribution than men, Provisional republican women began to band together to form community patrols. Without a telephone to warn their neighbours that the soldiers were on their way, the women resorted to a 'bush telegraph' of sorts; they found whistles and grabbed the lids off their rubbish bins. They formed groups called 'hen patrols' in response to army search groups, which had been dubbed 'duck patrols'. As the army conducted house searches groups of women followed them banging their bin lids and blowing their whistles to herald the army's presence in the neighbourhood. Maureen McGuinness remembered the hen patrols as a bonding experience:

> There were rotas and we'd go around the houses and ask who could go on hen patrols and what nights they could do ... you were up at four o'clock [for example] and then you were on 'til six or seven. And we didn't always walk down the streets. If it was quiet you'd stand at the corner and hear all the yarns about what was happening on the other streets. It was really exciting. [When the soldiers came] we followed them. If you saw them coming in the area you blew your whistle and hit the lids on the ground and made as much noise as you could, shouting, screaming, whatever.[72]

The bonding that women experienced during this period must not be underestimated; coming together to fight against a perceived common enemy through patrols contributed to a sense of empowerment.

Women engaged in psychological games against the 'duck patrols' by converging on them, blowing whistles, bashing their bin lids and then suddenly disappearing behind doors left open for them by local residents, only to re-emerge five minutes later and converge on the soldiers again. Women who took part in this activity describe the empowering feeling and shared delight at being able to frighten fully armed soldiers with such basic technology.[73] The soldiers they were acting against were often young men from working-class areas similar to Belfast and Derry. They had been trained for foreign combat and now, crucially, they could identify with and also understand the language of their adversaries, which in this circumstance could actually heighten their anxiety. McGuinness's comments comfirm this: '[We were] like their grannies and mammies. Yeah, they were afraid. They were really afraid.'[74] As these confrontations progressed barriers between the 'ducks' and 'hens' began to erode and confrontations erupted into physical violence.

Some women, in an effort to disarm the soldiers during violent confrontations, seized their weapons and passed them on to local IRA leaders. The security forces were convinced hen patrols had been an IRA front for arming the IRA from the beginning: 'the IRA uses women to pin-point the position of army sentries or patrols, particularly at night, by banging dustbin lids and blowing whistles. They harass and sometimes attack sentries, apparently with the aim of seizing their weapons.'[75] This patriarchal analysis denies women agency in what became a community effort to reject the British presence in Northern Ireland. On balance, the hen patrols were probably not conceived of as IRA operations but likely evolved into them once the first weapon was seized. As these confrontations became more routine, expectations of gendered behaviour soon blurred. By late 1971 two Cumann na mBan women were killed and another three republican women wounded by British soldiers as they patrolled the streets.[76] Unsurprisingly, Aretxaga concludes that the 'metaphoric [duck and hen] game ceased to be effective when the military figured it out' and began to shoot these women.[77] Overall, it was women's engagement in just such direct action coupled with their use of 'myth of innocence' that finally contributed to the erosion of their unique position within the community.

During that period a handful of women joined the movement as regular members of the Provisional IRA. Dolours and Marian Price were among the first to do so. Dolours had rejected the idea of joining Cumann na mBan in favour of playing an 'equal role to the male volunteers', as she saw it.[78] She believed that the reluctant decision to admit women into the IRA was made at the highest level by Sean MacStiofáin, who was in that period the Provisional IRA Chief of Staff. Though women were being recruited for the Official IRA as well, the emphasis on political action over militancy meant that female members of the Officials were more likely to engage the government through protest politics. The inclusion of women in the ranks of the IRA had the potential to stem the loss of men to internment, which was becoming an increasing problem as the security forces improved their intelligence. In the face of this new policy shift, it is noteworthy that the Provisional IRA was unconcerned about the issue of the changing roles of women in the movement. This contrasts with the Officials, who, as discussed in Chapter 5, were warming to the concept of feminism. This lack of awareness among the Provisionals is most likely the result of the concomitant chaos of the rapidly unfolding communal violence and the militant posture taken by the organization. Feminism was simply not on the radar for the Provisionals at this point because of where they were, what they were responding to, and how they styled their movement.

Bloody Sunday in January 1972 sealed the fate of community involvement in the Provisional IRA, when members of the Parachute Regiment killed thirteen apparently unarmed men (a fourteenth was mortally wounded) and wounded seventeen others during a NICRA march against internment. Ann Hope remembered the immediate aftermath of the shooting as she and Madge Davison made their way to Bridget Bond's home, which functioned as the local NICRA headquarters.

> As we walked toward Free Derry Corner we saw a row of men lined up against a wall … being guarded by soldiers. As we approached the soldiers automatically wheeled around and pointed their rifles at us … I can remember that Madge said something like 'don't worry, they are only shooting the men' and Madge and I kept walking and were not challenged. Madge's comment really caused the shock and horror to set in then … As it turned out, Madge was right, and it was only the men and boys who were killed that day. I now believe that this was a deliberate policy as it would have been difficult to accuse women of being nail bombers or having fired at the soldiers.[79]

Peter Taylor interviewed a British soldier who pointed out that when he had been previously stationed in Aden, shooting those who appeared to be ringleaders in a rioting crowd was a familiar method of riot control: 'If they didn't [disperse after a warning], then the man in charge, the sergeant-major, would say, "The man in the white turban, directly in the middle," and we all knew who he was. "Fire!" and someone would drop him … And then they'd all disappear.'[80] But in Northern Ireland the shootings at that anti-internment march simply perpetuated riots and armed activity. Richard English makes the point that after this event the Provisional IRA seemed to have more potential recruits than it could train.[81] The end of 1971 marked a new phase in community–gender relations between the Northern Irish Catholics and the British army. The British army shot three women at the end of

1971, which demonstrated that the unique status women enjoyed within the community was in a state of flux. This, combined with the events surrounding Bloody Sunday, meant that more and more women began to consider joining the Provisional IRA, which ensured they would become more integrated into a rapidly expanding organization.

With the increase of political violence, people joined the movement for a variety of reasons. Dolours Price remembered:

> Basically many people came into the republican movement who were not republican. They came into it because they wanted excitement in their lives. Some came into it because they were angry about the way the soldiers had treated them ... And some people came into it because of genuine feelings of Irishness that they were prepared to explore and articulate in that way.[82]

The end result was a rapidly expanding movement that took on recruits of varying republican commitment without comprehensively vetting them first. Rita O'Hare, who is one of the women who was shot at the end of 1971 and who is today a senior member of Sinn Féin, remembered back to that time: 'Nowadays membership checks are more stringent; then there was a tremendous openness ... In a way the openness was extremely bad. It gave the Brits the opportunity to plant spies and so on.'[83]

How did those women who did join reconcile their commitment to the republican movement and their domestic commitments? Women who consider joining armed political movements tend to cite anxiety about children or the possibility of motherhood as a possible barrier or mitigating factor in their decision to participate in political violence.[84] Many of the women who joined the IRA lived in tight-knit communities and had access to an extended family support network to help rear their children in their absence, which allowed them more freedom to join the movement. They also saw themselves as community defenders, which was seen as an extension of their domestic duties. Luisella de Cataldo Neuburger and Tiziana Valentini's study of Italian women militants has found that once women make the decision to join such movements, they appear to become more committed to the cause than many of their male counterparts.[85] Though we cannot easily apply this study of left-wing militancy to the events in Northern Ireland, there is certainly evidence that women's rhetoric reflected a high level of commitment during this period. One female member of the Official IRA said this of tarring and feathering a 15-year-old girl: 'If she was an informer they should have shot her. Tarring and feathering were too good for her.'[86] A woman in the Provisional IRA agreed: 'Me, I wouldn't waste time tarring and feathering and cutting her hair. I would shoot them in the leg or something, if they weren't going to be killed.'[87] These statements, printed in a New York pamphlet entitled 'Irish Women Speak', cannot be relied on solely for their content due to the anonymity of not only the subjects but also the editor. Nevertheless, they remain demonstrative of the changing roles of women and the increased commitment to the success of paramilitary operations no matter the human toll.

IRA women experienced a degree of resistance to their active participation. Some described males having difficulty with taking orders from women, but most pointed to acts of chivalry that hindered their sense of equality within the movement. For example, a statement by one woman illustrates the difficulties faced by both men and women regarding women's increased militancy: 'They might say to you, "I don't want a girl to come out on this operation ... If anything happens to you, if you get wounded, I'll want to stay behind and look after you, more so than if you were a male volunteer". It's a very slow process to convince them that you're equally capable of looking after yourself.'[88] The issue of ground combat chivalry was then and continues to be a significant obstacle to women's full military participation throughout the world.[89] Another impediment to achieving equal treatment within the movement was the fact that some women did not expect equal treatment. One post-internment Official IRA member's statement demonstrates how women themselves could encounter their own barriers to equality in the movement: 'Men know more about it – about the guns and the bombs and things like that. I think you need a man's guidance.'[90] These differing experiences and outlooks among women within the movement reflect a movement in transition still coming to grips with gender differences. Oftentimes, gender differences were minimized by those interviewed so as not to appear critical of the movement. This happened for two reasons. First, neither a women-centred consciousness regarding the layers of oppression to which women were subject in nationalist Northern Ireland, nor a feminist consciousness seeking to change the system had developed. Second, any statement interpreted to be disloyal to the movement might have left women open to retribution from within the movement, as in the case of Maria McGuire's *To Take Arms*, written while in hiding, about her year in the movement.[91] That so few women have achieved places on the Provisional IRA's Army Council speaks to the entrenched structural barriers to women's equal participation that are present even after the movement has undergone such significant changes to the gender regime.

Overall, republican women's roles within the movement underwent significant changes in the early 1970s mainly due to gender-based militancy and security activities. Internment raised the profile of women's street politics. Bloody Sunday copper-fastened women's activism because the casualties were all male. By focusing on men's activism for a period of a year and a half, the security forces and the administration contributed unwittingly to the rise of women's anti-state activism.

SECURITY DEVELOPMENTS AND WOMEN'S MILITANCY

By the end of 1972 the security forces began to realize that women's increased militant activism presented a particular problem. Official security policy began to change in response to the changes that occurred on the ground. There were few facilities in which to imprison women and there were no policies in place to usefully tackle their activity. Furthermore, the republican movement could play on traditional notions of women's roles to generate great propaganda if soldiers were seen to mistreat women. This kind of propaganda had been attempted unsuccessfully when Bridie O'Neill was interned in 1958, and it failed due to a lack of popular support for the movement. But now things were different. The broad support base the republican movement could now marshal, in conjunction with the civil rights groups, could galvanize the Catholic community and the world at large.

In 1972 the security forces began to figure this out. They began issuing soldiers and the police with a directive that 'females must not [sic] be arrested … simply for the purpose of interrogation'. Women were only to be arrested if caught red-handed, and in the event that they were arrested, the security forces were instructed that they must have a female officer with them because there was 'always a danger that an arrested female will subsequently allege that soldiers behaved indecently towards her'.[92] This directive quickly became policy, and it was re-emphasized in the following month's security standing order.[93] The wonder of this memorandum is that it shows the security community acknowledging the prevailing gender regime. Up until then the special treatment of women – the fact that they were not to be arrested simply for interrogation – had been common sense and unacknowledged, so powerful was the gender regime. The very existence of these directives outlining women's unique status suggests that the security forces were aware that the position of women in Northern Ireland had already begun to change.

The issue of recruiting more women police also surfaced during this period. Similar to the staffing problems faced by the IRA, as the level of violence increased, the Royal Ulster Constabulary needed new recruits. The possibility of recruiting more women reservists was floated at a 4 October 1972 meeting between the Secretary of State for Northern Ireland William Whitelaw and Sir Ian Fraser, chairman of the Police Authority of Northern Ireland. At subsequent meetings it was decided to recruit 500 more women at the customary 95 per cent of the male wage as soon as possible.[94] Unfortunately these memorandums do not reveal if the purpose of the drive to increase female recruitment was simply to make up numbers or to be able to make good on the standing security orders, which called for women security officers to be present at the arrest of all female suspects.

Throughout 1972 rumours that women would be interned abounded, even in the Republic. In December 1971 *Hibernia* began the public call for clarity on the issue when it asked if women would be next. It quoted a newsletter that had been circulating in the Turf Lodge area of Belfast saying that living in an area so bereft of its male members was 'living women's liberation – not talking it like our middle-class sisters in America: not burning bras but rattling bin lids'. The article went on to say that despite the fact that some women were obviously finding internment of their husbands liberating, how long was it going to be before the Northern Ireland security machine began to see women as a 'threat to Empire'?[95] This article, even in its dismissal of a shared experience among the world's women, reveals that some sense of second-wave feminism had begun to penetrate the consciousness of women embroiled in such an all-encompassing ethno-sectarian conflict. Interestingly, women who wrote about 'living liberation' highlighted the differences between themselves and their 'middle-class sisters in America', which gives rise to the question, why did they not draw parallels with the working-class feminist movements that became so pivotal to British feminism? A reluctance to draw parallels with the British feminist movement, despite some clear connections, points to the same type of underlying disinclination to identify with British radical politics that the Irish Women's Liberation Movement experienced in the Republic. Considering the context, this reluctance was not surprising.

For the moment, however, the main issue was the internment of women. The rumour of women's internment not only preoccupied Southern media sources, but it went to the highest level of the Republic's government. Soon after the Christmas period, Taoiseach Jack Lynch summoned British ambassador John Peck at short notice. According to Peck, Lynch complained about the intensification of the internment policy, mentioning the rumours of the internment of women. Peck reported to his superiors that Lynch conceded there might be some 'bad' women, 'but he was afraid that Irish traditions and attitudes being what they were we should turn the whole island against us if we interned them'. Peck added that he too, saw no strategic reason for interning women: 'It is hard to imagine what military advantage it could possibly have to outweigh the hostility it would arouse and the boost it would give to the IRA.'[96] Peck suggested that if it were a rumour, it should be killed quickly. But by the end of the month nothing had been done in this vein and Lynch was still worried. At a meeting with British Prime Minister Edward Heath in Brussels on 23 January, Lynch brought it up again and Heath changed the subject.[97] After that meeting, however, Peck was dispatched to assure Lynch that the introduction of internment for women was not on the table.[98]

The position was untenable once it became clear that more and more women were engaging in political violence on the same terms as their male counterparts, however. The security forces held out through a brutal contest of one-upmanship in 1972, but by the end of the year they began to contemplate a change in policy. The records suggest that without consultation with the Republic, or indeed significant 'in-house' discussion, the security forces interned the first woman, Liz McKee, on 1 January 1973. Heath was spared a protest against the decision to intern women by a distracted Lynch, who was on his way out of office and later predictably by newly elected Taoiseach Liam Cosgrave, a strong advocate of bi-partisan anti-terrorist measures. The decision to intern women caused an adverse response but not the wave of protest Lynch had earlier anticipated. The *Belfast Telegraph* reported that groups of female republicans had moved across the border to evade the security forces,[99] and though Cosgrave stood resolutely against paramilitarism, he decided not to intern. Instead, when he assumed power in March, he let recently enacted anti-terrorism legislation deal with those who were caught taking part in republican activity. In the North a situation report recorded a spontaneous demonstration over the new departure in policy demonstrated by the internment of Liz McKee.[100]

Once again Máire Drumm led a march of several hundred women in Andersonstown on 7 January.[101] During a speech she told the security forces: 'For every woman they try to intern, I am confident that another fifty women will step forward to take their place … The British can't put the women down.'[102] The myth of innocence was now almost fully eroded. A few days after McKee was interned, Drumm became the 'acting' president of Sinn Féin in place of a male leadership that was either interned or on the run. The contingency plan had worked: Drumm, despite her political provocations, had remained outside the security cordon while the rest of the leadership was interned. Much had changed in the past two years, however, and now that McKee was interned, Drumm had no guarantee that the security forces would continue to overlook her militant demonstrations.

Three months after the first female internee was detained, on International Women's Day, two of the first female Provisional IRA members, Dolours and Marian Price, along with another woman and eight men, embarked on a new phase of the campaign supervised by Dolours: bringing the violence to England. Marian Price later explained the reasoning behind the decision to bomb targets in England by commenting: 'It doesn't seem to matter if it's Irish people dying.'[103] They planted car bombs at symbolic targets guaranteed to shock the British public: the Old Bailey, New Scotland Yard, Whitehall and the British Forces Broadcasting Office. At their trial the group admitted their affiliation with the Provisional IRA and all were sentenced to life. The Price sisters and a few others undertook a hunger strike in order to be transferred to a jail in the North. At this point, with the bombing and the scale of negative propaganda a hunger strike would generate, women had now become a bona fide 'threat to the Empire' as full and equal members of the IRA. For Dolours Price the decision to undertake a hunger strike was informed by 'heaps of tradition, heaps of martyrdom ... We could be of service to the movement – we could sacrifice our life, our bodies, to promote our cause.'[104] This kind of thinking helped people like the Price sisters link their own militancy to those who took part in earlier republican hunger strikes in order to establish a sense of continuity. The hunger strike was a common weapon of last resort in Irish politics; these women saw themselves as taking their place among a long line of martyrs.

Though women were now joining the IRA as equal members, the relationship between republicanism and feminism remained nebulous. Through the pages of the Provisional movement's *Republican News* and surprisingly to a lesser extent, the Official movement's *United Irishman*, one can observe the beginnings of a debate about women's position within republicanism. Though the Official movement had begun passing resolutions in favour of contraception and women's equality,[105] and though Official Sinn Féin's most senior female member was also a founder of the Women's Liberation Movement during this period, *United Irishman* did not reflect this changing outlook. As discussed in

Chapter 5, the *United Irishman*'s failure to comprehensively engage in this issue in favour of other left-wing political issues meant that in an ironic twist the Provisionals' *Republican News* surfaced as the more egalitarian newsletter. Though both factions as a whole shied away from discussing controversial topics such as birth control and abortion, occasionally *Republican News* explored the equal pay debate and housing action.

In January 1973 Una O'Neill wrote a column for *Republican News* asking if women's liberation was relevant to her readership. Her argument fell broadly in line with Provisional thinking at the time: women were already liberated due to the 1916 Proclamation's call for Irishmen and Irishwomen to stand up for their cause. O'Neill's mild criticism that 'lordly menfolk' patronize women represented a small step towards a debate on equality.[106] Her assertion, that 'today the women of Ireland are liberated in the true sense of the word. They are not only willing to stand and fight beside their menfolk but also to die with them if necessary', would frustrate theorists such as Cynthia Enloe, who argue that entering into a patriarchal and militaristic organization does not represent a move towards the liberation of women. In fact, Enloe argues, it is quite the reverse. She rejects the idea that 'the military is so central to the entire social order that it is only when women gain access to its core that they can hope to fulfil its hopes and aspirations'.[107] But within republican circles in the early 1970s, joining the armed movement became the only way to work towards any sort of renegotiation of the gender regime. Moreover, the notion of enlisting in a paramilitary organization was born much more out of a reaction to communal violence than any women-centred or feminist consciousness that may have been ascendant at the outbreak of the violence. If feminists emerged, then they were inextricably linked to their political surroundings, which rendered the cultivation of a feminist consciousness that focused solely on feminism difficult, if not impossible.

More than a year had passed since the Price sisters and others had joined the IRA and in response the security forces were attempting to tackle the issue of how women's involvement impacted on them. The issue could no longer be ignored; Maria McGuire had just published her book about joining the republican movement and participating in arms deals on the Continent.[108] But according to the records, the Ulster Defence Regiment (UDR), a reserve security force, was the only force to discuss the dearth of women officers as a consequence of the rise of female militancy in 1973. Others had discussed hiring more women, but all had heretofore stopped short of attributing increased staffing needs to women's growing activism in the republican movement. By February 1973 R.A. Custis of the Ministry of Defence wrote a memorandum to most of the top officials, including the British Prime Minister, about recruiting women: 'In view of the increasing use of women in terrorist activities by the IRA (and possibly other extremist organizations) it is operationally important that the UDR, when manning check points, should be able to search women who, at present, mostly pass unchecked.'[109] This memorandum has the dubious distinction of being the first in a rather belated attempt at dealing with the changing nature of the republican movement. Though women's involvement in political violence still seemed to be sinking in among the RUC and the army rank and file, there may have been high-level intelligence about the Price sisters' involvement with the London operation, according to one news magazine.[110] If this is true, then it is difficult to understand why the security forces on the ground could have been so reluctant to tackle the issue of women's activism that it took them two years to articulate the reason for increases in female personnel.

Certainly, however, British politicians were shocked at this 'new' development in republican activity. On 27 March 1973 David Madel, conservative MP for South-West Bedfordshire, asked William Whitelaw in the House of Commons what information he had about women engaging in political violence. The Secretary of State for Northern Ireland's factual answer that thirteen women were presently serving sentences for offences such as causing explosions, possession of firearms and armed robbery, that eleven were awaiting trial for similar offences, that two women had been interned and two more had been issued with interim custody orders, underscores a shift in women's street activism towards increasing rates of participation in political violence.[111] What is significant, then, is the shock people felt when they learned women had now joined the movement on equal terms as republican men. Because women IRA members had been active for more than a year, the fact that the security forces and politicians were not ready for them reflects a kind of naïveté one might not expect from a major world power. Moreover, British military and intelligence sections knew quite well the power of the 'myth of innocence', judging from their experience with the F Section of the Special Operations Executive in the Second World War. After obtaining Cabinet approval for the use of women agents in France only, it sent over a group of women to act as couriers; their sex rendered them less likely to be searched.[112] In light of the past success of the F Section, the British security forces were slow to draw parallels and to recognize their vulnerability to female insurgency at the onset of the Northern Irish Troubles.

CONCLUSION

For nationalist women the first few years of the 1970s saw a renegotiation of the gender regime in ways that were heavily informed by their experience of the unfolding conflict in Northern Ireland. What began as a powerful force in street politics because of its ties to domesticity and the cult of Mary emerged as a collection of individuals expressing their power through their community activity and their choice to take up arms. Monica McWilliams, who went on to co-found the Northern Ireland Women's Coalition, points out that women were aware of this power that was linked to domesticity:

> In the 1970s women formed the backbone of most community action right across Northern Ireland, because problems in local areas were clearly affecting these women's lives and those of their children. Women had been brought up to see the home and the family as their primary responsibility, and the survival of these was being threatened increasingly by the state. It is paradoxical really, that our society should seek to keep women passive, yet by threatening the basis of that passivity, the society provokes action from the same women.[113]

The transition undertaken by women to reconfigure the gender regime within both strands of republicanism coincided with the advent of second-wave feminism, yet at the time it was rarely couched in feminist rhetoric. In joining the IRA as full members instead of the auxiliary Cumann na mBan group, women were beginning to express (but not verbalize) a dissatisfaction with the limits of their traditional roles. Once the first few women had joined both the Officials and the Provisionals as full IRA members (and they were able to do so without much discussion or debate due to depleted numbers and a surge in activity), others could do so as well without having to express a dissatisfaction with Cumann na mBan. Had it been a less chaotic period, there may have been more resistance to the integration of women, which may in turn have forced women to begin to adopt a women-centred consciousness and articulate feminist demands within the movement. This sensitivity to inequalities in the gender regime did not emerge, but women's street activism set the stage for it to do so as the conflict wore on and strip searches, no-wash protests and

Relatives Action Committee demonstrations became the order of the day.

Other groups within the community tore a page from Catholic women's activism by beginning to consider street politics as well. Women's peace groups began to hold vigils, marches and even negotiations with the Provisional IRA and Stormont MPs, and probably the most significant other group that sprang into action in the mid-1970s, the Loyalist Association of Workers, recruited and trained women to prepare for their province-wide strike in 1974. An analysis of loyalist post-1973 activism is necessary for a fuller understanding of province-wide street activism, but this lies outside the scope of this study. A few conclusions can be drawn from the available documents and interviews. Women were beginning to change their positioning within the gender regime during this period, as unfolding events demanded their increased activity. Because of how rapidly the political violence mounted, they were able to do so without significant resistance and without significant discussion as to why they sought to change their positions. Had it been a less chaotic period, then there may have been more debate, more discussion and more resistance to their membership in the IRA, and, in turn, that may have forced women to begin to articulate feminist demands within the group.

In the beginning of the 1970s there was an intercommunal tacit acceptance that the women of Northern Ireland held a separate, and perhaps even revered, status as managers of the private sphere; for both sides of the community this idea was based on religious tradition and social convention. What linked Irish Catholicism to the adulation of women in the domestic sphere was its emphasis on Mary-as-mother. So when women chose to penetrate the public sphere en masse, as they did during the Falls Road curfew, the social convention of the myth of innocence was respected. But as the campaigning intensified and internment without trial was introduced, women's unique status began to erode. In that liminal period at the commencement of internment, republican women occupied both strata of social roles; they utilized their power as a collective outside the army–republican paradigm hitherto reserved for men, and they began to engage in political violence on the same terms as their male counterparts, thereby entering that paradigm. A majority of women held on to their identities within the home, and a growing number sought to redefine their identities by engaging in paramilitary action.

Both the Northern Irish and the British governments seemed to be slow in responding to the changing roles of women and only began to see them as a threat to the state when major IRA operations involving females were already well underway. The security forces (and a large number of civilians) sustained significant casualties partly because they failed to interpret and act on the erosion of the tacit acceptance regarding women's unique position. By introducing gendered policies, such as the internment of men, and by taking gendered action such as imposing the curfew, engaging in house searches and killing a group of unarmed men in a mixed crowd, it was they, ironically, who unwittingly colluded with republicans to ensure that an increasing number of republican women were no longer content to remain auxiliaries in their father's army.

NOTES

1. Quoted in a Turf Lodge area newsletter from 1971, reprinted in *Hibernia*, 17 December 1971.
2. Interview with Ann Hope, Belfast, 30 June 2003.
3. Interview with Angela Nelson, Belfast, 2 July 2003.
4. Interview with Dolours Price, Malahide, 7 March 2003.
5. M. MacCurtain, 'Towards an Appraisal of the Religious Image of Women', in M.P. Hederman and R. Kearney (eds), *The Crane Bag Book of Irish Studies, 1977–1981* (Dublin: Blackwater Press, 1982).
6. G.D. Zimmerman, *Irish Political Street Ballads and Rebel Songs* (Geneva: Imprimerie la Sirine, 1966).
7. C.B. Shannon, 'Women in Northern Ireland', in Mary O'Dowd and S. Wichert (eds), *Chattel, Servant or Citizen? Women's Status in Church, State and Society* (Belfast: Institute of Irish Studies, 1995), p.245.
8. H. Brody, *Inishkillane: Change and Decline in the West of Ireland* (London: Faber, 1973), p.175.
9. M. McWilliams, 'The Church, the State and the Women's Movement in Northern Ireland', in A. Smyth (ed.), *Irish Women's Studies Reader* (Dublin: Attic Press, 1993), pp.82–3.
10. L. Edgerton, 'Public Protest, Domestic Acquiescence: Women in Northern Ireland', in R. Ridd and H. Calloway (eds), *Caught up in Conflict: Women's Responses to Political Strife* (Basingstoke: Macmillan Education in association with the Oxford University Women's Studies Committee, 1986), p.62.
11. J. Simpson, 'Economic Development: Cause or Effect in Northern Ireland', in J. Darby (ed.), *Northern Ireland: The Background to the Conflict* (Belfast: Appletree Press, 1983), pp.82, 101; J.M. Trewsdale, 'The Role of Women in the Northern Ireland Economy', in R.J. Cormack and R.D. Osborne (eds), *Religion, Education and Employment: Aspects of Equal Opportunity in Northern Ireland* (Belfast: Appletree Press, 1983), p.115.
12. *Regional Trends* (1992), cited in McWilliams, 'Church, the State and the Women's Movement', p.86.
13. L. Connolly and T. O'Toole, *Documenting Irish Feminisms* (Dublin: Woodfield Press, 2005), p.148.
14. J. Bardon, *A History of Ulster* (Belfast: Blackstaff Press, 1992), p.678.
15. P. Bew and G. Gillespie, *Northern Ireland: A Chronology of the Troubles* (Dublin: Gill and Macmillan, 1999), p.29.
16. *Irish Times*, 6 July 1970.
17. Interview with McAuley, Belfast, 25 June 2003.
18. C. Card, 'Rape as a Weapon of War', *Hypatia*, 11 (1996), p.47.
19. Anonymous quoted in H. Harris and E. Healy, *'Strong About It All': Rural and Urban Women's Experiences of the Security Forces in Northern Ireland* (Derry: North West Women's/Human Rights Project Publications, 2001), p.20.
20. B. Aretxaga, *Shattering Silence: Women, Nationalism and Political Subjectivity in Northern Ireland* (Princeton, NJ: Princeton University Press, 1997), p.57.

21. Ibid., p.59.
22. Memorandum to Prime Minister Edward Heath, 4 July 1970, London, NA PREM 15/100. For more on this tactic, see N. Klein, *The Shock Doctrine: The Rise of Disaster Capitalism* (New York: Metropolitan Books, 2007).
23. A. Oberschall, *Social Conflict and Social Movements* (Englewood Cliffs,NJ: Prentice-Hall, Inc., 1973), p.305.
24. E. Maloney, *A Secret History of the IRA* (London: Allen Lane, 2002), p.101.
25. Sunday Times Insight Team, *Ulster* (Harmondsworth: Penguin, 1972), p.221.
26. J.B. Bell, *The Secret Army: The IRA, 1916–1979* (Dublin: Poolbeg, 1990), p.377.
27. L. Fitzsimons, 'Liberty Is Strength' (n.d. c. late 1990s).
28. *Newsletter (Belfast)*, 6 July 1970.
29. Interview with Maureen McGuinness, Belfast, 27 June 2003.
30. *Irish Independent*, 6 July 1970.
31. P. Mukta, 'Gender, Community, Nation: The Myth of Innocence', in S. Jacobs, R. Jacobson and R. Marchbank (eds), *States of Conflict: Gender, Violence and Resistance* (London: Zed Books, 2000).
32. *Irish News*, 6 July 1970.
33. L. Dowler, 'No Man's Land: Gender and the Geopolitics of Mobility in West Belfast, Northern Ireland', *Geopolitics*, 6 (2001), p.161.
34. C. Cockburn, 'When Women Get Involved in Community Action', in M. Mayo (ed.), *Women in the Community* (London: Routledge & Kegan Paul, 1977), p.69.
35. See C. McAuley, 'Women in a War Zone: Twenty Years of Resistance' (Dublin: Republican Publications, 1989); Sinn Féin Women's Department, 'Women in Struggle' (1994).
36. *Irish News*, 9 July 1970.
37. L. Dowler, "'And they think I'm just a nice old lady": Women and War in Belfast, Northern Ireland', *Gender, Place and Culture*, 5 (1998), p.166.
38. *Newsletter (Belfast)*, 9 July 1970.
39. *Irish News*, 10 July 1970.
40. *Irish Independent*, 15 July 1970.
41. V.S. Peterson, 'Gendered Nationalism: Reproducing "Us" Versus "Them"', in L.A. Lorentzen and J. Turpin (eds), *The Women and War Reader* (New York: New York University Press, 1998), p.44.
42. C. Enloe, 'All the Men are in the Militias, All the Women are Victims', in Lorentzen and Turpin (eds), *Women and War Reader*, p.54.
43. Notes on Joint Security Committee meeting, 6 July 1970, London, NA, DEFE 13/730.
44. Ibid.
45. *Irish News*, 8 July 1970.
46. Aretxaga, *Shattering Silence*, p.59.
47. Interview with McAuley, Belfast, 25 June 2003.
48. Bardon, *History of Ulster*, p.678; D. Hamill, *Pig in the Middle: The Army in Northern Ireland 1969–1984* (London: Methuen, 1985), p.39.
49. Bardon, *History of Ulster*, p.683.
50. P. Hillyard, 'Law and Order', in J. Darby (ed.), *Northern Ireland: The Background to the Conflict* (Belfast: Appletree Press, 1983), p.37.
51. P. O'Malley, *The Uncivil Wars: Ireland Today* (Belfast: Blackstaff Press, 1983), p.208.
52. Bardon, *History of Ulster*, p.684; Bell, *Secret Army*, p.382; R. English, *Armed Struggle: The History of the IRA* (London: Macmillan, 2003), p.140; B. Feeney, *Sinn Féin: A Hundred Turbulent Years* (Dublin: O'Brien Press, 2002), p.271.
53. See *Report of the Inquiry into Allegations against the Security Forces of Physical Brutality in Northern Ireland Arising out of Events on the 9th of August 1971 (the Compton Report)* (1971).
54. Edgerton, 'Public Protest, Domestic Acquiescence', p.66.
55. Statement by Margo Collins and statement by Ann Hope to Bloody Sunday Inquiry, transcript available on www.bloody-sunday-inquiry.org .
56. Statement by Bríd Ruddy to Bloody Sunday Inquiry, transcript available on www.bloody-sunday-inquiry.org .
57. Northern Ireland Civil Rights Association Survey of Internees' families, undated, Derry, Harbour Museum, Derry City Council Archives, Bridget Bond papers, folder 25.
58. See F. D'Amico and L. Weinstein (eds), *Gender Camouflage: Women and the U.S. Military* (New York: New York University Press, 1999).

59. While the Political Hostage Action Committee is well documented in *Aretxaga Shattering Silence,* pp.71–4. the activities of Women Against Internment is less so. See 'Irish Women Speak' (1973).
60. Quoted in 'Irish Women Speak'.
61. Quoted in ibid.
62. Interview with McAuley, Belfast, 25 June 2003.
63. Though few records have been preserved, the growing popularity of the Provisionals indicates increasing recruitment levels. For more on this see Bardon, *History of Ulster*, p. 684; Bell, *Secret Army*, p.382; English, *Armed Struggle*, p.140; Feeney, *Sinn Féin*, p.271.
64. See *Belfast Telegraph*, 10 November 1971 and *Newsletter* (Belfast), 12 November 1971.
65. See 'Irish Women Speak'.
66. *United Irishman*, 4 April 1958. See also Chapter 1.
67. The last time a woman had been elected to such a powerful office was during the border campaign after the introduction of internment.
68. Feeney, *Sinn Féin*, p.268.
69. See Ch. 8 of Fitzsimons, 'Liberty is Strength'.
70. Bridie McMahon quoted in P. Wilson and R. Walsh (eds), *A Rebel Heart: Máire Bn. Uí Dhroma* (n.p. Belfast, 2001), p.15.
71. Edgerton, 'Public Protest, Domestic Acquiescence', p.66.
72. Interview with McGuinness, Belfast, 27 June 2003.
73. See Aretxaga, *Shattering Silence*, p.68.
74. Interview with McGuinness, Belfast, 27 June 2003.
75. IRA tactics, March 1972, London, NA, CJ 4/458.
76. D. McKittrick *et al.*, *Lost Lives: The Stories of the Men, Women and Children Who Died as a Result of the Northern Ireland Troubles* (London: Mainstream Publishing, 1999), pp.107–8.
77. Aretxaga, *Shattering Silence*, p.68.
78. Interview with Price, Malahide, 7 March 2003.
79. Statement by Ann Hope to Bloody Sunday Inquiry, transcript available on www.bloody-sunday-inquiry.org .
80. P. Taylor, *Brits: The War against the IRA* (London: Bloomsbury, 2001), p.31.
81. English, *Armed Struggle*, p.151.
82. Interview with Price, Malahide, 7 March 2003.
83. Quoted in E. MacDonald, *Shoot the Women First* (London: Fourth Estate, 1991), p.147.
84. See L. De Cataldo Neuburger and T. Valentini, *Women and Terrorism*, trans. Leo Michael Hughes (London: Palgrave Macmillan, 1996); MacDonald, *Shoot the Women First*.
85. De Cataldo Neuburger and Valentini, *Women and Terrorism*.
86. Quoted in 'Irish Women Speak'.
87. Quoted in ibid.
88. Quoted in ibid.
89. See for example L. Boussy, 'No Women in Ground Combat', *United States Naval Institute Proceedings*, 122, 11 (1996); M.E. Oelke and R.J. Vogt, 'Women in Combat Roles: Past and Future' (unspecified degree thesis, Air War College, Alabama, 1988).
90. Quoted in 'Irish Women Speak'.
91. See both S. MacStiofáin, *Memoirs of a Revolutionary* (Edinburgh: Gordon Cremonesi, 1975); M. McGuire, *To Take Arms: A Year in the Provisional IRA* (London: Macmillan, 1973).
92. Northern Ireland standing security instructions, November 1972, London, CJ 4/458.
93. Annex B to 1104G Commander Land Forces directive, 7 December 1972, London, NA, CJ 4/458.
94. See Women in RUC, October, 1972, London, NA CJ 4/128.
95. *Hibernia*, 17 December 1971.
96. Peck to Foreign and Commonwealth Office, 7 January 1972, London, NA, FCO 87/127.
97. Notes on meeting between Lynch and PM, 23 January 1972, London, NA PREM 15/1710.
98. Cabinet brief on internment, n.d., London, NA, FCO 87/56.
99. *Belfast Telegraph*, 2 January 1973. It is not possible to confirm if this statement reflects rumours or fact-based reports. Regardless, the article reflects the different approaches taken by the two governments.
100. Situation report, 3/4 January 1973, London, NA, PREM 15/1689.
101. Sinn Féin Women's Department, 'Women in Struggle'.

102. Quoted in Fitzsimons, 'Liberty is Strength', Ch. 8.
103. Quoted in English, *Armed Struggle*, p.163.
104. Interview with Price, Malahide, 7 March 2003.
105. Interview with de Burca, Dublin, 15 March 2004. See also (Official) Sinn Féin, 'Women's Rights in Ireland' (1975).
106. *Republican News*, 17 January 1973.
107. C.H. Enloe, *Does Khaki Become You? The Militarisation of Women's Lives* (London: Pluto Press, 1983), pp.16–17.
108. McGuire, *To Take Arms*.
109. Custis to PM, etc., 27 February 1973, London, NA, PREM 15/1690.
110. *Village*, 4–10 December 2004.
111. Northern Ireland press office notice, 27 March 1973, London, FCO 87/177.
112. For more on this see R. Kramer, *Flames in the Field: The Story of Four SOE Agents in Occupied France* (Harmondsworth: Penguin, 1996).
113. M. McWilliams, 'Women and Political Activism in Northern Ireland: 1960–1993', in A. Bourke, S. Kilfeather, M. Luddy, M. MacCurtain, G. Meaney, M. Ní Dhonnchadha, M. O'Dowd and C. Wills (eds), *Field Day Anthology of Irish Writing: Irish Women's Writing and Traditions*, vol. 5 (Cork: Field Day, 2002), Vol. 5, p.379.

Conclusion

Women's work within the radical activist milieu had a profound impact on Ireland's gender regime in the 1960s and 1970s. Their activism, which grew out of a concerted effort to radically restructure the state, spurred a comprehensive critique of power relations throughout Irish society. Did this work help to create the conditions for the second wave of feminism to take root? Yes. But the process was not the same in both regions. A women-centred consciousness, or an understanding of multiple layers of oppression experienced by women, developed in response to different precipitating conditions. Critically, however, these developments overlapped and influenced each other: they emerged in Ireland as part of international movements and they also developed out of historical and political factors that were unique to Ireland.

We cannot hope to understand the complexity of this social change while adhering strictly to geographic borders and/or isolated paradigms of study. While more problematic to conduct than state-by-state or issue-by-issue studies, we must insist on political analysis that mirrors its subject's fluidity. In this case, Irish activists often operated on both sides of the border, they read about contemporary global movements and they developed international and cross-group networks. By taking account of networks that existed on both sides of the border, that existed because of the border, or that chose to act only on one side of the border due to the contested status of the border itself, this study tells a story of the complexities of gender regime transformation within the radical and mainstream environment. There are similarities, parallels, shared relationships and differences within and among the developing activist agendas. The support and insight they shared was a key factor in each group's development and that of a wider radical movement. One person interviewed for this book remarked that membership in one group seamlessly led into another, while another said she could not have worked against state oppression without also working against women's oppression. If activists were beginning to make these connections to broaden their work, then researchers must respond by broadening their work to form a more organic analysis.

Gender, then, becomes a critical component to the exploration of any social change during this period. And not just for female historians. Without studying how women fit into the structure of society, how can we, as a discipline, hope to understand how that society functioned or how it changed? But we cannot simply stir women into the folds of history by recovering their stories. We must, as Joan Wallach Scott urges, expose the 'hidden operations of gender' within that society.[1] This study documents the transformation of the gender regime within the republican movement and the civil rights movement, as well as Irish society in general, through the germination of the feminist movement. It does so by inquiring into how women transformed the prevailing gender regime by bringing new concepts of equality from the margins of politics to the mainstream.

Anchoring research in its proper context is equally important. This study begins in the period preceding a major surge in activism in order to acknowledge the role of abeyance feminist organizations and radical organizations and to chart the rise of women's street activism. Throughout the 1950s abeyance feminist organizations such as the Irish House-wives Association provided movement continuity by continuing to lobby government ministers to consider implementing rights-based legislative changes. As the most significant radical political movement in the 1950s, republicans (male and female) understood women's roles to be so integral to the movement that their activism melded with their duties as responsible wives, mothers, sisters and daughters.[2] Female Sinn Féin members, Cumann na mBan members and family activists saw these roles as being so interconnected that they did not attach any particular significance to their activities. As in many nationalist movements,[3] whether it was rearing children to take up the cause, packing parcels and visiting jailed relatives, or providing safe-house facilities, republican women (and their male counterparts) generally viewed male militancy to be the single most notable factor in the family's activism. From their point of view, the women were simply carrying out their role within the family. In parallel to their abeyance feminist counterparts, republican women's activism, defined by the domestic sphere though it was, was crucial to preserving a sense of continuity for the movement. Rachel Ward, in her study on political activism among unionist and loyalist women in Northern Ireland, presents a similar analysis. According to her, women's involvement in political and community action was not confined to simply making the tea, and while 'national interests have been prioritized over gender', these women have tended to be politicized by threats to the domestic sphere.[4] Though republican women's roles were confined to a patriarchal gender regime, the women of the 1950s campaign provide an example of the radicalization of domestic roles at that time and a glimpse into radical politics in a setting hostile to street activism. They also provide a benchmark against which one can evaluate later radical activity.

The activity of the Homeless Citizens' League and the Campaign for Social Justice in the early 1960s reveals a similar trajectory of thought. These groups, however, also reframed women's activism (with uneven success) into a more female-oriented, media-savvy, political pressure group than the republican movement had contemplated. In dealing more directly with politicians, these groups challenged notions of their secondary status in the gender regime and the state. Their vitality is part of the reason they presented a formidable alternative to republicanism. And their success, creativity and ability to adapt tried and true political tactics ensured that their pivotal contribution to radical politics would be remembered, utilized and improved upon. But as much as many of these women worked to overcome the perception of their political innocence, they confirmed it by allowing themselves to be edged out of the groups, thereby reinforcing the gender regime and its hierarchies.

Irish society watched as these women achieved their successes and either withdrew or, as in the case of Patricia McCluskey, moved on to a less radical media campaign. This message was not lost on government officials, who also play a significant role in this study. This book documents the radical political changes women fought for during this period and how they changed the gender regime while doing so. But it is not enough to simply tell their story. In order to get at not just what happened *to women*, but to get to what *happened*, it is important to recognize that the government had a reflexive relationship with these groups and the women in them. In many ways the governments involved created the conditions for a rethink of the gender regime by starting on the process of European integration and attempting to reform antiquated legislation that affected women. Once that door was open, it was difficult to stave off calls for further reform. Government bodies also demonstrated a significant amount of intransigence during early calls for reform, and then a serious amount of heavy-handedness in their attempts to maintain order and break the radical movements of the early 1970s. As much as the radical movements of this period effected change in Irish society, the governments of Britain, Northern Ireland and the Republic of Ireland also played a significant role. Gendered policies, such as all-male juries in the Republic or male internment, radicalized women and gave them a *raison d'etre* to demand a renegotiation of the gender regime.

When did a women-centred consciousness develop and how did that spur second-wave feminism to take root? Just as anywhere else, it followed no recipe. There were, however, experiences common to women in both parts of Ireland. First, international news coverage of the American civil rights movement, the student movement and the women's movement played a significant role in setting the stage. It allowed activists the opportunity to make connections regarding power relations and the universality of oppressive tactics. It also set an example of ways in which to achieve radical societal and legislative change.

The radical press complemented news of international movements by allowing Irish activists to relate international issues to Ireland. By the mid-1960s the political paradigm of womanhood was being analysed and discussed comprehensively, not only with the Republic's radical press but also in a handful of mainstream publications. The breaking of social taboos and the expansion of topics such as familial roles, sexuality and family law educated an expanding cohort of women regarding their position within Irish society and the western world. This was a period of coalescence in the Republic where journalists began to expand their topics to expose the unspoken and unseen — a world very often associated with women. This period of consciousness-raising mirrored an international trend that preceded and corresponded with women's increased street activism. Though new political concepts were coming to the fore in Northern Ireland, the lack of a significant radical press and the segregated structure in the region muted this process of coalescence.

The period also saw a rapid proliferation of legislative and judicial activity designed to address systemic inequalities. Both the United Kingdom and Ireland were working towards gaining entry into the European Union, which meant they had to revamp their concepts of citizenship and rights to come into line with European law. This forced the Republic to begin grappling with concepts of equal work for equal value, the position of women in the family and inheritance law, and compulsory retirement upon marriage. While Northern Ireland had remained outside of most of Britain's equality legislation over the years, it had been included in postwar education initiatives, which meant that the generation that came of age in the late 1960s began to demand the same rights to which the rest of Britain was entitled. This legislation opened the door for agitation in favour of a more radical restructuring of both states.

Regardless of these steps, both governments responded to the rapidly mounting calls for change inadequately. Their intransigence (real and perceived) became the necessary foil for the respective activists to rally against, which only strengthened the different movements. As calls for reform went unaddressed, the government's intransigence evolved into heavy-handedness and ultimately abuse. In the North calls for an end to systematic discrimination against Catholics were initially ignored and then met with force. In the Republic housing agitation was met with the Prohibition Against Forcible Entry bill, which criminalized homeless squatters. Each account of government heavy-handedness or abuse, such as the Falls Road curfew and internment, acted as a recruiting agent for the movement involved. The movements then planned both reactive and proactive campaigns to address these issues.

A women-centred consciousness grew out of these experiences, as women's roles gained ground in their respective movements. Within the republican movement women played a key role in covert activities, no longer providing cover for men as they did in the border campaign but playing on notions of their political innocence to provide cover for themselves. After internment was introduced women civil rights activists immediately rose to the highest ranks of the movement; they could give speeches, walk the streets at night and lead marches with less fear of retribution from the security forces. Feminists in the Republic set upon raising that consciousness for the nation in their newspapers, on the 'Late Late Show' and on the streets. Their work in these movements spurred them to make connections between the movement's concept of oppression and their own. But this process did not progress evenly in both states, nor did it happen simultaneously. The Republic followed a similar pattern to other feminist movements throughout Europe. Northern Ireland's trajectory shared features of the American experience. In the chaos of evolving sectarianism, the formation of this consciousness was interrupted. Within the republican movement, the sense of community threat became so powerful that women rose up the ranks rather quickly. Perhaps had there been less chaos, the republican hierarchy might have resisted a bit more. Without that introspection, and in the gathering storm of tribalism, feminism was seen as a distraction. While it eventually did take root, it evolved into a very unique brand of feminism, having emerged amid a resurgence of nationalism and paramilitarism among the Catholic community.

A final question that might be asked is, where do we go from here? This research continues the historical narrative of women in Ireland by recovering strands of the radical street activist agenda as they relate to the development of women's roles. As more private and governmental records become available, there undoubtedly will be more to add. The inclusion of Protestant activists, the loyalist movement, the feminist movement in Northern Ireland and the decade directly following this study presents a variety of directions in which one could continue the discussion this research begins. The critical principle the researcher must keep in mind when attempting to widen the narrative to include these new strands of analysis, is that people, networks and ideologies invariably cross borders, patterning themselves into a tapestry that must be appreciated for all of its non-linear intricacies and backstitches. It is necessary to move beyond simplistic assumptions of movement unity and singularity of mind or purpose in analysing these social movements. By continually challenging paradigms of study, a more comprehensive story can be told.

NOTES

1. J. Wallach Scott, *Gender and the Politics of History* (New York: Columbia University Press, 1999), p.27.
2. For more on this phenomenon and how it interacts with nationalism, see N. Yuval-Davis and A. Anthias, *Women–Nation–State* (London: Macmillan, 1989).
3. Ibid.
4. R. Ward, *Women, Unionism and Loyalism in Northern Ireland* (Dublin: Irish Academic Press, 2006), pp.160–5.

Leabharlanna Fhine Gall

Select Bibliography

STATE ARCHIVES AND RECORDS

Derry City Council Archives, Harbour Museum, Derry
Bridget Bond Collection
National Archives of Ireland, Dublin
Department of Foreign Affairs – DFA
Department of Justice – DJ
Department of the Taoiseach – DT
National Archives, Kew Gardens, England
Foreign and Commonwealth Office – FCO
Ministry of Defence – DEFE
Northern Ireland Office – CJ
Prime Minister's Office – PREM
**National Archives and Records Administration of the United States of
    America, Maryland**
United States Department of State
Public Record Office of Northern Ireland, Belfast
Campaign for Social Justice Papers
Frank Gogarty Papers
Home Office Series
Kevin Boyle Papers

UNIVERSITY ARCHIVES AND LIBRARIES

Linen Hall Library
Microfilm Collection
NICRA papers
Political Collection
Morris Library, University of Delaware
Kay Boyle Papers

National Library of Ireland
Special Collections
Trinity Library
Special Collections

NEWSPAPERS AND MAGAZINES

An Phoblacht
Belfast Telegraph
Catholic Herald
Daily News
Daily Telegraph
Derry Journal
Dungannon Observer
Free Citizen
Hibernia
Independent
Independent on Sunday
Irish Echo
Irish Independent
Irish News
Irish Times
Irish People
Irish Press
Irish Woman's Journal
New Statesman
New York Times
News Letter (Belfast)
The Tablet
The Times
This Week
Tyrone Courier
United Irishman
Universe
Village
Woman's Way

INTERVIEWS, CORRESPONDENCE AND WITNESS STATEMENTS

Abortion Act 1967 Witness Seminar held 10 July 2001 (Institute of Contemporary British History, 2002, www.icbh.ac.uk/downloads/abortion.pdf).

Collins, Margo, witness statement to Bloody Sunday Inquiry, AC148 (4 April 2001), available on www.bloody-sunday-inquiry.org

Currie, Austin, interview, Dublin, Lucan, 1 September 2003

Dunlop, Ann, interview, Dungannon, 23 November 2003

Dinsmore, Susan, interview, Dungannon, 25 November 2003

De Burca, Máirín, interview, Dublin, 15 March 2004

Hope, Ann, witness statement to Bloody Sunday Inquiry, AH112 (8 April 2001), available on www.bloody-sunday-inquiry.org

Hope, Ann, interview, Belfast, 30 June 2003

Kavanagh, Noel, correspondence, 9 July 2009

Kenny, Mary, correspondence, 12 May 2004

Maher, Mary, interview, Dublin, 24 May 2004

McAuley, Chrissie, interview, Belfast, 25 June 2003

McCann, Eamonn, interview, Derry, 8 February 2003

McCluskey, Conn and Patricia, interview, Foxrock, 5 March 2003

McCrystal, Angela,interview, Dungannon, 31 March 2003

McGuinness, Maureen, interview, Belfast, 27 June 2003

McKeown, Ciaran, correspondence, 21 September 2005

Ó Nualláin, Máire, interview, Dublin, 3 December 2002

Price, Dolours, Malahide, interview, 7 March 2003

Ruddy, Bríd, witness statement to Bloody Sunday Inquiry, AR39 (8 April 2001), available on www.bloody-sunday-inquiry.org

Stewart, Edwina, interview, Belfast, 1 July 2003

Whelan, Rita, interview, Dublin, 2 April 2003

SECONDARY SOURCES AND OFFICIAL REPORTS

Anon., 'Caledon Was About Forcing British to Address Injustices in the North' (www.nicivilrights.org/?p=64, 14 July 2009).

Anon., 'Derry: The Walls Come Tumbling Down', *Fortnight* (7 October 1988).

Anon., 'From a Diary of Derry' (www.irelandsown.net/wire.htm, 7 May 2005).

Anon., 'Irish Women Speak' (n.p., New York, 1973).

Adams, G., 'A Republican in the Civil Rights Movement', in M. Farrell (ed.), *Twenty Years On* (Dingle: Brandon, 1988).

Almeida, L.D., 'A Great Time to be in America: The Irish in Post-Second World War New York City', in D. Keogh, F. O'Shea and C. Quinlan (eds), *The Last Decade: Ireland in the 1950s* (Cork: Mercier Press, 2004).

Anderson, B., *Joe Cahill: A Life in the IRA* (Dublin: O'Brien Press, 2002).

Arendt, H., *Crisis of the Republic* (San Diego, CA: Harvest/Harcourt Brace Jovanovich, 1972).

Aretxaga, B., *Shattering Silence: Women, Nationalism and Political Subjectivity in Northern Ireland* (Princeton, NJ: Princeton University Press, 1997).

Arthur, P., *The People's Democracy, 1968–73* (Belfast: Blackstaff Press, 1974).

Aunger, E.A,. 'Religion and Class: An Analysis of 1971 Census Data', in R.J. Cormack and R.D. Osborne (eds), *Religion, Education and Employment: Aspects of Equal Opportunity in Northern Ireland* (Belfast: Appletree Press, 1983).

Bardon, J., *A History of Ulster* (Belfast: Blackstaff Press, 1992).

Baxter, L., B. Devlin, M. Farrell and C. Toman, 'The People's Democracy: A Discussion on Strategy', *New Left Review* 55 (1969).

Beale, J., *Women in Ireland: Voices of Change* (Indiana: Indiana University Press, 1987).

Beccalli, B., 'The Modern Women's Movement in Italy', in M. Threlfall (ed.), *Mapping the Women's Movement* (London: Verso, 1996).

Bell, J.B., *The Secret Army: The IRA, 1916–1979* (Dublin: Poolbeg, 1990).

Bew, P., P. Gibbon and H. Patterson, *Northern Ireland, 1921–1996: Political Forces and Social Classes* (London: Serif, 1996).

Bew, P. and G. Gillespie, *Northern Ireland: A Chronology of the Troubles* (Dublin: Gill & Macmillan, 1999).

Bishop, P. and E. Mallie, *The Provisional IRA* (London: Heinemann, 1987).

Bolster, M., 'Women on the March: Women in the Civil Rights Movement in Northern Ireland in the 1960s', MA thesis (University College Dublin, 1991).

Bouchier, D., *The Feminist Challenge: The Movement for Women's Liberation in Britain and the USA* (London: Macmillan, 1983).

Boussy, L., 'No Women in Ground Combat', *United States Naval Institute Proceedings* 122.11 (1996), pp.42–4.

Boyd, W., 'Smoke Signals from Sinn Féin', *Hibernia* (February 1967).

Brody, H., *Inishkillane: Change and Decline in the West of Ireland* (London: Faber, 1973).

Brown, T., *Ireland: A Social and Cultural History, 1922–1985* (London: Fontana Press, 1985).

Buckley, S. and P. Lonergan, 'Women and the Troubles, 1969–1980', in Y. Alexander and A. O'Day (eds), *Terrorism in Ireland* (London: Palgrave Macmillan, 1984).

Buckman, P., *The Limits of Protest* (London: Little Hampton Book Services, 1970).

Butler, J., *Gender Trouble: Feminism and the Subversion of Identity* (New York: Routledge, 1990).

Campaign for Social Justice in Northern Ireland, 'Northern Ireland: The Plain Truth', 2nd edn (Dungannon: CSJNI, 1969; revised 1972).

—— 'Northern Ireland: Why Justice Cannot Be Done – the Douglas Home Correspondence' (Dungannon: CSJNI, 1964).

Card, C., 'Rape as a Weapon of War', *Hypatia* 11 (1996).

Carden, M.L., 'The Proliferation of a Social Movement Ideology and Individual Incentives in the Contemporary Feminist Movement', in K. Louis (ed.), *Research in Social Movements, Conflicts and Change: An Annual Compilation of Research 1* (Greenwich, CT: JAI Press, 1978).

CBS, 'Transcript of 60 Minutes', CBS television, 3 February 1970.

Central Statistics Office, *Census of the Population of Ireland* (Dublin: CSO, 1956).

—— *Statistical Abstract of Ireland* (Dublin: CSO, 1960).

—— *Statistical Abstract of Ireland* (Dublin: CSO, 1970–1).

Chappell, M., J. Hutchinson and B. Ward, '"Dress Modestly, Neatly ... as if you were going to Church": Respectability, Class and Gender in the Montgomery Bus Boycott and the Early Civil Rights Movement', in P.J. Ling and S. Monteith (eds), *Gender in the Civil Rights Movement* (London: Garland, 1999).

Christie, K., *Political Protest in Northern Ireland: Continuity and Change* (Reading: Link, 1992).

Clear, C., '"Too Fond of Going": Female Emigration and Change for Women in Ireland, 1946–1961', in D. Keogh, F. O'Shea and C. Quinlan (eds), *Ireland in the 1950s: The Lost Decade* (Dublin: Mercier Press, 2004).

—— *Women of the House: Women's Household Work in Ireland: 1922–1961* (Dublin: Irish Academic Press, 2000).

Cockburn, C., 'When Women get Involved in Community Action', in M. Mayo (ed.), *Women in the Community* (London: Routledge & Kegan Paul, 1977).

Communist Party of Northern Ireland, 'Ireland's Path to Socialism' (Belfast: programme adopted 1962, published CPNI, 1963).

Connell, R., *Gender* (Cambridge: Polity Press, 2002).

Connery, D., *The Irish* (London: Readers Union/Eyre & Spottiswoode, 1968).

Connolly, E., 'Durability and Change in State Gender Systems', *European Journal of Women's Studies* 10 (2003), pp.65–86.

—— 'The Republic of Ireland's Equality Contract: Women and Public Policy', in Y. Galligan, E. Ward and R. Wilford (eds), *Contesting Politics: Women in Ireland, North and South* (Oxford: Westview Press, 1999).

—— 'The State, Public Policy and Gender: Ireland in Transition, 1957–1977', Ph.D. thesis (Dublin City University, 1998).

Connolly, L., *The Irish Women's Movement: From Revolution to Devolution* (New York: Lilliput Press, 2002).

—— 'The Women's Movement in Ireland, 1970–1995: A Social Movement Analysis', *Irish Journal of Feminist Studies* 1 (1996), pp.43–77.

Connolly, L. and T. O'Toole, *Documenting Irish Feminisms* (Dublin: Woodfield Press, 2005).

Coogan, T.P., *The IRA* (London: Harper Collins, 2000).

Coote, A. and B. Campbell, *Sweet Freedom: The Struggle for Women's Liberation* (Oxford: Basil Blackwell, 1987).

Coughlan, A., 'Our Ideas', *Tuairisc: Newsletter of the Wolfe Tone Society* (31 August 1966).

Coulter, C., *The Hidden Tradition: Feminism, Women and Nationalism* (Cork: Cork University Press, 1993).

Crilly, A. (director), 'Mother Ireland', 52 minutes (Northern Ireland, 1988).

Crouch, C., *The Student Revolt* (London: Bodley Head, 1970).

Cunningham, M., *British Government Policy in Northern Ireland, 1969–2000* (Manchester: Manchester University Press, 2001).

Currie, A., *All Hell Will Break Loose* (Dublin: O'Brien, 2004).

Curtin, C., P. Jackson and B. O'Connor (eds), *Gender in Irish Society* (Galway: Galway University Press, 1987).

Daly, M.E., *Social and Economic History of Ireland since 1800* (Dublin: Education Company of Ireland, 1981).

——'"Turn on the Tap": The State, Irish Women and Running Water', in M. Gialanella Valiulis and M. O'Dowd (eds), *Women and Irish History* (Dublin: Wolfhound Press, 1997).

—— 'Women in Irish Trade Unions', in D. Nevin (ed.), *Trade Union Century* (Cork: Mercier Press in association with Irish Congress of Trade Unions and Radio Telefís Éireann, 1994); reprinted in A. Hayes and D. Urquhart (eds), *The Irish Women's History Reader* (London: Routledge, 2001).

—— 'Women in the Irish Workforce from Pre-Industrial to Modern Times', *Saothar* 7 (1982), pp.74–82.

D'Amico, F. and L. Weinstein (eds), *Gender Camouflage: Women and the US Military* (New York: New York University Press, 1999).

Darby, J. (ed.), *Northern Ireland: The Background to the Conflict* (Belfast: Appletree Press, 1983).

Davidson, S., 'Bernadette Devlin: An Irish Revolutionary in Irish America', *Harper's Magazine* (January 1970), pp.78–87.

De Beauvoir, S., 'France: Feminism – Alive, Well and in Constant Danger', in R. Morgan (ed.), *Sisterhood is Global* (New York: Anchor, 1984).

De Cataldo Neuburger, L. and T. Valentini, *Women and Terrorism*, trans. Leo Michael Hughes (London: Palgrave Macmillan, 1996).

DeClementi, A., 'The Feminist Movement in Italy', in G. Griffin and R. Braidotti (eds), *Thinking Differently: A Reader in European Women's Studies* (London: Zed Books, 2002).

DeFazio, G., 'Civil Rights Mobilization and Repression in Northern Ireland: A Comparison with the US Deep South', *The Sixties: A Journal of History, Politics and Culture* 2, no. 2 (2009).

Delaney, E., *Irish Emigration since 1921* (Dublin: Economic & Social History Society of Ireland, 2002).

Devlin, B., *The Price of My Soul* (London: Andre Deutsch, 1969).

Dhalerup, D., 'Three Waves of Feminism in Denmark', in G. Griffin and R. Braidotti (eds), *Thinking Differently: A Reader in European Women's Studies* (London: Zed Books, 2002).

Disturbances in Northern Ireland: Report of the Commission Appointed by the Governor of Northern Ireland (The Cameron Report) (Belfast: Her Majesty's Stationery Office, 1969).

Dooley, B., *Black and Green: The Fight for Civil Rights in Northern Ireland and Black America* (London: Pluto Press, 1998).

Douglas, S.J., *Where The Girls Are* (New York: Times Books, 1994).

Dowler, L., '"And they Think I'm just a Nice Old Lady": Women and War in Belfast, Northern Ireland', *Gender, Place and Culture* 5 (1998), pp.159–75.

—— 'No Man's Land: Gender and the Geopolitics of Mobility in West Belfast, Northern Ireland', *Geopolitics* 6 (2001).

Dowling, J., 'Interview with Cathal Goulding, Chief of Staff of the IRA', *New Left Review* (November/December 1970).

Downing, J.D.H., *Radical Media: Rebellious Communication and Social Movements* (London: Sage, 2001).

Edgerton, L., 'Interview between Lynda Edgerton and Betty Sinclair' (Belfast: Linen Hall Library Political Collection, 1980).

—— 'Public Protest, Domestic Acquiescence: Women in Northern Ireland', in R. Ridd and H. Calloway (eds), *Caught up in Conflict: Women's Responses to Political Strife* (Basingstoke: Macmillan Education in association with Oxford University Women's Studies Committee, 1986).

Eisenstein, Z., *The Radical Future of Liberal Feminism* (New York: Longman, 1981).

Elliott, M., *The Catholics of Ulster: A History* (Harmondsworth: Penguin, 2000).

Elshtain, J.B., *Women and War* (Chicago, IL: University of Chicago Press, 1987).

English, R., *Armed Struggle: The History of the IRA* (London: Macmillan, 2003).

Enloe, C., 'All the Men are in the Militias, All the Women are Victims', in L.A. Lorentzen and J. Turpin (eds), *The Women and War Reader* (New York: New York University Press, 1998).

Enloe, C.H., *Does Khaki Become You? The Militarisation of Women's Lives* (London: Pluto Press, 1983).

Etzioni, A., *Demonstration Democracy: A Policy Paper Prepared for the Task Force on Demonstrations, Protests and Group Violence of the President's National Commission on the Causes and Prevention of Violence* (New York: Gordon & Breach, 1970).

Evans, S., *Personal Politics: The Roots of Women's Liberation in the Civil Rights Movement and the New Left* (New York: Vintage, 1979).

Evason, E., *Against the Grain: The Contemporary Women's Movement in Northern Ireland* (Dublin: Attic Press, 1991).

Fairweather, E., R. McDonough and M. McFadyean, *Only the Rivers Run Free: Northern Ireland, the Women's War* (London: Pluto Press, 1984).

Farrell, M. (ed.), *Twenty Years On* (Dingle: Brandon, 1988).

Feeney, B., *Sinn Féin: A Hundred Turbulent Years* (Dublin: O'Brien Press, 2002).

Feeney, V., 'The Civil Rights Movement in Northern Ireland', *Éire-Ireland* (summer 1974), pp.30–40.

—— 'Westminster and the Early Civil Rights Struggle', *Éire-Ireland* (1976), pp.3–13.

Fennell, N., 'Irish Women: Agenda for Practical Action' (Dublin: Stationery Office, Working Party on Women's Affairs and Family Law Reform, 1985).

Fennell, N. and M. Arnold, 'Irish Women Agenda for Practical Action: A Fair Deal for Women, December 1982–1987, Four Years of

Achievement' (Dublin: Stationery Office, Working Party on Women's Affairs and Family Law Reform, 1987).

Ferriter, D., 'Mothers, Maidens and Myths: A History of the Irish Countrywomen's Association' (Dublin: Irish Countrywomen's Association, 1995).

—— *The Transformation of Ireland, 1900–2000* (London: Profile, 2004).

Finlay, A., 'The Cutting Edge: Derry Shirtmakers', in C. Curtin, P. Jackson and B. O'Connor (eds), *Gender in Irish Society* (Galway: Galway University Press, 1987).

Fitzsimons, L., 'Liberty is Strength' (privately printed, n.d., circa late 1990s).

Foster, R., *Modern Ireland, 1600–1972* (Harmondsworth: Penguin, 1988).

Freeman, J., 'Political Organization in the Feminist Movement', *Acta Sociologica* 18 (1975), pp.222–44.

Freeman, J. (ed.), *Social Movements of the Sixties and Seventies* (New York: Longman, 1983).

Friedan, B., *The Feminine Mystique* (London: Victor Gollancz, 1963).

—— *'It Changed My Life': Writings on the Women's Movement* (Cambridge, MA: Harvard University Press, 1977).

Gallagher, A., 'Women and Community Work', in M. Mayo (ed.), *Women in the Community* (London: Routledge & Kegan Paul, 1977).

Galligan, Y., *Women and Politics in Contemporary Ireland: From the Margins to the Mainstream* (London: Pinter, 1998).

Galligan, Y., E. Ward and R. Wilford (eds), *Contesting Politics: Women in Ireland, North and South* (Oxford: Westview Press, 1999).

Gamson, W.A., *Strategies of Social Protest* (Holmwood, IL: Dorsey Press, 1975).

Gardiner, F., 'The Impact of EU Equality Legislation on Irish Women', in Y. Galligan, E. Ward and R. Wilford (eds), *Contesting Politics: Women in Ireland, North and South* (Oxford: Westview Press, 1999).

—— 'Political Interest and Participation of Irish Women, 1922–1992: The Unfinished Revolution', *Canadian Journal of Irish Studies* 18 (1992), pp.15–39.

Gerhard, U., 'The Women's Movement in Germany', in G. Griffin and R. Braidotti (eds), *Thinking Differently: A Reader in European Women's Studies* (London: Zed Books, 2002).

Gerth, H.J. and C.W. Mills (eds), *From Max Weber: Essays in Sociology* (Oxford: Oxford University Press, 1946).

Gillespie, E. (ed.), *Changing the Times: Irish Women Journalists, 1969–1981* (Dublin: Lilliput Press, 2003).

Gorman, L. and D. McLean (eds), *Media and Society in the Twentieth Century: A Historical Introduction* (Oxford: Basil Blackwell, 2003).

Grieve, M., *Millions Made My Story* (London: Victor Gollancz, 1964).

Griffin, G. and R. Braidotti (eds), *Thinking Differently: A Reader in European Women's Studies* (London: Zed Books, 2002).

Halsaa, B., 'The History of the Women's Movement in Norway', in G. Griffin and B. Rosi (eds), *Thinking Differently: A Reader in European Women's Studies* (London: Zed Books, 2002).

Hamill, D., *Pig in the Middle: The Army in Northern Ireland 1969–1984* (London: Methuen, 1985).

Harkin, C., 'Come Back Mrs Pankhurst, we have not yet Overcome', *Ramparts*, Derry Labour newssheet (January 1969).

Harris, H. and E. Healy, *'Strong About It All': Rural and Urban Women's Experiences of the Security Forces in Northern Ireland* (Derry: North West Women's/Human Rights Project Publications, 2001).

Harris, R., *Prejudice and Tolerance in Ulster: A Study of Neighbours and 'Strangers' in a Border Community* (Manchester: Manchester University Press, 1972).

Hennessey, T., *A History of Northern Ireland, 1920–1996* (London: Macmillan, 1997).

Henry, M., 'Two Views', *Irish Woman's Journal* (April 1967).

Hess, D. and B. Marin, 'Repression, Backfire and the Theory of Transformative Events', *Mobilization: An International Journal* 11, no. 2 (2006), pp.249–67.

Hill, M., *Women in Ireland: A Century of Change* (Belfast: Blackstaff Press, 2003).

Hillyard, P., 'Law and Order', in J. Darby (ed.), *Northern Ireland: The Background to the Conflict* (Belfast: Appletree Press, 1983).

Hobsbawm, E., *The Age of Extremes: The Short Twentieth Century, 1914–1991* (London: Abacus, 1994).

Horgan, J., *Irish Media: A Critical History since 1922* (London: Routledge, 2001).

Hoskynes, C., 'The European Union and the Women Within: An Overview of Women's Rights Policy', in R. Amy Elman (ed.), *Sexual Politics and the European Union: The New Feminist Challenge* (Oxford: Berghahn, 1996).

Inglehart, M., 'Political Interest in West European Women', *Comparative Political Studies* 14 (1981).

Investment in Education. Report of a Survey Team Appointed by the Minister for Education in Conjunction with the OECD (Dublin: Stationery Office, 1967).

Irish Congress of Trade Unions, *Seventh Annual Report* (Dublin: ICTU, 1965).

Irish Congress of Trade Unions, *Tenth Annual Report* (Dublin: ICTU, 1968).

Irish Congress of Trade Unions, *Twelfth Annual Report* (Dublin: ICTU, 1970).

Jackson, A., *Ireland 1798–1998* (Oxford: Basil Blackwell, 1999).

Johnston, R., *Century of Endeavour: A Biographical and Autobiographical View of the Twentieth Century* (Carlow and Dublin: Tindell Publications in association with Lilliput Press, 2006).

—— 'Manuscript Dealing with Sinn Féin Ard Comhairle Minutes' (held by Richard English, 2001).

Jones, M.A., *American Integration* (Cambridge: Cambridge University Press, 1960).

Kaplan, G., *Contemporary Western European Feminism* (London: UCL Press, 1992).

Kearney, R., *Postnationalist Ireland: Politics, Culture, Philosophy* (London: Routledge, 1997).

Keating, M., 'Pregnant from Ireland', *Woman's Way* (19 July 1968).

—— 'Those who don't go away', *Woman's Way* (19 July 1968).

Kennedy, F., *Cottage to Crèche: Family Change in Ireland* (Dublin: Institute of Public Administration, 2001).

Kenny, M., *Goodbye to Catholic Ireland* (Dublin: New Island, 2000).

Keogh, D., *Twentieth-Century Ireland: Nation and State* (Dublin: Gill & Macmillan, 1994).

Klein, N., *No Logo* (London: Flamingo, 2000).

—— *The Shock Doctrine: The Rise of Disaster Capitalism* (New York: Metropolitan Books, 2007).

Kramer, R., *Flames in the Field: The Story of Four SOE Agents in Occupied France* (Harmondsworth: Penguin, 1996).

Lawrence, R., *The Government of Northern Ireland: Public Finance and Public Services, 1921–1964* (Oxford: Clarendon Press, 1965).

Lawson, R. and S.E. Barton, 'Sex Roles in Social Movements: A Case Study of the Tenant Movement in New York City', in G. West and R.L. Blumberg (eds), *Women and Social Protest* (Oxford: Oxford University Press, 1990).

Lee, J.J., *Ireland, 1912–1985: Politics and Society* (Cambridge: Cambridge University Press, 1989).

Lefebvre, H., 'The Right to the City', in E. Kofman and E. Lebas (eds), *Writing on the Cities* (Oxford: Basil Blackwell, 1996).

Lenin, V.I., *Collected Works*, Vol. 5 (London: Lawrence & Wishart, 1960).

Lerner, G., *The Creation of a Feminist Consciousness* (Oxford: Oxford University Press, 1993).

Levine, J., 'Marriage is a Woman's Business', *Irish Woman's Journal* (October 1967).

—— *Sisters: The Personal Story of an Irish Feminist* (Dublin: Ward River Press, 1982).

—— 'The Women's Movement in the Republic of Ireland: 1968–1980: Introduction', in A. Bourke, S. Kilfeather, M. Luddy, M. MacCurtain, G. Meaney, M. Ní Dhonnchadha, M. O'Dowd and C. Wills (eds) *The Field Day Anthology of Irish: Irish Women's Writing and Traditions*, vol. 5 (Cork: Field Day, 2002).

Litton, F., *Unequal Achievement: The Irish Experience, 1957–1982* (Dublin: Institute of Public Administration, 1982).

Lovenduski, J., *Women and European Politics: Contemporary Feminism and Public Policy* (Brighton: Wheatsheaf, 1986).

Lovenduski, J. and P. Norris, *Women in Politics* (Oxford: Oxford University Press, 1996).

Luddy, M., 'The Labour Movement in Ireland', in A. Bourke, S. Kilfeather, M. Luddy, M. MacCurtain, G. Meaney, M.Ní Dhonnchadha, M. O'Dowd and C. Wills (eds), *Field Day Anthology of Irish Writing: Irish Women's Writing and Traditions*, Vol. 5 (Cork: Field Day, 2002).

Lyons, F.S.L., *Ireland since the Famine* (London: Fontana, 1973).

Macardle, D., 'Some Irish Mothers and their Children', *Irish Press* (14 September 1931).

MacCurtain, M., 'Towards an Appraisal of the Religious Image of Women', in M.P. Hederman and R. Kearney (eds), *The Crane Bag Book of Irish Studies, 1977–1981* (Dublin: Blackwater Press, 1982).

MacDonald, E., *Shoot the Women First* (London: Fourth Estate, 1991).

MacStiofáin, S., *Memoirs of a Revolutionary* (Edinburgh: Gordon Cremonesi, 1975).

MacSwiney, T., *Principles of Freedom* (London: Kennikat Press, 1970).

Maguire, F.B., 'Women against the World', *Irish Woman's Journal* (August 1967).

Mahon, E., 'From Democracy to Femocracy: The Women's Movement in the Republic of Ireland', in P. Clancy, S. Drudy, K. Lynch and L. O'Dowd (eds), *Irish Society: Sociological Perspectives* (Dublin: Institute of Public Administration, 1995).

—— 'Women's Rights and Catholicism in Ireland', in M. Threlfall (ed.), *Mapping the Women's Movement* (London: Verso, 1996).

Maloney, E., *A Secret History of the IRA* (London: Allen Lane, 2002).

Mary Ellen O'Doherty Appreciation (http://www.springtowncamp.com /files/news/2008/may/02.html, 29 June 2009).

Mayes, E., 'The 1960s and '70s, Decades of Change', in S.M. Parkes (ed.), *A Danger to the Men? A History of Women in Trinity College Dublin, 1904–2004* (Dublin: Lilliput Press, 2004).

Mayo, M. (ed.), *Women in the Community* (London: Routledge & Kegan Paul, 1977).

McAliskey, B., 'A Peasant in the Halls of the Great', in Michael Farrell (ed.), *Twenty Years On* (Kerry: Brandon, 1988).

McAllister, R., *From EC to EU: An Historical and Political Survey* (London: Routledge, 1997).

McAuley, C., 'Women in a War Zone: Twenty Years of Resistance' (Dublin: Republican Publications, 1989).

McCafferty, N., *Nell* (Dublin: Penguin, 2004).

—— *Peggy Deery: A Derry Family at War* (Dublin: Attic Press, 1988).

McCann, E., *War and an Irish Town* (London: Pluto Press, 1993).

McCluskey, C., *Up off their Knees: A Commentary on the Civil Rights Movement in Northern Ireland* (Ireland: Conn McCluskey and Associates, 1989).

McEnroy, M., 'Divorce in Ireland', *Woman's Way* (2 February 1968).

—— 'Equal Work ... Equal Pay', *Woman's Way* (12 April 1968).

—— 'Failure of a Revolution', *Woman's Way* (7 June 1968).

—— 'Family Planning', *Woman's Way* (1 March 1968).

—— 'Left on Her Own', *Woman's Way* (3 March 1967).

—— 'National Attitudes to Women', *Hibernia* (June 1967).

McGuire, M., *To Take Arms: A Year in the Provisional IRA* (London: Macmillan, 1973).

McKeever, C., 'The Forgotten Women', *Woman's Way* (12 January 1968).

McKeown, C., *The Passion of Peace* (Belfast: Blackstaff Press, 1984).

McKittrick, D., S. Kelters, B. Feeney and C. Thornton, *Lost Lives: The Stories of the Men, Women and Children Who Died as a Result of the Northern Ireland Troubles* (London: Mainstream Publishing, 1999).

McKittrick, D. and D. McVea, *Making Sense of the Troubles* (Harmondsworth: Penguin, 2001).

McShane, L., 'Day Nurseries in Northern Ireland', in C. Curtin, P. Jackson and B. O'Connor (eds), *Gender in Irish Society* (Galway: Galway University Press, 1987).

McWilliams, M., 'The Church, the State and the Women's Movement in Northern Ireland', in A. Smyth (ed.), *Irish Women's Studies Reader* (Dublin: Attic Press, 1993).

—— 'Women and Political Activism in Northern Ireland: 1960–1993', in A. Bourke, S. Kilfeather, M. Luddy, M. MacCurtain, G. Meaney, M. Ní Dhonnchadha, M. O'Dowd and C. Wills (eds), *Field Day Anthology of Irish Writing: Irish Women's Writing and Traditions*, Vol. 5 (Cork: Field Day, 2002).

Meenan, J., *The Irish Economy since 1922* (Liverpool: Liverpool University Press, 1970).

Michels, R., *Political Parties* (Glencoe, IL: Free Press, 1949).

Miller, R.L., R. Wilford and F. Donoghue, *Women and Political Participation in Northern Ireland* (Aldershot: Avebury, 1996).

Milotte, M., *Communism in Modern Ireland: The Pursuit of the Workers' Republic since 1916* (Dublin: Gill & Macmillan, 1984).

Mitchell, J., 'Women: The Longest Revolution', *New Left Review*, 40 (1966).

Morgan, M., 'The Catholic Middle Class: Myth or Reality', *L'Irlande Revue Politique et Sociale* 1, no. 3 (1987), pp.95–114.

Morgan, V., 'Women and the Conflict in Northern Ireland', in A. O'Day (ed.), *Terrorism's Laboratory – the Case of Northern Ireland* (Aldershot: Dartmouth, 1995).

Morrissey, H., 'Betty Sinclair: A Woman's Fight for Socialism', *Saothar* 9 (1983), pp.121–32.

Moyer, B., J. McAllister, M.L. Finley and S. Soifer, *Doing Democracy: The Map Model for Organizing Social Movements* (Gabriola Island, BC: New Society, 2001).

Mukta, P., 'Gender, Community, Nation: The Myth of Innocence', in S. Jacobs, R. Jacobson and R. Marchbank (eds), *States of Conflict: Gender, Violence and Resistance* (London: Zed Books, 2000).

Mulholland, M., *Northern Ireland at the Crossroads: Ulster Unionism in the O'Neill Years, 1960–9* (Basingstoke: Macmillan, 2000).

Murphy, H., 'Woman's Place ... Again', *Irish Woman's Journal* (January 1968).

Nagle, J., 'From "Ban-the-Bomb" to "Ban-the-Increase": 1960s Street Politics in Pre-Civil Rights Belfast', *Irish Political Studies* 23, no. 1 (2008), pp.41–58.

Neugebauer, M.E., 'Domestic Activism and Nationalist Struggle', in J. Turpin and L.A. Lorentzen (eds), *The Women and War Reader* (New York: New York University Press, 1998).

Nolan, W., 'Is Housewifery an Art or Craft?' *Irish Woman's Journal* (December 1967).

Norris, P., 'Gender Differences in Political Participation in Britain: Traditional, Radical and Revisionist Models', *Government and Opposition* 26, no. 1 (1991), pp.59–63.

Northern Ireland Civil Rights Association, '"We Shall Overcome": A History of the Struggle for Civil Rights in Northern Ireland, 1968–1978' (Belfast: NICRA, 1978).

Ó Dochartaigh, N., '"Sure, it's hard to keep up with the splits here": Irish-American Responses to the Outbreak of Conflict in Northern Ireland 1968–1974', *Irish Political Studies* (1995), pp.138–60.

Ó Glaisne, R., *Saoirse Na mBan* (Dublin: Cló Grianréime, 1973).

Oakley, A., *Subject Women* (New York: Pantheon, 1981).

Oberschall, A., *Social Conflict and Social Movements* (Englewood Cliffs: Prentice-Hall, 1973).

O'Connor, E., *Reds and the Green: Ireland, Russia and the Communist Internationals, 1919–43* (Dublin: University College Dublin Press, 2004).

O'Dowd, L., 'The Church, State and Women: The Aftermath of Partition' in C. Curtin, P. Jackson and B. O'Connor (eds), *Gender in Irish Society* (Galway: Galway University Press, 1987).

O'Dowd, M. and M.G. Valiulis (eds), *Women and Irish History* (Dublin: Wolfhound Press, 1997).

Oelke, M.E. and R.J. Vogt, 'Women in Combat Roles: Past and Future', unspecified degree thesis (Alabama: Air War College, 1988).

O'Faolain, N., *Are You Somebody? The Life and Times of Nuala O'Faolain* (Dublin: New Island, 1996).

(Official) Sinn Féin, 'Women's Rights in Ireland' (Dublin: Official Sinn Féin, 1975).

O'Halpin, E., *Defending Ireland* (Oxford: Oxford University Press, 1999).

O'Hanlon, G., 'Population Change in the 1950s: A Statistical Review', in D. Keogh, F. O'Shea and C. Quinlan (eds), *Ireland in the 1950s: The Lost Decade* (Dublin: Mercier Press, 2004).

O'Malley, P., *The Uncivil Wars: Ireland Today* (Belfast: Blackstaff Press, 1983).

Orpen, A., 'Irish Women as Wives', *Irish Woman's Journal* (August 1966).

O'Sullivan, S., 'Sex Segregation?', *Irish Woman's Journal* (September 1968).

Owens, R.C., *A Social History of Women in Ireland: 1870–1970* (Dublin: Gill & Macmillan, 2005).

Patterson, H., *The Politics of Illusion: A Political History of the IRA* (London: Serif, 1997).

Peterson, V.S., 'Gendered Nationalism: Reproducing "Us" Versus

"Them"', in L.A. Lorentzen and J. Turpin (eds), *The Women and War Reader* (New York: New York University Press, 1998).

Portelli, A., *The Order has been carried out: History, Memory and Meaning of a Nazi Massacre in Rome* (New York: Palgrave Macmillan, 2003).

Prince, S., *Northern Ireland's '68: Civil Rights, Global Revolt and the Origins of the Troubles* (Dublin: Irish Academic Press, 2007).

—— 'The Northern Irish Civil Rights Movement in Context', lecture (Belfast: Queen's University, October 2008).

Pugh, M., *Women and the Women's Movement in Britain* (London: Macmillan, 2000).

Purdie, B., *Politics in the Streets: The Origins of the Civil Rights Movement in Northern Ireland* (Belfast: Blackstaff Press, 1990).

—— 'Was the Civil Rights Movement a Republican or Communist Conspiracy?', *Irish Political Studies* 3 (1998), pp.33–41.

Randall, V., *Women and Politics: An International Perspective* (Basingstoke: Macmillan, 1991).

Regional Trends (London: Office for National Statistics, 1992).

Report of the Council of Education as Presented to the Minister for Education: The Curriculum of the Secondary School (Dublin: Stationery Office, 1960).

Report of the Inquiry into Allegations against the Security Forces of Physical Brutality in Northern Ireland Arising out of Events on the 9th of August 1971 (The Compton Report) (London: Her Majesty's Stationery Office, 1971).

Report on Emigration and Other Population Problems, 1948–1954 (Dublin: Stationery Office, 1954).

Report on Irish Education (Dublin: Stationery Office, 1975).

Reinharz, S., *Feminist Methods in Social Research* (Oxford: Oxford University Press, 1992).

Ridd, R., 'Powers of the Powerless', in R. Ridd and H. Calloway (eds), *Caught up in Conflict: Women's Responses to Political Strife* (London: Macmillan, 1986).

Rohan, D., *Marriage: Irish Style* (Dublin: Mercier Press, 1969).

Rooney, E., 'Transitional Intersections: Gender, Sect and Class in Northern Ireland', in E. Grabham, D. Cooper, J. Krishnadas and M. Harmon (eds), *Intersectionality and Beyond: Law, Power and the Politics of Location* (London: Routledge Cavendish, 2008).

Rosaldo, M., 'Women, Culture and Society: A Theoretical Overview', in M. Rosaldo and L. Lamphere (eds), *Women, Culture and Society* (Stanford, CA: Stanford University Press, 1974).

Rose, C., *The Female Experience: The Story of the Woman Movement in Ireland* (Galway: Arlen House, 1975).

Rose, R., *Governing without Consensus: An Irish Perspective* (London: Faber, 1971).

Rottman, D.B. and P.J. O'Connell, 'The Changing Social Administration', in F. Litton (ed.), *Unequal Achievement: The Irish Experience, 1957–1982* (Dublin: Institute of Public Administration, 1982).

Sammon, T., 'Back to Work', *Irish Woman's Journal* (April 1967).

Shannon, C.B., 'The Woman Writer as Historical Witness: Northern Ireland, 1968–1994. An Interdisciplinary Perspective', in M.G. Valiulis and M. O'Dowd (eds), *Women & Irish History* (Dublin: Wolfhound Press, 1997).

—— 'Women in Northern Ireland', in Mary O'Dowd and S. Wichert (eds), *Chattel, Servant or Citizen? Women's Status in Church, State and Society* (Belfast: Institute of Irish Studies, Queen's University Belfast, 1995).

Shannon, E., *I Am of Ireland: Women of the North Speak Out* (London: Little, Brown, 1989).

Simpson, J., 'Economic Development: Cause or Effect in Northern Ireland', in J. Darby (ed.), *Northern Ireland: The Background to the Conflict* (Belfast: Appletree Press, 1983).

Sinclair, B., 'Ulster Women and the War' (Belfast: Communist Party of Northern Ireland, 1942).

Sinn Féin Women's Department, *Women in Struggle* (Belfast: Sinn Féin Women's Department, 1994).

Smyth, A., 'The Contemporary Women's Movement in the Republic of Ireland', *Women's Studies International Forum* 11 (1988), pp.331–41.

—— 'Feminism in the South of Ireland, a Discussion', *Honest Ulsterman* (summer 1987), pp.41–58.

Spender, D., *For the Record: The Meaning and Making of Feminist Knowledge* (London: Woman's Press, 1985).

Springtown Camp and Civil Rights' Women (http://www.nicivilrights.org/?p=30, 29 June 2009).

Sreberny-Mohammadi, A. and K. Ross, 'Women MPs and the Media: Representing the Body Politic', in J. Lovenduski and P. Norris (eds), *Women in Politics* (Oxford: Oxford University Press, 1996).

Staunton, E., *The Nationalists of Northern Ireland, 1918–1973* (Dublin: Columba Press, 2001).

Stetler, R., *The Battle of the Bogside* (London: Sheed & Ward, 1970).

Sullerot, E., *Women, Society and Change*, trans. Margaret Scotford Archer (New York: McGraw Hill, 1971).

Sunday Times Insight Team, *Ulster* (Harmondsworth: Penguin, 1972).

Sweetman, R., *On Our Knees* (London: Pan Books, 1972).

Taillon, R., *The Women of 1916: When History was Made* (Belfast: Beyond the Pale, 1996).

Taylor, P., *Brits: The War against the IRA* (London: Bloomsbury, 2001).

—— *Provos: The IRA and Sinn Féin* (London: Bloomsbury, 1997).

Thody, P., *An Historical Introduction to the European Union* (London: Routledge, 1997).

Thompson, P., *The Voice of the Past: Oral History* (Oxford: Oxford University Press, 2000).

Threlfall, M. (ed.), *Mapping the Women's Movement* (London: Verso, 1996).

Tobin, F., *The Best of Decades: Ireland in the 1960s* (Dublin: Gill & Macmillan, 1984).

Travers, P., 'Emigration and Gender: The Case of Ireland, 1922–60', in M. O'Dowd and S. Wichert (eds), *Chattel, Servant or Citizen? Women's Status in Church, State and Society* (Belfast: Institute of Irish Studies, Queen's University Belfast, 1995).

Trewsdale, J.M., 'The Role of Women in the Northern Ireland Economy', in R.J. Cormack and R.D. Osborne (eds), *Religion, Education and Employment: Aspects of Equal Opportunity in Northern Ireland* (Belfast: Appletree Press, 1983).

Trewsdale, J.M. and M. Trainor, 'Womanpower: A Statistical Survey of Women and Work in Northern Ireland' (Belfast: Equal Opportunities Commission for Northern Ireland, 1979).

Turner, R.H., 'The Public Perception of Protest', *American Sociological Review* 34 (1969), pp.815–31.

Tweedy, H., *A Link in the Chain: The Story of the Irish Housewives Association* (Dublin: Attic Press, 1992).

Useem, B. and M.N. Zald, 'From Pressure Group to Social Movement: Organizational Dilemmas of the Effort to Promote Nuclear Power', *Social Problems* 30 (1982), pp.144–56.

Valiulis, M. G., 'Neither Feminist nor Flapper: The Ecclesiastical Construction of the Ideal Irish Woman', in M. O'Dowd and S. Wichert (eds), *Chattel, Servant or Citizen? Women's Status in Church, State and Society* (Belfast: Institute of Irish Studies, Queen's University Belfast, 1995).

Van Voris, W.H., *Violence in Ulster* (Amherst, MA: University of Massachusetts Press, 1975).

Viney, M., *The Broken Marriage: A Study in Depth of a Growing Irish Social Problem* (Dublin: Irish Times, 1970).

Violence and Civil Disturbances in Northern Ireland in 1969 (The Scarman Report) (Belfast: Her Majesty's Stationery Office, 1972).

Walby, S., 'The European Union and Gender Equality: Emergent Varieties of Gender Regime', *Social Politics* 11, no. 1 (2004), pp.4–29.
—— *Theorizing Patriarchy* (Oxford: Basil Blackwell, 1990).
Wallach Scott, J., *Gender and the Politics of History* (New York: Columbia University Press, 1999).
Ward, M., 'Marginality and Militancy: Cumann Na mBan, 1914–36', in A. Morgan and B. Purdie (eds), *Ireland: Divided Nation, Divided Class* (London: Ink Links, 1980).
—— *Unmanageable Revolutionaries: Women and Irish Nationalism* (Dingle: Brandon, 1983).
Ward, R., *Women, Unionism and Loyalism in Northern Ireland* (Dublin: Irish Academic Press, 2006).
West, G. and R.L. Blumberg, 'Reconstructing Social Protest from a Feminist Perspective', in G. West and R.L. Blumberg (eds), *Women and Social Protest* (Oxford: Oxford University Press, 1990).
White, R.W., *Ruairí Ó Brádaigh: The Life and Politics of an Irish Revolutionary* (Indiana: Indiana University Press, 2006).
Whyte, J.H., *Church and State in Modern Ireland* (Dublin: Gill & Macmillan, 1971).
—— *Interpreting Northern Ireland* (Oxford: Oxford University Press, 1990).
Wilford, R., 'Women and Politics in Northern Ireland', in J. Lovenduski and P. Norris (eds), *Women and Politics* (Oxford: Oxford University Press, 1996).
Williams, K., *'Get me a murder a day!' A History of Mass Communication in Britain* (London: Edward Arnold, 1998).
Wilson, E., 'Women in the Community', in M. Mayo (ed.), *Women in the Community* (London: Routledge & Kegan Paul, 1977).
Wilson, P. and R. Walsh (eds), *A Rebel Heart: Máire Bn. Uí Dhroma* (n.p., Belfast, 2001).
'Women in Civil Rights Conference' (http://www.springtowncamp.com/ files/news/2008/may/03.html, 29 June 2009).
Yuval-Davis, N. and A. Anthias, *Women–Nation–State* (London: Macmillan, 1989).
Zimmerman, G.D., *Irish Political Street Ballads and Rebel Songs* (Geneva: Imprimerie la Sirine, 1966).

Index

public policy and, 2, 30, 178–81, 195–8
republican movement and, 37–8, 40–9, 55,
117–18, 125–7, 130–1, 208, 249
Second World War and, 187
women's legal status, 185, 190–1, 192, 204,
251
gender roles, 1–2, 3, 9–10, 12, 15, 122, 130,
41–2, 156–7, 163–4, 166, 167
Derry riots (August 1969) and, 156–9, 166
in farming, 111–12
leadership and _see_ leadership roles, women in
military operations and, 125, 228, 229, 234–6,
238
in Republic of Ireland, 102, 125, 207, 251
republican movement and, 2, 6, 12, 14–15,
40–9, 55–6, 117–19, 125, 130, 228–36,
249–50, 252
Second World War and, 34–5
traditional _see_ patriarchy; traditional gender
roles
the Troubles and, 8–9, 62, 66, 213–16, 217–18,
219–24, 226–36, 242–4
see also gender regimes
'Gentle Revolution' in Dublin (late 1960s), 124,
182
gerrymandering, 63, 64, 87, 137, 140
Gillespie, Elgy, 110
Gogarty, Frank, 153–4
Gonne, Maud, 5
Goulding, Cathal, 42, 92, 116, 117, 119, 123,
127, 182, 184
Government of Ireland Act (1920), 84, 90
Greaves, C. Desmond, 91
Grehan, Ida, 107
Grieve, Mary, 22

H

Hamill, Desmond, 224
Harkin, Cathy, 138, 156
Harris, Rosemary, _Prejudice and Tolerance in
Ulster_ (1972), 25
Haughey, Charles, 111, 180
Heaney, James, 128
Heath, Edward, 218, 238
hen patrols, 231–2
Hennessey, Thomas, 27–8
Hibernia, 129, 164, 173, 183, 196, 197–8, 237
Hill, Bernie, P2
Hill, Myrtle, 2, 114, 158
Hillery, Patrick, 108, 180
Hobbs, Mary, 203
Hobsbawm, Eric, 102, 136, 174
Hoffman, Abbie, 200
Holland, Mary, 29, 156
Holmes, Erskine, 165
Home, Alec Douglas, 84–5, 88
Homeless Citizens League (HCL), P2, 14, 64, 70,
71–80, 94, 96, 97, 120, 138, 150

compared to CSJ, 81, 83–4
Fairmount Park squat and, 74–8, 82, 87, 94, 95
gender and, 72–3, 75–7, 78–9, 80, 82, 84, 94,
96, 120, 250
social class and, 14, 70–1, 73, 76–7, 78–9, 81
82, 94–5
Hope, Ann, P6, 146, 154–5, 213, 214, 226, 233
Horgan, John, 109, 174
Hoskynes, C., 21
housing in Northern Ireland, 14, 34, 36, 53,
137–9, 140, 143, 240
Caledon sit-in (1968), 94, 140
discrimination against Catholics, 34, 61, 63,
64–6, 71, 72, 137, 140, 215
O'Neill's five-point plan and, 147
overcrowding issues, 64, 67, 70
Second World War and, 34, 63
Springtown camp housing action (Derry,
1959), 5, 68, 79, 138
see also Dungannon housing activism
(1963); Homeless Citizens League (HCL)
housing in Republic of Ireland, 108, 127, 129
Irish Women's Liberation Movement and,
191–2, 193, 201, 203–4, 205, 208
'one family, one house' demand, 191–2, 193
203, 204
overcrowding issues, 119, 120
Prohibition of Forcible Entry Bill (1971),
184–5, 201, 203, 208, 252
republican movement and, 117, 118, 119–22,
129–30, 182, 191, 193, 203–5, 207, 208,
209
see also Dublin Housing Action Committee
(DHAC)
Hull fishing trawlers, 105
Humanae Vitae (papal encyclical, 1968), 114–
15, 118–19, 195
Hume, John, 144
Humphries, Rosemary, 188
hunger strikes, 9, 239

I

Iceland, 20, 102, 106, 177
Inglehart, Margaret L., 9, 45
International Alliance of Women, 111
international contexts, 5, 10, 15–16, 19, 55, 185
gender regimes, 2, 4, 5, 10, 248
radical media, 4, 15, 131
radicalism and, 102–6, 129, 131, 146, 183,
248
revolution of culture (late 1960s), 102–6, 136
second-wave feminism and, 9, 10, 103–6, 131
168, 174–8, 207, 248
see also student movements, international
International Labour Organization (ILO), 115
internment
during border campaign, 39, 43–4, 45–6, 55,
236